Hegel's Moral Corporation

# Hegel's Moral Corporation

Thomas Klikauer
*University of Western Sydney, Australia*

palgrave
macmillan

First published 2016 by
PALGRAVE MACMILLAN

Palgrave Macmillan in the UK is an imprint of Macmillan Publishers Limited, registered in England, company number 785998, of Houndmills, Basingstoke, Hampshire RG21 6XS.

Palgrave Macmillan in the US is a division of St Martin's Press LLC, 175 Fifth Avenue, New York, NY 10010.

Palgrave Macmillan is the global academic imprint of the above companies and has companies and representatives throughout the world.

Palgrave® and Macmillan® are registered trademarks in the United States, the United Kingdom, Europe and other countries.

ISBN: 978–1–137–54738–5

This book is printed on paper suitable for recycling and made from fully managed and sustained forest sources. Logging, pulping and manufacturing processes are expected to conform to the environmental regulations of the country of origin.

A catalogue record for this book is available from the British Library.

A catalog record for this book is available from the Library of Congress.

*To*

***Rosa Luxemburg***

*(Rosalia Luxemburg, Polish: Róża Luksemburg; 5 March 1871, Zamość, Vistula Land, Russia – 15 January 1919, Berlin, Germany)*

*Before World War I, Rosa Luxemburg advocated that German workers should not shoot at French workers. But German conservatism and nationalism decided otherwise. Instead of following Rosa Luxemburg, they started two World Wars and created Nazism. Today, a German call to arms against France would be met with utter disbelief. Finally, Rosa Luxemburg's dream is reality. If only German conservatism would have listened to Rosa Luxemburg instead of murdering her . . .*

# Contents

# List of Tables and Figures

## Tables

## Figures

# Preface

This book is not predominantly a philosophical book but a book about two versions of a corporation – one business oriented and dedicated to shareholder-value and profit-maximisation and one dedicated to moral life – *Sittlichkeit*, in Hegelian terms. The book is not written by a philosopher but by an author who has delivered a substantial critique on managerial capitalism in *Managerialism – Critique of an Ideology* (Klikauer 2013; Clegg 2014; Jaros 2014). In any case, merging Hegelian philosophy, ethics, and corporations is not as easy as it might appear. This is for several reasons: Hegel is widely recognised to be one of the most complicated philosophers. Hence an engagement with Hegel's ethics provided a number of challenges when, for example, specific Hegelian terms such as *Geist*, *aufheben*, and *Sittlichkeit* needed to be used appropriately either in their original German form as applied by Hegel and/or with their general German meaning. Perhaps Hegel's concept of *Geist* is the single most challenging one (*Geist* in Hegel does not mean spirituality – it has next to no religious connotations). A book on *Hegel's Moral Corporation* needs to separate Hegel's ethics from his general philosophy because only Hegel's ethics, ethical life, and *Sittlichkeit* is of concern for the book. If one seeks to apply Hegel's ethics to the world of business, management, and corporations, his ethics needs to be stripped down to the absolute core, separating the 'essential' from the non-essential and 'accidental' as Hegel would have it.

While there are Hegel interpretations from very different perspectives and orthodoxies, the book follows the British philosopher Houlgate's (2011:1) notion that 'no single orthodox . . . is presented here'. What is sought instead is a comprehensive picture of Hegelian ethical philosophy that is closest to a truthful representation of Hegel's work. Hegel's sometimes rather complex and difficult originals (primary literature) are clarified through using contemporary Hegel-interpretations (secondary literature). But even on interpretations, Hegel's philosophy has issued certain contextual demands that had to be taken into account when writing on Hegel, as German philosopher Marcuse (1941:72f.) has outlined. Hegel appears to be one of those philosophers who have generated a considerable volume of secondary literature and several schools of thought called Hegelians, all of which have developed significant insights into Hegel's philosophy. Those who have developed Hegel's philosophy further (e.g. Marx, Feuerbach, Stirner, Adorno, Anderson, Habermas, Honneth, Marcuse, Taylor) had to be separated from those who predominantly have had an interest in interpreting Hegel's philosophy (e.g. Hartmann, Henrich, Jameson, Kojève, Neuhouser, Pippin, Wood).

Since Hegel has only ever published four books, some of his philosophy is only available as lectures and lecture notes; hence, a quest for historical documents became unavoidable. Conflicts between Hegel's original German versions and sometimes diverging English translation(s) also had to be solved. Many initial translations of German literature have been undertaken by using 'translate.google.com' which more often than not provided a rough idea which demanded significant adjustments rather than a comprehensive translation. Additionally, most journals in English-speaking countries had been digitalised by the time of the writing of this book while access to German journals such as the all-important 'Hegel Studies' demanded the manual checking of volume by volume in libraries in Germany.

There are conflicting accounts inside the community of philosophers who are considered 'Hegel experts'. These conflicts have been left aside in order to focus on the task at hand – Hegel's Moral Corporation – relying on the most commonly recognised version of Hegel's ethics. The outcome of the examination of Hegel's ethics was applied to management, business, and corporations. Since Hegel's ethics deals mostly with human beings, the book necessarily deals more with the human side of the corporation (e.g. Human Resource Management, organisational theory, organisational behaviour, organisational psychology, and organisational studies) than with its rather technical-engineering side. If corporations are to be understood in their affirmative textbook version – often written by those who Baritz (1960) has called 'The Servants of Power' – the emerging picture of corporations would be highly one-dimensional. Therefore non-textbook sources had to be used in order to provide a comprehensive and truthful representation of 'what corporations are'.

One of the most exact representations of what corporations do has been developed by former *Harvard Business Review* editor Magretta (2012). Since most academic and non-academic (e.g. *Harvard Business Review*) management and business journals provide most uncritical pro-corporate research findings, more than these sources were required. But Hegel's dialectical requirement not to focus solely on positives but also to include the negatives (to see both sides: positive and negative) demanded the extensive use of critical non-textbook-like literature on corporations.

# Acknowledgements

Initially, my 2007 book *Communication and Management at Work* led to the first engagement with the world of moral philosophy, a theme that was carried forward in *Management Communication – Communicative Ethics and Action* (2008), and was more generally approached in *Critical Management Ethics* (2010), *Seven Management Moralities* (2012), and *Seven Moralities of Human Resource Management* (2014). *Hegel's Moral Corporation* continues this exploration of ethics by focusing on the moral philosophy of German philosopher Georg Wilhelm Friedrich Hegel (1770–1831). For their original and continuous support I would like to thank all those who have given me their time and assistance in the initial conception of this book and by providing constructive criticism throughout the writing period. Special thanks go to Andreas Arendt (ultra-fast scanning and forwarding of material), Stephen Ackroyd, Sybol C. Anderson, Joe Berendzen, Jay Bernstein, Karin de Boer, Petra Gehring, Gerhard Göhler, Ágnes Heller, Lisa Herzog, Stephen Houlgate, Douglas Kellner, Wolfgang Kersting, Hannes Kuch, Piotr Markowski, Jan Müller, Stefan Müller, Albena Neschen, Ulrike Pappert, Terry Pinkard, Paul Redding (for assistance and discussions), Jürgen Ritsert, Tina Röck, Nathan Ross, Christoph Schmidt am Busch, Alison Stone, Allen Speight, Kenneth R. Westphal (extensive email contact and guidance), Richard Dien Winfield, and Allen Wood (commenting favourably on some of my previous Hegel publications).

In compiling this book I am in debt to Khalida Malik for providing editorial assistance on initial drafts which were in a convoluted version of Germanic-English and, above all, my lovely wife Katja for proofreading the entire book twice. I am even more obliged to our two children – Noah and Lara – whose demand for playtime injected life into an otherwise relative lifeless academic work. Thanks also go to my sister, Bettina Hammann, to the German IT expert David Claybourne, and to Frankfurt University Library IT-specialist Armin Wenz for furnishing me with German literature on Hegel and to the people of UWS' Document Delivery Service for providing a valuable service. This has been enhanced through several 'self-funded' research trips to Germany.

Despite the public image of being a technologically advanced country, Germany lags behind when it comes to digitalising academic journals.

By the time of this research (2011–2015), digitalisation was still being done only by individual publishers that digitalised some journals but not others, some volumes but not others. Some publishers did it but most did not. This made it necessary to go through volumes of philosophical journals and often dust-covered books in 'four' maze-like medieval German libraries (with some built in the year 1547) at Technische Universität Darmstadt. I am grateful to UWS for a few weeks of 'self-funded' research (2011–2015) and for supporting my attendance at the Hegel Congress 2011 (before cuts to conference attendance) in Stuttgart (Hegel's birthplace) where I was able to meet many world-renowned Hegel scholars who provided an indispensable source of knowledge for this project.

The ability to speak German and access German Hegel sources has been indispensible. Machine-translation (www.translate.google) faulted immediately when facing Hegel's language (e.g. *den Rahmen des Staates zu sprengen* does not mean to 'blow up the state'). Hence, all translations had to be my own, done to my best ability as the closest approximation to the truth. I am also indebted to the employees of the 'US-Congress Library' who have catalogued books to perfection.

My appreciation also goes to those colleagues at UWS who shielded me from the worst excesses of Managerialism. My foremost gratitude, however, goes to my parents. Without their support my transition from being a local country boy attending Hauptschule (and an engineering apprenticeship) to the world of academia would never have been possible. I am endlessly indebted to the German trade union foundation, the Hans-Böckler-Stiftung. Finally, I would like to thank Palgrave's team, especially Liz Barlow, Kiran Bolla, and Maddie Holder.

# 1

# Introduction: Hegel's Philosophy of Corporations

*The corporation is the only institution of civil society upon which Hegel unqualifiedly bestows the epithet 'sittlich'.*[1]

Business ethics is often seen as an oxymoron because business and ethics seem to be mutually exclusive. Perhaps this is even more so when moral philosophy is being linked to corporations. Reading through standard business ethics textbooks, one finds it is hard to avoid the impression that the field of business ethics is aware of this. It appears as if business ethics shields business and corporations from moral philosophy, reducing it to a few introductory pages that superficially 'highlight' selected elements of business ethics. As a consequence, it has become quite common in books and textbooks on business ethics, management, and corporations to focus on so-called key ethical themes such as virtue ethics, Kantian ethics,[2] utilitarianism, and perhaps occasionally on Rawls' ethics of 'Justice as Fairness'. Most textbooks, however, quickly proceed with a short overview of other ethical issues (marketing, wellbeing, whistle-blowing, etc.). In other words, one finds 'the relegation of moral and political problems and value judgements to the extreme margins of [managerial] textbooks'.[3] The issue of management ethics seems to be a surface-structure rather than a deep-structure issue (Chomsky 1957). Remaining at the surface, standard management literature rarely finds managerial themes such as corporations discussed in the light of specific philosophers.[4]

As a consequence, it appears rather unusual for a scholarly book in the general area of management to engage with a specific aspect of moral philosophy, for example, Hegel's *Sittlichkeit*,[5] linked to a specific managerial institution: the corporation.[6] But a book on Hegelian *Sittlichkeit* linked to corporations can illuminate today's role of management in relation to corporations because 'Hegel has especially positive things to say about the corporation'.[7] Such a book is not an overall examination of management ethics found in standard textbooks on management, nor is it a critical assessment of management on the base of a wide range of moral philosophies.[8] In contrast to more general books on management, this book examines one single institution of management – corporations – from the standpoint of a specific philosopher: German philosopher G. W. F. Hegel (1770–1831).[9] This is in line with the fact 'that Hegel wishes philosophy to confront "reality" i.e., economics in general and political economy in particular'.[10] To honour this Hegelian commitment, this book investigates Hegel's engagement with modern economy within which Hegel placed the corporation.[11] In essence, this book is concerned with just six paragraphs – *Philosophy of Right* (1821:§§250–256) – of Hegel's entire philosophical work.

There appears to be a near total neglect or 'veil of ignorance'[12] when it comes to including Hegelian philosophy in management ethics.[13] This applies across the board to nearly all writers of textbooks on management ethics and even more so to standard management textbooks. If management ethics is viewed from the perspective of one of the most used models in management, the SWOT (strengths, weaknesses, opportunities, and threats) analysis that operates with defender, prospector, analyser, and reactor, for example, the following picture emerges.[14] The field of management ethics carries connotations of being Miles and Snow's 'defender' rather than their 'prospector' because management ethics appears to defend its position enshrined in the narrow box of the perceived three to four so-called key themes of ethics which are virtue ethics, deontology, utilitarianism, and perhaps Rawls' 'Justice as Fairness'.[15]

Many publications of management ethics (the morality of management seen as an internal issue) and business ethics (focusing more on external issues) do not prospect beyond the much trumpeted standard range of four to five key themes. Unlike these, this book on Hegel and corporations seeks to engage with moral philosophy outside the three standard themes of virtue ethics, Kantian ethics, and utilitarianism. It is because of this self-imposed limitation or, as Rawls might see it, 'veil of ignorance'[16] that the field of business ethics hardly ever ventures deeper into moral philosophy and contemporary developments within it.

In other words, the standard approach of business ethics shows the very opposite of what the US television show *Star Trek* has popularised as 'to boldly go where no man has gone before'. The final frontier of most management ethics writers is to stay inside the box of what is perceived to be standard ethical theories. Management ethics is not on a mission to explore new worlds. It does not seek out new life and new ethical theories nor does it 'boldly go where no man has gone before'. In other words, management ethics remains asphyxiated inside its defender status; it displays ignorance towards what lies beyond the confinements of its three to four key themes, and the field is characterised by a staunch avoidance of prospecting beyond the well-documented depth of traditional and contemporary moral philosophy. Given that, it is not surprising that management ethics is a field that shows total ignorance towards Hegelian philosophy (cf. Klikauer 2013a). This is in spite of the fact that Hegel wrote comprehensively on morality, ethics, and ethical life.[17] Hegel remains the only classical philosopher who directly engaged with the corporation – *Die Korporation*.[18]

Since its invention, management ethics has remained in blissful ignorance of even those philosophers who have extensively dealt with one key managerial issue: corporations.[19] Perhaps the only significant exception is Alister MacIntyre's article on 'Why are the Problems of Business Ethics Insolvable?' (1983) and his work is not even directed towards the corporation. No modern philosopher has dealt with corporations in the way Hegel has.[20] Not surprisingly, Hegel is not only the first but remains the only modern philosopher ever to engage with corporations on a systematic (*Philosophy of Right*, 1821),[21] philosophical (through his overall work), and ethical level (*Phenomenology*, 1807).[22] Most importantly, he engaged corporations from the standpoint of his moral philosophy that he calls *Sittlichkeit*, which is Hegel's key term [*Schlüsselbegriff*] and which is commonly translated into moral life.[23] No other modern philosopher who has developed a comprehensive ethical system has included corporations in such a system.[24] Hegel remains the only philosopher to have achieved this. In the words of American philosopher William Maker (1987:22), 'Hegel is a thinker of modernity who has conceptualised the family, economics [and corporations], society, and the state in a distinctively modern and original way.'

This book first examines Hegel's link between corporations and his ethics of *Sittlichkeit* or ethical life. This is the morality link between *Sittlichkeit* and corporations. It closes the gap in standard management literature. Secondly, it presents somewhat of a critical extension of Hegelian moral philosophy on corporations because it reaches well beyond Hegel's outlines of Hegelian corporations in the early 19th century. In other words, it is not Hegelian but Neo-Hegelian in its approach because it does not remain within the confines of Hegel but applies his philosophy to the corporations of the 21st century.[25] It fulfils what more recently Herrmann-Pillath & Boldyrev (2014:6) have noted as 'modern corporations have something to learn from the Hegelian model of *Korporationen.*' To achieve this, one needs to contrast Hegel's *sittliche* corporations against modern business corporations.[26] Perhaps more than almost all classical writings on business corporations,[27] it was the corporate CEO of the world's largest insurance corporation (AIG) – Hank Greenberg – who best summed up the basic moral philosophy of corporations:[28]

> All I want in life is an unfair advantage.

Contrasting this with Hegel's *sittliche* corporation as outlined in his *Philosophy of Right* (1821) is in itself a very Hegelian approach.[29] But it is also, as Hegel's predecessor Kant would have said, a project that contrasts 'what is' ('unfair corporations', Greenberg) with 'what ought to be' (*sittliche* corporations), thereby extracting the essence of corporations.[30] To sharpen the contrast between Hegel's '*sittliche* corporation' and the 'modern business corporation', one must acknowledge that modern business corporations have positive aspects; for example:[31]

> corporations bring lighting, air conditioning, automobiles, jetliners, and clothing, computers, smart phones, plasma screens televisions, video games, and movies.

The overall picture of modern business corporations in this book still tends to focus on the critical aspects of the business corporation. This enhances the task of the book found in contrasting Hegel's moral–philosophical concept of a *sittliche* corporation with the modern business corporation. But all of this is not to be understood as an 'old versus new' issue as Hegel's moral philosophy and his *sittliche* corporation carry forward ethical demands onto today's business corporations. And neither is Hegel's philosophy an issue for history books.

In the words of German philosopher Glockner (1965:420), 'In truth, Hegel has created only one work. It has not appeared in bookstores. It is living and working in his mind.' It is today's task to carry forward Hegelian philosophy and to apply it in order to analyse present-day phenomena such as the business corporation.[32] As Italian Neo-Hegelian philosopher Ferrarin writes, 'What matters in the study of the ancients [and Hegel as well] is thus not so much the degree of fidelity and authenticity with which we reconstruct past philosophies, but rather the relation between our own philosophy and its time.'[33] This is a very Hegelian statement.[34]

The value of this becomes most obvious in the chapters of this book. Ferrarin (2011:436) continues with 'the history of philosophy for Hegel is thus not a matter of retrieving givens, but of engaging in a living exchange with our predecessors'.[35] Perhaps this is exactly what, in the words of British philosopher Zygmunt Bauman (1987), divides legislators from interpreters. In short, there are those who can interpret Hegel. Sometimes they do so with the utmost precision. And then there are those philosophers who understand Hegel's philosophy in order to move beyond the narrow confinements of Hegel's specific words to become 'legislators' in their own right. This occurs when they create their own philosophy based on Hegel's work. They create their own philosophical view by reaching beyond Hegel. In Ferrarin's words they engage in a 'living exchange with our predecessors' to develop their own philosophy. They are philosophers – not mere interpreters – who engage in philosophical theories rather than theoretical interpretations.

This book provides access to Hegel's ethical philosophy on corporations from the standpoint of *Sittlichkeit*. It is also written in the Hegelian *Geist* or spirit.[36] 'Hegel, unlike Fichte, did not have much confidence in teaching philosophy to the masses [but writing on philosophy one] must recognise that the people might possibly elevate themselves to it [philosophy]; but it must not lower itself to the people.'[37] In line with Hegelian writing, this book is an attempt to teach Hegelian philosophy to those inside management studies who can think 'outside the box' of the so-called four key ethical themes. Nevertheless, it also honours Hegel's demand not to lower itself to the level of standard management studies. Hence, this book might be underwhelming to serious philosophers and a bit overwhelming to management students, perhaps because it concerns the – at times – almost incomprehensive writings of Hegel.

Understanding the philosophical writings of German philosopher Georg Wilhelm Friedrich Hegel remains unthinkable without understanding his immediate predecessors, his influential group of friends, and his historical period.[38] 'Hegel was a child of his time'[39] and throughout his life he had a strong and close working relationship with his contemporaries. This extended also to one of his best known predecessors. It is not helpful to understand Hegel's concept of *Sittlichkeit* and how it relates to corporations in isolation from Kant's Trilogy of Critiques – *Critique of Pure Reason* (1781), *Critique of Judgement* (1790), and *Critique of*

*Practical Reason* (1788).[40] Hegel can be said to be faithful to Kant's critical theory.[41] Apart from Kant, Aristotle was in many respects Hegel's great model and master philosopher.[42] Building on Aristotle and Kant, Hegel came to be seen as without a doubt one of the towering figures of modern thought.[43] On the downside, he has been called obscure,[44] difficult to understand,[45] and highly intellectualistic.[46]

On the upside, 'Hegel magisterially exploits the resources of the German language of his day' (Rockmore 1997:4) and is not easy to translate into English. He uses specific German terms such as *Geist* and *Sittlichkeit* that are sometimes non-translatable and for some other terms the English language only provides close approximations: *Sittlichkeit* is not just ethical life and *aufheben* does not only mean to sublet. It is quite conceivable that this is also the reason why Hegel is one of those very rare philosophers who has a dictionary in his name for explaining Hegelian terms.[47] Given those complexities, it is not at all surprising that Hegel has been misunderstood, misinterpreted, misappropriated, misused, abused and seems to be one of the most demonised philosophers.[48] However, this becomes less of a problem when digging deeper into Hegel's philosophy of *Sittlichkeit* and his writings on corporations because very few philosophers have ever dared to venture into the complex, dense, and demanding philosophical specifics of Hegelian *Sittlichkeit* in relation to corporations.[49]

From the outset it is important to focus our attention on the fact that Hegel's moral philosophy represents a philosophy of freedom [*Freiheitsphilosophie*][50] – 'the category of freedom pervades all areas of Hegel's philosophy'.[51] He wrote his philosophy of freedom as far as this was possible to achieve given the circumstances of his life under Prussian authoritarianism and censorship.[52] Hegel was born in a part of the southern hinterland that was to become Germany.[53] During Hegel's time Germany was still defined by Germanic miniature states [*Kleinstaaten*] before it became a full-fledged unified country. This occurred after Hegel's death. His life at the dawn of Enlightenment in Germany was dominated by a depressing mixture of militarism, chauvinism, backwardness, religion, conservatism, and authoritarianism that forced Hegel to be constantly aware of the watchful eyes of the totalitarian Prussian censorship.[54] This might explain his avoidance of the most feared word among 19th-century – and perhaps even early-20th-century – German authorities: democracy.[55] It may also explain his writings on religion and his work on the state.[56] On the other hand, there is an assessment of Hegel as argued by German philosopher Horkheimer, who states,[57]

> Hegel's work did more serious harm to that reactionary institution than all the use of the latter could derive from this formal glorification. Reason is a poor ally of reaction. A little less than ten years after Hegel's death (his chair remained unoccupied that long), the King appointed a successor to fight the 'dragon's teeth of Hegelian pantheism', and the arrogance and fanaticism of his school.

In other words, 'formal glorification' (Horkheimer) and the avoidance of Prussian censorship might well account for Hegel's dense, inaccessible, and at times highly unintelligible writing style that made it possible for Hegel to engage with the philosophy of freedom while simultaneously avoiding detection by the Prussian censors. One might even suspect that the unsophisticated state-servants [*Staatsbeamte*] of the official and secret police simply gave up on Hegel's texts and failed to understand them, deeming his work incomprehensible and therefore insignificant.[58]

In short, Hegel managed to get his work past the censor while still being able to write on human freedom, one of the most dreaded words in the dictionary of German conservatism. The ability to sidestep censorship while writing on human freedom might well be his greatest and remaining achievement. It kept him employed in various – and for a serious philosopher perhaps rather demeaning – positions such as house tutor, newspaper editor, school principal, etc. Only very late in his life did Hegel become a full tenured professor.[59] One might regard Hegel's short-term precarious employment situation as always on the edge of joining the ranks of the working poor. Despite all this, employment tended to ease a lifetime of financial problems while simultaneously reallocating valuable time away from philosophy. Nevertheless, it assured that Hegel's writings on human freedom, for example, were not lost. This occurred during a time when German conservatism did everything in its power to prevent the freedom movement – that originated in the French Revolution of 1789 – from entering German states and, worst of all, German minds as a beautiful sunrise.[60] In the words of American Neo-Hegelian philosopher Robert Pippin (2010:43),

> It is easy to summarise in Hegel's own terms his answer to the 'How important is freedom?' question: absolutely important. Everything Hegel writes about, from the history of religion to the relations between universal and particular, has to do in one way or another with the realisation of the freedom problem, and his entire philosophy could be summarised in one phrase, however, initially opaque: that the Absolute is freedom.

Hegel's philosophy sees freedom as the absolute (*das Absolute*). Yet it was birthed in the 19th-century authoritarian German states fearful of human freedom. The historic freedom versus authority conflict must have been daunting for Hegel who was well aware that engaging in a philosophy of freedom might disable his dream of teaching and writing philosophy at university level. The very same fear has been expressed by nearly everyone who sought to teach Hegel's philosophy of freedom after Hegel's death. Perhaps the very same applies today when someone seeks to teach Hegel's philosophy of human freedom at a management school.[61] Unlike 19th-century authoritarian censorship, today's management schools 'publicly' honour academic freedom in their official ethics codes, that is, the right to publish books on Hegel, human freedom, *Sittlichkeit*, and corporations. However, such schools also reserve their right to hire and promote those who contribute directly to management's quest for shareholder-value and profit-maximisation, code-worded 'The Real Bottom Line' (Magretta 2012:129–140), those whom Baritz has called The Servants of Power.[62] The Servants of Power might not view Hegel's ethics of freedom as a contribution to management studies, let alone to management.

## Hegel and Hegelianism

There is a blissful and perhaps systematically engineered ignorance by The Servants of Power and management studies towards Hegel's philosophy of human freedom and *Sittlichkeit*. And it happens in spite of Hegelianism as a well-developed body of scholarly research,[63] and despite the existence of Hegel societies and Hegel study groups in most English-speaking countries, as well as rafts of journals dealing with Hegelian philosophy including specific Hegel study journals such as the *Owl of Minerva* (USA), *The Bulletin of the Hegel Society of Great Britain*, and *Hegel-Studien* (Germany). Today, there are numerous philosophers who either have written on Hegel or are outright Hegel experts. And there are also relatively high numbers of Hegel followers and philosophical themes that started during Hegel's lifetime. Many of those who continued after his death are reaching into today's world inside and outside of philosophy and general academia. In terms of management and business studies, nevertheless, most Hegelian themes are still blissfully ignored, just as any history of thought that led to today's management ethics is ignored. Also ignored is the fact that Hegel was one of the main philosophers of the 19th century and that he had a substantial number of followers in Germany, France, Italy, England,

Australia, the USA, and so on. Hegel's followers were that substantial in numbers that they even split into diverging subgroups after Hegel's death in 1831.[64] The first of these groups of Hegel followers became known as the 'Young Hegelians' who carried forward Hegel's philosophical heritage after his death.[65] They are commonly divided into two groups as shown in Table 1.1.

Table 1.1 shows five types of Hegelians. The table starts with the famous chasm of Hegelian philosophers who lived either at the time of Hegel or shortly afterwards. These 19th-century Hegelians can be divided into two opposing groups: the Left and Right Hegelians. Those philosophers who lived during the 20th century and carried forward Hegel's philosophy might be termed modern Hegelians. While the early part became weaker with the death of most of its main proponents, the remaining philosophers tended to focus on Hegel's work. Those philosophers who are currently engaging with Hegelian philosophy and/or developed Hegel's philosophy further are shown as two 21st-century groups. One group consists of purely Hegelian philosophers while the second group is often called 'Neo'-Hegelian philosophers. The dividing line between both can be found by using the terms

*Table 1.1* The Hegelians

| Period | Names given | Some of the main representatives |
|---|---|---|
| 19th century | Right or Old Hegelians | Heinrich Leo, Herrmann Lübbe, Michelet, Karl Friedrich Göschel, Hermann Friedrich Wilhelm Hinrichs, Johann Edward Erdmann, Eduard Gans, Carl Ludwig Michelet, Georg Andreas Gabler and Karl Rosenkranz |
| 19th century | Left or Young Hegelians | David Friedrich Strauss, Edgar and Bruno Bauer, Friedrich Feuerbach, August von Ciszokwski, Max Stirner, Moses Heß, Arnold Ruge, Kierkegaard, and a certain Karl Marx |
| 20th century | Modern Hegelians | Alexandre Kojève, Jean Hyppolite, George Lukács, Theodor Adorno, Herbert Marcuse |
| 21st century | Current Hegelians | Stephen Houlgate, Charles Taylor, Axel Honneth, Bruce Gilbert |
| 21st century | Current Neo-Hegelians | Robert Pippin; 'Pittsburgh Neo-Hegelians' (Brandom & McDowell); Paul Redding, Kenneth Westphal |

'Neo-Hegelian': for philosophers who have an interpretation of Hegel that tries to render Hegel compatible with some broader contemporary set of normative considerations about how to engage with philosophy.

'Hegelian': for philosophers who are more or less convinced that Hegel 'got it right' and does not need the type of accommodation to the present that Neo-Hegelians attempt.

But before this development could occur, many of the 19th-century Hegelians were censored, prosecuted, isolated, became jobless or marginalised, and were forced to live in exile culminating in the Young Hegelians' exile in Paris and Marx's émigré in England. Later two key 20th-century Hegelian philosophers, Theodor W. Adorno and Herbert Marcuse, escaped to the USA when German Nazis burned books first and people later (Klikauer 2011). Meanwhile, many Right Hegelians embraced mainstream supporting positivism.[66] This challenged the critical wing of Hegel's legacy on philosophical grounds inside and outside of Germany. Today, Hegelian philosophy is well anchored in many of Germany's universities (Frankfurt, Berlin, Heidelberg, etc.).

Essentially, German society of the 21st century is somewhat more representative of Hegel's philosophy of *Sittlichkeit*, for example, when compared to Hegel's 19th-century *Kleinstaaten* with their feudal leftovers of authoritarian–militaristic mini-emperors. In most European countries and modern societies, many of Hegel's institutional teachings such as family, civil society, the state, and other selective aspects of his philosophy such as human freedom and even parts of Hegelian *Sittlichkeit* have become part of society. Nevertheless, other parts of Hegelian philosophy remain unchanged. While the foundation of ruling has changed from 19th-century authoritarianism to 20th-century democracy, both – albeit in different ways – still establish rulers and the 'to be ruled'. In other words, we might have changed from hitting one another until the strongest ruler remained standing to the use of a pen under the equation: 'x = democracy', but the ruler versus ruled dichotomy remains. In Hegelian terms, there are still masters and slaves, there are still rulers and the ruled (over), and there are still management and employees. In short, Hegel's master–slave dialectics remains prevalent in corporations, society, and politics.[67]

The political applications of selective moments in continental philosophy are designed to secure political and economic rule. Originally developed as Kantian and Hegelian, critical philosophy was converted into 'positive' philosophy. This came as a reaction to Hegel's insistence that 'the negative' is relevant to understand the truth.[68] Hegelian philosophy is thoroughly dialectical demanding to examine both sides that, rather oversimplified, have been seen as 'positive and negative' and 'pros and cons'.[69] Any blunt rejection of the negative element in Hegelian philosophy resulted in a one-dimensional focus on the positive. This one-dimensional view aided the invention of positivism and empiricism (Marcuse 1966). While previously being an insignificant subarea of philosophy, today positivism has been accelerated to an unquestioned and all-guiding paradigm.

The dominance of this paradigm made the origins of critical rationalism that started with Kant's Trilogy of Critiques disappear in many areas. Despite this, Hegel developed Kantian philosophy as speculative philosophy. His speculative philosophy focuses on negativity and dialectics.[70] In historical terms, the development of 18th-century Kantian and 19th-century Hegelian philosophy occurred, just as Enlightenment itself, as a reaction to the monistic authority of religious belief-systems that supported the Dark Ages, the Inquisition, and the Ancient Regime.[71] While France ended all this with the French Revolution of 1789, Germany only ever experienced a 'revolution'[72] of the *Geist* and this only in parts of an educated and enlightened class.[73] During the 19th century and in some cases well after World War II, various German counter-forces directed against Enlightenment still sought to prevent modernity, Kantianism, and even more so Hegelian philosophy.

But neither Kantian nor Hegelian philosophy simply presented a counter-opinion. 'In philosophy, we cannot just use one position to oppose another position . . . that is opinion [according to] Luthers' 'here I am, I cannot help it' . . . in philosophy, however, criticism has to be rational . . . another philosophical conception cannot simply be destroyed by criticism, but it must be *aufgehoben*.[74] Philosophical concepts like this not only have historical significance but are also important for today, for our understanding of the world, the way civil society, management, and corporations work. Hegelian philosophy might mean for management and business studies what is described in the following.

When management and business studies reject critique and Hegel's 'dialectical negative' outright, they do not view processes such as 'thesis → anti-thesis → synthesis' as rational – which is something Greek philosophy did roughly 2,000 years ago and which continues until today.[75] Simultaneously, this rejects philosophical attempts to unify positives and negatives under Hegel's dialectic of reconciliation. Instead, management studies view critique that includes positives and negatives in Martin Luther's opinionated way, 'Here I am, I cannot help it.'

This expresses an opinion, not a philosophical–rational critique based on the inclusion of negatives. Management studies' rejection, marginalisation, isolation, and dislike of critique and the negative have been designed to prevent a critique that outlines the inextricable part of anything that exists, namely, the negative: there is no day without night; no darkness without light; no birth without death; no management without employees; and no strategic management without the management of daily affairs.

Inside managerial thinking every critique is re-framed simply as opinion versus opinion rather than the philosophical–rational critique of positive → negative → synthesis. Those who have been assigned the job to protect management from critique – Baritz's The Servants of Power – are organised under the heading of management studies. They re-frame any philosophical–rational critique as mere opinion. This is the task of management studies and once accomplished an opinion can attack any non-managerial and anti-Managerialism view.[76] All this is, perhaps, a five-centuries-old Lutheran idea (Martin Luther, 1483–1546) but management studies not only cling to it but also ignore the philosophical–rational critique of Hegel (1770–1831). In sum, dismissing, marginalising, and rejecting a philosophical–rational critique on management as mere opinion perceived as an attack on management shows opinionated thinking rather than an understanding of European Enlightenment, continental philosophy, and the Hegelian project (Moggach & Lledman 1997:540). Hegelian philosopher Pippin (2010:110) summarised this in the following way:

> Looking at the Hegelian project . . . of course, leads us to a decisive and somewhat unstable turning point in European or what we now call Continental philosophy, the point where Kant's great inventions, his attempts to re-conceive a purely rational philosophy in the face of the collapsing authority of traditional rationalism and the unsatisfying modesty of modern empiricism, inventions like his notion of transcendental subjectivity, or of only 'practical reality', are being reconceived in this developmental way, and that means also socially and historically, and where his self-legislating moral subject is reconceived as such more than a practically necessary idea and is instead animated with an historical life.[77]

In order to prevent 'the collapsing authority' and the rise of Kant's 'self-legislating moral subject', King Frederick William IV of Prussia

(1795–1861) commissioned German philosopher Schelling to destroy the dragon seed of Hegelianism.[78] To some extent the Prussian/Schelling programme of destroying Hegel had actually succeeded during the 19th century. German philosopher Dieter Henrich (1971:7), for example, begins his book on *Hegel in Context* [*Hegel im Kontext*] with the following: 'For more than a century, those who wanted to understand Hegel were alone. They found no guiding analysis which would have helped in reading Hegel.'[79]

The Prussian/Schelling programme was to annihilate Hegel's philosophy of phenomenology as outlined in Hegel's masterpiece: *The Phenomenology* (1807). It developed a philosophy in which the phenomenon examines the relationship between appearance and truth [*Schein und Wahrheit*] that seeks to look through an appearance to ascertain truth. In the functional world of pure positivism that has set up ideological belief-systems such as 'facts speak for themselves', pure science, objectivity, neutrality, and the like, any philosophical examination that carries one deeper into what is made-up and presents itself as pure appearance is not welcomed.[80] However, misleading and ideological claims such as the infamous self-speaking facts, for example, can be exposed as ideological through simple common sense:[81] facts cannot speak for themselves for two reasons – they have no mouth to speak with and always depend on the human interpretation of these so-called objective facts to make sense of them. This always incurs a human factor in the form of a needed interpretation of the facts which is inextricably linked to subjectivity (Kant). Despite all this, positivism, pragmatism, functionalism, system theory, and most ideologies of management studies and Managerialism seek to convince us that the managerial interpretation of facts under the banner of value neutrality, for example, is not an ideology but the reality. And that this is TINA reality – there is no alternative. In reality, however, this represents no more than a managerially constructed view of a specific form of reality. In short, Hegelian philosophy drills through the appearance [*Schein*] of managerial ideologies to uncover the truth.[82]

## Hegel's corporation and the modern corporation

Nevertheless, keeping up the appearance – commonly known as 'Impression Management' (Rosenfeld et al. 1995) – is a near perfect description of management studies. This has direct spillover effects from management studies into real academic fields and society. Under

Managerialism, the latter are increasingly forced to remain within the boundaries of positivism.[83] Management studies seek to pretend that management is a positive and neutral subject. While the ideology of neutrality stems from the engineering ideology, the positive carries two values: (i) positive as in positivism and (ii) positive as in good, that is, not negative. In line with this, management studies teach management as a global-managerial subject operating on valid laws. Academics within management studies often represent The Servants of Power.

One way of supporting management and the ideology of Managerialism is claiming that management is non-historical and universal. It is the claim that management has always existed. Supporting evidence for this ideology comes directly from the 'horse's mouth' so to speak when former *Harvard Business Review* editor Magretta (2012:4) wrote a surprisingly open book – her non-textbook work on *What Management is – How it Works and Why It's Everyone's Business* (2012) – that in a 'tell-it-all' mode is as close to a perfect description of management as one can find. She writes, for example, 'society has always had managers'. This is no more than an ideological attempt to make us believe that management is therefore neutral to historical processes. If management has always existed, one might wonder about the following:

- Were Egypt's pyramids built under the economic system of managerial capitalism?
- Were pharaohs shareholders?;
- Did they operate a corporation called 'Pyramid Construction Ltd.'?;
- Did their corporate management include financial controlling, marketing, and operations management techniques (e.g. worldwide sourcing, supply chain management, and global production networks)?;
- Did their corporation use ROI (return on investment)?;
- Did their corporation have a sophisticated corporate governance structure?;
- Was their strategic management more akin to Whittington's (2001) classical or systemic approach?;
- Did those who built the pyramids operate under cost-cutting, performance management systems, the infamous KPIs (key performance indicators), and performance-related pay systems?;
- Were those people called human resources governed by Human Resource Management?
- Were those people members of a trade union operating under the international labour standards as prescribed by the International Labour Organisation (ILO)?

It appears that this was not the case. Hence, The Servants of Power can never grow tired of pretending otherwise. They can also never stop claiming that corporate management operates on universally valid laws and is timeless. But corporate management is a 20th-century invention that was only made possible under capitalism 'after' ownership and administering corporations separated.[84] As such, management is quite a modern invention operating as a socially constructed and ideologically secured particularity.

In short, The Servants of Power need to secure management against a Hegelian demolition job that balances management studies' overt positivism with the other side of reality: Hegel's philosophy of dialectics that includes the negative side of things. To avoid this, management studies need to be one-sided (positive and positivism). By contrast, Hegel's two-sided approach (+/–) always includes negatives.[85] But excluding one over the other might also mean that management studies can never be a truly scientific enterprise but has to – almost by definition – remain ideological. To clarify the terminology of corporate management further, it needs to be distinguished from its three bedfellows: management studies, Managerialism, and managerial capitalism. This is necessary because originally management was simply an office (19th century) that turned into administration and bureaucracy (20th century) and has then mutated into corporate management. Later it added two ideological support mechanisms to its portfolio: management studies and Managerialism. In other words, when one uses 'corporate management' today, a raft of institutions, ideologies, images, and expressions can be conveyed (Morgan 1993).

Seen from this perspective, management takes on at least four subforms. These are managerial regimes, management studies, Managerialism, and managerial capitalism. To begin with the most immediate level, managerial regimes operate inside corporations. They are the clearest and most direct expression of corporate management and managerial rule-making. This is because of corporate management's task to oversee companies, corporations, and the like. This creates management's institutional setup commonly framed as 'organisation' by The Servants of Power to eclipse and ideologically neutralise the profit-making character of companies (Klikauer 2007:144). Management's most direct expression of managerial regimes is self-invented, authoritarian, and non-democratic (Soederberg 2010:74). Hence, it incurs the self-invented image of illegitimacy. And this not because of democratic illegitimacy but because of its self-invented status of being a depoliticised entity solely constructed out of engineering science, technical, neutral, and value-free elements.[86]

This includes the self-assigned 'right to manage' and an inverted focus on itself that is found in management studies and even more so in business studies. As a result, those over which management rules – workers and employees – are by and large excluded. This sets up the managerial prerogative with perhaps Macho-Management as one of its worst modern-day expressions.

The event of modern management could only occur 'after' the 'separation of ownership and control' when a non-owning class of corporate managers displaced their capitalist predecessors, thereby creating the industrial bureaucrat with an extensive administrative apparatus.[87] These are the structural imperatives that confine corporate management to so-called 'organisational objectives' which is the code word for profits. To hide the primacy of profits, managerial language uses such terms as shareholder-value, profit-maximisation, organisational goals, competitive advantage, the Triple-Bottom Line (PPP = Profit, People, Planet), The Real Bottom Line, and many more managerial buzzwords to cloak what corporate management is really about: profit.[88] But corporate management not only works for corporations, it also works for itself because 'growth, sales, technical efficiency, a strong competitive position are at once inseparable managerial goals and the determinants of high corporate profits – which in turn are the prerequisite of high managerial income and status' (Zeitlin 1974:1096).

## The thought experiment: two versions of the corporation

Perhaps more than anything, this book is an invitation to a 'thought experiment' on a moral–philosophical discussion reaching beyond the deeply ingrained 'Hegel's corporations are different' that is commonplace in Hegel studies and to – somewhat – modernise Hegel by examining today's business corporations in the light of Hegel's *sittliche* corporations. If Hegel was correct and philosophy's task is indeed 'to comprehend our own time in thoughts', then, and this is to follow Hegel, one cannot lock corporations away as a historical factotum that only ever existed in Hegel's books.[89] Historically at least, Hegel's moral corporations did not make it even though they did exist in various forms.[90] What survived though are what we now know as today's corporations. It is the task of Hegelian philosophy to discuss these modern corporations in the light of philosophy. This might be Hegel's legacy [*Auftrag*] for today.

The aim of the book is not to present a precise organisational comparison between Hegel's *sittliche* corporations and today's corporations as Hancock and Tyler, for example, delivered in *Managing Subjectivity and the Dialectics of Self-Consciousness: Hegel and Organisational Theory* (2002). Instead, it focuses on the ethics of *Sittlichkeit* and Hegel's *sittliche* corporations. It aims to understand the basic ethical lessons gained from a discussion of Hegel's corporations and his 'system of *Sittlichkeit*' and to apply these to modern corporations. The argument presented here is somewhat similar to Socrates', Plato's, and Aristotle's moral philosophies. Their moral philosophies are not dismissed because Greek city states [the *polis*] have changed massively during the last 2,000 years. Similarly, the Hobbesian *bellum omnium contra omnes* (1651) is not dismissed because we no longer live in the state of civil war. The institutional backgrounds (slavery for Plato and Aristotle and feudalism for Hobbes) have truly changed but the lessons of their moral philosophies are still discussed today. Much closer to today, we find Hegel's 1821 writings on moral life [*Sittlichkeit*] offering moral insights even though Hegel's – like Socrates', Plato's, Aristotle's and Hobbes' – time has passed.

In order to do that, perhaps the institutional setup of today's corporations remains best depicted in Bakan's *The Corporation – The Pathological Pursuit of Profit and Power.*[91] As is often the case in Hegelian philosophy, the corporation, understood as a profit-making institution, is not what Hegel had in mind when discussing the early 19th-century *Korporation* (the corporation) in his *Philosophy of Right* (1821). To begin with, Hegel's moral corporations existed 'before' modern corporations took shape.[92] In the words of Hegelian philosopher Schmidt am Busch (2011a:233), for example, 'Hegel's term corporation does not refer to a particular historical phenomenon.' Hegel's *sittliche* corporations are not synonymous with today's business corporations. He saw the *sittliche* corporations of his day very differently.

Hegel's original concept of the corporation carried strong connotations to *Stand*, a German word that can be translated into 'status' or 'class', or, in a political context, into 'estate'; and Hegel uses this term to cut across all dialectical phases of *Sittlichkeit* according to Hegel, therefore, the political estates 'still retain in their own function the class distinctions already present in the lower sphere of civil life' (PR, 304). Class distinctions have 'familial, economic, and political significance' (Gallagher 1987:172f.). Hegel's corporations also carry connotations to associations, guilds, cooperatives, trade unions, business estates, professional associations.[93] Despite the significant differences between Hegel's *sittliche* corporations and business corporations there are also 20 strong, important, and compelling similarities (Table 1.2).

*Table 1.2* Twenty similarities between business corporations and *sittliche* corporations

| No. | Both business corporations and Hegel's moral corporations . . . |
|---|---|
| 1 | are organisations in the understanding of management studies and organisational theory, |
| 2 | are socially created by human beings participating in the corporation, |
| 3 | corporations are economic entities that fall inside the political economy, |
| 4 | are places for the production of societal necessary goods and services,[a] |
| 5 | have human beings as members solely based on labour market capabilities, |
| 6 | exclude peasants, nobility, and public servants from membership, |
| 7 | relate to the external world largely in economic but also in social terms, |
| 8 | have similar internal organisational principles, |
| 9 | develop their own culture as an internal organisational culture, |
| 10 | deal with internal conflicts between individuals and the organisation, |
| 11 | deal with the tensions between individual freedom and organisational demands, |
| 12 | have to deal with internal arrangements and external demands, |
| 13 | have to deal with the external world: society, NGOs, states, etc. |
| 14 | function at level two of Hegel's *Sittlichkeit*, i.e. both are part of civil society, |
| 15 | are part of a sub-section of civil society, namely, the economic sphere, |
| 16 | function under economic imperatives and conditions of competitiveness, |
| 17 | are overseen by the state through regulations and laws, |
| 18 | are also part of *Sittlichkeit*, |
| 19 | can also be in conflict with the moral goals of *Sittlichkeit*, and |
| 20 | include human beings and therefore are inextricably linked to ethics. |

[a] Schmidt am Busch (2011a:234).

In other words, these 20 similarities significantly counteract the rather simplistic and thought-preventing claim of some dogmatic and orthodox letter disciples [*Buchstabenschüler*] that Hegel's corporations have nothing to do with business corporations. In a way, positioning Hegel's *sittliche* corporations against business corporations can be seen as a 'thought experiment' aligned to German philosopher Theodor Adorno's (1903–1969) concept of 'making the ineffable effable'.[94] In other words, the project at hand – Hegel's *sittliche* corporation – also reflects Hegel's own idea (Schmidt 2007:18) that 'everyday, I am more convinced that theoretical work accomplishes more in the world than the practical'.[95]

While acknowledging that Hegel's 19th-century corporations carried some distinctively different features when compared to today's corporations, the strong and compelling similarities between both justify an examination of modern corporations – like any other social institution inside civil society – under Hegelian ethics as outlined in his system of

*Sittlichkeit.*[96] In addition, only by relating Hegel's *sittliche* corporations to business corporations can an assessment of the morality or *Sittlichkeit* of business corporations be made when conducted from the standpoint of Hegel's system of *Sittlichkeit.* In philosophical–dialectical thinking – what became somewhat of an urban myth shortened as 'thesis → anti-thesis → synthesis' – Hegel's *sittliche* corporation might be seen as a thesis put forward by Hegel; today's business corporation represents an anti-thesis to Hegel's *sittliche* corporation. A subsequent assessment of today's business corporations under Hegel's *Sittlichkeit* can be seen as a concluding synthesis. The key to such a 'thought experiment' remains Hegel's philosophy of *Sittlichkeit.* It is his ethics of *Sittlichkeit* under which all institutions of all societies fall – including all economic institutions such as corporations. This is irrespective of whether they existed in the 19th century or are currently in existence in the 21st century. Under Hegelian philosophy, all corporations have to be organisations dedicated to *Sittlichkeit.*

Perhaps Hegel remains the only philosopher who has ever dealt explicitly with 'the corporation' in the context of a moral system.[97] He linked his philosophy of corporations to a comprehensive system of morality enshrined in his *Sittlichkeit.*[98] After he had established the basic parameters of his philosophy in his *Phenomenology* (1807), Hegel's subsequent system of *Sittlichkeit* was outlined in his second major book: *Philosophy of Right* (1821). In it corporations are outlined in such a way that they carry significant elements of what we today call modern corporations. In order to fully appreciate Hegel's concept of corporations, one has to overcome the present understanding of corporations that has been somewhat tarnished by the imperatives of Managerialism. Once the view has been cleared from the ideologies of Managerialism, corporations can also be viewed from a different standpoint. As a moral philosopher, Hegel linked corporations to freedom and morality. These links are established in a section of his book entitled 'The Ethical System'. Hegel saw freedom to be established through his 'System der *Sittlichkeit*'.[99]

Hence, corporations are part of ethical life [*Sittlichkeit*]. In historical terms, all this comes from a time when moral philosophy and economics were not segregated entities. In historic terms, it links Hegel to, for example, Adam Smith (1723–1790). While today Adam Smith is made to appear like the Machiavellian 'Prince' of neo-liberalism, originally he was seen quite differently.[100] After all, he was a Professor of Moral Philosophy outlining morality in 'The Theory of the Moral Sentiments' (1759).[101] This is a fact that many of his apostles happily seek to neglect, diminish, and deny. While Adam Smith never addressed corporations specifically, Hegel did.[102] In line with moral philosophy, Hegel also saw the corporation as being part of an ethical life and not the other way around as today's proponents of Managerialism and corporations seek to make us believe.

In other words, Hegel, perhaps even more so than Adam Smith and Immanuel Kant, did not see morality (Kant) but *Sittlichkeit* as moral life (Hegel) as the prime philosophy under which institutions such as the law, families, states, schools, universities, and corporations exist.[103] Managerial capitalism – with the assistance of the ideology of Managerialism broadcasted by corporate mass media – has reversed this from 'morality → corporation' (ethics) to 'corporation → morality' (Managerialism). In line with today's management studies, The Servants of Power have been eager to invent catchphrases and managerial buzzwords such as corporate social responsibility to make one believe that corporations are the centre of morality (Raman & Lipschutz 2010). While The Servants of Power seek to eclipse the reality of corporations, Nobel Prize-winner Milton Friedman expressed the reality of corporations in a short but very truthful way (1970):[104]

> The social responsibility of business is to increase its profits

The real world seems to be more akin to the world of Friedman than to that of The Servants of Power. In today's real world of corporate capitalism, 'When Corporations Rule the World', corporations and profits come first while morality (Kant) and *Sittlichkeit* (Hegel) come second.[105] Morality (Smith and Kant) and *Sittlichkeit* (Hegel) have been reduced to mere add-ons, appendices, and prefixes that corporate management has taken on in order to pretend to give consideration to external community expectations of being a good corporate citizen with corporate social responsibility.[106]

Quite contrary from the dominant view on profit-maximising corporations (Friedman), Hegel's ethics sees corporations – together with families and states – as roots of ethical life [*Wurzeln der Sittlichkeit*]. Today's corporations that have next to no interest in social pathologies such as poverty – which Hegel outlines in his chapter on corporations in his *Philosophy of Right* (1821) – view poverty as an externality. In the managerial orbit of corporate management, poverty is neither created by corporations and managerial capitalism nor in any form related to both. Hegel, on the contrary, saw poverty as a pathology of a market-based economy that includes corporations.[107] Unlike today's corporate management, Hegel was concerned with this issue. Contemporary Hegelian philosopher Honneth (2007:4) argued, for example, 'that social philosophy is primarily concerned with determining and discussing processes of social development that can be viewed as misdevelopments [*Fehlentwicklungen*], disorders, or "social pathologies"'.[108] Undoubtedly, such misdevelopments, disorders, social pathologies, and 'negative consequences of capitalist development can be found inside and outside of corporate management'.[109]

The study of the role of corporations viewed from Hegel's system of *Sittlichkeit* engages an ethical perspective that examines several moral linkages. These are between Hegel's philosophy of freedom, his system of *Sittlichkeit*, corporations, corporate capitalism, and social illnesses such as precarious work arrangements, working poor, unemployment, crime, violence, alcoholism, welfare dependency, homelessness, and poverty. Today, the negative side of managerial regimes and managerial capitalism are, for example, called Organisational Pathology and 'misdevelopments [*Fehlentwicklungen*], disorders, and social pathologies'.[110] During the 19th century, many started to notice the negative impacts of 'free' markets, business organisations, and corporations. In his *Philosophy of Right* (1821), Hegel saw these as 'poverty, unemployment, and extreme inequality' (PhR, §§185, 200, 230–245). These evils cannot but evoke 'discontent and moral dissatisfaction' (Neuhouser 2011:287).

As a mechanism to deal with such social–economic ills created by corporations and by corporate capitalism, Hegel suggested the state and – more specifically – what is today called the social-welfare state. But his ethics did not exclude corporations from their 'moral duty' (Kant) in society. Corporations are part of ethical life and hence Hegel's philosophy of *Sittlichkeit* relies on the preventative role of families, corporations, and the state so that people do not enter into poverty. In short, Hegel saw corporations inside his system of ethical life structured in such a way that people are protected from becoming rabble, commoners, or a mob which Hegel termed *Pöbel*. Hence, Hegel noted:[111]

> Die Korporation als zweite Familie hat für ihre Mitglieder nicht nur die Sicherung der Subsistenz, sondern auch die Standesehre und die soziale Anerkennung zu garantieren.

With this Hegel means that 'the corporation is like a second family'. This is not to be understood in managerial ideologies such as 'we are all in one boat' and 'our company is one big (happy) family'. Under Managerialism, this invokes the following ideological equalisations: families, like corporations, are a natural given. However, this is not the case as families are socially structured whilst corporations are managerially created. Nevertheless, a conservative illusion remains that equalises corporations with families. Despite significant differences between families and corporations – families are for mutual support while corporations are for profits – a nonsensical equalisation of a father as the head of a family and a CEO as head of a corporation persists. Such an irrational equation (father = CEO) as invented by Managerialism may assist corporations ideologically but does not reflect reality and borders on the perversion of morality. One is part of an organic family while the other is on top of a managerial hierarchy designed to achieve profits (Klikauer 2014b). In short, corporations (competition and profits) are not equal to families (mutual aid). Any attempts to equalise the 'non-equalise-able' is pure ideology. The equation of 'corporations = family' is not what Hegel's philosophy is about when stating 'the corporation is like a second family'. Unlike managerial ideologies, Hegel seeks to express that both – families and corporations – are located precisely where he located them, inside ethical life [*Sittlichkeit*]. The primary role of both – families and corporations – is to enhance ethical life. 'Families, for example (along with corporations), cushion the blows that unlucky or ill-equipped participants in the market economy are bound to endure (PhR, §§238, 252)'.[112] By the term 'second' Hegel meant that the corporation is an institution that follows on from family life into the public arena. Hegel saw the family as the first step into society while corporations are part of the second level of ethics which is civil society. As outlined in his *Philosophy of Right* (1821), civil society includes the economic sphere which includes corporations. But like the first institution – families – the corporation's role remains exactly the same. It has to contribute to an ethical existence of its 'members'. Again, Hegel did not intend to say that these members are 'organisational members' in today's managerial sense as conforming, de-humanised, and de-personalised 'Organisation Men' (Whyte 1961) or as alienated 'human resources' but as members of an ethical institution.

The two final points Hegel makes in this passage of his *Philosophy of Right* (1821) are that the corporation's role is not only to secure the livelihood (subsistence) of its members (managers and employees) but also to guarantee their honour [*Standesehre*] and their social recognition.[113] The term *Standesehre* that he uses is a pre-bourgeois term originating from a pre-modern system where society was divided into *Stände*, estates, classes, and casts. It defines the social position of an individual based on either a profession, the work one did (e.g. peasant, worker), or a place one was assigned (e.g. clerical, nobility; Bürger divided individuals into bourgeois versus citoyen, and peasants) by a ruling authority.[114] Key to Hegel's use of *Standesehre*, however, is not the term *Stand* but *Ehre* meaning honour and dignity. Hegel saw corporations as one of the main institutions guaranteeing the dignity of human beings. In sharp contrast to today's managerial understanding of corporations, Hegel saw their main role not in profit-making but in providing a moral framework inside which actors can achieve ethical life [*Sittlichkeit*]. Even when discounting truly unethical corporations such as Enron, WorldCom, British Petroleum, and Exxon, the non-headline-grabbing and non-evil corporation is not what Hegel envisioned.[115] To elaborate on this in a truly Hegelian way, one needs to reflect on what has been termed 'norm versus norm' that is very different from 'fact versus fact'.

## *Sittlichkeit* and corporations: the structure of the book

To examine the critical tensions between Hegel's *sittliche* corporations and business corporations, the proceeding nine chapters are structured as follows: the introductory notes, provided in chapter 1 on Hegel's ethics of corporations, are followed by a general comparison between business corporations and Hegel's *sittliche* corporations (chapter 2). Since the academic view on corporations has been largely shaped by university scholars in the field of management studies rather than managers, chapter 3 deals with an analysis of issues, namely, the ethics of management studies itself and the position of management studies inside Hegel's system of *Sittlichkeit*. The next chapter (4) discusses 'corporations and Hegel's three ethical institutions' because Hegel's system of *Sittlichkeit* includes three societal institutions, namely, the family (level one), civil society with economics and corporations (level two), and the state (level three). Between family (below) and states (above) Hegel emphasises the institutions of civil society, economy, and corporations as being located at the second or middle level. He saw this second level as the location that creates poverty and that also encompasses those Hegel called *Pöbel* – roughly today's working poor. Chapter 4 finishes with a brief discussion on Hegel's *Pöbel* in relation to the social function of corporations. Chapter 5 extends this to two other areas of concern to corporations, namely, the Hegelian suggestion for a supervising institution that oversees corporations and Hegel's philosophy on property and investment.

To a large degree, *Sittlichkeit* relates not only to property and investment but to the internal management of corporations. The field of management studies calls this corporate governance. As a consequence, chapters 6 and 7 relate corporate governance to Hegel's ethics of

*Sittlichkeit* and discuss corporate governance in relation to Hegel's concept of 'the power of the whole'[116] and his writings on labour. Managers, just as non-managerial staff, work in corporations. Chapter 8 relates all of the above outlined issues to Hegel's overall theme of *Sittlichkeit* by focusing on Hegel's concept of 'ethical bonds', economic freedom, and Hegel's universal spirit of the *Geist*.[117] Chapter 9 concludes the book by emphasising four interrelated issues: (i) Hegelian philosophy, (ii) American ethicist and psychologist Kohlberg's scale of morality (cf. Klikauer 2014a), (iii) the role of Hegel's *sittliche* corporation and the business corporation, as well as (iv) the place both occupy in Hegel's system of *Sittlichkeit* and Kohlberg's scale of morality (Klikauer 2012, 2014c). Chapter 1 outlines some of the basic parameters of Hegel's ethics of *Sittlichkeit*.

# 2
# Modern Corporations and Hegel's Ethical Corporation

*The fate of property has become too powerful for us to tolerate reflections on it, to find its abolition thinkable.*[118]

Written about 200 years ago, the early quote of Hegel shown above demonstrates that Hegel's philosophy remains timeless. But such a claim would be highly un-Hegelian because in Hegelian terms philosophy is always linked to time. Hegel has warned us against what he called *Zeitgeist*. In Hegel's understanding, as expressed in his *Phenomenology of Spirit* (1807), *Zeitgeist* denotes something like 'the spirit of the time' or 'the spirit of the age'. It is a general cultural, intellectual, ethical, philosophical, and political climate within which certain writings and philosophies – along with a general ambience, morals, socio-cultural directions, and moods associated with an era – take place. *Zeitgeist* combines the German word *Zeit* [time] with *Geist* [spirit]. *Zeitgeist* remains best known in relation to Hegel's philosophy of history (Houlgate 2009). Nevertheless, the origins of the concept of *Zeitgeist* go back to one of Hegel's predecessors: Johann Gottfried Herder (1744–1803). In 1769, Herder introduced the word *Zeitgeist* into German (spirit of the age). For Hegel *Zeitgeist* means that one is aware of one's time but reflects critically on it in order not be asphyxiated by the spirit of that particular time and historical period. In an almost classical form of Hegelian dialectics, Hegel asks us to overcome something to which we are bound. This includes a thesis [*Zeitgeist*] and an anti-thesis in the form of reflection and overcoming of the *Zeitgeist*.

Quite apart from *Zeitgeist*, his above quoted words – the fate of property has become too powerful for us to tolerate reflections on it, to find its abolition thinkable – indicate a number of things: firstly, in a true understanding of *Zeitgeist*, Hegel was aware of the importance of property in civil society[119] and perhaps even more so for the economic sphere with corporations constituting one of the main expressions of property-owning in the form of shareholders who own the business;[120] secondly, Hegel correctly assessed the role of property in civil society and economy by stating that property has become too powerful. Perhaps the moral dilemma and trouble with property started with land-ownership as outlined by Rousseau in his *Discourse on the Origins of Inequality* (1755):[121]

> The first man who, having enclosed a piece of ground, bethought himself of saying 'this is mine', and found people simple enough to believe him, was the real founder of civil society. From how many crimes, wars, and murders, from how many horrors and misfortunes might not any one have saved mankind by pulling up the stakes or filling up the ditch.

The negative impacts of property-owning might have developed in three stages:

1. firstly as feudalism's land-owning property that had replaced the previous slave-owning society;
2. later as machinery and factories under early liberal capitalism, and
3. thereafter in the form of corporations under corporate capitalism.[122]

The economic importance of land-ownership under feudalism marks the development of land as property 'before' capitalism made land-owning secondary to factory-ownership. Hegel saw the rising importance of property as a 'fate' which carries highly negative connotations in its original use. German writers would always see fate as something unavoidable that impacts negatively on human beings. Hence, the 'fate of property' indicates that something negative is attached to property such as Rousseau's 'many crimes, wars, and murders [and] how many horrors and misfortunes'. In Hegelian dialectics, one might argue, it is not only human beings who own property but also property that 'owns' human beings.

In other words, 'property thus results from a mental act' because a person assigns a will to a thing converting this thing into a possession or property.[123] But this assignment of a will to a thing works both ways. It is property that enforces its will onto human beings, for example, through the need to protect this property. In the case of corporations, this is the force of investing in it for ROI, the return on investment, only to re-invest it as an endless and mindless treadmill. This is a very Hegelian thought because it shows the dialectical relationship between individuals and property. Perhaps one of the clearest expressions of this aspect of Hegelian philosophy has been made by one of 20th century's key philosophers working in the critical tradition of Hegelian philosophy, namely, the German social-philosopher Erich Fromm (1900–1980). Hegelian philosophy expressed in the quote above may have been brought to perfection in Fromm's work on *To Have or To Be?* (1995).

Hegel also tells us that this fate has become too powerful. In other words, property and the belief in property are too dominant in society.[124] In turn this also means that we should find ways to reverse the pathological belief in property as invented by Managerialism, corporations, and corporate capitalism and sustained by corporate mass media. Perhaps most importantly, the blinding faith in property has also affected human thinking and this in a highly undesirable way. Once an aspect of society such as, for example, property has become so powerful that it no longer tolerates reflections, 20th-century Neo-Hegelian philosopher Adorno's words become very appropriate:[125]

> There is no right way to live in a false world.

If a world disallows reflection because of a pathological belief in property, it is a false world. It also means that if the power of ideology as engineered by corporate mass media and Managerialism has become so powerful that any reflection on property has become impossible, philosophy is needed because it makes us aware of this and reflects on it. It also means that the quasi-academic field of management studies, for example, needs to reflect on the non-reflective. So far it has deliberately avoided reflecting on property because management studies represent a system-stabilising critique (if at all) from within but never about property. It is merely an ideology. Finally, Hegel's strongest emphasis on this comes in the form of 'to find its abolition thinkable'. This, for example, means that a book, perhaps one written from the perspective of Hegelian philosophy on corporations advocating, for example, the abolition of corporations, has been made unthinkable by the prevailing paradigm of Managerialism. It can only exist outside of the one-dimensional paradigm of management studies. Today, management studies – and society as a whole – have been made to reach obscene levels of conformity, non-critique, and non-reflection.[126] This no longer allows reflections on an institution that owns substantial property: the corporation. As a consequence, almost any suggestion towards abolishing corporations has been eliminated and Marcuse's one-dimensional thinking has become reality (1966). In line of that, Hegel's initial statement leads to two things:

1. It highlights the hegemonic power of corporate mass media and Managerialism that has made reflections, and even more so the mere thought of abolition of property and corporations, unthinkable. This is the triumph of one-dimensional thinking.
2. It also shows that once reflection on property has been made impossible and advocating the abolition of corporations has been rendered intolerable, Managerialism has established a totalitarian society in which non-reflection is rewarded.

This leads to the death of reflection, critical philosophy, critique, and eventually thought itself. But it also annihilates ethics as such and Hegel's *Sittlichkeit*.[127] Hegel's philosophy of *Sittlichkeit* depends on an open debate that is not restricted by whatever Managerialism and management studies deem permitted to be reflected on. It demands the exact opposite by encouraging reflections on property and, if necessary, advocating its abolition. The way such an open debate can occur has, for example, been outlined by 20th-century Hegelian philosopher Habermas (1997). His communicative philosophy denotes the concepts of communicative action and ideal speech (Klikauer 2008). This secures civil society against totalitarian threats such as the denial of thinking, the enforcement and rewarding of unthinkable issues, and reflecting on those taboos. The elimination of reflection on those issues that have been declared a taboo by those in a hegemonic power position (e.g. Managerialism and management studies) destroys Hegel's 'System der *Sittlichkeit*'. These managerial institutions have become ideological institutions that enhance one-dimensional, totalitarian thinking resulting in totalitarianism in its last consequence. Instead of that, Hegel's philosophy of freedom and his three-level 'System der *Sittlichkeit*' are specifically set up to prevent the one-dimensional and totalitarian thinking that has been engineered by corporations and Managerialism.[128]

Hegel's sphere of *Sittlichkeit* comprises three elements, namely, family, civil society, and state. Corporations are located at the second level which is sub-divided into a civil and an economic sub-sphere. Inside the second sub-sphere of level two, political or preferably social economics [*wohlfahrtsstaatliche Ökonomie*][129] as Hegel would say, we find companies, firms, business enterprises, holdings, joint ventures, trusts, cartels, and of course Hegel's *Korporation* – the moral corporation.[130] Hegel's philosophical and today's modern corporations have their origins in the first half of the 19th century. This was the time when the legal system began to support corporations with a statutory framework that was and still is based on a fiction, namely, the idea that business corporations are legal persons. Roughly 150 years after that invention and the legal certification of corporations, Korton (1995) formulated the following question: 'When [do] Corporations Rule the World?' His question has long been answered (Rowland 2006). Recently, 51 out of the top 100 economic entities were corporations: Exxon Corporation, for example, was bigger than Denmark![131] Exxon Corporation, like any other corporation, is managed by corporate managers as individuals and by management as an institution covered by Managerialism as an ideology.[132]

Corporations and corporate management can be viewed from several perspectives: historical, anthropological, legal, economic, sociological, neo-liberal, environmental, Marxist, cultural, political, managerial, philosophical, and ethical.[133] Hegel's perspective on ethics as outlined in his *Sittlichkeit* views corporations from a moral or ethical perspective. Hegel engaged the question of corporations at a philosophical, moral, and systematic level.[134] He remains the only philosopher ever to examine the morality of corporations at the dawn of their existence (Hegel 1821).[135] The ethical view of examining modern corporations from the standpoint of Hegel's *Sittlichkeit* is very much in line with the recent argument made by Italian Neo-Hegelian philosopher Alfredo Ferrarin (2011:435–436):

> What matters in the study of the ancients is thus not so much the degree of fidelity and authenticity with which we reconstruct past philosophies, but rather the relation between our own philosophy and its time [and] the history of philosophy for Hegel, is thus not a matter of retrieving givens, but of engaging in a living exchange with our predecessors.

Hence, the argument on the morality of corporations is not about a precise interpretation of a historical reconstruction of the exact configuration of Hegel's corporation of his time. In the words of American political scientist Fatton (1986:582), 'He [Hegel] knew that his philosophy was the philosophy of his age, the age of capitalism [and] that every individual is a child of his time; so philosophy too is its own time apprehended in thoughts.' In other words, Fatton's age of capitalism has not passed, even though 19th-century liberal capitalism has transformed itself into corporate capitalism. Hence, Hegel's examination of corporations as conducted in his *Philosophy of Right* (1821) was a study of corporations of Hegel's time. Equally, a study of today's corporations is necessarily a study of corporations of today's time.

The ethical corporation of Hegel's time as outlined in his 'System der *Sittlichkeit*' was a moral concept of corporations of Hegel's time. A discussion of today's corporations within the moral concept of Hegel's system of *Sittlichkeit* has to have today's corporations at its centre, not Hegel's corporations of the early 19th century. Simultaneously, if Hegel's statement 'philosophy too is its own time apprehended in thoughts' is correct, a study of modern corporations has to produce a philosophy apprehended in thoughts of today's time. As a consequence, Hegelian philosophy demands an examination of today's corporations from the standpoint of philosophy when it seeks to be a philosophical study. It cannot merely be a historical account of Hegelian corporations of the early 19th century. As a result, Hegel's *Sittlichkeit* has to be applied to modern corporations, not to the historical configurations of early 19th-century corporations. The ethical corporation Hegel had in mind was quite different from today's business corporations. These early corporations were not equal to today's corporations as many Hegel experts have pointed out.[136] There is no 'corporation = corporation' formula in historical–philosophical terms. For this reason, many scholars of Hegelian philosophy have correctly pointed out what Wallace (1999:431) has expressed as follows:

> These Korporationen are not profit-making enterprises but more like trade associations, unions, churches, and municipalities; self-governing participatory organisations that aim to include a whole sector of the society and to provide welfare services to its members.

The project of examining modern corporations under the conditions of Hegel's *Sittlichkeit* is not designed to follow what Hegelian philosopher Dieter Henrich (1971:215) called being a letter-disciple of Hegel [*Buchstabenschüler Hegels*]. Instead of surgically dissecting every nuance of every word in Hegel's original texts, the aim of discussing modern corporations from the standpoint of Hegel's *Sittlichkeit* is to retrieve Hegel's thoughts and philosophies on corporations in order to 'engage in a living exchange with them' (Ferrarin 2011). In line with that, it is an application of Hegel's philosophy of *Sittlichkeit* to the business corporation. In the words of British philosopher Zygmunt Bauman (1987), such a project is more reflective of being a 'legislator' than being merely an 'interpreter' of Hegel's thoughts. Instead of interpreting Hegelian philosophy, it is used 'legislatively' so that business corporations can be measured against Hegel's *Sittlichkeit*. To achieve this, the best place to start is the beginning of what today is called the corporation.

Initially, corporations were off to a bad start when the British East India Company was set up on 31 December 1600 (Robins 2006). This first ever corporation came to symbolise the dazzlingly rich potential of corporations. But it also symbolised the new methods of business that are both brutal and exploitive. Modern corporations followed the footsteps of the infamous East India Company. The birth of present-day corporations dates back to a more recent time. These are the early days of Hegel's 19th century when the Boston Manufacturing Company of 1813 constituted the first significant American industrial corporation. By 1819, the US Supreme Court granted corporations a plethora of rights they had not previously enjoyed. In 1886, the US Supreme Court ended the childhood period of corporations by granting them the status of full legal persons.[137] With that, corporations were protected by the 14th Amendment of the US Constitution. From then on corporations had 'rights to due process of law and equal protection of the laws'.[138] In short, the first contractions leading to the birth of corporations coincided with a time when Hegel constructed his philosophy of *Sittlichkeit*. While US forms of corporations transmuted into what we know corporations to be today, continental concepts of corporations differed vastly from that. For example, Hegel's contemporary Eduard Gans noted:

> The varieties of worker's corporations that emerged in early-nineteenth-century France . . . these corporations were no longer hierarchically organised jurandes or maîtres controlled by masters but were societies or associations composed exclusively of workers.[139]

In other words, the history of corporations is not as linear as Managerialism tries to make it out. In line with that, one needs to remember that Hegel's concept of the corporation as outlined in his 'System der *Sittlichkeit*' diverged from what we today know corporations to be.[140] By the time of Hegel's writings, only a very limited number of business corporations existed but these, nevertheless, carried features of today's corporations. Hegel examined these organisations at the dawn of a new age, the age of capitalism and modernity. He did so largely from the writings of the early economists, economic reports, early business-oriented magazines, and newspapers. In Hegel's philosophy, however, corporations merged with socio-economic institutions resembling something like a guild [*Zunft*] while not constituting a *geschlossene Zunft* – a closed association.[141] Nevertheless, Hegel's corporations are, like today's corporations, positioned between family and state.[142] And they represent, like today's corporations, selfishness, economic egoism, and all the excesses and pathologies Hegel attributed to them.[143]

This made it necessary for Hegel to see corporations inside a comprehensive *Sittlichkeit* that included states, civil societies, and families. In short and despite some significant differences between Hegel's *sittliche* corporations and today's business corporations, at a more fundamental level, Hegel's concept of the corporation was right on the mark. He correctly outlined many of the key characteristics of the modern corporation. In Kantian terms, Hegel correctly described what a corporation is (Kant's 'what is').[144] But Hegelian corporations also included Kant's philosophy of 'what ought to be'. His corporations are not, for example, cooperatives.[145] Retrospectively, Hegel correctly emphasised, 'it is the task of our time to build corporations'.[146]

Hegel's interest in the corporation was a result of his study of the leading writers of economic thought during his time.[147] These included the British–Scottish Enlightenment thinkers James Steuart (1770), Adam Ferguson, David Hume, David Ricardo, and above all a professor of moral philosophy by the name of Adam Smith.[148] Even during the rise of liberal capitalism and industrialism of the 18th- and mid-19th centuries, many early for-profit organisations carried defining characteristics of what corporations were to become: today's multinational business corporations. In many ways, these early corporations, especially corporations like the British East India Company (1600–1874), were always linked to what was then called imperialism and what has been re-framed as globalisation under Managerialism and neo-liberalism.[149]

Then, as today, corporations – not only the British East India Company – remain business institutions of a national as well as a global economy. But they are also part of ethics because economic actors such as corporations and corporate management impact on human beings in numerous ways and thus engage in morality (Kant) and *Sittlichkeit* (Hegel).[150] Once an action affects human beings, inevitably ethics is involved. Despite the best efforts of Managerialism and management studies, and those Baritz (1960; Brief 2000) has termed The Servants of Power, there is no escaping from this (Singer 1994). The linkage between human beings, management, and ethics cannot be explained away as a mere externality as Managerialism and management studies have it. Nevertheless, the relationship between corporations and morality may be described as[151] corporations need morality but morality does not need corporations.

As such, ethics, and with it Hegelian ethics, is linked to corporations which in turn are linked to the economic system in which corporations operate. Hegel's 19th-century terminology of the 'system of needs' describes what is today called political economy.[152] In Hegel's economic arrangement of a 'system of needs', he viewed the satisfaction of human needs and corporations as entities of a sub-sphere attached to civil society. Contemporary Hegel expert Herzog[153] noted, 'civil society for Hegel includes the "system of needs", the "administration of justice", and the "police and corporations"'. In other words, Hegel's economic sphere which is part of civil society includes non-economic actors and economic actors such as corporations that together constitute civil society. To view corporations from the Hegelian perspective of his *Sittlichkeit*, four issues are immediately relevant:

1. **Hegel's corporation and today's business corporation**
   Hegel's understanding of

> the corporation [*Korporation*] applies especially to the business class, since this class is concentrated on the particularities of social existence and the corporation has the function of bringing implicit similarities between various private interests into explicit existence in forms of association. This is not the same as our contemporary business corporation but rather a voluntary association of persons based on occupational or various social interests such as professional and trade guilds.'[154]

On this, Schmidt am Busch (2011:78) noted, 'when using the expression "corporation", Hegel does not refer to a particular historical phenomenon. Thus his theory of corporations cannot be read as a plea for the social rehabilitation of corporations.' Perhaps, in Hegel's and Schmidt am Busch's view, corporations are beyond rehabilitation. On the other hand, Ross (2008b:47f.) noted Hegel's 'prescriptive mode for the role of the corporation in the economy . . . that is still applicable today'. He also noted that Hegel's corporation was

> rooted in the 19th century legal reality and bears little similarity to what we today call a corporation . . . Hegel considered the corporation not as a single business entity, but as representing

> the interests of all of the members of a special kind of industry. (Ross 2008b:55f.)

Two aspects need to be clarified: firstly, the legal and managerial configurations of today's corporations are not equal to the Gestalt of Hegel's corporation: there is no A = B; secondly, today's corporations are not a historical continuation of Hegel's corporations. Also, today's corporations did not develop out of the Hegelian concept: there is no A → B. Nevertheless, six arguments need to be made in favour of viewing today's corporations from the perspective of Hegelian *Sittlichkeit*:
Table 2.1 shows six arguments in favour of viewing business corporations from the standpoint of Hegel's system of *Sittlichkeit*. A concurrent view is also found in a plan devised by one of Hegel's main predecessors, namely, German philosopher Gottfried Wilhelm Leibniz (1646–1716).[155] Hegelian philosopher Hans Heinz Holz (1968:22, 24) who investigated the philosophical continuities between Leibniz and Hegel noted,

> In einem sehr frühen Plan [Leibniz] ist die allmähliche Überführung der Productionsstätten in die Hand einer ohne Profit tätigen Genossenschaft vorgesehen, insofern alle technischen Erfindungen eben nicht mehr privater Nutzung überlassen, sondern einer solchen Genossenschaft übertragen werden sollen.

In other words, while shareholder-value and profit-maximisation are the only guiding principle for today's corporate management, Hegel's 17th-century predecessor Leibniz advocated a gradual transfer of production-related facilities [*Produktionsstätten*] into the hands

*Table 2.1* Hegel's *sittliche* corporations and his system of *Sittlichkeit*

| No. | Descriptions and arguments |
|---|---|
| 1 | Corporations are part of the economic system of capitalism (Hegel's system of needs). |
| 2 | They are part of Hegel's institution of civil society. |
| 3 | They are not part of Hegel's first moral institution (families). |
| 4 | They are not part of Hegel's third institution (states). |
| 5 | They are part of Hegel's *Sittlichkeit*. |
| 6 | This demands that both can be examined from Hegel's ethics of *Sittlichkeit* because the moral imperatives of ethical life apply to all institutions and all corporations in exactly the same way. |

of non-profit cooperatives. Even technological inventions should not be used for private profit gains but should be assigned to such cooperatives. These ideas can be found in Hegel's concept of corporations which are not designed as 'profit-making machines' but as institutions that mirror the ethics of *Sittlichkeit*.[156]

2. **The corporation's external and internal ethical affairs**
Corporations are part of an economic structure and of civil society. In the words of Hegelian philosopher Schmidt am Busch (2011:78), 'Corporations . . . are essentially responsible for structuring the sphere of production.'[157] Viewed from the perspective of corporate management, corporations engage with two spheres: internal and external. This concerns business ethics as well as management ethics. The former deals primarily with a corporation's external relations (suppliers, customers, markets, communities, NGOs, state regulation, trade unions, etc.) while management ethics focuses on internal affairs (e.g. managerial regimes) such as employees, middle- and line-management, departmental structures (marketing, accounting, Human Resource Management [HRM], operations management), functionalities (multi-divisional corporations, geographical structures, etc.), hierarchies, and so on.[158]

3. **Corporate management and corporate governance**
When a corporation's internal relationships are examined from the philosophical–ethical perspective of *Sittlichkeit*, management ethics, for example, deals with issues such as the morality of corporate governance. Corporate governance is commonly seen as a set of processes, customs, policies, laws, and institutions affecting the way corporations are directed, administered, or controlled. The *Financial Times Lexicon* (lexicon.ft.com) defines it as follows:

> Managers are paid professionals with their own self interests. In order to prevent managers from making decisions that benefit themselves but that are detrimental to others, a system of checks and balances is put in place. This system is called 'corporate governance'. At a minimum, governance systems include a board of directors (to hire, fire, and compensate management) and an external auditor (to make sure financial statements are accurate). Other constituents such as creditors, customers, suppliers, labour unions, the media, and regulators also play a role in corporate governance by making sure that management behaves appropriately.

The World Bank's International Finance Corporation notes, 'Corporate governance refers to the structures and processes for the direction and control of companies.'[159] This means that when corporate management and the institution of corporate governance direct and control corporations, they also direct and control the morality of corporations.

### 4. The corporation and Sittlichkeit

Corporations and their external relationships need to be placed in Hegel's holistic 'System der *Sittlichkeit*' (1803/4). *Sittlichkeit* is a uniquely Hegelian concept exceeding Kant's individualistic formalism of, for example, categorical imperatives.[160] Unlike Kant's individualistic notion of morality, Hegel's *Sittlichkeit* combines philosophy, ethics, economy, and society.[161] Hegel has distinguished his non-individual morality of the societal ethical life as *Sittlichkeit* in his *Phenomenology* (1807). In his second major book, the *Philosophy of Right* (1821), Hegel described the institutional configurations, structure, and role corporations play inside his *Sittlichkeit* [System der *Sittlichkeit*] in more detail. Like all other societal institutions, corporations too 'have a role to play in the moral development of their members', noted Hegelian philosopher Cullen (1988:29) correctly. Positioning corporations inside a philosophical–ethical perspective raises the immediate question: can corporations have ethics at all? Economist Milton Friedman (1970), for example, thought that

> corporate executives' responsibility is . . . to make as much money as possible while conforming to their basic rules of the society, both those embodied in law and those embodied in ethical custom . . . adding . . . the only entities who can have responsibilities are individuals . . . A business cannot have responsibilities. So the question is, do corporate executives, provided they stay within the law, have responsibilities in their business activities other than to make as much money for their stockholders as possible? And my answer to that is, no, they do not.[162]

In other words, when viewed from a neo-liberal, pro-business, and managerial perspective, because it is just individuals inside corporations who are morally responsible.[163] Arguments like this have been used by management, management studies, and Managerialism to relinquish moral responsibility in a MADD-like fashion – moral attention deficit disorder.[164] As a consequence, morality has been made to appear as a question of individual managers, not of management or the corporation (e.g. Johnson 2012). Viewed from the sociological structure versus agency theory, this means that management studies and Managerialism have displaced ethics from management (structure) to individuals (agency) and thereby relieve management from its moral obligations. This might be successful in rhetorical and ideological terms by setting up managerial belief-systems but it does not work in reality (Klikauer 2007, 2008). Inside such managerial belief-systems as engineered by Managerialism, cases like Enron, World.Com, Bernie Madoff's Ponzi-scheme, Exxon Valdez, Shell's Brent Spar, Nike's sweatshops, Nestlé's baby formula deaths, Thalidomide, BP's oil spill, Union Carbide's Bhopal, the infamous textbook case of Ford Pinto, and many more have nothing to do with corporations (Benson 2012). The immoralities above are due to individuals. On the other side of the same coin there is a more comprehensive view. It does not artificially segregate individuals from the institutions they shape, administer, run, and manage. In the words of one of the founding fathers of modern management (Fayol 1916): management's task is to 'plan, organise, command, delegate, and control'. As much as Managerialism and its loyal servants in management studies seek to pretend that corporations are merely technical, well-engineered, and machine-like institutions that have nothing to do with ethics, since institutions such as corporations always involve human beings, these institutions are inevitably linked to morality and ethics. They remain socially constructed entities. Human beings have invented, constructed, assembled, bought and sold, and dissembled corporations. As such, corporations can never exist independent of, outside, next to, separated from, or apart of the imperatives of moral philosophy.

## Corporations and philosophy's love of wisdom

A perspective that is not outright pro-business, somewhat less ideological, does not set up fake belief-systems, is not linked to Managerialism, and does not serve a managerial agenda comes from a philosophical–ethical perspective. This is a perspective aligned to the very tradition of philosophy. Philosophy originated in 'philosophia' from the Greek φιλοσοφία meaning love of wisdom. In Hegelian philosophy, for example, philosophy's love of wisdom is seen as the purest form of thinking because it exists only for itself and serves nobody. In this perspective, moral philosophy is not just another idea that can be appropriated to support management. As a consequence, there are two totally diverging answers to the initial question raised above 'can corporations have morals?' One is managerial–ideological and one is philosophical–ethical.

Contemporary American business ethics philosopher Peter A. French (1979), for example, sees corporations in the following way: 'Corporations came into being through a legal fantasy that assumes corporations are like a legal person.'[165] In other words, if corporations want to be like a legal person, that is, like human beings, they also carry human ethics. Corporations cannot have the one without the other. Once business institutions like corporations have been separated from morality, severe pathologies emerge. Historically, the quest of being awarded legal person status gave corporations a human-like character that inextricably links corporations to human ethics. The granting of this, as demanded by corporations, links the human invention of corporations to a legal framework that underwrites the existence of corporations. In other words, capitalism needed to give corporations a human appearance in order to make them functional – buying and selling – but when it comes to the human concept of ethics, corporations and their Servants of Power seek to make us believe that corporations can suddenly be taken out of the equation.

In short, The Servants of Power want to have it both ways: corporations are like a legal person with human-like qualities (buying and selling) but they should not have the human quality of morality. For decades, Managerialism has tried consistently to portray corporations as somehow outside of human morality. Only an ideology like Managerialism seems to be able to cover up obvious contradictions like these. 'Hegel, by contrast, contends that these contradictions provide positive insights into reality.'[166] Highlighting these contradictions brings to light the internal contradictions of Managerialism and corporations. But neither Managerialism nor management studies are interested in 'providing positive insights into reality'. Their interest is not truth and philosophy's love of wisdom (philo- and -sophy) but the advancement of management directed towards The Real Bottom Line. Hence, Managerialism – with the assistance of management studies – represents an ideology that seeks to eliminate contradictions relinquishing the interest in truth and wisdom.

By doing so, management studies transform themselves from pretending to be a 'science' into being an ideology. It comes as no surprise that ideologies like that have accompanied management ever since it left the simple and narrow confinements of being merely the administration of factories which itself is no more than an advanced version of the overseer's whip of the 18th and 19th century.[167] With the historical rise of management and corporations came the rise of Managerialism and management studies as paralleling ideologies supporting management. Since the rise of industrial, managerial, and eventually corporate capitalism, most if not all modern legal systems are supportive of corporate capitalism by giving corporations a person-like legal status. This has been done despite the fact that corporations – unlike real people – are not naturally born and never die a natural death.[168] Instead of a human birth–maturity–death trajectory, the corporate mantra is rather eternal and dedicated to the infinite growth paradigm with grow, grow, grow, both in size and in market share. According to Rowland (2006:99),

> There is no ultimate limit to corporate size, no ideal number, though it is often in the corporation's interest to stop short of achieving full monopoly power in order to maintain the fiction of market competitiveness. This is done for both ideological and regulatory reasons. As long as the company can argue that its market remains free, it can credibly fend off public indignation and regulatory backlash, each of which has the potential to damage profits.

But the legal fiction has serious consequences. Like real people, corporations can buy and sell commodities and property, hire and fire employees, commit moral and immoral acts, and have legal obligations which can be limited. The business form of 'Ltd', for example, has been invented to limit a corporation's liability. Corporate managers like to extend these limited liabilities to morality in what became known as MADD, moral silence, moral deafness, moral blindness, and moral amnesia.[169] Despite the legal fiction, the status of corporations as economic business organisations has real consequences and carries real moral responsibilities. In short, and this is despite the best efforts of management studies and Managerialism, corporations remain part of the economy, society, and ethics. In general ethics, as expressed in Hegel's *Sittlichkeit*, these three are inextricably linked and, as a consequence, corporations can only exist inside the arena of morality.

Nevertheless, 'corporations and morality' are two sets of ideas that, at least in the mind of many, are hard to unify. And this is not a recent phenomenon. Already during Hegel's time, many did not see for-profit corporations as having ethical norms as their foundation. The superiority of profits over ethics remained unchanged during the course of the 20th century. If anything, the concentration in corporate ownership continued relentlessly. 'In 20th century America, for example, 90 percent of all corporate stock was held by 10 percent of shareholders while the top 1 percent of shareholders owned half of all stock. Almost all of these large shareholders are other corporations, such as pension funds, mutual funds, and insurance companies. Only a very few are individuals' (Rowland 2006:105). The high degree of corporate ownership of other corporations is seen by many as an ethical problem in itself. The concentration or near monopoly of corporate-to-corporate ownership limits not only market freedom and the freedom to own property, but also freedom in general. Being the philosopher of the 'ethics of freedom', Hegel highlighted the dilemma of 'corporations versus ethics'. In Hegelian philosophy, only one is geared towards achieving human freedom.[170] Just one example can demonstrate this: Hegel's *Sittlichkeit* is a system that is enacted by participants in the full conscious of their actions. On the other hand, 'the economic law of markets [of which corporations are a part] operates behind the backs of all without being enacted by anyone'.[171] As a consequence of Hegel's awareness of market capitalism and corporations, he faced a serious dilemma between two opposing entities:

(a) corporations based on shareholder-value and profit-maximisation and
(b) society based on moral values, which Hegel called *Sittlichkeit*.[172]

To solve this dilemma, Hegelian ethics would, first of all, distinguish between economic freedom – the freedom to engage in business, free markets, competition – and human freedom.[173] The second freedom is the freedom of self-determination which remains a key term of Kantian philosophy pre-dating Hegelian philosophy. Hegel took Kant's philosophy on. But he also expanded it to self-actualisation that carries societal connotations and demands towards the actualisation of freedom, that is, a real movement towards what Kant had called 'Kingdom of Ends' and Hegel calls *Sittlichkeit*.[174] In Hegelian philosophy, human freedom also means the absence of alienation and the overcoming of the 'master–slave' dialectics.[175] Hegelian philosophy would view work relationships under corporate managerial regimes as 'master–slave' relationships.[176] This remains Hegel's most famous section in his *Phenomenology* (1807) and is the key to understand work relations in modern business organisations. Historically, Hegel's recognition of a master–slave relationship [*Herr und Knecht*] originated in the philosophy of Gottfried Wilhelm Leibniz (1646–1716).[177] Leibniz called it 'lord and bondsman'.[178] German Hegelian philosopher Siep (1979:252) noted,

> What Hegel's theory of recognition most certainly excludes is exploitation in the sense of a lordship and bondage relationship.[179]

But this builds exactly the key of all managerial regimes. According to British philosopher Jameson, Hegel's philosophy of a struggle between master and slave is 'surely the first time in the history of philosophy in which the problem of the Other is thematised as such'.[180] Hegel's master–slave dialectics remains imperative for his philosophy of freedom because his philosophical concept of freedom can never accept that 'human beings are subservient to strangers'.[181] In his *Philosophy of Right* (1821), Hegel noted, 'Freedom is only by itself when nothing but freedom refers to itself and when everything that creates dependence falls away.'[182] In other words, Hegel's freedom can only flourish when it depends on nothing but itself. Business corporations, however, engineer the opposite – a dependency on management.

The destructive pathologies that reside in dependencies of Hegel's freedom in modern economies have not gone unnoticed. Perhaps the single most influential introduction to Hegel's master and slave dialectics remains the one from Russian–French philosopher Alexandre Kojève (1902–1968). Kojève (1947) saw the master–slave opposition as an 'inscription of class struggle'.[183] Kojève and most other Hegelian philosophers place a somewhat higher currency on Hegel's master–slave dialectics. Not surprisingly, it remains the single most important, referenced, quoted, and discussed part of Hegel's *Phenomenology* (1807). Whatever the correct assessment of Hegel's work on *Herr und Knecht* may be, it has withstood the critique of time showing an alluring permanency. Hegel's work on master and slave is highly relevant to today's corporations. In corporate terms, the master–slave dialectics is shown in the continuing existence of management on the one side and what management calls non-managerial staff on the other.

Today, corporations do not represent Hegel's exact words as there are neither lords nor bondsmen in corporations. Nevertheless, the fundamentals of what Hegel had outlined continue to exist, albeit with different names. The predecessor of a business administrator was a factory overseer (of Satanic Mills)[184] while the predecessor of today's management was administration. The administrative origins of today's management can still be seen in the title of the prime management degree issued by management schools – the MBA: Master of Business 'Administration'. Meanwhile in the non-managerial side of corporations, labourers became workers who were converted into employees and eventually human resources and human capital.[185] Despite a multitude of name-changes, the underlying structural and asymmetrical relationship remained unchallenged. Perhaps Hegel's master–slave relationship is a case of an Orwellian notion. According to George Orwell (1949:210), 'From the point of view of the low, no historic change has ever meant much more than a change in the name of their masters.' This is manifested in the clear-cut division between management and non-managerial staff/employees and in hierarchies depicted in every organisational chart of every corporation and in the power relationships that work inside corporations.[186]

Despite the frequent name-changes paralleled by the continuous relevance of Hegel's master–slave dialectics, Hegelian ethics would always insist on placing human beings and human freedom at the centre from which guiding principles for ethical life [*Sittlichkeit*] emanate. In contrast, corporations are based on managerial thinking, instrumental rationality, and what contemporary Hegelian philosopher Kersting (1988L:3) calls selfish calculations [*selbstsüchtiger Kalkulationen*]. The German term *selbstsüchtig* is particularly interesting. It is a merger of two words: *selbst* and *süchtig*. The former means self while the latter is the more interesting term, meaning addiction. In other words, *selbstsüchtig* means an illness, a kind of pathological addiction to oneself. Once combined, the true pathological character of selfish calculations comes to light. In management, such selfish calculations are enshrined in means–ends, cost–benefit, the bottom line, cost-cutting, efficiency, value-adding, downsizing, outsourcing, shareholder-values, and profit-maximisation, all of which are designed to further the managerial self and this, according to Kersting (1988L:3), is a pathological illness.

In Hegelian philosophy, *Sittlichkeit* represents the extreme opposite to selfish calculations. *Sittlichkeit* is the place where Hegel links corporations, economy, and civil society to ethics (1821). As a consequence, the original Kantian but also Hegelian concept of moral duties applies to corporations and corporate management and to all spheres of Hegelian *Sittlichkeit*. There are moral duties of members of families, of society, and of corporations. Hence, 'corporate members acquire duties towards fellow members, such as the corporate provisions of welfare' (Cullen 1988:32). The ethical concept that corporate members have moral duties to one another based on their membership in a corporation is extremely alien to corporate management. But it is even more abhorrent to corporate management to include 'corporate provisions of welfare' in such moral duties. Welfare is something seen as an externality by corporate management, viewed as an issue belonging to the sphere of states but not to the sphere of corporations. Nevertheless, Hegel's *Sittlichkeit* advocates the exact opposite to what corporate management has in mind when confronted with terms such as moral duty and welfare. Secondly, a moral understanding of these terms is contradictory to the managerially defined duty of corporate employees in the understanding of management. Kantian and Hegelian duties are always 'moral' duties and as such they clash with the 'organisational' duties as invented and prescribed by corporate management. In other words, this is the precise location where two norms collide: moral–ethical duties versus organisational–managerial duties. Corporations are where these two norms meet.

As a consequence, an investigation into modern corporations from the perspective of Hegel's *Sittlichkeit* is not about 'fact versus fact' that place one empirical fact against another. It is not about, for example, factually destructive corporations versus factually non-destructive ones. Secondly, it is also not about 'norm versus fact' that places a norm against a fact. A 'norm versus fact' investigation, for example, would place normative aspects such as Hegel's philosophy of ethical life [*Sittlichkeit*] against facts (e.g. corporate misbehaviour, corruption, white collar crime, or environmental destruction; Benson 2012). Instead of these two options this investigation places the norms of Hegelian philosophy against the norms of corporations. As such, it is about 'norm versus norm' because it is concerned with corporate norms such as shareholder-value and profit-maximisation, The Real Bottom Line, competition, and 'Competitive Advantage' (Porter 1985). The corporate norm of The Real Bottom Line is set against another norm, the ethical norm of Hegelian *Sittlichkeit*. In short, a philosophical investigation into 'Hegelian *Sittlichkeit* and the modern corporation' represents a philosophical engagement with two norms: corporate norms versus moral norms. This is underpinned by the recognition that Hegel remains perhaps the only philosopher who systematically engaged with corporations placing them inside his 'System der *Sittlichkeit*'. To achieve that, he developed clear parameters for his *sittliche* corporation.

For Hegel the primary image of a corporation is not a profit-generating machine (e.g. Milton Friedman 1970) but a moral institution. Hence, a corporation should be an institution that guarantees social recognition [*soziale Anerkennung*] of its members.[187] This denotes that the corporation sees itself primarily as a social–moral actor rather than a business entity. Corporations exist inside an ethical system that is part of life in general. In Hegel's own words, corporations are an organ of the general society.[188] Therefore, one of corporation's moral tasks is to enhance the system of ethical life. Hegel's concept of ethical life consists of a number of social institutions one of which is the corporation. In Hegel's *Sittlichkeit*, corporations exist within and as an organic part [*ein Glied*,

Hegel] of civil society. As such, civil society is not merely an externality as Managerialism has it. Instead, there is a moral and organic relationship between corporations, the economic sphere, civil society, and *Sittlichkeit*.

This also means that Hegel's *Sittlichkeit* does not leave any space for 'corporate social responsibility' (CSR). CSR is of one of the newest 'management fashions' (Abrahamson 1996). It fits well into the managerial orbit, the ideology of Managerialism, and corporations because CSR represents no 'clear and present' danger to corporations. For CSR, the moral responsibility of corporations does not originate in society, in moral philosophy, or in Hegel's *Sittlichkeit* (May et al. 2007). CSR is not based on moral philosophy. There is no overarching moral structure, moral theory, and moral philosophy. Instead, CSR is a corporation-centred view aligned to management and Managerialism and lacking the credibility of moral philosophy. It is not Managerialism's idea that corporations have a moral responsibility towards civil society even when such a 'moral' responsibility is reduced to a mere 'social' responsibility and morality is devalued to merely being 'a' responsibility among others. For Hegel, it is not Managerialism's 'corporations → CSR → society' but '*Sittlichkeit* → corporations'. Norm-setting institutions are *Sittlichkeit* setting moral norms. By contrast, corporations can never be such norm-setting institutions. Corporations exist under this. *Sittlichkeit* defines the corporation, not the other way around. In Hegel's philosophy of *Sittlichkeit*, corporations cannot have CSR because they merely represent a mirror image of a larger, ethical, and determinant structure, namely, *Sittlichkeit*. The determination of corporations comes from *Sittlichkeit*. It is the structure of Hegel's 'System der *Sittlichkeit*' or system of ethical life that defines at least seven key aspects of corporations:

Table 2.2 shows how corporations are shaped by *Sittlichkeit*. This has at least seven implications for corporations, ranging from the actual form of a corporation as a business organisation to its ethical life. *Sittlichkeit* also determines the internal structures and affairs of corporations, namely, the way corporate management works, the setup and function of corporate governance, and how managerial regimes (corporate culture, relationships to employees, trade unions, management's right to manage, hierarchies, power relationships, domination, etc.) are organised. On managerial regimes, for example, Hegelian philosophy would emphasise that the exposed position of management as the sole non-democratic rule-giver and authoritarian 'leader' over corporations and employees denotes that corporate management is reflective of a 'despot, not a free man, not a man' because it establishes a regime in which a

*Table 2.2* The shaping of corporations via *Sittlichkeit*

| | **Areas defined by *Sittlichkeit*** |
|---|---|
| 1 | The actual shape of corporations, business organisation, etc. |
| 2 | Their internal affairs, i.e. corporate management, corporate governance, managerial regimes, etc. |
| 3 | Their place in civil society and inside a corporation's sphere of economics |
| 4 | The moral standing of corporations |
| 5 | Their relationship to other actors and institutions inside civil society |
| 6 | Their relationship to the two other levels of *Sittlichkeit*: family and state |
| 7 | The ethical life of corporations |

'few are free and not man as such'.[189] The Hegelian conditions, as outlined by philosopher Fatton (1986), issue severe challenges for corporations. These are the fact:

1. that non-democratic and even anti-democratic management is despotic;
2. that this means a despotic institution cannot be free; and
3. that managerial regimes are regimes in which 'few are free and not man as such'.

Perhaps it even means that corporations, when measured against just three elements of Hegel's *Sittlichkeit*, are immoral or, as Hegel would say, *unsittlich*. But *Sittlichkeit* also determines a corporation's place inside two spheres: (i) inside the economic sphere and (ii) inside the sphere of civil society of which economics is part. This, in turn, shapes how corporations are perceived by other social and economic actors in the spheres of civil society and economy. It determines the moral standing of corporations. Finally, this is also established by the moral relationships between corporations and other institutions inside civil society (e.g. NGOs and mass media) as well as the relationship of corporations to Hegel's other two levels of *Sittlichkeit*: families and states.

Inside Hegel's ethical system [*das ethische System*] demarcations between corporations, the economic sphere, and civil society are largely non-existent because corporations are an organic part of society and ethical life with the task of enhancing both. Hence corporations can be seen as a kind of special institutional setup that assists a society in achieving and maintaining ethical life. As such, boundaries between society and corporations carry minor, largely insignificant, and subsidiary roles. The institutional character of corporations can never be defined as anything but institutional setups to enhance ethical life. Being such an institution determines that corporations exist as subsidiaries to society. They do not exist in a 'camera obscura' fashion that is the other, immoral, and wrong way around as is currently the case (cf. Gadamer 1966). The '*Sittlichkeit* → corporation' relationship sets guiding principles for corporations. It defines everything corporations are and do. Perceived from the standpoint of Hegel's ethical life, managerial issues such as corporate citizenship, CSR, and stakeholders are largely rendered meaningless. Such terms can only gain relevance in an unethical system where corporations are not part of an ethical life and where they have been artificially segregated from civil society and *Sittlichkeit*.

Management, Managerialism, and management studies' inventions of stakeholders, shareholders, CSR, corporate citizenship, and others can only exist when corporations see themselves as something different, separated, and disconnected from *Sittlichkeit*. This can only be the case when they have established relationships to external actors that are determined from the standpoint of corporations rather than from the moral standpoint of Hegel's *Sittlichkeit*. This also renders Managerialism's ideology of management as being 'standpointless', neutral, natural, engineering-like, purely rational, objective, a scientific enterprise, and so on nonsensical. While Managerialism claims to be without standpoint, it simultaneously has an ideological perspective that sees anything from the position of management.

It turns everything non-managerial simply into an externality, into something that exists in the external world and outside of management. This is the ideological position of corporations and management. It is not the perspective of Hegel's *Sittlichkeit*. In short, beneath the ideology of being standpointless lurks the ideological and one-dimensional standpoint of management itself. In Hegel's ethics the managerial standpoint of 'Me-First' Management (Crittenden 1984) is contradictory to ethical life as enshrined in *Sittlichkeit*. This also leads to a second point Hegel makes on corporations. Corporations are no more than a form of a social and ethical sub → sub → sub institution to *Sittlichkeit*. In other words, *Sittlichkeit* determines the place of corporations inside *Sittlichkeit* (→), inside civil society (→), and inside an economy (→):

*Sittlichkeit* → civil society → economy → corporations

From this position, it is the moral duty of corporations to recognise all other actors and institutions of Hegel's *Sittlichkeit*. Just like the whole *Sittlichkeit* and any entity within it, corporations too are responsible for social recognition and for recognising everyone and every other institution inside Hegel's *Sittlichkeit.*[190] In Hegelian ethics, this means that individuals and society recognise the moral institution of corporations while corporations recognise society and individuals at a mutual and equal level.[191] This is contrary to the faked ideology of individualism as propagated by Managerialism and HRM; instead, 'the corporation serves the very definite function of acknowledging the intrinsic worth of the individual "as a somebody"' (Nederman 1987:516) and not as a nameless human resource with a corporate ID number attached. But this also means that Hegel's corporations recognise their members and, equally, their members recognise corporations. As a consequence, corporations cannot treat corporate members merely as human resources (internally) and customers (externally).

The corporation's relationship to society is defined by an altruistic purpose [*uneigennützige Zweck*] that defines the corporation's entire interest and efforts [*ganzes Interesse und Bemühungen*] as outlined in Hegel's *Phenomenology*. In Hegelian ethics, a corporation is part of ethical life that mutually recognises Hegel's 'others' as equals. The purpose of a corporation is solely defined in relation to ethical life.[192] It is imperative to recognise Hegel's altruistic purpose of a corporation that is diametrically opposed to any sort of one-dimensional focus on profit-maximisation, managerially code-worded as shareholder-value, organisational goals, performance outcomes, and so on. And, more importantly, Hegelian ethics denies any 'a bit of both' answer. It is not a case of both but a clear case of one purpose, the one of altruism [*uneigennützig*, Hegel]. Hegel's use of the German word 'uneigennützig' excludes self-interest [*Eigennutz*]. His concept of corporations as 'uneigennützige' institutions as defined by *Sittlichkeit* has to be manifested in corporations, managerial regimes, Managerialism, corporate management, and management studies.

# 3
# The Morality of Management Studies

*People in top business schools believe their own propaganda; they – perhaps out of self-preservation and certainly out of self-promotion – have not grasped the idea that good management education can occur without business schools or that they should serve broader interests than those of the management caste.*[193]

Hegel's *sittliche* corporation is a non-self-interested altruistic corporation that has virtually no interest beyond ethical life. In order to achieve this, corporate management would need to recognise this while management studies simultaneously would need to refocus attention on researching and teaching it because this is what defines corporations, corporate management, and management studies itself. In other words, corporations are dedicated to *Sittlichkeit* when they engage in socio-economic activities. This means that management studies would need to teach the role of corporations not merely as businesses but predominantly as moral institutions. A very different picture of corporations emerges once examined from the standpoint of Hegelian ethics. Hegel's ethical–normative picture of moral corporations (thesis) represents a truly Hegelian contradiction to what is perceived to be the norm for business corporations (anti-thesis). This is the non-conceptualised moral problem of management ethics, management studies, corporate governance, and, above all, Managerialism. Such contradictions are not even visualised in the standard academic literature of management studies and never taught in the prime institution that trains managers who then manage corporations: the business school.[194]

The management of corporations has originally been 'pre'-scribed rather than 'de'-scribed by the management writers Frederic Taylor and Henri Fayol.[195] Managerialism provides a supportive ideology to this. Once management was linked to its prime ideology of Managerialism, one of the 20th century's most successful support regimes had been built. As a third actor, both are legitimised by business schools. These 'schools' (!) represent schooling in the strictest understanding of the term.[196] They operate rather differently from what universities and universal education are designed to achieve. Management schools are certainly not to be understood in the Latin *universitas magistrorum et scholarium*, meaning a community of teachers and scholars who are engaged in a quest for education, knowledge, truth, and what philosophy calls the 'love of wisdom'. In the original *universitas magistrorum et scholarium*, 'love of wisdom' was the main if not only aspect contained in curricula. In historical terms, *scholarium* started with the reconciliation of classical philosophy and medieval Christian theology. As a tool and method of external and internal criticism for learning and researching, it placed emphasis on dialectical reasoning – rather than religious belief-systems – providing guidelines through scientific synthesis.[197]

In contrast to this, management studies are weak on dialectical reasoning while successfully appropriating Enlightenment's philosophy of criticism (Kant) inside a system-cybernetic model of self-reinforcing elements designed to legitimise, justify, and sustain management and its ideology of Managerialism inside its semi-critical wing Critical Management Studies.[198] Instead of *universitas magistrorum et scholarium*, management schools employ experts drawn from neutral-sounding 'industry' – management itself – to deliver so-called 'practical knowledge'. They are not designed to educate people in Aristotelian 'virtue ethics' inside a moral community of friends with virtuous character. Instead, they provide functional and ideological training while simultaneously representing 'competition' in their actual organisational structure. They have been attached to universities to create an aura of 'morally neutral human science' and the impression of value-freeness linked to scientism while teaching the 'scientific' value of 'making money'.[199] In other words, 'instead of cultivating their own nature, man now seemed satisfied to accumulate wealth and external conveniences'.[200]

Supported by a crypto-scientific setup, business schools' and management studies' rather one-dimensional task focuses on supporting – not criticising – management.[201] Most important for management has been a steady stream of managerial and ideologically trained graduates employed into the ranks of management to supply functional knowledge and ideological justification. The inbreeding of management school teachers with managerial experience carries connotations of what HRM calls 'internal' recruitment; that is, managers hire graduates from 'their' management schools. This is a circular motion of a closed self-reinforcing cybernetic system of self-sustaining inputs with a strictly protected '*management school ⇆ management*' interface. These managers have been code-worded 'industry experts'. In this three-way interaction all participating institutions subscribe to the same ideological 'glue': Managerialism. To the outside world, this setup creates a multitude of ideological impressions.

Table 3.1 shows an incomplete list of links based on the ideology of Managerialism and therefore exposes – perhaps necessarily – several contradictions. These contradictions range from the 'science versus practicality' opposition to the 'real world versus ideology' contradiction (Göhler 1974:103–200). In general, it demands elimination, reduction, and simplification of anything theoretical into something practical and applicable. Hence, there are neither 'basic' nor 'grounded' theories in management studies. Virtually everything done in management studies is reduced to 'KISS – keep it simple, stupid!' As the former *Harvard Business Review* editor Magretta (2012:6) emphasised, 'Management's real genius is turning complexity and specialization into performance.' In other words, management studies must be able to convert human complexities into managerial simplicities so that these can be managed and made useful for management.

Managerialism's TINA (there is no alternative) has created its own ideology: 'Doing well in today's world . . . requires that we all learn to think like managers, even if that's not what we're called' (Magretta 2012:3). Only successfully attending a management school can achieve what Magretta has outlined. Teaching this inside management schools leads to the mutual benefit of those institutions under the umbrella of Managerialism. In the simplistic terms of Managerialism's beloved prisoner dilemma, it is a win-win situation in which everyone inside is a winner as long as one sticks to the overall ideology.[202] The win-win situation supports external research funding, publications in so-called prestigious management journals, promotions, and the attraction of management students through an accreditation with one of Managerialism's lobbying bodies.[203] This setup expresses system theory to the letter because all parts subscribe to the established cybernetic equilibrium of Managerialism (Dickey 1987:215). The 'doctrine of Managerialism' (Peter Drucker) is a one-dimensional ideology.[204] In sharp contrast to management studies that need to maintain the appearance of neutrality, objectivity, and

*Table 3.1* The link between management schools and management

| Impressions | Descriptions |
|---|---|
| Scientific | There is the impression of being scientifically based using spillover effects from natural science. |
| Recruiting fresh ideas | It also supports the factually important delivery of new ideas by people conditioned to think inside the ideological box of Managerialism enshrined in the sole determination of how to create better profits, more successful companies, and the increase in the extraction of surplus value from labour (Holz 1968:58). |
| Practical and real world link | The impression of being 'practice based' and connected to 'the real world' (Löwith 1962:15). This supports the strong anti-theoretical stance of management studies by delivering 'real results for real people', not theories. |
| Selling degrees | This assists management schools in their marketing to attract management students who are not interested in theory, ethics, the quest for knowledge, and who have no love for wisdom. Their one-dimensional interest lies in converting their ideological and functional degrees into tangible benefits (high salaries). |
| Buzzwords and weasel words | A steady supply of new managers into management schools who are equipped with the latest managerial buzzwords, weasel words, and managerial ideologies. |
| Accreditation and curriculum | There is a sophisticated setup between teaching curricular and managerial agencies that strongly influence – dictate – quasi-academic learning through the process of 'accreditation'. In return, this assists business schools in marketing their degrees. The mutually beneficial arrangement largely determines what is taught at business schools while simultaneously limiting academic freedom on the teaching side. |
| Corporate funding | Management teaching is greatly supported through a decline in university and state funding for research based on Managerialism's ideology of deregulation, privatisation, and tax-cuts. Hence, management schools are successful in attracting so-called 'industry partnerships'. These have an ever increasing relevance in research funding. The decline in state funding and the parallel increase in corporate funding 'shapes' – determines – research programmes of most management schools. |
| Management journals | Such management-supportive and often corporately financed 'research' is often published in so-called 'high-quality', A-class, or star journals run by gatekeepers (i.e. journal editors). These are peer reviewed in a circular, self-supporting, and cybernetics-like motion geared towards supporting management as an institution and management studies as a subject. |

(*continued*)

*Table 3.1* (continued)

| Impressions | Descriptions |
|---|---|
| Academic promotions | Virtually all of the above is linked to promotion that has been made dependent on the attraction of external funding. Through the managerial invention of key performance indicators codified in performance management plans to assess managerial academics; promotions are linked to an annual 'number' of so-called 'high-class' publications. On that the perceived reputation of a journal and numbers are important. Together with attracting external funding, this is the main tool that ensures that the academics inside management studies remain supportive of management and Managerialism. |
| School rankings | It is almost natural that strategic management tools such as the well-known 'positioning school' (that seeks to determine the place of a corporation inside a market) has been applied to management schools to position these schools. Rankings of a management school's position in the 'educational market' show prospective students (preferable candidates in distant learning MBA programmes because of their high ROI, cf. Locke 2011:108) where 'their' management schools stands. This determines job prospects for graduates, salaries, and promotion prospects of the managerial academic. |

scientific scholarship, Managerialism is much freer when advocating its ideology because it has institutionally separated itself from management studies (Apel 1980:253). Simultaneously, Managerialism can rely on 'independent research' supplied by management studies which delivers 'sound science'. All of this is designed to eclipse its ideological orientation.

In sum, both management studies and Managerialism are important for corporations because they create an affirmative climate, a pro-business atmosphere, and positive public images of corporations (Enzensberger 1974). This is further enhanced by image consultants and corporate PR experts.[205] Such an affirmative atmosphere, one-dimensional pro-corporation *Zeitgeist*, and pro-business climate are greatly supported by the structural self-interest of 'corporate' mass media and the media's favourable attitude towards Managerialism.[206] As a result, managerial capitalism can operate relatively unhindered from unwarranted influences such as NGOs, trade unions, state regulations, and consumer protests. These are not destroyed but largely rendered irrelevant, serving merely as tokens to show that managerial capitalism is open to 'marginalised' critique that has been incorporated or is simply ignored.[207]

To achieve the full level of ideological support, corporations depend on functioning relationships to Managerialism and consumer capitalism. Historically, this has been achieved with the transformation of 18th- and 19th-century liberal capitalism into 20th-century consumer capitalism. Unlike liberal capitalism, consumer capitalism is based on Fordism's standardisation, mass-production, and mass-consumption (Dorary 1988). Fordism delivered somewhat of a *drive-by death* to liberal capitalism. Consumer capitalism created a raft of new agencies gaining rapid importance as it progressed. These agencies sustain mass-consumerism such as corporate mass media and a $120bn worldwide marketing industry.[208] Both have been rolled out globally. Since the successful demise of former state-socialist countries and European-style welfare states, corporations have expanded relatively unhindered to become a worldwide model for all societies. The colonisation of everyday life through global corporations was re-framed under Managerialism: gone are the evils of 'imperialism' (Orwellian Oldspeak) when one can have 'globalisation' (Newspeak) instead.[209]

Despite Orwellian Newspeak cloaking the reality of corporate colonisation, the way in which corporations expand remains the traditional way: opening up and organising markets, supplying consumer goods, and a complete and corporate destruction of traditional ways of life.[210] The linguistic move from evil imperialism to good globalisation signifies not only Managerialism's success but also a noteworthy shift. Colonisation no longer occurs through the battleship but through semi-corporate financial institutions. Corporations also have managed to create external political supporting agencies that flank their worldwide triumph (e.g. EU, NAFTA, ASEAN, APEC). While 20th-century mass-consumerism has been linked to 21st-century globalisation, the latter has also added new initiatives to capitalism while its key features remain unchanged – exploitation of labour and ownership of capital. However, what has changed is a strong reliance of corporations on corporate mass media to entice people to consume without which corporate capitalism is not sustainable.[211]

More than ever before, it has combined productive with media capital. Evidently, this has created many new areas in which corporations have to show presence: corporate mass media, advertising, marketing, consumer psychology, financial services, global business strategies, and so on. This explains the parallel rise of Managerialism, management studies, and management schools because corporations need scientific methods to achieve The Real Bottom Line in an ever more complex business environment. According to the predominant mantra of Managerialism, there is only one organisation that can make this possible: the corporation. Corporations are administered through corporate management that has successfully departed from its original sphere of simple factory administration. Perhaps the 'A' in MB'A' (Master of Business 'Administration') is one of the last reminders of the administrative factory origins of management. Managerialism has ideologically disconnected management from its brutal history of factory regimes depicted in the *Satanic Mills* and stretching from 19th-century Europe to 21st-century developing countries. As a matter of fact, all variants of management such as corporate, strategic, HR, and corporate, are essentially no more than hyped-up ideological versions of tyrannical factory administration. Today, nothing reminds one of the historical brutalities of the overseer's whip. It is because of Managerialism's ideological success that – in the best tradition of Hegelian philosophy – managerial concepts [*Begriffe*] relevant to corporations have to be clarified and distinguished.[212] An attempt to achieve this is made in the following brief but incomplete overview.

Table 3.2 shows that management takes on, at least, four relevant forms. Firstly, there are managerial regimes inside corporations as the clearest and most direct expression of corporate management. It signifies management's unchallenged 'positions of institutional power'[213] creating the most authentic and relevant institutional setup. In management studies, these managerial regimes are commonly re-framed as 'organisations' by those Baritz has termed The Servants of Power.[214] The term 'organisation' eclipses and ideologically neutralises the profit-making character of corporations.[215] These organisations and managerial regimes are self-invented, authoritarian, and non-democratic.[216] From the standpoint of Kant's ethics of self-determination, for example, management possesses an illegitimate 'right to manage' because those over which management rules are excluded from rule-making (Harris 1982). In Hegelian terms, there is no self-actualisation inside corporations (Siep 2007:20f.). Management's ideology of a 'managerial prerogative' and its 'right to manage' are designed to pave over management's illegitimacy. An even stronger ideological cover for management's illegitimacy comes in the form of 'Macho-Management'. In spite of an obviously non-existing legitimacy, management's task remains to manage the affairs of owners and shareholders with shareholding as the most common way of corporate ownership.

*Table 3.2* The four forms of management

| Forms | Institutional setup | Expressions | Task |
|---|---|---|---|
| Managerial regimes | Firms, companies, corporations, holdings, joint-ventures, etc. | Managerial policies and culture, right to manage | Profits: managing affairs of owners<br>Ideologies: work hard, individualism |
| Management studies | Management and business schools | Academic publications reports and consultancy | Hidden ideologies cloaked as 'scientific' through university links |
| Ideology of Managerialism | Lobbyists, think tanks, employer associations, business federations | Lobbying governments, popular business press | Openly ideological: free market, no state, competition, deregulation |
| Managerial capitalism | Societies, geographical regions, globalisation, multi-national agencies | Ownership of capital corporate mass media | Profits: production and selling of commodities and services |

This occurred after the 'separation of ownership and control' when a non-owning class of corporate managers displaced their capitalist predecessors, thereby creating industrial bureaucrats and extensive administrative apparatuses.[217] Their self-invented role of representing owners confines management to so-called 'organisational objectives', the code word for achieving profits. 'Managerial language' uses terms such as shareholder-value, profit-maximisation, organisational goals, competitive advantage, the Triple-Bottom Line, PPP = Profit, People, Planet, The Real Bottom Line, and several others designed to cloak what management is really about: profits.[218] This sense and purpose of corporations has been depicted in Bakan's *The Corporation – The Pathological Pursuit of Profit and Power*.[219] In Hegelian philosophy, however, *die Korporation* (Hegel 1821) is not understood as merely a profit-making institution. Not surprisingly, Hegelian corporations are placed under 'the ethical system of *Sittlichkeit*'.[220] This is a fact that Adam Smith's apostles happily neglect, diminish, and deny. Hegel saw the corporation as being part of *Sittlichkeit*.

He saw *Sittlichkeit* as the prime institution under which all other institutions such as law, families, states, schools, universities, and corporations exist. But managerial capitalism – with the assistance of the ideology of Managerialism as broadcasted by corporate mass media – has reversed this. In today's world of corporate capitalism 'Corporations Rule the World': corporations come first and *Sittlichkeit* (Hegel) second, if considered at all.[221] Morality has been reduced to an appendix and a prefix that management has to have to show considerations of external community expectations and to create corporate citizenship with CSR.[222]

Not surprisingly, these managerial buzzwords are seen as an 'in-subject', being 'ethical chic', just another fad, a 'Sunday school subject not worthy of serious investigation', 'sweet music', a 'soft marginal subject' often perceived as 'useless and separated' from real management, or it is seen as 'good public relations'.[223] 'It is true', as the world's most quoted management writer Drucker said, that business ethics 'provides speeches at conferences, lecture fees, consulting assignments, and lots of publicity'.[224] In the words of *Harvard Business Review* writer Albert Carr, ethics is often fostered through phrases such as 'it pays to be ethical or sound ethics is good business. Actually, this is not an ethical position at all; it is a self-serving calculation in disguise.' Perhaps US comedian Groucho Marx hit the nail on the head when he observed:[225]

> Good business is all about honesty and fair dealing; if you can fake that, you've got it made!

In other words, business leaders and corporations have learned to live with society's demands for ethics. Viewed as an externality, they have responded to such requests largely through Managerialism's newest invention of CSR.[226] Just as Carr (1968:148) outlined, the pretence that 'ethics is good business . . . is not an ethical position at all; it is a self-serving calculation in disguise'. The favourable proclamation of the former, paralleled by the conveniently ignored second section of Carr's quote, has allowed management studies to invent their own internal, mild, and non-consequential critique. This has been achieved through the inclusion of CSR into management studies and management's newest sideshow of Critical Management Studies.[227] The successful reduction of moral philosophy to CSR and its shelving inside Critical Management Studies has allowed corporations to operate as usual without significant modifications in order to appear ethical. Just as the BBC (Smale 2006:2) noted:

> Former energy giant Enron won a host of awards for its CSR work

Management studies no longer need to forcefully eliminate – usually 'controversial' framed – opinions. Instead, they can deal with a critique that flows from moral philosophy in predominantly six ways: moral philosophy is reduced to an opinion; it is framed as CSR; it is taken on board if useful for management; if moral philosophy leads to a substantial critique of management and it is considered threatening to management, a veil of ignorance befalls it; this is not a cut and dried issue. Hence, a refined system of stratification has been invented so that critical thinking in the mode of 'about' management that functions as a system-corrective is successfully marginalised. Simultaneously, quasi-critical thinking that is system-stabilising – for example, Critical Management Studies – is placed at a safe distance from 'hard-core' management. As an outcome of the stratification of critique on management, Managerialism has virtually no need to call in the state (surveillance, censorships, blacklisting, withdrawal of university funding, dismissing academics, etc.) to protect management.

In sharp contrast to the Prussian censorship of Hegel's lifetime (*D'Hondt* 1988), today's deregulated state agencies no longer include harsh censorships positioned against those who critique management and Managerialism. The successful isolation and marginalisation of anti-managerial views has extended deep into the realm of corporate mass media. For example, today, nobody inside management studies and corporate mass media uses the term 'democracy' in connection with corporations, management, and corporate governance.[228] Terms such as democratic management and democratic corporations have simply been eliminated under the simple but successful Orwellian logic of 'if there are no words, there are no thoughts, there is no critique, and subsequently there is no rebellion against the prevailing one-dimensional paradigm of Managerialism'. A near total silence has been established. Democracy in the context of where people spend eight plus hours per day has been successfully exterminated.

The need to isolate democracy might indicate that it still causes fear in the minds of corporations. This is different compared to Hegel's 19th century. During Hegel's lifetime, he was unable to attack his masters by explicitly outlining their staunch anti-democratic orientation. Today one is somewhat freer in emphasising the lack of democracy inside corporations and their strong anti-democratic stance. Today, a discussion on why corporations are anti-democratic institutions can occur openly. One is even free to suggest that the dominance of these anti-democratic managerial institutions has led to a non-democratic society. Unlike Hegel, one does not necessarily need to fear Prussian censorship and personal demolition when discussing democracy in relation to corporations. It is exactly because the tools of marginalisation and the stratification of knowledge inside the managerial paradigm have become so refined and successful, that one can, for example, discuss Hegelian philosophy to show the morality and immorality of business corporations quite openly. It is largely inconsequential – meanwhile corporations march on.[229] One can highlight the immorality of corporations, for example, by contrasting just five key institutions linked to corporations to show how these relate to key terms of Hegelian philosophy.

Table 3.3 relates five managerial institutions to themes in Hegelian ethics. While it is obvious that Hegel's terms [*Begriffe*] cannot be restricted to an exclusive application inside such a classical sociological '2-by-2 matrix' as depicted above, it still shows those parts of corporations to which Hegelian terms predominantly relate. In Hegel's philosophy, freedom is understood as a central and normative commitment of modernity. Hegel understands freedom as human freedom. It is a non-economic and non-corporate understanding of freedom seen as 'the hermeneutic circle of undemanding and evolution'.[230] Aligned to that, 'Hegel regards the market economy as an inadequate arena of freedom.'[231] His concept of freedom inside his *System der Sittlichkeit* (Schmidt 2007) does not mean 'economic' freedom. It is 'human' freedom rather than the freedom to manage (managerial prerogative) or business freedom (market freedom, etc.). 'The ultimate goal as Hegel saw it was freedom [which is] the achievement of personal freedom' (Davis 1987:196ff.). As a consequence, Hegel's philosophy of freedom applies universally. But it immediately challenges the freedom of corporate managers to engage in markets that set the terms and conditions of managerial actions. Human freedom, under the conditions of *Sittlichkeit*, contradicts supposed self-determination of corporate management (Hyman 1987). The ability to be self-determined is highly limited by markets.

*Table 3.3* Management and key Hegelian ethics themes

| Corporate management | Hegel's key ethical themes |
|---|---|
| Corporate governance | Freedom, recognition, self-determination |
| Managerial regimes | Alienation, self-actualisation, master–slave dialectics |
| Management studies | Truth, system of logic, subjectivity, rationality |
| Managerialism | Appearance, essence, reality (*Wirklichkeit*) |
| Corporate capitalism | Ethical life, *Sittlichkeit* |

Inside managerial regimes, human freedom under the condition of *Sittlichkeit* means that human beings are to develop autonomous self-actualisation instead of 'a loss of individual autonomy' (Schmidt am Busch 2001:756) – seen as 'how human freedom can be realised' – in the absence of alienation.[232] It also means that such human beings are recognised as human beings, not as human resources (HR) managed by Human Resource Management. When placed inside sociology's 'structure versus agency' model, for example, it denotes a move away from structural determinants such as cost–benefit, instrumental rationality, and cost-cutting towards a human self-actualising agency. Hegelian philosophy also determines that the human agency is 'non-HR', a human being living a life of *Sittlichkeit* that includes the overcoming of Hegel's 'master–slave' dialectics.[233] All of this incurs a total restructuring of management studies away from an ideology providing agency. Under *Sittlichkeit*, management studies can no longer supply corporations with quasi-scientific knowledge that is not directed towards 'truth' but towards The Real Bottom Line (Magretta 2012). Instead of favouring The Real Bottom Line, it would need to favour human freedom. Inside management studies meanwhile, Hegelian ethics means to have the freedom to research, teach, and publish on, for example, human freedom. In management schools and management studies, the self-actualisation of academic freedom, for example, would mean

1. 'the goal of the individuals in Hegel's civil society is not wealth but education (197) and recognition (254:255A)',[234]
2. to be independent from external interferences such as corporate finance and controlled research,
3. university degrees are not financial instruments saleable to educational customers by university management (Bird & Waters 1989:73),
4. degrees are no longer accredited by corporate lobbying institutions,
5. publications are no longer certified through corporate gatekeepers (journal editors of journals owned by multi-national publishing corporations),
6. promotion and salaries are not linked to attracting corporate funding and the number of publications in – perceived and hearsay reputation of – so-called 'good' journals, and
7. proper peer reviewing processes outside a circular self-referencing of 'old boys' networks.

For Managerialism, it would mean that ideology no longer supersedes reality.[235] The Hegelian 'truth of a thing' can no longer only be allowed when representing a 'corporate truth'. Research, degrees, publications, teaching curricula, and so on, are no longer to be adjusted to what Hegel calls thing-world [*Dingwelt*] and to Managerialism ending 'HMV' (his masters' voice) so that academics can speak their own – instead of their masters' – voice in the form of corporate funding bodies and university management.

It would mean the reversal of all ideological adjustment processes. If a thing is found to be unethical, it has to be changed. This does not mean adjusting ethics to the demands of corporations to gain the appearance – not the essence – of being ethical (Rosenfeld et al. 1995). Instead, managerial capitalism is to be based on *Sittlichkeit* so that it defines ethical corporate life. Life can no longer be condensed to consumer-'life' (!) in an unethical society in which ethics is merely a marketing appendix 'for' Managerialism and consumerism. Instead, a *sittliche* society represents self-actualisation and human freedom expressed in Hegel's ethical 'world spirit' [*Weltgeist*] of a universal, collective, self-reflective, and self-conscious ethical mind.[236] In sum, Hegelian themes such as universal human freedom, self-determination, self-actualisation, and, most importantly, mutual and equal recognition touch all four managerial spheres, namely, corporations, governance, managerial regimes, and managerial capitalism. Simultaneously, acting ethically in Hegelian terms means that those in management studies who critique management are not exposed to demolition, censorship, loss of income, denial of promotions, and other restrictions.

Throughout most of his life, Hegel sought to avoid academic and private attacks as instigated by his enemies and demagogues (D'Hondt 1988:65–178). Hegel was able to narrowly avoid attacks and attempts to demolish his personal reputation (D'Hondt 1988). Quite often that came at the price of having to switch jobs, moving to new cities in another miniature state, and living just above the poverty line. Next to the surveillance by Prussia's censors, and the sustained attacks through chauvinistic Germanic student fraternities (D'Hondt 1988:83–118), Hegel was able to write philosophy in which he used many concepts that originated in the writings of German philosopher Johann Gottlieb Fichte (1762–1814) ranging from self-determination to recognition. Hegel skilfully avoided ever stating a 'philosophy of democracy' during years of profoundly antidemocratic state oppression that only ended – after the brief 1919–1933 intermezzo of the Weimar Republic – during the late 1960s of post-World War II Germany. Avoiding the suspicion of his authoritarian masters and employers, Hegel managed to envision a modern society based on *Sittlichkeit*, mutual recognition, law, and institutions of 'living ethicality'.[237]

The 20th-century Hegelian philosopher Marcuse (1941), for example, argues that 'Hegel's system brings to a close the entire epoch in modern philosophy that had begun with Descartes and had embodied the basic ideas of modern society'.[238] The basics of the epoch 'before' Hegelian philosophy traces back to René Descartes (1596–1650) and to Descartes' contemporary Galileo Galilei (1564–1642). Both critiqued an outdated belief-system to find new philosophical, mathematical, and physical principles that explain the world. This resulted in sustained conflicts with what Mills would call 'The Power Elite' (1956). For Galileo Galilei, it came through the 'torturing' (!) disapproval of the Catholic Church. Both Galilei and Descartes remain masterminds of modernity and their writings and philosophies became precursors to Hegel's philosophy. In some way, their philosophies also mark the closing of a pre-Hegelian epoch inside what became known as modern philosophy. In it, Hegelian philosophy became a key to modernity. As a consequence, his general philosophy and his specific writings on corporations are signifiers of modernity. Corporations – just like Hegelian philosophy – are part of this modernity.

Hegelian philosophy remains a modern tool to analyse and critique modernity itself. As such, it applies expressions of modernity such as corporations to corporations themselves. Corporations only appear in modernity and as such they are exposed to Hegelian philosophy because his *Sittlichkeit* embodies basic ideas of modernity. Today, nobody would argue that corporations are not part of modernity and equally nobody would dispute that Hegelian philosophy is not part of modernity. At first glance, however, corporations and philosophy appear to be opposites. Hence, one is hard pressed to imagine terms such as 'corporate philosophy' and 'philosophical corporations' in management studies. If management uses the term 'philosophy', it appears as an appendix or prefix to management. Unsurprisingly, the word 'philosophy' does not mean philosophy in the philosophical sense when used by management. Under Managerialism, it appears as 'our corporate philosophy is to sell A & B' and 'it is our philosophy to create a competitive organisation'. Under Managerialism, philosophy is reduced to simple statements of managerial intentions which often appear to be linked to The Real Bottom Line. Management and management studies never relate 'philosophy' to the philosophical understanding of the 'love of wisdom'. Yet despite Managerialism's distortions, philosophy and moral philosophy remain highly relevant to corporations.

## The relevance of ethics to corporations

While Managerialism and corporations misappropriate the term philosophy to state managerial intentions, there are, nevertheless, The Servants of Power inside management studies who carry highly negative attitudes towards philosophy. This can be seen on an ordinary example of a book on business ethics that is by no means exceptional. Managerial academic Norman E. Bowie is a professor of strategic management and *philosophy*.[239] Here is what the 'professor of philosophy' (!) said in 'his' preface to Jeffery Smith's *Normative Theory and Business Ethics* (2009): 'my annoyance' is with authors who are philosophers 'rather than a person doing empirical research'. Never mind that empirical research has been founded by a philosophy called epistemology (Dickey 1987:210). Business writer Bowie meanwhile frames a serious and systematic philosophical engagement with business as 'attacks . . . that I find extremely off-putting'. In short, serious philosophy is reduced to 'my annoyance [and being] off-putting'. Statements like these qualify anyone in the crypto-academic field of management studies as an unbiased and outstanding scholar. In addition, the book's editor (Jeffery Smith 2009:6) makes it even more obvious: 'Normative theories [e.g. ethics and philosophy] in business thus need to be built around the norms of the market, because the market is the institutional home of business.'

In other words, managerial–empiricist ideologies disqualify philosophy and ethics because both are accused of not being based on empirical research; they are seen as attacking management, and they are simply 'annoying and off-putting', indicating an ideological rather than scientific engagement (DeVos 1996:101). Furthermore, Smith (2009:6) advocates that when philosophy and ethics are to engage with business, corporations, and management, they have to do this on managerial 'terms and conditions' which are business and management, and, above all, 'the market'. In the managerial world of The Servants of Power, it is the market rather than philosophy that sets the terms to which philosophy and ethics have to contribute. After all they are 'the institutional home of business'. This reverses the position of philosophy in relation to markets. Simultaneously, it eliminates the entire history of philosophy and moral philosophy ever produced by human beings because these philosophies are not 'built around the norms of the market'. It renders the work of most, if not all, philosophers worthless.

None of these philosophers have built their philosophies around the market. In the world of The Servants of Power in management studies, almost the entirety of all human philosophies produced during the course of the last 2,000+ years are irrelevant. Meanwhile, they constitute substantial parts of the complete body of human philosophy telling us what it means to be human. Finally, statements like those made by eminent figures of management ethics – Bowie and Smith – assist corporations and Managerialism because of their ideological and perhaps abusive character.[240] Simultaneously, they destroy the moral philosophy of the two most important ethical philosophers ever, Aristotle and Kant. Neither Aristotle's virtue ethics nor Kantian deontology is 'built around the norms of the market'. Managerialism's ideology that ethics needs to be 'built around the norms of the market' would annihilate virtually all ethics ever produced. But not even The Servants of Power in management studies can seriously advocate the abolition of virtue ethics and deontology. Perhaps it is enough to stick with the abuse – 'my annoyance' and 'off-putting' – and seek to reverse the 'ethics → management' relationship.

In short, some advocates of management and business ethics demand the denial of moral philosophy and, perhaps more importantly, a reversal of philosophy in which the latter no longer sets the terms and conditions for all other academic disciplines, including management studies. Philosophy and ethics are only to engage with business and management under what Marcoux (2000) called a 'business-focused business ethics' in the above-mentioned edition. It demands a self-reinforcing circular and cybernetic relationship in which ethics is to be viewed from the standpoint of management in support of management and conducted by crypto-academics inside Managerialism and management studies. Their sole function is to support and legitimise the task to achieve *competitive advantage* as one of Managerialism's foremost management gurus, Michael Porter (1998), asserted. The overall objective is not philosophy's 'love of wisdom' and moral philosophy but to increase shareholder-value. In the words of former *Harvard Business Review* editor Magretta (2012:27), management's key task remains 'as mundane as profit-making'. In short, and despite all the managerial ideology of Baritz' (1960) The Servants of Power, it is philosophy and moral philosophy that set the terms of markets and corporations, not the other way around as management writers would like to have it. From a historical perspective, management and its ideological legions of management studies including its entourage of servants have only been possible in modern times. These are the times when the profit-motive became not only an overriding hegemony,[241] but also a widely accepted, unchallenged, and never questioned ideology of advanced capitalism.

Only advanced capitalism includes corporate governance, thereby allowing a sophisticated division between capital-owners (shareholders) and capital-managers. Only advanced capitalism has business freedom permitting businesses to thrive and advance themselves to a stage where this separation signifies modernity (Marglin 1974). But any investigation into the morality of corporations from a Hegelian perspective demands two further steps. Firstly, the inclusion of *Sittlichkeit* that links corporations to society so that one cannot end where traditional management studies likes to end – inside corporations. Hegelian philosophy demands to include the corporations–society link. Nevertheless, the prime expression of management in society is not so much the colonisation of society through managerial thinking engineered by Managerialism. It is rather the existence of large, multi-national corporations that are made to appear as if floating in an unconnected orbit. They are portrayed as centrepieces of a managerial orbit that has somehow nothing to do with society.

Secondly, the insistence on truth remains the key to all philosophies. An investigation into the truth of corporations needs to distinguish between reality and rhetoric, between truth and ideology, and between Hegel's essence [*Wirklichkeit und Wesen*] and appearance [*Anschein*]. The same applies to the 'textbook-truth' of management that can never represent management's reality.[242] The textbook version of managerial knowledge needs to be compared to those versions of management that are a closer approximation to the truth.[243] Hegelian philosophy demands the avoidance of any one-sided view by looking at the affirmative positive side of corporations and at the non-affirmative negative side. Being a post-French Revolution and post-Kantian philosopher, Hegel's epistemological philosophy of truth follows well-defined formulas such as thesis → anti-thesis → synthesis. These can hardly be established by people who 'think inside the managerial box', demanding the market to be the only guiding principle. It demands the exact opposite. Hegelian philosophy advocates an examination of corporations from outside the box of Managerialism and management studies. It demands a viewing of corporations from the moral framework of *Sittlichkeit*. Only such a view can prevent the self-limiting restrictions of an 'in-box' mindset as defined by Managerialism. Hegel's demand adheres to the *Bauhaus* architect Walter Gropius (1883–1969):

> The human mind is like an umbrella, it works best when open.

Such openness of the mind cannot be established when it is confined to markets, when limited to thinking inside Managerialism and management studies, and when philosophy is deemed 'annoying and off-putting'. But this is not only a self-limitation of thinking. It is also a self-limitation of the freedom to think and of freedom as such. Being a *Philosopher of Freedom*, Hegel's interest in four questions of freedom is noteworthy (Pippin 2010:i):

1. What is freedom?
2. What would it be to act freely?
3. Is it possible to act freely?
4. How important is leading a free life?

These questions are central in Hegelian philosophy because they are highly relevant to philosophy and testify to the single most relevant event in Hegel's life: the French Revolution of 1789 that moved Europe towards freedom, thus marking Enlightenment, truth, and modernity and leading directly to Hegel's philosophy on human freedom. Freedom remains the most enduring feature of Hegel's entire philosophy. Throughout his life, Hegel faced two opposing forces, a philosophical one and one that came as a direct threat to his philosophy. One was Hegel's long-term interest in human freedom introduced to Europe's centre stage via the French Revolution. The other one was authorities preventing human freedom as much as possible. Ironically, these institutions were quite often those employing the philosopher Hegel. Then, as today, philosophers remain unlikely to find employment in a corporation. Hegel had to prove to his employers and state-authoritarian control and censorship masters that he presented no danger to the prevailing order of his time.

Finally, Hegel experienced a number of dying regimes of pre-Germanic midget-states [*Zwergstaaten*] that were on the edge of being swept away by freedom, democracy, German unification, and modern economic systems. To balance these diverging forces was perhaps one of Hegel's greatest lifetime achievements.[244] As a consequence, his philosophical project of human freedom does not follow standard formulas that have defined management ethics ever since its invention. In Hegelian philosophy there is no

1. simple adding of ethics (E) to management (M) as a prefix to create management ethics (ME) (E + M = ME);
2. there is also no 'adjustment' and 'subjugation' of ethics to management; and
3. there are no managerially made-up quasi-moral formulas such as corporate policies, mission statements, and CSR, seeking to invent morality in otherwise non-*sittliche* corporations that lack Kant's self-determination and self-actualisation.[245]

An application of ethics to corporations demands that ethics takes on the prime role from which every issue – including the corporation itself – is examined. It is moral philosophy that provides the supreme and only Litmus Test against which corporations are measured. In sum, management ethics and the *Sittlichkeit* of corporations are nothing more than a version of applied ethics. It applies the ethical standards of *Sittlichkeit* to corporations. This is what Hegel did in the 19th century and this is what can be done to corporations of the 21st century. In both Hegelian *Sittlichkeit* and today's corporations, ethics remains the key starting point that finally results in a three-way programme: thesis → anti-thesis → synthesis.[246]

In terms of Hegelian freedom, it is human freedom (thesis) against which corporations (anti-thesis) are measured to arrive at an assessment (synthesis) of corporate freedom (positive) or corporate unfreedom (negative). This could very well also be seen from the sociological 'structure versus agency' dictum or the philosophical question of 'Are We Ever Free?'[247] Viewed from these perspectives, 'corporate freedom' remains a term that does not exist. Instead, Managerialism subsumes corporate freedom under Smith's 'invisible hand' of markets that dictates corporate actions externally while shareholder-value and profits limiting internal actions (cf. Eecke 1980:98). As a consequence of a first and perhaps most preliminary measure of corporations on Hegel's ethics of freedom, the Hegelian synthesis is that corporations are unfree; they are not free to act. This also answers one of philosophy's most enduring questions as expressed by Sample et al. (2004:213–276), 'Are We Ever Free?', in the negative. In sum, corporations exist under the dictate of capitalist markets and a managerial structure that destroys human freedom to act because both structural imperatives work against human freedom. They are largely invented and supported by management studies and as such they damage Hegel's ultimate goal of freedom (cf. Davis 1987:196).

Not 'despite', but 'because of' the fact that corporations override human freedom, thereby producing corporate unfreedom, the two options presented above (E + M = ME & adaptation) remain heavily used by The Servants of Power. Under management studies, the Hegelian philosophy of human freedom is covered up with a blissful ignorance towards this philosophy.[248] Nonetheless, if affirmative writers of management ethics had their way with Hegelian philosophy, the following two scenarios would be most likely: in the case of 'E + M = ME', Hegel's ethics of freedom, for example, would simply be added to corporations to create corporate freedom under the formula 'freedom plus corporations equals corporate freedom' with freedom not being 'human' but managerial freedom. In a further step, reasons would have to be invented to justify why and where corporate freedom exists (e.g. markets) and why corporations are ethical. In the second, more common, and more ideological version, places between ethics and corporations would be reversed so that corporations and markets would become the prime institutions that set the goalposts which determine ethics.

In this version, ethics would be adjusted or subjugated to corporations and management. This also reverses the historical 'Order of Things' (Foucault) because philosophy has set norms for all other faculties since roughly 2,500 years. Nevertheless, it fits the a-historical mode of management studies denying moral philosophy's history. Simultaneously, management ethics also denies the historical contingency of the brutality of early factory regimes which are still found in corporate sweatshops 'outsourced' to the developing world. Baritz' The Servants of Power – who occupy the managerial orbit – tell management that everything can be managed: from suppliers to consumers, from employees to environmental standards, and even ethics (Akers 1989:74). This reduces ethics to a manageable entity which fits managerial thinking better than reality. A typical example representing this approach is, for example, Smith's (1985:86) demand that 'one way of making business ethics more relevant to management decision-making is to restate the issue from the manager's perspective'. This is designed to achieve at least five things.

Table 3.4 shows five key aspects of what is achieved and what is denied, neglected, and annihilated when ethics is viewed from the standpoint of management studies. Ethics is converted into an ideology and made subservient to management studies. It is successfully downgraded to the level of any other issue that management manages. From that perspective, ethics can be successfully neutralised so that Hegel's ethics of freedom, for example, can become business freedom seen as the freedom to engage in business (external). Internally, it becomes managerial freedom as the 'right to manage' enshrined in the ideology of a 'managerial prerogative'. Simultaneously, those over whom management rule are conveniently forgotten. The treatment of Kant's philosophy by management studies can serve as a concluding example. Kant remains the world's second foremost philosopher of ethics, after Aristotle (Seymour-Smith 1998). Part of Kant's key ethics is his categorical imperative:

> Act in such a way that you treat humanity, whether in your own person or in the person of any other, always at the same time as an end and never merely as a means to an end

*Table 3.4* The relevance of ethics to corporations

| | What is the claim of relevance achieves |
|---|---|
| 1 | Before even starting an investigation into ethics in relation to corporations, ethics is skilfully reduced to business ethics – an applied version of ethics so that any serious engagement with moral philosophy is rendered obsolete. |
| 2 | It reverses places so that ethics can be subsumed under corporations – it can be surrendered and rendered worthless and meaningless so that it causes no challenge to the prevailing paradigm of Managerialism. |
| 3 | It downgrades ethics to 'making it relevant to management' while real ethics' has only one telos: truth which is in line with the original concept of philosophy, namely, the love of wisdom. |
| 4 | It simultaneously narrows ethics down to a subject of decision-making that fits nicely to the managerially preferred and thought-limiting construct of the prisoner dilemma (Nowak & Highfield 2011; Klikauer 2012a). |
| 5 | 'Restate the issue' opens up opportunities for The Servants of Power to 're-frame' an issue so that they can weaken its ethical content in line with managerial thinking; an ethical question simply becomes a managerial question and attention is diverted away from moral philosophy. |

Kant's categorical imperative has been neutralised by The Servants of Power and business ethics shift from Kant's 'means–ends' imperative towards general ideas on what is often called 'human nature'. Once Kantian ethics is eliminated, human beings can be converted into HR and can be treated and exploited purely as a 'means' as long as management shows 'some' respect towards them. But Kant's categorical imperatives are freestanding, self-contained, self-explanatory, and law-like formulas designed to guide human behaviour. The categorical imperative above consists of 38 words. It does not include the word 'respect' which business ethics usually introduces at this point. Nowhere does Kant mention 'respect' in the context of this categorical imperative (Korsgaard 1996). Because of this, management studies had to artificially introduce 'respect' while simultaneously ignoring Kant's German original and classical texts on Kantian ethics. All this is done in order to weaken the categorical imperative and make it adjustable to management.

By diluting the real content, management studies have been able to re-direct the attention away from Kant's categorical imperative and towards the newly introduced term 'respect'. Through this, the managerial treatment of people as a 'means' becomes merely a question of 'respect'. In a second step, management is often ideologically re-phrased as 'you' to increase the distance between the institutions of management and Kant's categorical imperative and to personalise a rather formal version of moral philosophy precisely at a place that disallows personalisation. In a third and even more ideological step, readers of textbooks on management ethics are told that as long as management 'respects' people they adhere to Kantian ethics. Again the term 'people' is used for two purposes: to make it sound general – something we (the people) all do – and to avoid the term management uses, HR, because this term carries strong connotations to 'means' and 'tools' which is to be avoided for ideological reasons (Klikauer 2010:5). This converts ethics into an ideology. The link between treating human beings as human 'resources', 'tools', and 'means' has to be avoided when one seeks to ideologically distort Kant's philosophy. With this, writers of managerial ideology – rather than ethics – have achieved six goals. They have

1. diminished all critical powers of Kantian ethics through their ideological re-interpretation,
2. introduced the term 'respect' indicating that showing respect is enough to carry on with exploitative relationships;
3. made themselves indispensable to management because they can re-interpret Kantian ethics and make it look as if Kantian ethics supports management;
4. made Kantian ethics applicable to management without any consequence for management;
5. personalised Kant's ethics so that it appears as an issue of respect between two people; while simultaneously,
6. taking out management and therefore eliminating management from the scene of morality.

This is done in full view of Kantian philosophy that demands to treat everyone 'always as an end'. An ideological re-interpretation has achieved the seemingly unachievable. Quite often such re-interpretations are framed as 'these words are usually interpreted to mean we should respect other people (and ourselves!) as human beings' (Klikauer 2010:5). The 'usually interpreted' stands for 'trust us experts and textbook writers'. Humanity is a term comprehensively ignored by management studies when writing management textbooks on ethics and teaching business ethics. Contrary to today's modern corporations and the teachings in business schools, for Hegel, the corporation is an important process as it ensures 'the elevation of man from his natural particularity to the rational universality of humanity' (Ashton 1999:7). In other words, while Hegel advocates corporations to be institutions directed towards humanity, standard management practices and teaching seeks to avoid it.

The avoidance of terms such as 'humanity' has a long tradition in management studies. Next to no management text, for example, mentions 'humanity'.[249] During the nearly nine decades of the *Harvard Business Review* the term 'management humanity' does not appear even once. Neither is the term 'humanity' found in two recent examples of standard management textbooks.[250] But textbooks often include 'humane orientation' and the 'humanistic perspective' with relevant sections divided into three short parts starting with the reduction of humanity to the so-called

1. 'human relations movement' manifested in the Hawthorne experiment that created the *Myth of the Docile Worker* (Bramel & Friend 1981). This is followed by the
2. 'human resources perspective' that converts human beings into resources, tools, and means. Just as Kantian ethics has warned against, this part also includes
3. 'the behavioural approach': On his own approach of behaviourism, Skinner (1983; Antoniou & Cooper 2011) noted, 'what a fascinating thing! Total control of a living organism. The underlying assumption [of behaviourism], according to one critic, seems to be that the semi-starved rat in the box, with virtually nothing to do but press on a lever for food, captures the essence of virtually all human behaviour';[251] the final section is dedicated to
4. 'humane orientation': deceptively under the title appears 'Other Cultural Characteristics' reducing their humane orientation to a one-liner: 'The final dimension refers to the degree to which a society encourages and rewards people for being fair, altruistic, and caring.' Again, it is not about humanity. Instead, ethics is framed as a typical managerial exchange: encourage and reward 'for' being fair, altruistic, and caring. These are not moral duties as Kant and moral philosophy argue; instead, they are reduced to managerial exchange characteristics that 'have to be' displayed in order to be rewarded. It is not moral philosophy but managerial exchange theory.

Just one short excursion into a typical management textbook has shown that humanity simply does not exist in management studies. There simply is no management humanity; hence management is better off eliminating this key element of Kantian philosophy. Instead, management studies have invented 'respect' because it eradicates humanity. The two examples – Kant's categorical imperative of 'means–ends' and Hegel's ethics of freedom – have highlighted the key difference between moral philosophy and management studies where standard texts on management ethics follow ideological pathways. As a consequence and in order to be truthful to a most authentic representation of Hegelian philosophy, a philosophical rather than a managerial–ideological approach is necessary to ascertain the role of modern corporations in Hegel's *Sittlichkeit*. The subject area remains moral philosophy and the philosophy of Hegel in particular. A truthful investigation that honours moral philosophy does not invent terms to legitimise Managerialism. It does not weaken original philosophical concepts as outlined by Hegel's *Phenomenology* (1807) and *Philosophy of Right* (1821) and his views on *sittliche* corporations. It presents Hegelian ethics in the most authentic approximation to his philosophy using an approach that is pragmatic rather than ideological–managerial.

'Only' current and established interpretations of Hegel's original writings, recognised translations, and the original German version related to *sittliche* corporations have been used in this book. On the downside, a pragmatic approach to Hegel's writings on corporations still does not save one from the complexities of Hegelian philosophy constituting a relentless challenge even to the philosophically educated mind. Hence, the overall task is to authentically represent Hegelian ethics on corporations and *Sittlichkeit*. Moral philosophy and Hegel's *Sittlichkeit* are retaining their norm-setting characteristics. This approach does not simply add ethics as a prefix to management to create the appearance of being ethical. Neither does it seek to weaken Hegelian philosophy through ideologically motivated re-interpretations, the introduction of new terms, or a distortion of Hegelian philosophy in order to adjust it to management. Instead, it examines critical tensions and contradictions (Hegel) between *Sittlichkeit* and business corporations. Equipped with a clear understanding of the danger of managerial re-interpretations and ideologically motivated adjustment processes, the moral philosophy of Hegel's *Sittlichkeit* becomes imperative. This is the exclusive standpoint from which the institutional setting of the business corporation is examined.

# 4
# Corporations and Hegel's Ethical Institutions

*To deprive your will of all freedom is to deprive your actions of all morality.*[252]

It is in Hegel's *Philosophy of Right* (1821) where he developed the institutional details for the concept of moral life or *Sittlichkeit* that views everything in society – including corporations – as socially constructed. Three levels of morality are necessary to establish *Sittlichkeit.*[253] Hegel places corporations at the second level between families and states. The first level of morality is that of the family or *Familiensittlichkeit.*[254] This is the most immediate and natural form of social coexistence and cooperation because families are the first social entity of mutual and equal recognition. This is the place where human beings experience parental love, intimacy, closeness, mutual support, 'the solidarity of families', and Hegel's ethics of recognition.[255] Canadian philosopher Charles Taylor (1994), for example, stresses just how important recognition is for human beings: recognition is 'a vital human need'.[256]

In families, parents recognise their children while children recognise their parents, husbands and wives recognise one another, just as siblings, uncles, and cousins do. Today's mini-families just as Hegel's extended families create 'bonds of recognition'. There is what Hegel calls a 'bond of blood' among family members as well as a 'bond of intimate social relations'.[257] One might be called a 'natural' bond while the other is the 'social' bond.

In the evolution of human life that started roughly somewhere around 2.5 million years ago, these two bonds remained absolutely necessary for human existence because they enabled families to establish 'Mutual Aid as Super-Cooperators'.[258] Families operate on mutual love and intimacy, not on competition. Ideologically, the idea of competition as manifested, for example, in management's preferred prisoner dilemma would have meant that children who compete with parents for food would have died in a strictly competitive world of Hobbes' 'war of all against all' (1651). Competition and the paralleling ideology of the 'survival of the fittest' encounter very serious problems in explaining evolution and biology.[259] Contemporary evolutionary science has come to understand that theories of cooperation have the stronger explanatory power. Hegelian philosophy supports the evolutionary concept of mutual aid, altruism, and cooperation by outlining that 'the family is the sphere of altruism and love within which the individual behaves (not as an independent person) but as a member'.[260] Hegel defines families as '*sittliche* institutions' formative for Hegel's second level, namely, civil society.[261] The link between families and civil society has been outlined by American philosopher William Maker (1987:24; cf. Blaschke 1974:312) when emphasising that 'civil society shows itself as the "continuation" and "transformation" of the ethical life of the family'. This is shown in Figure 4.1.

Figure 4.1 shows *Sittlichkeit* progressing through three stages of moral development: 'family → civil society → states'. It also depicts two transition points: (i) between family and civil society and (ii) between civil society and states. On the basis of level 1 (family) and 2 (civil society), morality is carried over into Hegel's third level of the state. At the third level, Hegel saw the state representing Rousseau's general will – *volonté générale* – and Kant's universal will as the most universalistic aspects of ethical life because they represent the self-actualisation of people. Like families, states exist for non-competitive and non-profit-making reasons. While families strive towards the common good of family members, states strive for the common good of state members. But there is also a crucial difference between families and states. States are shaped by their members via democratic elections creating institutions for the benefit of its members. This constitutes today's interface between civil society and the state.[262]

In civil society we find elections, political parties, and what Habermas (1988, 1997) calls 'public sphere' and lifeworld. The state comprises

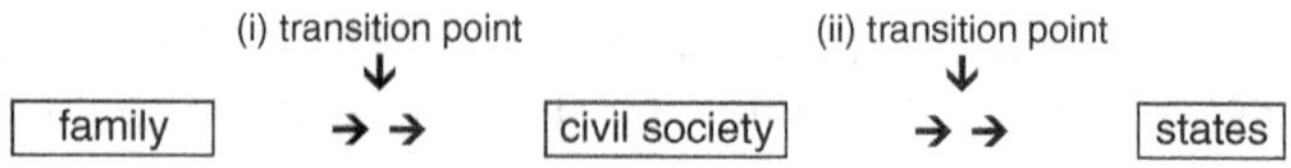


*Figure 4.1* Hegel's three levels of morality and their transition points

administrative states governed by elected representatives. Civil society and state members recognise one another through equality and, as Hegel would emphasise, through mutual and equal recognition: one person – one vote. Without equal recognition, cooperation, and mutual aid, families, civil society, and states would not exist. As an outcome, modern states recognise their members mutually and equally, for example, through the rule of law. The democratically established 'rule of law' is always an expression of what Kant calls self-determination and Hegel's self-actualisation. In addition, there is also mutual recognition between members and institutions of democratic states. In sum, Hegel's two moral entities of family and state deliberately exclude the third entity: corporations. Unlike business corporations based on shareholder-value, The Real Bottom Line, and competition, Hegel's two institutions of families and states are based on cooperation, recognition, mutuality, and ethics.[263] These levels of *Sittlichkeit* are depicted in Table 4.1.

Table 4.1 shows the moral levels of family, civil society with economics and corporations, and the states that establish *Sittlichkeit*. German philosopher Römpp (2008:211) has argued that Hegel's trilogy of institutions mutually compensate for deficiencies evident at each level. The shortcomings of family morality, for example, are individualism, a lack of sociality, and universalism (Ashton 1999:3). These are compensated for by civil society and states. The shortcomings of societal morality are a lack of intimacy and insufficient universalism because of a focus on a specific society. These are compensated for by the intimacy of families and the universalism of states. Finally, state-based morality lacks intimacy and socially established morality via communities.[264] These

*Table 4.1* The corporation in Hegel's *Sittlichkeit* and freedom

| Ethical institutions | Hegel's freedom | Expressions of human freedom |
|---|---|---|
| Family | Individual–subjective | Early educational development of human freedom and self-actualisation inside families, development of 'I' identity, social relations to family and peers |
| Corporation | Social–economical | Freedom of markets, freedom of corporate membership (labour markets), economics of *Willkür* [chances], master and slave dialectics, end of alienation |
| State | Democratic–legal | Universal human self-legislation, democracy, participation in moral institutions, self-regulation of society: regulator and regulated |

are compensated for by the family's intimacy and the social morality of a living community. Yet, in Hegel's system of mutually compensating moralities, corporations still occupy a problematic position.

*Sittlichkeit* wedges corporations between families and states, viewing families as the moral nucleus of society that prepares individuals to participate in *sittliche* corporations and democratic-universal states. For Hegel, corporations remain somewhat awkward and artificial institutions because of their particularity and sectarian interest as an economic institution.[265] Corporations have a very different foundation when compared to families and states and are entirely different from *Sittlichkeit*'s first and second levels. For one, corporations do not constitute a holistic sphere of morality (Göhler 1974a:356). Rather, they are particular economic institutions of an economic sub-sphere of civil society. Hegel saw civil society as a full sphere of morality inside which corporations are just 'one' element. Despite this, civil society, economics, and corporations remain prime institutions that connect families to states within the framework of ethical life. In summary, Hegel saw the first, non-corporate level in natural families and regarded democratic states as the most universal form of morality. This is contrasted by artificial corporations because they are neither 'natural' like families nor 'democratic' like states. The way Hegel constructed the relationship between all three and morality is shown in Figure 4.2.

The key to understanding *Sittlichkeit* (Figure 4.1) is that levels 1 and 3 operate virtually on the same ethical principles of mutual and equal recognition, freedom, mutual aid, and cooperation. The economic subsection (level 2), however, remains the 'odd one out'.[266] Natural families and democratic states do not exist because of narrow profit motivations, self-interest, selfishness, 'pathological self-love', egoism, shareholder-value, profit-maximisation, The Real Bottom Line, and organisational objectives, competitive advantage and a raft of other code words

| Levels | Form of Morality | Institution | Expression & Foundation |
|---|---|---|---|
| Level 1 → | Cooperation & Mutual Aid | Families | Natural Bonds via Blood & Intimacy |
| Level 2 → | Competitive Advantage & Profits | Corporations | Artificial Bonds via Selfishness & Egoism |
| Level 3 → | Cooperation & Mutual Aid | Democratic States | Universal Bonds via Participation & Elections |

*Figure 4.2* Hegel's three levels of morality and the position of corporations

designed to cloak 'profits'.[267] In sharp contrast to families and states, business corporations are part of a sphere that is dominated by markets. In the words of Herzog,[268]

> Hegel's market is not the peaceful, self-adjusting mechanism that Smith had described. Instead, it is a battlefield of everyone against everyone else – and hence the relic of the state of nature . . . and of each against the common interests of the community.

Hegel did not see markets – where corporations operate – as a system that creates equilibrium but one that is more akin to a battlefield. One might argue that his philosophy is not analogous to 'system theory' that assumes a cybernetic-like framework of mutually compensating forces creating a perfect equilibrium. Rather, Hegelian philosophy is more akin to 'conflict theory' with conflicting interests inside society and economics.[269] Meanwhile, the aim of management in the market battlefield of corporations 'is about winning the battle, the war' (Magretta 2012:77). This is not the interest of a family, civil society, community, or the state. Hegel goes even one step further by calling the marketplace a 'relic of the state of nature'. Today, the brutality of the 'state of nature' has been converted into the brutality of markets. Hegelian philosophy sees nature and markets as domains of 'unfreedom' where Hegel's self-actualisation cannot be achieved and institutions are exposed to forces beyond human control.[270]

In the first domain, human beings and the 'reality of their *sittliche* organisations' (Schmidt 2007:140) are forced to hand their freedom over to the brutality of nature. In the second domain, human beings have been made to – somewhat 'involuntarily' – hand over their freedom to the brutality of markets that are made to exist beyond human control. The domination through nature and markets destroys Hegel's self-actualisation, human freedom, and *Sittlichkeit*. In Hegelian philosophy, there can never be *sittliche* life inside an unconsciously existing market that reduces human beings to reacting to markets. Hegel's concern with 'unfreedom' resulted in an awareness of the initial existence of human beings in an untamed nature blindly following animalistic instincts.[271] Both are elements found in market economies as expressed in Hegel's *Writings on Politics and Philosophy of Right* where he notes,

> Blind totality of the market, whose workings are those of a wild animal . . . Thus, according to Hegel, the market creates a necessary inequality [which] causes a relationship of domination. Such

> domination, he argued, condemns the individual to the rawness of life and the dullness in labour and poverty, so that others could amass fortunes.[272]

Besides a deliberate replacement of being determined by natural forces with being determined by the blind and blinding forces of market domination, both destroy self-actualisation. Relinquishing the human free will, Kant's self-determination, and Hegel's self-actualisation in favour of Adam Smith's invisible hand of market determinations is seen by Hegel's contemporary, the philosopher Moses Hess (1845:56), as 'in a world defined by a petit-bourgeois business world [*Krämerwelt*] the highest level of animalism, namely the hunter, defines the level of consciousness'. Hess added, 'today's *Krämerwelt* represents the conscious and principal form of egoism'. But not only Hegelian philosopher Hess, Hegel himself issued a critique of market domination that condemns participants to the rawness of an egoistic existence in an economic system. Together with handing over one's own individual will to blind market forces, capitalism – *Krämerwelt* (Hess) – also leads human beings into 'dullness and poverty'. In markets, 'poverty' is deliberately engineered, so that others can 'amass fortunes' (Hegel). Perhaps with this in mind Hegel summarised the core pathologies of capitalism. But Hegel was hitting the nail on the head when he stated,[273]

> Factories and manufacturers base their existence on the misery of a class.

Today, these 'factories and manufacturers' have mutated into global modern business corporations but their existence is still based on profits in exchange for the misery of a class, namely, those labouring in distant sweatshops, artificially disconnected from corporations via geographical distancing structures that include sub-contracting and GPN – global production networks (Schmidt am Busch 2002:139). Being a philosophy of freedom, the key to this is not even 'the misery' (Hegel) that corporations create and the relocation of such misery to the distant corners of Davis's *Planet of Slums* (2007). It is the dilemma this creates for Hegel's key philosophy of freedom. The second dilemma of modern economy and modern business corporations has been outlined by Hegel himself (Fatton 1986:588):

> The spirit of complete mercilessness and the domain of crass and cruel materialism in which currency must be honoured, but family,

> welfare, life etc. all may perish . . . the labourer, according to Hegel, becomes, through the work of the machine, more and more machine-like, dull, spiritless.

For a phenomenological philosopher, the spiritual damage done to human beings under market capitalism is of grave concern.[274] Hegel outlines a complete mercilessness of markets establishing 'crass and cruel materialism'. In his *Philosophy of Right* (1821), this 'crass and cruel materialism' is linked to *Sittlichkeit*'s second level, namely, economy and corporations. It is not linked to the non-economic part of civil society, nor to families or states. Nevertheless, it has implications for all levels because the 'cruel materialism' of market economies and corporations leads to a way of life in which only 'currency must be honoured'. This explains the high esteem currency traders, bankers, merchant and investment bankers, fund managers, money traders, shareholders, portfolio managers, hedge-fund managers, and so on receive in today's society. It also is in line with the honour Managerialism gives to financial institutions.

And, at least partly, it explains why 'family, welfare, life etc. all may perish' (Hegel) because corporate capitalism is a system in which families – contrary to consumers and labour-supply – are largely rendered irrelevant. Hence, there has been a destruction of what was once an 'extended family'. This occurred roughly between Hegel's time and today. Today, a breakdown of families flanked by a stratospheric rise of single-person households which already have become the norm in some cities can be detected. This is paralleled by a substantial increase of the ideology of individualisation and the invention of DINK 'double income no kids'. The demise of family and family life (e.g. a marked decline in the once common family dinner) is of course also flanked by the conservative ideology of family-values that ideologically sustains the slow death of families. Simultaneously, the romantic illusion of family life is played out on silly TV shows produced by corporate mass media.

The family as a moral unit is of no use to corporations other than being consumers and to sustain the re-productive sphere of corporate capitalism. The slow death of families might continue until the sphere of families can be completely moved into a consumptive sphere comprising atomistic individuals.[275] They are placed in a commercial structure in which eventually all social relationships become commercial exchanges where commercial goods and a tremendous amount of private consumer gadgets replace family members.[276] The replacement of family members with consumer electronics in a totally commercialised world will perhaps be the final triumph of neo-liberalism and Managerialism.

Meanwhile, on 'the human condition' (Arendt) inside managerial regimes, Hegel noted that 'the labourer . . . , through the work of the machine, becomes more and more machine-like, dull, spiritless'.[277] During the rise of industrialism, this meant the manufacturing machinery. But with the conversion of manufacturing capitalism into the service industry and knowledge capitalism, these machines have changed from 'automated manufacturing machines' to 'International Business Machines' (IBM) and subsequently into desktop and laptop computers and software. The machine has changed but the *Geist*-spirit-numbing work remains. Put bluntly, work on the steam engine (19th century) or the metal stamping-press (20th century) is as mind-numbing as is hacking endless numbers into an Excel spread sheet or a 'cut and paste job' of another corporate policy downloaded from the Internet to be signed off by a boss (21st century). Hegel's 'machine-like, dull and spiritless' work manifests itself in today's computer programmes. Steam engines, stamping presses, and computer programmes have never allowed human beings to actualise human freedom. Instead, corporations and corporate management have relentlessly applied these machines for shareholder-value, that is, profit-maximisation, rather than for the development of the human spirit [*Geist*] or *Sittlichkeit.*

In addition to the direct impact of markets and the mind-destroying way corporate management organises machine-computerised work, a more serious ethical dilemma is lurking. The 'unfreedom' of the rawness of markets under modernity continues the 'unfreedom' of the animalistic instincts enforced by the rawness of nature (Hegel). The moral dilemma of human self-actualisation versus markets lies at the heart of Hegelian philosophy. Neither in the bestiality of natural instincts nor in the arbitrariness [*Willkür*] of markets are individuals able to find *Sittlichkeit.*[278] Instead, the 'unfreedom' of a 'fight of all against all' in nature has been replaced by the 'unfreedom' of the 'fight of all against all' inside markets.[279] In both, freedom cannot be achieved because the free will of individuals is relinquished in favour of external forces.[280] The dilemma of the non-natural sphere of modern economics and corporations has been summed up by Greer (1999:573): 'Economic freedom operates by blind necessity and is not any individual's conscious creation.' This renders the ideological notion of an 'individual' moral responsibility of individual managers nonsensical. Management studies have never acknowledged or discussed the ethical problem of 'Hobbes versus Hegel' as 'a war of all against all' (Hobbes 1651) versus *Sittlichkeit*. In the words of Hegelian philosopher Cullen,

> The economic bellum omnium contra omnes [is] the battlefield where everyone's individual private interest meets everyone else's, where each self-seeking individual is primarily absorbed in satisfying his or her own selfish ends, without respect for the common good. Hegel recognises that civil society is to save the pursuit of interest from omnium bella omnium – the war of all against all [hence it is] the task of civil society to provide the institutions that allow individuals to realise their interests through a normative interaction of freedom.[281]

What Hobbes (1651) and Cullen (1988) have described as battlefield, the former editor of the *Harvard Business Review* Magretta has presented as 'like all wars, these [business battles] too have their civilian casualties'. This links militaristic language and thinking to management and corporations (Klikauer 2007, 2008). Like the military's artificial needs for weapons, killing, and destruction, Hegel noted that corporations also invent two kinds of artificial needs: internally, these are profits, wages, promotion, and bonus while, externally, they are consumer goods, consumerism, commodities, and services sold in markets. Such artificial internal and external needs play on individual self-interests while simultaneously annihilating moral cooperation (families) and universal morality (states).[282] But Hegel was unable to solve this dilemma. It remains what Hegel has called the 'tragedy in ethical life' and a contradiction between two diverging spheres: the ethical and the business sphere (Schmidt 2007:58).

> The 'ethical sphere cannot accept the bourgeois sphere [of economics with corporations] as legitimate. At the same time, however, the ethical sphere has to admit its necessity. The only way it may "master" it is "to cede and to sacrifice a part of itself" to the bourgeois sphere' of economics with corporations.[283]

The sphere of economics and its focus on monetary gains (profits and wages) and consumerism (commercial goods) locates corporations in what Hegel called thing-world [*Dingwelt*] where an individual is forced to 'turn oneself into an object'.[284] This only occurs at Hegel's second level of civil society and here in the sub-section of economics and corporations. In Hegelian ethics, families and states are supportive of ethics rather than of the reification of human beings (Honneth 2005). Both are based on ethical principles such as blood and democratic bonds creating morality in support of *Sittlichkeit*.[285] But they also have to deal with the odd one out: corporations. How Hegel thought the relationship between family/states and corporations is structured is shown in Figure 4.3.

Figure 4.3 simplifies what Hegelian philosophy would define as a key ethical dilemma. All three levels of *Sittlichkeit* should be based on 'cooperation for mutual benefit'. The problematic level of corporations, however, exists outside of *Sittlichkeit* or at least it has a tendency to position itself externally to *Sittlichkeit*. This is because its underlying mechanism, organisational structure, and normative constitution are not based on 'cooperation for mutual benefit'. Instead, these are 'competitive market relations' in which corporations seek to increase shareholder-values based on markets. *Sittlichkeit*, however, can only be created by moral actors and moral institutions. They can never be created by an abstract 'invisible hand' of rather elusive markets mysteriously linked to individual self-interest. Equally, it can never be created through the relinquishing of human self-actualisation in favour of market forces. This point has been clarified by Fatton when emphasising that[286]

> he [Hegel] knew that there was no invisible hand capable of generating the collective good of society from the private passion of interest of atomised individuals.

The problem of individualism, selfishness, and self-interest versus the common welfare of society remains an unsolvable dilemma of all those economic systems that are based on markets. This remains a moral dilemma for market economies and for corporate organisations inside these market economies. The moral dilemma of corporations inside modern civil societies and *Sittlichkeit* is indicated by an arrow (←) at the centre of Figure 4.3, indicating two diverging spheres. This remains a 'contradiction' because 'the harmony of the private and

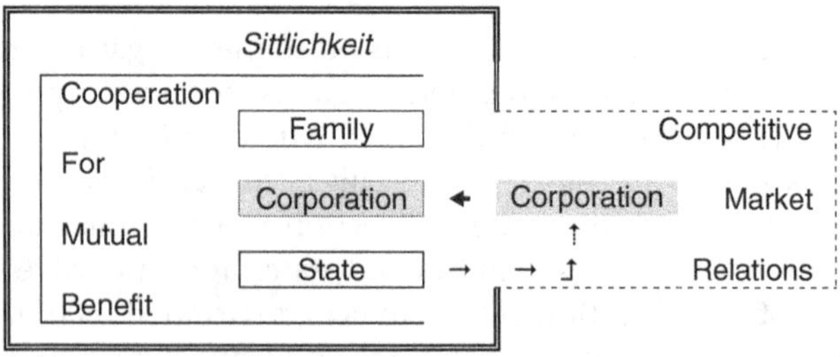


*Figure 4.3* Hegel's *Sittlichkeit* and corporations

the public was an issue that Hegel never solved'.[287] Civil society, economics, and corporations are unable to solve the issue of poverty and organisational and social pathologies.[288] Hegel had simply given up on solving poverty and the pathologies created by market institutions like corporations.[289]

Adding to Hegel's painful awareness of the ethical dilemma of 'poverty versus *Sittlichkeit*', his ethics of *Sittlichkeit* demands the elimination of poverty and its resulting social pathologies and moral injuries.[290] But the sphere of economics and corporations which is 'unquestionably a sphere where narrow particularity and self-interest hold sway' is unable to eradicate poverty.[291] In addition, the sectarian interest of corporations is incapable of solving this problem. Instead, it actively contributes to poverty, misery, and pathologies because of corporation's narrow, particular, sectarian, and one-dimensional focus on what Milton Friedman (1970) has correctly described as 'it is the social responsibility of business to increase its profits'.

But this is not only the case for corporations; it carries wider ramifications. 'The business class is essentially concentrated on the particular' and to serve such a particular interest 'corporations are especially appropriate' (Fatton 1986:593). Not only are corporations interested in sectarian issues, namely, profits, but the business class as a whole is interested in profits.[292] For that, Managerialism has paved the ideological road to shareholder-value and The Real Bottom Line. What has been created is a uniformity of a one-dimensional interest, just as Friedman outlined. This is shared by everyone in the vicinity of management and corporations. Virtually all managerial institutions and ideologies operate contrary to *Sittlichkeit* that demands universalism while corporations follow a narrowly defined particular interest in a highly sectarian way. To a large extent, Hegelian ethics illuminates the dilemma between *Sittlichkeit* and civil societal institutions such as corporations.

## Institutions of civil society and corporations

*Sittlichkeit* makes it very clear that inside civil society we find economics and, as a sub-section, corporations. While modern corporate management reduces civil society to a market, Hegelian philosophy sees it as the exact opposite. Civil society is a key feature of *Sittlichkeit* inside which economics and corporations represent just 'one' element. As a consequence, 'Hegel views civil society and its economy as subordinate, and not the determinative features of a just society'.[293] This has mainly two implications: (i) a 'just' society carries elements of what

American philosopher Rawls calls 'Justice as Fairness';[294] and (ii) the determining feature of a 'just' society remains *Sittlichkeit* rather than corporations.

Hegel's civil society is just, fair, and democratic and takes place in what German philosophers Edmund Husserl (1936) and Jürgen Habermas (1988, 1997) have termed 'lifeworld' constructed as an 'open public sphere'. Institutions inside civil society and the lifeworld are bodies of *Sittlichkeit*. In that, corporations represent no more than an institutional sub-section placed inside the sphere of economics which itself is a sub-section of civil society representing only one level of *Sittlichkeit*. In Foucault's *Order of Things* (1970), this would be as represented in Figure 4.4.

Figure 4.4 focuses only on Hegel's second institutional level placed between family and states. Inside civil society, there is an economic sphere that has corporations as 'one' part, on which two issues are relevant: firstly, Hegel's middle level can be split into a social, that is, non-economical civil part of society – what Habermas calls 'the lifeworld' (1997; cf. Flynn 2014) – and into an economic sphere. What remains inside civil society are the non-economic lifeworld, the economic realm, and corporations inside both. Habermas's concept of a lifeworld remains essential because it explains why civil society still includes social 'human-to-human' relationships that – under neo-liberalism – are not 'yet' fully converted into market relations. But civil society also has economic parts such as markets and corporations. Both main sub-sections – lifeworld (non-market) and economy (market) – create the civil society. According to German philosopher Kersting (1988:1), Hegel's civil society has three levels:

1. the satisfaction of the needs of all members of such a civil society;
2. protecting property through a legal system; and
3. social welfare to support those arbitrarily and negatively impacted by the economy so that the common interest of a community

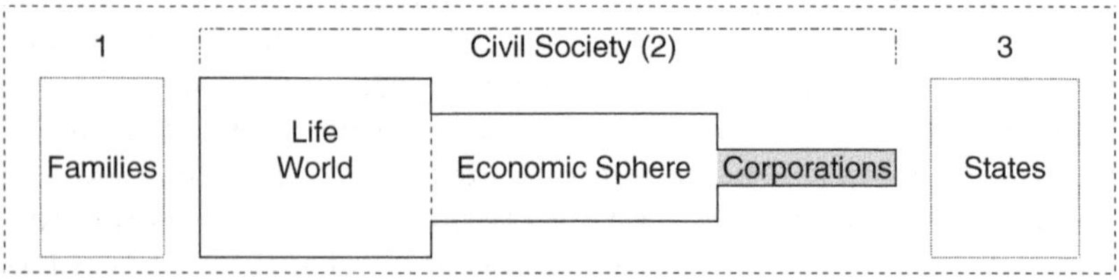


*Figure 4.4* The corporation inside Hegel's sphere of civil society

> [*eines Gemeinsamen*] is protected. This is the task of corporations and the *Wohlfahrtspolizei* [welfare-police] which is a 19th-century German idea of a merger between polic'e', social polic'y', and welfare.[295]

Inside these three, Hegel sees corporations as being 'embedded' in the modern economy. 'Civil society is such that the economic relations fall within it.' On this Hegelian philosopher Gallagher (1987:179) emphasised, 'Economic and social institutions are embedded in the objective ethical order; the ethical order is objective freedom; and these economic and social institutions are "the pillars of public freedom".'[296] In comparison to the *Sittlichkeit* of families and states, the sphere of economy and corporations is marred by at least three dilemmas:

1. 'solidarity versus competition',
2. 'cooperation versus competition', and
3. 'lifeworld versus market relations'.

Despite Hegel's awareness of the problematic character that corporate competition and market relationships have on *Sittlichkeit*, there is, nevertheless, still a 'socialising function that Hegel finds in the economy'.[297] There is the dilemma of 'solidarity versus competition' between Hegel's levels 1 + 2 and 2 + 3. This is paralleled by the same dilemma that also exists inside level 2, namely, between civil society's 'non-competitive' and the 'competitive' section. Figure 4.5 seeks to clarify these counterforces. It shows the core dilemma between corporations and virtually all other elements, spheres, and levels of *Sittlichkeit*.

Figure 4.5 shows first of all *Sittlichkeit* as the frame inside which all other actors are positioned and illustrates the three levels of morality at a vertical dimension. It depicts Hegel's middle level as more exposed than levels 1 and 3 because in that way the position of corporations becomes clear. Once all key actors of *Sittlichkeit* are in place, arrows indicate their

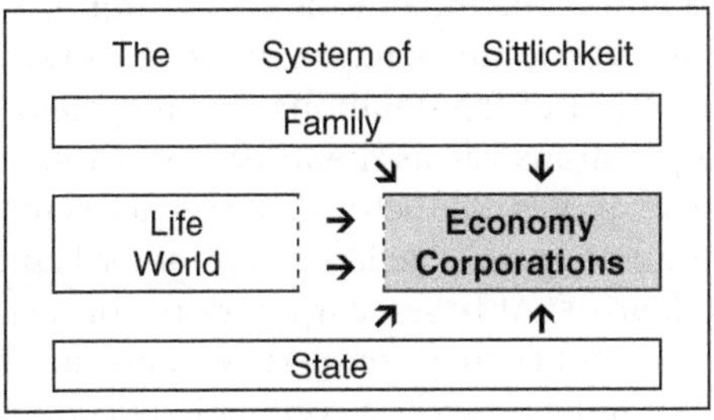


*Figure 4.5* Cooperation versus competition in *Sittlichkeit*

relationships to corporations. The multitude of arrows indicates a number of social–moral institutions based on a different normative constitution compared to that of corporations. Predominantly, these are the moral levels of family and states and the first half of civil society, namely, the lifeworld. Lifeworld, family, and states follow recognitive and moral relations (*Phenomenology*, 1807). Inside *Sittlichkeit*, the anomalistic institution remains the corporation as indicated on the right (Figure 4.5, grey shade). Hegel was aware that the entire structure was exposed to disintegration because of the centrifugal and destructive forces of markets and corporations working against *Sittlichkeit* (Westphal 2002:313). Hence, he envisioned other societal elements working towards keeping corporations within *Sittlichkeit* as indicated through arrows (Figure 4.5). These designate that virtually all other levels work towards keeping corporations within *Sittlichkeit*. The moral dilemma of 'corporations versus lifeworld' is most directly manifested in 'society versus capitalism'. This comes as a conflict between two sub-spheres working against one another, namely, 'solidarity versus competition'.

To complicate matters further but to complete the picture, one more contradiction has to be outlined. This contradiction comes as a moral dilemma 'inside' the economic sphere because this sphere is based on competition, not cooperation, mutualism, and equal recognition.[298] This creates two more dilemmas: inside civil society and the economic sphere. These can be conceptualised as follows:

1. **Markets versus Non-markets**
   There is a moral conflict between those sections of civil society that are engaged in market relationships, such as economic sphere and corporations, and those that are not, such as NGOs, trade unions, churches, boy scouts, environmental groups, and citizen planning committees.
2. **Corporations versus Capitalism**
   There is also a moral dilemma inside the economic sphere itself consisting of purely economic actors. This is, for example, manifested in the contradiction of 'corporations versus system' (the interest of individual corporations versus the interest of capitalism as a whole). To this, Hegel attributes competition as well as elements of solidarity as 'socialising functions'. Hegelian philosopher Plant (1980:59) calls this 'social solidarity'. At times, corporations form cartels in 'solidarity' while at other times they compete with one another.

   The second moral conflict is a conflict between 'individual corporations' versus 'the system of capitalism'. Both do not always share the same motives and behaviours. Corporations, for example, tend to follow more individualistic pathways as prescribed by shareholder-value, ROI as the return on investment, profit-maximisation, and The Real Bottom Line. Corporations are foremost interested in themselves. This has been perfectly expressed by the Noble Prize winner Milton Friedman (1970): 'It is the social responsibility of business to increase its profits.' On the other side of the coin, the system of capitalism needs to survive and thrive. Just two examples illustrate the contradictions of 'corporations versus system':

1. **Wages**
   For corporations, workers' wages are costs that have to be kept low. Hence, corporate management invented measures to achieve these organisational objectives.[299] There are strong incentives for management to reduce wage costs. Increases in profits are often paralleled by a bonus for management and the total value of 'their' corporation. On the other hand, there is the system of consumer capitalism that thrives on workers' wages as disposable income when converted into spending power, that is, consumption, resulting in two contradictions: 'corporate wage-reduction versus wages for consumerism' and 'corporations versus capitalism'.
2. **Education**
   The second example comes from education understood as a form of moral character building. Corporate management has reduced the concept of a broad and universal education of the spirit [*Geist*] to training for a narrow, functional, and ideological purpose. Such training schemes are opposed to what, for example, Aristotle's thought of education is, namely, the forming of the human character so that human beings can enter a human community in the spirit of morality and friendship. In spite of this, corporate training, nevertheless, is a costly affair and therefore always exposed to cost reduction measures (Magretta 2012:126–127).

These cost implications are accompanied by the second fact that works against corporate education, namely, the managerial belief that a corporation's 'most important assets – people' (Adonis 2010) might leave an organisation after training, thus resulting in a financial loss: a trained asset (tool, machine, apparatus, and investment) is gone. In sum, there is a reduction of education to functional training that is largely of no value to individuals but of high value to corporate management; the corporate cost factor works against education and a trained human resource's potential exit-option which represents the ultimate loss to a corporation. On the other side, there is the need for the system of capitalism as much as for corporations to employ trained and functional human resources. This results in severe contradictions for corporations.

These two examples show some of the individual 'corporation versus economic' system contradictions. It does not come as a total surprise that Hegel foresaw these 'corporations versus society' as well as 'corporations versus morality' contradictions. They can be made visible when contrasted to the classical dilemma of 'solidarity versus competition'. In this model, corporations are at odds with not only Hegel's moral family and states but also many institutions inside civil society that are not specifically dedicated to markets. These non-competitive and non-market-driven institutions are not 'forces of unfettered individualism and economic competition'.[300] Hence, 'the problem then confronting Hegel was to explain why the centrifugal forces of private interests did not tear peoples and their states apart' (Davis 1987:196). Hegel sought to achieve this by linking *Sittlichkeit* to 'the general will'. Many institutions of civil society are reflective of what Rousseau called 'the general will' – *volonté générale*. Once Hegel had added Rousseau's concept to *Sittlichkeit*, it began to take shape. On the downside, institutions of *Sittlichkeit* that do not represent a *volonté générale* are characterised as immoral. Institutions representing a 'general will' are likely to be trade unions, political parties, democratic parliaments, NGOs, churches, religious organisations, book clubs, bird watcher associations, public broadcasting, universities, and so on. These do not operate on a competitive basis but for the mutual benefit of their members, for solidarity, and for human enjoyment.

As a consequence, the dividing line between civil society and economy has to be seen as stronger compared to that between economy and corporations (Figure 4.5). But corporations can never be a determining factor because they operate on even narrower principles compared to the economy and because of the 'corporation versus system' problem. On the whole, the above outlined contradiction of 'capitalist system versus individual firm' remains the core problem. In addition, there are goals, such as the provision of welfare for all, that severely contradict a corporation's narrow focus on profit-maximisation. In Hegelian terms, the concept of economy – geared towards the welfare of all – remains close to the universal goals of *Sittlichkeit*. 'Welfare means the welfare of others [which is a] moment of universality.'[301] As a consequence, the sectarian interest of modern corporations works against welfare and universality. This remains one of the single most important dilemmas that capitalist economies based on markets, competition, and competitive advantage face. Nonetheless, Canadian Hegelian philosopher Gilbert (2013:163) suggests that 'Hegel thinks that work in professional associations called "corporations" enables this transformation [from individual towards universal] to take place'.

In addition to the 'individual versus universal' contradictions, there is also a dilemma that is played out within markets and in particular those markets that supply human resources, that is, labour markets. Labour market and economic policy issues are useful in order to elaborate the wage-dilemma by refocusing on corporations. Firstly, there are those economic activities and policies that have an interest in establishing a broad middle class that can be converted into consumers in order to sustain corporate capitalism. They are needed to sustain consumer capitalism under the non-neo-liberal equation of 'high wage equals high consumption'. Secondly, inside corporations, however, high wages have essentially three meanings:

1. **Rewarding top-management:**
   Top-managers and CEOs have been able to self-reward their very own constituencies for not always achieving organisational goals as Kothari's *Executive Greed: Examining Business Failures* (2010) has shown. The top-managerial mechanisms of self-rewarding are Magretta's (2012:31) 'soaring compensation packages and such perks as corporate jets'. For those who define themselves as 'managers [who are] people in positions of institutional power' substantial rewards have been possible. Managerialism seeks to justify the stratospherically high remuneration packages of CEOs largely on three grounds: management's hallucinations that 'we do an excellent job'; the international labour market for CEOs pays well; and a skilfully engineered uncoupling of shareholders and CEOs.

   Unlike everyone else in a corporation, CEOs are hardly ever exposed to performance management (Kramar et al. 2014). They, and often top-management as well, have managed to skilfully de-link their own pay from fluctuations of corporate profits. Simultaneously, CEOs have been able to link their pay to 'other' positive achievements when corporate profits are down so that shareholder voting does not negatively impact on their standing and, more importantly, on their salaries. Perhaps, it is even more important to note that shareholders of corporations are often other business corporations that share an interest in 'the enslaving function of ideologies' such as Managerialism (O'Neill 1996:19). Perhaps this is also because CEOs have accrued a high level of institutional power (Magretta 2012) over all others in a corporation which allows them to operate relatively freely. This is supported by the ideological image they have fostered about themselves which Bolchover (2005) has labelled 'The Great Leaders'.

2. **Cost reduction and cost leadership**
   For non-managerial staff the situation is different because their wages are seen by management purely as cost factors that have to be reduced. Managerial ideology uses 'cost leadership' for that (Samson & Daft 2012:309f., 2012a:251f.). Management has invented numerous instruments to achieve this, often viewing it as a zero-sum prisoner dilemma: their wage gain = my loss of bonus and a devaluation of my shares; and their loss in wages = my next bonus and an increase in the value of 'my' corporation, which gives me a favourable image in the business community and press, enabling me move to the next 'better paid' position.
3. **The positioning school**
   The demand of a never challenged ideology of cost leadership also means that CEOs must also always be cost leaders on the never-ending treadmill of dual competition and cost reduction. The managerial equation is 'the lower the cost, the higher a corporation's competitive advantage and vice versa'. These cost pressures are often used by management to reduce the cost of employees via wage reductions, outsourcing, downsizing, unpaid overtime, and so on. In some cases, top-management even plays Drucker's 'mindless and ruthless game' of *Sophie's Choice* with underlings.[302] This game is supported by Managerialism's prisoner dilemma and by management studies' rational choice model. It is not a game but management tends to view 'playing with underlings' as a game. This 'playing of games with underlings' has been expressed by one of the world's foremost management gurus, Peter Drucker, as 'a seemingly mindless game of chance at which any donkey could win provided only that he be ruthless' (Magretta 2012:1). Management's *Sophie's Choice* game-plan goes something like this: either you reduce 'your' wage costs by 20 per cent or your department will be restructured.

The rhetoric 'you' means an 'underling' in charge of a department, for example; the 'you' in reduce 'your' wage costs is the code word for the wages of those in a department; 'by 20 per cent' is often simply invented by top-management; and 'your department will be restructured' is the code word for being destroyed. Sometimes these statements are paralleled by HRM's 'or you will be performance managed out of here!', meaning her/his position will be terminated (cf. Klikauer 2010:118). In managerial ideology, this is 'purely' (!) geared towards competitiveness but can and has been used for more sinister reasons as Schrijvers (2004) has so masterfully depicted. Apart from management's more menacing reasons, the reduction of wage costs 'can' lead to an increase in the value of the corporation because of the one-dimensional managerial thinking of those involved in the process under the linear formula of 'less heads equals more profits that equals higher share prices and company value'. This is the underlying assumption of Managerialism. This, in turn, determines a corporation's position against other corporations as outlined by management's 'positioning school'.

But when seen from the perspective of the system of consumer capitalism, high wages are positive even though they simultaneously represent a negative for management. In recent decades the power of an economy geared towards the welfare of others (Hegel) has been shifted towards the welfare of corporations under a decisive offensive by neoliberalism and Managerialism. In the age of Managerialism, corporations have become a one-dimensional driving force of economic and political affairs. Eventually socially conscious economies of the 20th century mutated into corporate capitalism (21st century). This enhanced contradictory forces as economic pathologies increased. As a consequence, Managerialism demanded much stronger efforts by corporate mass media to eclipse the rising wage gaps and inequalities in societies paralleled by the deliberate creation of the working poor. These are Hegel's *Pöbel* and today's working poor suffer in precarious employment conditions while being abused by corporate mass media.[303]

This indicates that the position of corporations is no longer restricted to the economic sphere. Instead, they carry significant spillover effects into civil society. This is akin to what Habermas (1997) called 'the colonisation of the lifeworld'. In institutional terms, corporations remain in fact nothing other than a minor sub-section of an economy that itself is a sub-section of civil society. Civil societies, however, are to an overwhelming extent not yet defined by 'unfettered market forces' that have been 'unleashed' (Cullen 1988:23). Hegel was aware of market and corporate power and he became the first philosopher who systematically discussed the ethical dilemma between modern markets, corporations, and *Sittlichkeit*. This has been correctly noticed by many contemporary Hegelian philosophers. Maker (1987:8), for example, emphasised, 'As Stillman, Winfield, Plant, and Westphal especially stress, the market is in certain ways a domain of "unfreedom" and its benefits are not unqualified.'

Despite Managerialism's best efforts to invent an ideological dividing wall between markets and society, markets remain inextricably linked to *Sittlichkeit*. Nevertheless, the 'market versus *Sittlichkeit*' relationship carries several contradictory elements. Perhaps one of the foremost problems is that the market 'compels them [corporations] to focus on narrow economic concerns' (Maker 1987:8). Such a reduced focus is highly counterproductive to an understanding of the location of corporations in Hegel's *Sittlichkeit*. *Sittlichkeit* and civil society are designed to support universal *Sittlichkeit* via civil society as a whole rather than the particularity of corporate interests. Even when considered from the standpoint of civil society, corporations should not exist outside of the latter because civil society is based on *Sittlichkeit*, not on 'the force of unfettered economic competition that has been unleashed' (Cullen 1988:23). When viewed from the ethical standpoint of *Sittlichkeit*, corporations ought to be linked to *Sittlichkeit* because *Sittlichkeit* represents a universal ethics that applies to everyone and every institution inside its sphere.

In Hegelian as in Kantian philosophy, universal ethics always supersedes the managerial order of 'any' particular institution. *Sittlichkeit*'s universal interests overlay the particular and sectarian interest of corporations. Hegelian ethics demands that corporations – like any other socially constructed organisation – must remain inside *Sittlichkeit*. This assists in avoiding poverty which Hegel saw as an element with the potential to damage *Sittlichkeit*. Poverty is a social and economic issue resulting in what Hegelian philosopher Honneth calls 'pathological misdevelopments' [*pathologische Fehlentwicklungen*].[304] In *Sittlichkeit*, corporations are part of the economic sphere and therefore, at least partly, responsible for creating poverty. Modern business corporations do this through precarious working conditions, destruction of trade unions, outsourcing, mass-retrenchments, plant-closures and re-locations, and so on.

## Corporations, poverty, and the *Pöbel*

*Sittlichkeit*'s problematic issue remains the corporation because of several negatives that corporations create in the economic sphere. Hegel was well aware of the pathological impact the middle level has by producing what he called fragmentation, disruptiveness, atomisation, and disconnectedness of society.[305] He expressed his awareness that a market economy based on private property will be unable to satisfy the needs of everyone in society.[306] Hegelian philosopher Winfield (1987:58) explains,

> Neither non-profit nor profit-making corporations, private nor public enterprises, corporate nor worker in self-managed firms can prevent differences in wealth from arising [and] any free enterprise system entails social injustices and must be rejected. This applies not only to a system of unregulated private capitals but to any social order that seeks to resolve the problem of economic welfare through a principle of organisation internal to the economy.

Since much of Winfield's list is mere history today, we are left with 'profit-making corporations and private enterprises'. For one, modern business corporations are not 'self-managed firms' (Azevedo & Gitahy 2010). Managerialism has made sure that a term such as 'self-managed' has been eradicated from the public sphere.[307] Hence, corporations have been able to exclude any public input in their affairs focusing instead on their sole one-dimensional goal of profit-maximisation resulting in the above-mentioned *Fehlentwicklungen.* But the asymmetrical distribution of wealth is accepted and perhaps even actively encouraged by corporations and Managerialism. Historically, as today, Hegel remains absolutely on the mark when emphasising on the 'development of systematic economic inequalities, extreme poverty and unemployment, and eventually the cultivation of a social class that feels completely deprived of the benefits of the society around it and thus incapable of participating in a common political life'.[308] According to Davis (1987:202), 'Hegel and Thurow (1980) have pointed out: there cannot be winners in the distribution of economic resources without at the same time there being some losers.' Hegel noted further that if 'these evils' cannot be controlled, 'discontent and moral dissatisfaction' will be the consequences.[309] One such consequence is, for example, 'the objective dimension of poverty [that] is the actual distress of those who are impoverished' (Davis 1987:201).

In the age of corporate outsourcing the people who are 'actually distressed [are also] those who are impoverished'. They have been placed far away from the glamorous headquarters of multi-national corporations. Courtesy of corporate mass media, 'people in actual distress' and 'the descent of the masses into the cruel hell of squalor' (Fatton 1986:580) remain largely unseen, confined to distant corners of the *Planet of Slums.* Some of these outsourced factories – mirroring 18th-century 'Satanic Mills'– produce many of those items corporations sell through glamorous advertising.[310] In other words, a child in a plastic hut without schooling and healthcare in some of 'our' Planet's Slums is the hidden dark side of the next great super sale discount at 'your' local store with a $5 shirt made by the 'Boys without Names'.[311]

Then, as today, this remains what Hegelian philosopher Fatton (1986:579) calls 'the riddle of poverty', albeit 'for Hegel the market creates poverty'.[312] But it is not simply the market that creates poverty, corporations also participate in it and both together do more than that. According to Hegelian philosopher Bohman (2010:443), 'Poverty in civil society also raises issues of domination.' For one, domination through markets severely damages Hegel's ethics of recognition; secondly, human freedom requires non-domination; and, thirdly, domination is a grave form of 'non-recognition' and therefore highly destructive to recognition.[313] This occurs because poverty ruthlessly restricts an individual's ability of self-actualisation, self-determination, and mutual and equal recognition. Adam Smith, for example, 'talks about the exclusion of workers from public participation in terms of the lack of social good such as a linen shirt, which makes it impossible to "appear in public without shame"'.[314] Adam Smith's 18th-century 'no linen shirts' for the working poor have been replaced by cheap trainers and discount tracksuits but poverty continues. No matter whether Smith's linen shirt or a tracksuit is concerned, we know that wealthier, better educated people are more likely to participate in public debates and elections while poor, less educated, marginalised, isolated, atomised (Hegel), and disenfranchised people are less likely to do so.[315]

In the words of Herzog (2011:164), the 'market cannot create more mutual recognition and social inclusion . . . citizens aren't citoyens but only bourgeois'.[316] It is this marginalisation created by markets and corporate capitalism that represents the very opposite of Hegel's 'mutual recognition and social inclusion'. It creates bourgeois, or worse, petit-bourgeois with non-democratic, authoritarian, selfish, and egoistic attitudes rather than the *sittliche citoyen* of altruism, welfare, and community spirit. In other words, markets create 'no stable practice of recognition' because they are vertical structures of domination. They are games of seeking commercial advantages over the other side rather than instruments of mutual and equal recognition on a horizontal level. The outcome of non-horizontal, vertical forms of damaged recognition is the creation of great riches and great poverty, bourgeois, and petit-bourgeois, market winners and losers, and those who have been called riffraff and rabble.[317]

Hegel called the class that cannot 'appear in public without shame' (Smith) rabble, pauper, and *Pöbel* which translates into mob, populace, riffraff, and hoi polloi. He noted that 'poverty is one of the most disturbing problems which agitate modern society'.[318] One of Hegel's more outstanding students, a certain Left Hegelian by the name of Karl Marx

(1818–1883), later called them *Lumpenproletariat.*[319] Today, the class of the working poor is marginalised, atomised, isolated, and abused by corporate mass media as anti-social, parasites, and welfare-cheats under the 'blame the victim' ideology. For Hegel, the continuous existence of isolated and marginalised *Pöbel* under modern capitalism created enormous ethical problems. Hegel noted a 'rabble' mentality consists in a loss of the sense of right and wrong, of honesty and the self-respect' – an *Entsittlichung und Pöbelhaftigkeit.*[320] Once the 'sense of right and wrong, of honesty and the self-respect' has been destroyed by marginalisation, poverty, and 'blame the victim' ideologies, participation in Hegel's *sittliche* community becomes impossible.[321]

Hegel's discussion of poverty and the poor in relation to corporations also includes, nevertheless, a rather surprising element. He excluded day labourers from corporate membership.[322] On the other side, Hegel also thought that such day labourers 'typically work in the same industry, and often in the same factory. Once that regularity is established such labour is no longer casual and it merits recognition through labour contracts and ultimately through corporate membership'. In short, while Hegel saw day labourers as external to corporations, they can become part of a corporation through regular employment. Today, corporate management works towards the annihilation of such regular forms of employment. There is an increased casualisation of labour, sub-contracting, outsourcing, precarious work arrangements, and unstable forms of work. These have been invented and 'ruthlessly' (Drucker) applied by corporate management.[323] The casualisation of labour by corporate management, for example, carries significant pathologies for society ranging from missed school-to-work transitions to, for example, denials of bank loans because of short-term employment contracts invented and used by corporate management.

Exclusions like these are manifested in the fact that economic agents are reduced to being economic figures on a chessboard moved by economic forces that exist independently of them. Individuals in modern capitalism continue to be excluded from shaping economic affairs that are driven by anonymous markets over which no individual person, no individual corporation, no group of people – least of all the *Pöbel* – has any influence. Instead of self-actualisation, people in modern capitalism are subjugated by these forces. In the *Philosophy of Right* (1821) Hegel noted, 'The isolated individual, so far as his duties are concerned, is in subjection.' This subjection of corporate human resources, underlings, and subordinates includes suppression through managerial regimes. They exist inside an immoral organisational structure reducing them to human resources while their existence inside an immoral economic structure includes a deliberate creation of systematic 'imperfections' of labour markets, limited access to employment, unequal pay structures, and many more pathological features.

Nevertheless, it remains imperative to understand one of Hegel's prime concerns about market economies, namely, that markets – in which corporations operate – create unpredictable, arbitrary, and random behaviours of actors and organisations. Both are confined to erratic and rapidly changing markets. Hence, corporations are forced to follow economic and consumer trends blindly. Hegel expresses what management calls 'a marketing mindset', 'a capitalism-centred view of the world', and 'playing the market', as 'entire branches of industry go bankrupt, and thus throw a huge population . . . into helpless poverty'.[324] In other words, management's competition game creates winners and losers. For Peter Drucker, this is a game in which[325]

> [b]usiness can look like a seemingly mindless game of chance at which any donkey could win provided only that he be ruthless.

The managerial goal of this game is to sustain corporate profitability. This is the essence of profit-seeking behaviour leading to employing resources. Deviations from profit-maximising behaviour lead to a lower market price of corporate stocks and make corporate management an attractive and vulnerable target for takeovers that can have the replacement of management as a consequence.[326] Management has at least two reasons to increase shareholder-value (profits): firstly, profits keep shareholders happy who are, after all, the owners of the business (Magretta 2012); and, secondly, profits protect corporate management from possible annihilation in the form of takeovers, mergers, and acquisitions. This shapes the behaviour of management. It must constantly strive to prove its usefulness to the demands of markets and shareholders, nailed to the treadmill of a never-ending pursuit of competitive advantage (Porter 1985). This negates Hegel's ethics of self-actualisation because the individual 'free will' of management has been handed over to abstract and largely uncontrollable market forces inside which management is exposed to competition.[327] Relinquishing one's 'free will' sustains serious damage to *Sittlichkeit*. Nevertheless, corporate management does exactly that in favour of 'the marketing mindset' (Magretta 2012:27) albeit this mindset does not really have a mind according to Drucker's 'mindless game'. But the 'marketing mindset versus mindless game' comparison has never stopped any ideology, let alone Managerialism. Hegel was well aware of the pathologies of unhindered competition. Subsequently, his *sittliche* corporations are designed to diminish competition. This is very different from Managerialism's way of excluding it:

> Business executives are society's leading champions of free markets and competition. Truth be told, the competition every manager longs for is a lot closer to Microsoft's end of the spectrum than it is to the dairy farmers. All the talk about the virtues of competition notwithstanding, the aim of business strategy is to move an enterprise away from perfect competition and in the direction of monopoly.[328]

Hegel suggests that a *sittliche* corporation should not be exposed to 'the ruinous competition between corporations that has unpleasant consequences for affected workers and industrialists' (Greis 1995). In other words, while today's corporations are, to some extent, in competition with one another, Hegel's *sittliche* corporations should be excluded from ruinous competition as much as possible. Externally, this largely defines how these *sittliche* corporations relate to other corporations; internally, it influences the way how they organise their own affairs.

# 5
# The Morality of Corporate Relationships

*No man has natural authority over his fellow men.*[329]

In corporations most managerial relationships are not managerial but human relationships. Despite this, present-day corporate management reduces human relationships and human beings to pure human resources. This constitutes a corporate de-recognition of human beings.[330] It demolishes not only Kantian ethics of human beings as 'ends-in-themselves' but also *Sittlichkeit* of self-conscious and self-reflective human beings; in addition, it destroys Adorno's (1971) idea of 'mature–enlightened–self-reflective' [*mündige*] individuals.[331] In corporations, a human being is merely an appliance, a resource, human capital, a means (Kant), and an instrument exposed to unconscious markets. In this, corporate management sees itself as the sole force of transmission converting market determinations into 'organisational reality' – the Orwellian terminology for managerial domination. Inside corporations, this is manifested in managerial regimes. Externally, it means surrendering to labour markets. To enhance the surrender of individuals and ethics to the anonymity of markets even further, corporate management has created its own ideological prison through 'instrumental rationalities'.[332]

Contrary to Managerialism's 'human → resource' ideology that asphyxiates individuals inside a managerial toolbox, *Sittlichkeit* argues the very opposite. In his *Phenomenology*, Hegel maintains a 'transition from necessity to freedom'.[333] However, corporate management has reversed this into a 'transition from freedom to necessity' so that virtually all human beings/resources inside a managerial orbit are confined to the singularity of managerial rationality. Under management, there can be no 'free will' or human freedom that determines human action.[334] Instead, human action must be defined by management and the sole purpose of corporations, namely, the increase of shareholder-values. Hence, managerial ideology offers an endless array of ideologies constructing and supporting managerial instrumental rationality.[335] Overall, however, the destruction of the human free will and freedom is not management's prime objective. Managerial instrumental rationality has two key objectives.

Table 5.1 shows that corporate management faces two key dilemmas when viewed from *Sittlichkeit*: management has abandoned the 'human free will' in favour of instrumental rationality and blinding market determinations, and it has relinquished the 'human free will' by inventing an ideology that serves its interest of self-preservation and Porter's 'competitive advantage'. This has been covered up by Managerialism's ideological offensive called 'strategic management'. In sum, management has largely surrendered its ability to self-determine (Kant) and self-actualise (Hegel) its own affairs in favour of instrumental rationality. With this, management – at least partly – abandons ethics. Having successfully established its own (ir)rationality and ideological legitimising instruments, it is up to the market while morality vanishes into thin air.[336] Management excuses itself as a moral agency in two ways: it favours anonymous market forces that cannot be determined and creates layers of internal hierarchical structure that disallow apportioning moral responsibility. Above that, management uses self-engineered ideologies to move from 'agency to structure' supported by Adam Smith's mythology of an 'invisible hand' of market forces.[337] Paradoxically, at the same time management insists that it possesses (i) 'The Right to Manage' (Harris 1982), and (ii) an ability to forecast markets inside a theme called 'strategic management'.[338] But management's 'agency → structure' move also produces significant contradictions.

*Table 5.1* Corporate rationality and legitimacy

| Issue | Description |
|---|---|
| Rationality | It creates Hegel's constraint [*Sachzwang*] based on invented necessities that largely shape managerial decision-making seen as serving 'the' (!) market and shareholders |
| Legitimacy | It serves as a legitimising ideology that corporate management uses against its potential opponents: employees, shareholders, state regulations, trade unions, competitors, suppliers, customer advocates, NGOs, etc. |

The move towards a de-personalised, de-humanised, and immoral structure renders managerial rationality and legitimacy to being ideological tools, thereby creating a 'moral exclusion zone'. Corporations represent the 'agency→structure' move in which 'individual corporate managerial agents' are subsumed under 'corporate–internal and market–external structures'. Management uses this as supporting evidence for an approach known as MADD – moral attention deficit disorder.[339] Management sees de-personalisation and de-humanisation as important factors for its ability to excuse itself from moral responsibilities. In short, managerial ideology is built on mythical markets as pre-scribed by the belief in the invisible hand. Adam Smith's invisible hand fable however does not solve a corporation's real internal contradiction. In fact, it is also unable to solve two external contradictions.

The first level of Table 5.2 shows the continued existence of what moral philosophy calls 'moral selfishness and moral egoism' (Pinkard 2014:210). In managerial terms, this is based on a profit-motive that exists in stark contradiction to the common welfare of a society. At the second level, the unsolved dilemma of management's drive towards cost-cutting of wages, for example, contradicts the need for high consumptive levels for the survival of consumer capitalism.[340] Both contradictions represent a *Catch-22* situation for corporate management and corporate capitalism. Since they cannot be unravelled, they can only be eclipsed through ideology. In the hierarchical thinking of management, the invisible hand of market forces, for example, has assumed a God-like status to which many negative managerial decisions can be attributed in order to relinquish managerial responsibility. But this does not relate exclusively to a corporation's externalities. Inside corporations, the affairs of management mirror this ideology as well.

Internally, hierarchies, power, and functionalities also prevent *Sittlichkeit*'s 'ethical life'. The surrender of a managerial order in favour of markets affects one part of management in particular, namely, HRM.[341] It results in HRM's prime ideology of reducing human beings to corporate

*Table 5.2* The two main contradictions of corporations

| Institution | | Contradiction | | Institution |
|---|---|---|---|---|
| Corporate Selfishness | ← | Versus | → | Society's Common Welfare (Niji 2014:291) |
| Individual Corporations | ← | Versus | → | System Imperatives of Consumer Capitalism |

tools or human resources. These corporate resources are 'lifeless figures' as Immanuel Kant once noted (Klikauer 2010:82). They are forced to move on a managerial chessboard through invisible market forces via the guiding hand of corporate management. Management has established itself as the sole agency to understand these forces and has set up a belief-system that underwrites its claim to manage them. In short, an external market-driven 'agency→to→structure' move is paralleled by an internal 'human → resource' move. This managerial double-move creates ideologies resulting in what Hegelian philosopher Honneth calls pathological misdevelopments [*pathologische Fehlentwicklungen*] in line with Kant's radical distinction between 'pathology' and 'morality'.[342]

Managerialism makes the culprit that engineers such pathological misdevelopments disappear. The ideology of Managerialism uses the above outlined double-move to eject management from morality while simultaneously creating social and economic pathologies. In conclusion, corporate management has handed over its free will to the imaginary tale of markets, thereby creating a highly supportive ideology. Simultaneously, it has eliminated its own moral responsibilities through the 'double-move' that leads to pathological misdevelopments. Hegel noted some of these contradictions created by markets and economic institutions such as corporations and management. Unlike Managerialism, Hegel could never blindly accept these pathologies because of their threat to *Sittlichkeit*. To circumvent the looming danger of an unrestricted reign of markets and corporations, he saw the need to supervise corporations.

## Supervising corporations

Hegel was not unaware of the corrosiveness that markets and, within them, economic organisations such as corporations have on *Sittlichkeit*. Hence, he supplied special provisions designed to tame the negative impacts that the pathologies of capitalism have on Hegel's *Dreiteilung* [triage] of *Sittlichkeit*, as Dutch-American philosopher Peperzak (1991:261) called it. Hegel's triage includes families at level 1, civil society including corporations at level 2, and the state at level 3. Provisions that tame the negative impacts of capitalism are designed to protect the following institutions and actors:[343]

1. at level 1: children, individuals, families and members of extended families;
2. at level 2a: the non-economic side of civil society such as voluntary organisations;

3. at level 2b: the economic side of civil society (e.g. market failure) and economic actors such as corporations, trade unions, business associations;
4. at level 3: the states that include the judiciary, the legislature, and the executive, administration, bureaucracies, parliaments, perhaps even supra-national organisations (UN, EU, etc.); and finally
5. the system: this includes not just the above three levels but also Hegel's entire 'system of *Sittlichkeit*' setting moral imperatives for ethical life that covers all spheres.

Theoretically, economic theories such as those of Adam Smith and others offered next to nothing to domesticate markets, tame business corporations, or achieve *Sittlichkeit.* As a consequence, Hegel saw only one way to purge economic and corporate pathologies. He envisioned the regulative powers of state authorities as a mechanism able to discipline the arbitrary, random, non-human, non-ethical, and even pathological character of corporate decisions.[344] For that, Hegel's *sittliche* corporations needed to be corporations that were 'independent corporations' (Nederman 1987:512). But 'the conflict between business corporations and family/civil society is reconciled by a rational state' overseen by *sittliche* corporations.[345]

Given the power of corporations, Hegel saw the legal, regulative, and legislative power of states as central to the moral universality of *Sittlichkeit.* Historically, as today, and despite the populist image and ideology of a 'footloose' corporation, business corporations remain inextricably linked to states. For one, they need a place from which they can act, headquarters, production sites, and what the inventor of strategic management, Alfred Chandler, called militaristic 'field-units'.[346] These places remain within states that have legal jurisdictions over corporations from which no corporation can escape. Corporations are aware of that and, therefore, have invented ideologies such as 'footloose' corporations while equally claiming 'corporate social responsibility' and being a 'good corporate citizen'. In Hegelian philosophy, however, the term 'citizen is defined by a concept of autonomous personality that is realised only in developed political and cultural communities' of 'a genuine political order [based on] the civic virtues or public sentiment of its citizens'.[347] In the ideology of Managerialism, however, business corporations:

1. can never be 'autonomous' inside a socially constructed 'I versus society' interface;
2. they are not part of a developed political and cultural community;

3. the ideology of a business community does not reflect the Aristotle–Rousseau–Hegel concept of a cultural, moral, and political community;
4. they have no civic virtues beyond the profit-motive; and
5. no public sentiment beyond a shareholder sentiment.[348]

In short, 'Hegel championed . . . community over a system of egoism' (Buchwalter 2012a:56) while corporations represent the exact opposite. While publicly proclaiming to be a 'good corporate citizen' who follows the rules and is law-abiding, in private, a CEO admitted that[349]

> we would not knowingly break the rules anywhere. We always employ one set of experts to tell us what they are and another set to tell us how to get around them . . . it is the job of the government to make the rules, and ours to find the loopholes.

The gap between ideology and reality has created awareness among some that corporations are 'Organisations of Hypocrisy'.[350] They are hypocritical two-faced *Janus*-like organisations claiming to be law-abiding while 'privately' admitting to circumventing laws. They do not seek to establish a balance between the interest of the state and themselves but are trying to manipulate state regulations – through lobbying and corporate PR – by-passing laws wherever possible.[351] Hegelian philosophy strongly rejects this. Hegel saw a 'strong state as supervisor' over corporations.[352]

His strong state is 'not' to balance corporate powers as Managerialism might have it. The relationship between corporations, state, and *Sittlichkeit* is not horizontal as Managerialism envisions it with corporations on one side and states on the other as 'equal' partners. Instead, Hegel saw this as a vertical relationship with a clear hierarchy positioning states above corporations so that 'the corporate spirit [*Korporationsgeist*] transforms itself into the spirit of the state'. States are based on their ability to be truly universal actors. They represent the ethics of universalism having ethical and legal powers 'over' corporations. Ottow (2001:474) emphasises 'that corporations are subordinate to the higher interests of states'. For Hegel, states are the strongest and best placed institutions to ensure that corporations remain inside *Sittlichkeit*. It is the role of states to ensure that *Sittlichkeit* remains above corporations as a defining element. In that way, corporate managers are guided by *Sittlichkeit* overseen and supervised by the state. In *Sittlichkeit*, this structure can never be reversed. It remains the task of the moral state to maintain ethical life [*Sittlichkeit*]. Even though 'the role of the state is to guarantee economic wellbeing', this can never overrule the pre-eminence of *Sittlichkeit*.

But the role of Hegel's state is not to be an overtly regulative superstate in Foucault's (1995) panoptic vision, one that suffocates corporations. Instead, 'the Hegelian state is the organ and the protective cuirass of propertied power'.[353] In other words, the Hegelian state remains a supporter of propertied power – such as corporate power and corporate ownership – but, nevertheless, regulates and secures the function of corporations through its regulative powers over corporations. Once underwritten, supervised, overseen, chartered, and controlled by a moral state, corporate managers can never become independent of ethical life.[354] In the words of Hegel, 'They [corporations] need to stand under the surveillance of the public authority otherwise they might ossify, build themselves in, and decline into a miserable system of castes.'[355] Hegel specifically issued three requests to supervise corporations. Firstly, there needs to be a form of surveillance. Secondly, Hegel did not want corporations to become ossified. He was afraid that corporations would 'build themselves in'. But this is exactly what business corporations do. In the words of perhaps the world's foremost investment guru:[356]

> Warren Buffett, the legendary investor, who describes his company, Berkshire Hathaway, as a castle of capital, put it this way in remarks cited in the *New York Times*. Other people want to take our castle away . . . I reward my managers for building a moat around our castle and then making the moat deeper, wider and filling it with alligators.

While Hegel warns against corporations that 'build themselves in', management wants corporations to do exactly that – build themselves in – and even top it up with the demand that corporations erect a high wall and moat filled with alligators around them. This represents the complete opposite of *Sittlichkeit*. Third, and finally, and this comes despite Hegel's dire warning, today we might well be on the way to have modern corporations representing a 'miserable system of castes'.[357] Hegel noted that only the state can protect us from descending into such a system. But business corporations, and even more so markets, work towards such a 'miserable system of castes' because of their divisive powers that stratify society.[358]

Together with some actors in civil society such as NGOs, the state 'practices trade and market supervision, protects consumer interests, and prevents the adverse social use of types of freedom' (Kersting 1988:6). Hegel saw the state as the key institution that practises trade and market supervision guaranteeing that business corporations do not create monopolies to circumvent markets. In the conflict between individual corporations versus the system of corporate capitalism, for example, Hegel knew that the centrifugal powers of corporations would eliminate competition and the market with it. He knew that Hobbes' economic *bellum omnium contra omnes* as an unrestricted and unlimited fight of all against all would result in the domineering powers of a few corporations.[359] In the words of Hegelian philosopher Plant, 'Non-intervention in the system of needs [Hegel's term for economy] would be disastrous because all that would then exist would be blind and irrational forms of economic and corporate transactions.'[360]

In many ways, the idea of state-supervised business corporations is to protect the corporations from themselves. In order to do that, Hegel needed a strong state because business corporations themselves are as incapable as 'industry self-regulation' is. Hence, the state's involvement was required for three reasons. Firstly, remnants of Hegel's concept of 'protecting corporations against themselves' are still found in the legal statutory books of many state governments under headings such as 'competition commissions', 'non-monopoly authorities', and 'anti-cartel provisions'. Some of them still exist as institutions 'to be deregulated', exposed to an onslaught of neo-liberalism and Managerialism. But corporations, as outlined by Magretta (2012:81), work towards the exact opposite to an existence under competition:

> All the talk about the virtues of competition notwithstanding, the aim of business strategy is to move an enterprise away from perfect competition and in the direction of monopoly.

Secondly, protecting consumer interests is a state task (Plant 1980:78). It is still found in state agencies such as 'departments of fair trading' and 'consumer protection authorities'. Despite the deliberate under-funding engineered by neo-liberalism's ideology of less state, no more red tape, and deregulation, many states still uphold consumer protection. In this role, states are designed to do more than just watching; they are active. The Hegelian state is not reduced to what Managerialism calls a 'necessary evil' reminiscent of an 18th-century 'night watchman' of Liberalism and 21st-century neo-liberalism.[361] In the words of Greer (1999:573), 'Like Aristotle, Hegel conceives the state as an end in itself, not as a necessary evil that serves as a night watchman.' The concept of a state as an 'end-in-itself' (Kant) is highly alien to corporations and Managerialism that see states purely as externalities impacting negatively on corporations. For example, through consumer protection, states often prescribe health and safety standards. These are costly for corporations which are driven by cost minimisation. The pharmaceutical 'industry' – 'industry' is Managerialism's code word for corporations – is at the forefront of corporate immorality. Quite apart from the pharmaceutical 'industry', one of the most infamous cases remains the 'Ford Pinto' immorality as a prime example of a cost–benefit analysis that safeguards corporate profits but kills people.[362] For corporations, regulating immoralities such as 'Ford-Pinto' remains an unnecessary evil. Hence, the reduction of states to the status of a night watchman is – although contrary to Aristotelian and Hegelian morality – exactly what corporations and Managerialism has in mind.

Thirdly, and perhaps most importantly, states should also 'prevent the adverse social use of types of freedom'. By this Hegel did not mean Managerialism's conversion of human freedom into business freedom. Business corporations tend to reduce freedom in a carved-up version of a sectarian business freedom (the right to make money). In Hegelian philosophy, the perpetual drive to make money results in the fact that

> civil society represents the superficial world of money relations . . . the core of degradation, the 'spectacle of excess, misery, and psychological and social corruption' . . . in civil society the full horrors of the exchange market are unfolded, the basis of which is the accumulation of private wealth proceeding through the impoverishment of the labouring class. (Hegel, 1821:§185, 243, 244)[363]

While this is contrary to universal human freedom, it damages *Sittlichkeit*, and Hegel's philosophy of universal ethics. In other words, the managerial idea of 'the freedom to buy and sell what one wishes is a degenerate case of freedom'.[364] Hegel saw that narrow choices of buying and selling and unrestricted market forces have devastating impacts on civil society, *Sittlichkeit*, and human beings. Market forces and buy-and-sell ideologies are powerful enough to potentially destroy *Sittlichkeit*. In addition, 'Hegel [also] posits that market relations exert a far-reaching and profound impact on individual consciousness [and that there is] a higher mode of freedom than economic freedom' (Greer 1999:568). Hegel's human freedom enables 'individual consciousness' to flourish. In contrast, Managerialism's version of corporate freedom represents the ability of corporations to sell and buy commodities. This is a highly sectarian form of freedom related to corporations, ownership, shareholding, property, and investment.

## Hegel on property and investment

Being a philosopher of self-consciousness and *Geist*, it is human freedom that is of great relevance to Hegel's *Sittlichkeit*. For Hegel, *Sittlichkeit* needs the state to ensure that the higher moral aim of human freedom is achieved. In order to accomplish this, corporations need to be kept inside the sphere of *Sittlichkeit*. According to Winfield, 'Corporations and a just economy must be supplemented by a public administration of civil law.'[365] For Hegel, public administration represents the state and civil law. But the moral state is more than a direct expression of *Sittlichkeit*. In Hegelian ethics, states are a kind of functionaries of *Sittlichkeit*. It is *Sittlichkeit* that remains Kant's ultimate goal of a *Kingdom of Ends*.[366] Today, as during the Kantian–Hegelian 18th–19th centuries, the *Kingdom of Ends* and *Sittlichkeit* still remain distant possibilities. Instead, powerful business corporations have joined the fight against what Hegel calls *Sittlichkeit*. Predominantly, and in terms of morality, corporations do this in at least three ways:

1. like a camera obscura, business corporations have reversed the primacy of ethics over all other affairs towards what American linguist and philosopher Noam Chomsky calls 'Profit over People' (1999);
2. business corporations have replaced morality through the managerial substitution of instrumental rationality; and
3. they have reduced morality to just another issue in their management portfolio next to marketing, operations management, employment relations, and so on.[367]

It is imperative to remember that Hegel, being a moral philosopher, views all socially created institutions such as corporations from the ethical perspective of *Sittlichkeit* (Hegel 1803/04). These institutions can only exist when embedded in social practice that forms the very foundation of *Sittlichkeit*. Hegel's system starts with the family even though he eventually came to the conclusion that 'natural' family ties have been significantly weakened through the rapid social change in the wake of rising industrial capitalism that converted traditional rural peasant families to fractured, dislodged, and atomised proletarian families in impoverished urban areas.[368] Hegel's conclusion has been recognised by Hegelian philosopher Adriaan Peperzak who noted, the modern economy had 'torn the individuals off from their family bonds'.[369] But the rise of industrial capitalism and its eventual conversion into corporate capitalism also converted living rural communities into fractured and displaced industrial labour. Hegel recognised these corrosive effects.

Consequently, 'he [Hegel] is not convinced that the unintended bonds of community and solidarity generated in civil society provide enough of an educative and corrective basis' to keep corporations in check.[370] The impact of capitalism on family bonds has also been noticed by 19th-century industrialist and philosopher Friedrich Engels.[371]

With sociological sharpness and precision Engels (1892) outlined the destructiveness of capitalism on families in his seminal work *The Condition of the Working Class in Britain in 1844*.[372] Despite the devastation industrial capitalism has on families, the early proletariat tried to convert 'natural family bonds' into 'socially established bonds'. The outcome of this became known as the 'proletarian milieu' (Brecht & Ottwald 1932). The 20th-century Hegelian philosopher Plant (1980:70) sees these socially established bonds that have defined the early industrial proletariat as 'the bonds of social solidarity'. Perhaps it was a proletarian attempt to compensate against the corrosion of 'natural family bonds' during the rise of capitalism. This may have been – at least partly – successful during the 18th and 19th centuries, but the conversion of the working class into a petit-bourgeois middle class with all the trimmings of petty-consumerism and individualism further damaged family bonds and early forms of social bonds. As a result of the disintegration of families and society, Hegel was forced to view the family/socially established bonds as not strong enough to curb the looming pathologies of market capitalism which today includes business corporations.

The weakening of families and society occurred throughout the rise of industrialism and rapid capitalist advances, only to be enhanced by the subsequent pathological effects of consumerism. As a consequence, Hegel was forced to rely on the third level (states). Therefore, states almost 'had to' become the sole guarantor of corporate *Sittlichkeit*. For Hegel, it could only ever be the universally moral state that is strong enough to force corporations firmly inside *Sittlichkeit*. Not surprisingly, Hegel's ethical notion of 'universal freedom and equality of the Geist' remains contradictory to the present corporate structure.[373] For Hegelian philosopher Neschen, economic societies [*Ökonomiegesellschaften*] and corporations create substantial inequalities.[374] Given all that, Hegel tended to judge corporations negatively when viewed from the standpoint of the *sittliche* people's spirit [*Volksgeist*] that represents the collective *Geist*/spirit of an enlarged community.[375]

Despite the contradictory relationship between *Sittlichkeit* and corporations and attempts to convert Hegel's civil society into a pure

*Ökonomiegesellschaft* with all human relations expressed as economic exchange relations, Hegel's philosophy of *Sittlichkeit* remains overwhelmingly positive. In terms of British philosopher Isaac Berlin (1909–1997) Hegel's *Sittlichkeit* is not about 'negative' but 'positive' liberty (1969), namely, the 'freedom to act'. Hegel's positive definition of liberty, freedom, and *Sittlichkeit* contains a number of elements such as the notion that *Sittlichkeit* is alive during 'times of happiness' when economic hardship and excessive inequalities of wealth are absent.[376] But even during Hegel's 'times of happiness', certain levels of discomfort, hardship, and poverty remain in liberal and corporate capitalism.[377] In the *Philosophy of Right* (1821) Hegel summarised this:

> It hence becomes apparent that despite an excess of wealth civil society is not rich enough, i.e. its own resources are insufficient to check excessive poverty and the creation of a penurious rabble.

In other words, even the richest societies appear to be incapable or unwilling to exist without poverty.[378] For Hegel, 'poverty means both physical deprivation and an internal sense of alienation from society on the part of those who are poor'.[379] The growing 'injustice, social inequality [leads to] what generally Hegel calls a loss of moral life'.[380] Bobbio (1974:97) quotes Hegel's *Philosophy of Right* (1821:§185) describing this as 'physical and moral ruin' [*physisches und sittliches Verderben*]. In Hegelian philosophy, obscene levels of personal and corporate wealth, greed, and corruption that furnishes corporate crime are understood as 'extravagance'.[381] While in today's society the state is envisioned as the supervisor of business corporations preventing corporate crime – or not when neo-liberalism's hallucination of industrial self-regulation takes hold – Hegel saw his *sittliche* corporations doing the very opposite. Because his corporations are based on *Sittlichkeit*, they are able to provide 'supervision of the public power'.[382] Such a supervision could prevent today's CEOs from becoming Crime Executive Officers.

The signifier for such a 'C'EO and corporate crime became the 'CEO of the Tyco Corporation who had spent $6,000 for a shower curtain'.[383] The obvious contradictions between wealth and poverty found in corporate capitalism became already visible during the early 19th century when Hegel studied British political economy.[384] Corporations have not been able to change that – if anything, they have been an enhancing force. Hardship and excessive wealth have accompanied three centuries of capitalism.

*Table 5.3* Three centuries of capitalism

| Historical period | Description |
|---|---|
| 18th and 19th centuries | Liberal capitalism, free markets, early corporations, brutal suppression of workers, Satanic Mills |
| 20th century | Social-welfare capitalism flanked by mass-consumerism accompanied by the rise of corporations and their development into mature multi-national corporations |
| 21st century | Corporate capitalism flanked by global marketing corporations and global corporate mass media |

Table 5.3 shows three centuries of capitalist development paralleled by inequalities between rich and poor countries (www.poverty.com) and between rich and poor inside capitalist countries.[385] If anything, these gaps have been widened during the shift from liberal to corporate capitalism.[386] This includes income inequalities between CEOs and workers.[387] Despite Managerialism's ideologies such as the infamous 'rising-boat' ideology that lifts all up and the 'trickle-down effect' (wealth trickles down to everyone), stratospheric levels of inequalities – diagnosed by Hegel as extreme poverty and exorbitant wealth – remain a constant feature of capitalist economies. For Hegel, poverty and exorbitant wealth severely limit *Sittlichkeit*[388]

1. by preventing people from achieving mutual, and equal recognition,
2. by splitting society into rich and poor, haves and have-nots, owners and non-owners (Adam Smith's linen shirt becomes today's discount tracksuit),
3. by alienating, atomising, fracturing, and marginalising people, and
4. by destroying the *Sittlichkeit* of mutual aid and cooperation in favour of Adam Smith's market competition and Porter's (1985) competitive advantage.

But Hegel's critique *also extends* to 'the modern property-owning bourgeois with a sole interest directed towards securing and accumulating wealth'.[389] Today, this has created two extremes: (i) there is an ownership class that exists as shareholders (capitalists) and (ii) a petit-bourgeois class directly – or potentially – exposed to poverty which even extraordinary levels of trivial consumerism paralleled by a pro-business ideology and engineered through corporate mass media can only ever partly eclipse.[390]

These two extremes plague civil society because any division into two opposing classes affects *Sittlichkeit*'s entire structure of families, society, and states even though it took a certain Left Hegelian philosopher by the name of Karl Marx (1818–1883) to make this explicit.[391] Even before Marx, Hegel placed owners of capital or what today is called corporate shareholders, businessmen, and capitalists in the first class. For them the equation 'property equals freedom' stands. Hegel correctly 'recognised property ownership as essential for freedom' (Maker 1987:5). In the words of Hegelian philosopher Alan Patten,[392] this describes what might be named a Hegelian 'developmental thesis' denoting that 'having at least a minimum amount of private property is essential to the development and maintenance of the capacities and self-understanding which make up free personality'. The level of property ownership allows this class a level of individual freedom unseen in any economic system prior to corporate capitalism. While capitalism – Hegel calls it a 'system of needs' – depends on property, he 'sharply distinguishes property from possessions'.[393] Davis (1987:189), for example, has most correctly outlined the quintessential contribution of Hegel's philosophy on property, possessions, and freedom:

> For Hegel property is 'the primary mode of freedom', and is thus 'in itself a substantive end' – that is, an end in itself [Hegel, 1821, 33 & 45]. In the course of his analysis, Hegel distinguished property from mere possessions by the necessary introduction of the presence of the will in the former category. Possession means only having power over a thing outside oneself, but in property one becomes an object to oneself, one recognises oneself herein and is recognised by others as well. In crossing the threshold from possession to property – and in so doing the element of self-consciousness (as contrasted, for example, with sense-consciousness) is required – one becomes for the first time an actual will.

In other words, the key difference between possessions and property, as outlined by the philosopher of phenomenology [*Geist*], is, to put it in simple terms, possessions are things we have while property are those things to which, in managerial terms, ROI – return on investment – is assigned. What creates property and possessions is a mental process – an act of the *Geist*. For example, the house we live in is not a property. It is a possession because we do not own it for ROI. An investment property in which we do not live is property because it is owned for ROI. Only when the human *Geist* assigns such a will (ROI, for example) to possessions do they become property. In the 'use versus exchange value' model, for example, possessions are for use but when owned for exchange, they become property. This is an important and perhaps somewhat Kantian distinction because we assign certain *geistige* (Hegel) intentions (Kant) to material objects. One implication of this might be that Hegel cannot be seen as a straightforward supporter of property-owning capitalism. Hegel clearly distinguishes between commercial property and private possessions with his emphasis being on possessions when discussing freedom. 'Indeed, since Hegel assumed that private [possessions] are the embodiment of personality, it can only be concluded that a vast mass of the population is condemned to life as less than humane existence' (Fatton 1986:589). During the 19th century, this applied to early liberal capitalism as it applies to today's global corporate capitalism.[394]

Hegel acknowledged that the result of this 'is the dependence and distress of the masses'. The distressing experience of poverty comes from being poor – a 'lack of possession' (Hegel) – and being forced to live with the bare minimum of personal possessions, exemplified by not even having a 'linen shirt' (Adam Smith). Being forced into such a position means to be rendered 'incapable of feeling and enjoying the broader freedoms and especially the intellectual benefits of society' (Fatton 1986:589). A satisfying level of ownership of private possessions assists freedom because it relieves individuals from absolute and relative poverty.[395] Hence, Hegel suggested 'a minimum on possessions' to enable individuals to exist, be *sittlich*, and live a life in relative happiness.[396] On the other hand, commercial and corporate property is expressed by the fact that most shareholders of corporations are corporations themselves.[397] Since this is inextricably linked to corporate capitalism, Hegel has frequently emphasised the pathological consequences of trading commodities via markets. All this does not mean, however, that Hegel was an unquestioning advocate of capitalism. As Maker noted,[398]

> Most fundamentally, a subjective will whose only interest lies in and whose only actions are directed towards the satisfaction of personal inclinations and desire is still unfree and undeveloped, a slave either to these desires and inclinations or to arbitrary caprice.

In other words, following markets and carrying out the illusive and often self-invented demands of capital under the managerial heading of The Real Bottom Line (Magretta 2012:129–140) does not render management free. Neither (i) the satisfaction of personal inclinations to work towards The Real Bottom Line; (ii) nor the desire for shareholder-value and profit-maximisation, (iii) nor following 'arbitrary' markets will make corporate management free. In fact, it results in the exact opposite of Hegelian freedom. It is the 'unfreedom' of an existence rather than moral life [*Sittlichkeit*] that has been handed over to the arbitrary forces of uncontrollable markets. In Magretta's terms (2012:32), it is 'the unrelenting discipline of the capital markets' that tells corporations what to do. It eliminates the much acclaimed managerial ideology of 'corporate decision-making' as signified, for example, by management studies journals such as the *Journal of Management and Decision Making* and *Strategic Decision Making – A Journal of Management.*

These journals, the overall ideology of Managerialism, and the crypto-academic setup of management studies are dedicated to the ideological procrastination of managerial choices flanked by rational choice models and the ever-present prisoner dilemma. These are part of 'Impression Management' (Rosenfeld et al. 1995) seeking to pretend that management is really in control of capital, ownership, markets, and corporations. Most importantly, the illusion of managerial decision-making enhances the legitimacy of management. These ideologies are supportive of an administrative need left open by a gap between business owners on the one hand and corporate management of corporations on the other after the historic split between ownership and corporate management.

In historical terms, Hegelian ethics originates from a time 'before' capital was divided into ownership of capital with control over capital institutionalised through shareholders on the one hand and corporate management on the other.[399] To shareholders and CEOs top-management can be added because shareholders, owners, CEOs, and top-management show high levels of interest-symbiosis. This interest-symbiosis is transmitted to everyone in the managerial orbit through Managerialism. Hegel calls this the business class. The business class includes corporate management running business corporations but they do so in stark contrast to Hegel's *sittliche* corporation. On the relationship between a business class and Hegel's *sittliche* corporations, Canadian philosopher Renato Cristi (1989:729) noted,

> The natural selfishness of the business class is to be tamed by [Hegel's *sittliche*] corporations. Corporations should instil a spirit of solidarity among their members and eliminate conspicuous consumption, which he interprets as a compensation for the modern loss of status and sentiments of honour.[400]

Then, as today, Hegel was correct to describe those in the vicinity of Managerialism as business class (Mills 1956). Equally, he was accurate in ascertaining their behaviour as 'selfish' and creating pathologies that have to be 'tamed' (cf. Samuel 2010). However, unlike Hegel's *sittliche* corporation, business corporations do not 'instil a spirit of solidarity' among their members and they do not eliminate conspicuous consumption. Corporate management achieves this in two ways: (i) through their strict division of corporate members into management and non-managerial staff defined as underlings, subordinates, human resources, etc.; and (ii) through a relentless enforcement of competition and individualism. Both are capable of diminishing the ethical 'spirit of solidarity'. Externally, corporations – for example, corporate mass media – broadcast the exact opposite to solidarity: competition, conspicuous consumption, and hyper-individualism. Media-corporations are financed through advertising revenue created to encourage conspicuous consumption (McChesney 2008). Today multi-national media corporations behave *unsittlich* by encouraging conspicuous consumption. They can never cut off their method of financing (Kieran 1997). This represents a clear 'norm versus norm' contradiction in the form of two diverging norms, namely, '*Sittlichkeit* versus profits'. As a consequence, *Sittlichkeit* would eventually lead to the demise of media corporations in the present form. Business and media corporations work towards the exact opposite, thereby enhancing organisational and societal pathologies.

Hegel describes the pathological behaviour of a business class as 'the luxury of the business class and their passion for extravagance and wastefulness'.[401] Of interest is his term *Verschwendungssucht* which is a combination of *Verschwendung* [wastefulness] and *Sucht* (addiction). Once combined, it means 'an addiction to wastefulness' reminiscent of a socio-pathological behaviour. The previously mentioned case of the Tyco CEO exemplifies a deeply ingrained and highly common behaviour of 'an addiction to wastefulness' among top-management. An equally visual image of top-management's 'infinite greed' has been most exquisitely depicted in Oliver Stone's movie *Wall Street* (1987) and the 2010 sequel *Wall Street: Money Never Sleeps*.[402]

Along with business owners, CEOs, and top-management, there is a second group that plagues *Sittlichkeit*. This is the non-managerial class of employees and workers who – after liberal capitalism turned into consumer capitalism – mutated into the class of petit-bourgeois.[403] Marx argued that the rise of industrial capitalism would lead to a rise in the proletarian class followed by increasing conflicts between capitalists and workers which, eventually, will result in an overthrowing of capitalism.

Hegel, on the other hand, foresaw the exact opposite of Marx's prediction in what might be called a 'petit-bourgeois fraction'. He argued that the working class will take on bourgeois values such as pettiness, selfishness, and individualism and become petit-bourgeois themselves. During the 19th century, Hegel and Marx were unable to imagine the exact configurations of capitalism's future development from 19th-century liberal to 20th-century mass-consumer to 21st-century consumer capitalism. The current form of capitalism relies on corporate mass media as an accompanying ideology fulfilling two functions – consumerism and ideological support – via the political sphere of consumer capitalism (Rowbottom 2010). Hegel foreshadowed that capitalist societies would take quite a different route to what Marx suggested 'after' Hegel's death.

Today, 20th-century middle-class petty 'commodity fetishism' (Winfield 1987:47) has mutated into a form of 'influenza-sickness', termed *Affluenza* that converts the *Affluent Society* into a sickness.[404] Given the development of capitalism since the 19th century, one is tempted to argue that Hegel was right. Bourgeois societies have indeed mutated into middle-class society with petit-consumerism in which corporate mass media engineer individualist values, selfishness, and egoism. In Hegelian ethics, however, 'the individuals do not live as private persons for their ends alone'.[405] According to Hegel, when 'individuals' interests [are] given free rein, accidental caprices and subjective desires put people at risk, and make the satisfaction of their needs 'a matter of luck'.[406] Perhaps this is exactly what the ideology of 'consumer choice' fosters. It gives individuals a free shopping reign which has been successfully associated with individual freedom by corporate mass media.[407]

In a consumerist society, the ever diminishing degree of real life choices has been further reduced to the accidental caprice of consumerism when life choices become mere consumptive choices. While human beings have next to no choice other than to oscillate between work and consumerism, they are offered an endless choice on types of toothpaste. The enforced 'choice' to exist in consumer and corporate capitalism exposes individuals to 'risks' rendering their lives to 'a matter of luck' (Hegel). In sum, the ideology of a false individual freedom over consumer choices inside middle-class existence has successfully removed Hegel's *sittliche* solidarity that once existed in communities of a proletarian working class. These communities are no longer able to counterbalance free-market ideologies, thereby driving towards life as an endless chain of risks, changes, and luck.

On top of that, corporate mass media have effectively annihilated even the slightest memory of Marx's proletariat fighting against class society and creating universal health cover, unemployment benefits, an economy of full employment, public schooling, social security, free universities, Occupational Health & Safety (OHS) regulation, and so on.[408] What occurred during the 20th century was not a revolutionising of workers but their pacification in a process that ended Berthold Brecht's (1898–1956) proletarian milieu as a *Farewell to the Working Class*.[409] Neither Hegel nor Marx could have foreseen 20th century's *Fordist* mass-production and mass-consumption. While both were keen students of Enlightenment philosophy and economy, Hegel's writings on society appear to be on the mark. Perhaps this might also explain the fact that British and Scottish Enlightenment philosophers and economists had great influence on Hegel's philosophy. But Hegel's main predecessor, at least in philosophical terms, remains Aristotle (Ferrarin 2011) closely followed by Hegel's more contemporary philosophical counterpart, the French philosopher Jean-Jacques Rousseau (1712–1778). After all, it was Rousseau who wrote in his *A Discourse on the Origin of Inequality* (1755):

> The first man who, having enclosed a piece of ground, bethought himself of saying 'this is mine', and found people simple enough to believe him, was the real founder of civil society. From how many crimes, wars and murders, from how many horrors and misfortunes might not anyone have saved mankind, by pulling up the stakes, or filling up the ditch, and crying to his fellows, 'Beware of listening to this impostor; you are undone if you once forget that the fruits of the earth belong to us all, and the earth itself to nobody.'

Rousseau's *Discourse* left a deep impression on Hegel (Ilting 1974:66). But it was the former's writings on democracy that alerted Hegel to an issue barely mentioned by Hegel: democracy![410] While Hegel seems to have a general distrust of parliamentarian democracy,[411] what today is called 'deliberative democracy'[412] might represent an ideal vehicle for an ethics that sees institutions like corporations as democratic institutions governed by its members to achieve *Sittlichkeit*'s self-determination and self-actualisation.

Today, to a somewhat limited extent we find parliamentarian democracy in modern consumerist societies successfully sidelined and perhaps shelved into the formal political sphere of occasional voting spectacles as guided by corporate mass media with many years between them. This is paralleled by a stunning absence of democracy in daily lives, in managerial regimes, and in corporations (Riedel 1981:240, 251). In short, individuals spend eight hours almost every day in institutions with absolutely 'no' democracy while ticking a box every four years. Above that, we are made to believe that this is democracy and this is widely accepted. It is perceived as normal and remains unquestioned, unchallenged, un-uttered, and un-spoken (Poole 2006). Already, Hegel's *Geistes*/mental-link between corporations and democracy has been made unthinkable while 'democratic management' remains an oxymoron just as much as the 'democratic corporation'. These links have been disconnected and rendered impossible.[413] Despite the introduction of democracy into many countries, corporations have successfully avoided becoming democratic institutions. Hence, management runs anti-democratic corporations. They are organisations that Hegel would call 'mercantile money aristocracy'. Despite the corporate totalitarianism that rejects democracy, these anti-democratic corporations influence the affairs of democratic society. Managerialism seeks to convert the whole of society into 'mercantile money aristocracy' guided by market-exchanges and what Hegel calls *Willkür*.[414]

## Hegel's political economy, markets, and *Willkür*

In 1797 Hegel moved to Frankfurt, Germany's dominant city of the mercantile money aristocracy, where he experienced a rising money-capitalism first-hand which led him to a more detailed study of British economics. But he also engaged in a fundamental critique of Kantian morality. Hegel argued that Kantian ethics suppresses human needs and desires through artificial commandments [*lebensfremde Gebote*]. For Hegel, this turned morality into something alien and dead. He viewed Kantian categorical imperatives as lifeless, as the so-called 'laws of capitalist exchange' governing corporations. Mysteriously, many of these 'laws' are based on nothing but an invisible hand. To Hegel the invisible hand was an attempt to cover up the economic contradictions inherent in capitalism but while Adam Smith sought to cover them up, Hegelian philosophy highlights them by emphasising them in his writings on *Sittlichkeit*. Invisible-hand-like and ideologically motivated cover-ups prevent *Sittlichkeit*. Hegel argued that only when an economic structure is truly supportive of an ethical system can *Sittlichkeit* be achieved. But the real problem of market's preventative effects on *Sittlichkeit* rests in Adam Smith's economic selfishness.

Capitalism and corporations thriving on selfishness alienate Hegel's 'holistic character of human beings' that remains a necessity for *Sittlichkeit*. The raw economic dependency created by markets that individuals experience as a lifeless mechanism is contradictory to *Sittlichkeit*.

Hegel emphasised that market-determined private property represents a 'lifeless dividing force' set up against human beings. As a result, its overt focus on market-driven exchanges relinquishes a 'public' in favour of a 'consumptive-private' sphere reflective of a Greek *oikos economy*.[415] It attests to the overtaking of *citoyen* by bourgeois, thereby leading to a destruction of democracy.[416] The citoyen is needed for democracy and *Sittlichkeit* while the bourgeois is (i) a destructive force, (ii) set against the former, and (iii) prevalent in capitalist societies and business corporations. Reflections like these make Hegel the only philosopher of German idealism who engaged systematically and philosophically with economic theories, corporations, and the Industrial Revolution and their impact on *Sittlichkeit* (Hegel) and *The Human Condition* (Arendt 1958; Riedel 1974c:818). Hegel correctly saw the Industrial Revolution in the light of philosophy and Enlightenment, viewing it as the beginning of a new historical epoch.

In the wake of these changes, Hegel realised that human life was forced to surrender to external material–economic forces that exist beyond the realm of individual influences and severely hamper human self-actualisation. Rather than establishing human freedom, people become subjugated to the egoism of ownership [*Egoismus des Habens*]. This destroys the *Sittlichkeit* of a human being as a holistic sensual–spiritual unity (Neschen 2008:85). To achieve such a unity, Hegel demanded that economic affairs be subservient to *Sittlichkeit*. Otherwise the wealth of modern societies would not be distributed equally, thus resulting in economic and societal inequalities in which individuals without linen shirts (Adam Smith) are unable to participate. Contrary to *Sittlichkeit*, what we find under corporate capitalism is that 'disproportionate riches', capital, and wealth are concentrated in the hands of a few, resulting in pathologies and damaged and unethical lives.[417]

Hegel's ethics highlights this as a central point: economic affairs are to be placed below *Sittlichkeit*. For Hegel, it is the human quest for freedom that sets the history of mankind in motion. This motion is directed towards the realisation of *Sittlichkeit*.[418] The 20th-century Hegelian philosopher Marcuse (1941:231) noted that in Hegelian philosophy, the final destination of history is 'not simply progress to freedom, but progress in the self-consciousness of freedom'. What Hegelian philosophy emphasises is more than a simple progress towards human – rather than neo-liberalism's economic – freedom. Being a phenomenological (1807) philosophy of the *Geist* and idealism, Hegelian philosophy always insists on the progress of human self-consciousness as an essential necessity for human beings. In turn, 'progress in the consciousness of human freedom' is to be paralleled by progress in the consciousness of economic freedom. By themselves, however, economic affairs and economic freedom are incapable of historic movements.

Economic affairs can never exist disconnected and independent of the holistic concept of human freedom and *Sittlichkeit* which are holistic concepts [Hegel's *sittliche Ganze*]. As a consequence, Hegel's system of *Sittlichkeit* represents an all-encompassing philosophical system.[419] With it, Hegel remains one of the last great philosophers who has developed an entire, complete, holistic, and self-contained system of philosophy. In this philosophical system, corporations are no more than just 'one' aspect. For Hegel, this aspect of economics cannot be 'left to its own destiny' because of 'the bestiality of absolute economic thought and action' (Neschen 2008:121). This bestiality is found in three distinctive outcomes of liberal market economics:

1. its factual expressions in widespread poverty that accompanies market economics;
2. in the sheer unpredictability and randomness [*Willkür*] of economic affairs;[420] and
3. in corporations operating inside free and, therefore, unpredictable markets.

The Hegelian notion of the randomness of economic activities and its negative effects on human beings appears in several places in his philosophical writings. Viewed from his famous 'master–slave' dialectics, Hegelian philosophy frequently analyses why workers rather than management have been on the receiving end of seemingly uncontrollable poverty cycles.[421] Above that, Hegelian ethics argues that 'man's ethical life, having its principle in freedom, is elevated above all necessity and chances' (Peddle 2000:127). While his ethics advocates the absence of randomness, arbitrariness, risks, and changes, corporations, however, are based on the exact opposite. For management guru Peter F. Drucker (1909–2005), for example, corporate management first of all is a mindless game of chances at which any donkey could win provided only that he be ruthless.[422]

Once Hegel's ethics of 'elevating human beings above necessity and chances' is brought into contrast with management's 'mindless game of chances' (Drucker), it becomes evident that management exists in contradiction to *Sittlichkeit*. *Sittlichkeit* can never be in favour of a 'mindless game of chances' that relinquishes the human 'free will' for the 'unfreedom' of an always alienating market.[423] It highlights the fact that markets, societies, and corporations are not simply made up of atomised individuals that simultaneously are being made economically dependent on one another (Sartre 1996:90). Management's atomising individualism is further enhanced and enforced through rafts of HRM techniques.[424] In contrast to the individualism propagated by management, Hegelian philosophy emphasises that 'labour cannot be an idiosyncratic, individual act; rather, the economic imperatives of civil society must govern it [(labourers) in order to] make themselves links in this chain of social connexion' (Greer 1999:564). Hegel sees the totality of work which includes managerial work not as Managerialism's competitive game, but as a cooperative arrangement.[425] This carries, at least, three meanings for management:

1. work as such and even managerial work is not as individualised as management and Managerialism would like to have it; instead,
2. work is part of a social chain that provides the economic fundamentals of civil society; and
3. the social existence of work as well as its economic function is established through a 'chain of social connexion' that is socially constructed.[426]

On the negative side, however, Hegelian philosophy emphasises that among the managerially atomised corporate individuals no social welfare, mutual care, moral trust, or solidarity can exist. It is because of this that Hegelian ethics describes the outcomes of these managerial processes geared towards the individualisation as atomised and selfish individuals. In business corporations, individual selfishness and moral egoism can be found in human resources and in corporate management as fostered by management and HRM (internally). Externally meanwhile, the historical trajectory of generations of pacified former working class members together with authoritarian schooling (Bowles & Gintis 1976) and all of this linked to the ideological effects of corporate mass media have 'pre-prepared' human beings in such a way that they enter managerial regimes willingly and without questioning (Klikauer 2008:33, 75, 131ff.).

Being exposed to the ideological forces of Managerialism creates a sort of behaviour that resembles what Hegelian philosophy calls a 'swarm of arbitrary actions'. This is what Hegel meant by *Wimmeln von Willküren* [swarming arbitrariness] in his *Philosophy of Right* (1821:§189).[427] Inevitably, a *Wimmeln von Willküren* leads to damaged and inauthentic choices. In the words of Herzog,[428] arbitrariness or *Willkür* can be seen in a 'pursuit of [managerial and corporate] self-interest [that] leads to a situation that looks chaotic and disorganised at first glance, an apparently scattered and thoughtless sphere'. The 'scattered and thoughtless sphere' which is the sphere of corporate management creates relentless problems for *Sittlichkeit.*[429] The way corporations are governed often represents moral peevishness [*moralische Verdriesslichkeit*] for Hegelian *Sittlichkeit.*[430] The systematically engineered *moralische Verdriesslichkeit* and disconnection between *Sittlichkeit* and business corporations destroys Hegel's concept of a moral good. It is this 'moral good' rather than a corporation's *moralische Verdriesslichkeit* that is represented in the idea of human freedom and *Sittlichkeit*, seeking to actualise itself as the world's final destination. In Hegelian philosophy, this destination remains self-actualisation and freedom, not economics, corporations, and The Real Bottom Line. The role of corporations in this move towards the world's final destination is not to be a business corporation but a *sittliche* corporation.

The role of corporations, capitalism, markets, and economy along the way towards *Sittlichkeit* has been discussed by many Hegelian and Neo-Hegelian scholars. According to the Hegelian philosopher Neschen (2008:279), for example, 'Hegel does not reject liberal market economies outright' while Ross (2008b:51) emphasised Hegel's argument in favour of 'the freedom of labour and the open pursuit of economic activities' (Holz 1968:58). On the other hand, Greer (1999:562) argues that 'while Hegel basically shares the economic liberalism of classical political economy, he offers a vision of the *telos* of society that differs markedly from this school'. Nakano (2004:33, 49; cf. Plant 1980:86) noted, 'Hegel's economic thought is not a form of economic liberalism [but more like] Keynesian macroeconomic policy.' This assessment is in line with Fatton who noted that[431]

> Hegel was a bourgeois political economist . . . his awareness of capitalist exploitation and injustice never led him to reject capitalism itself [and] Hegel was not some sort of early social democrat.

Certainly, Hegel was pro-capitalism but this does not mean that he was a neo-liberal in economic and political terms. Herzog (2011:83), for example, argues that 'Hegel does not really want to leave the economy free'. Meanwhile, German philosopher Schmidt am Busch suggests a sort of middle way between state and free market when arguing that Hegel favoured a *korporativ verfasstes modernes Gemeinwesen*,[432] a kind of 'corporately constituted community'.[433] While Hegel's moral corporation might also carry connotations to what political science theory calls 'corporatism',[434] it is perhaps more likely to see *sittliche* corporations as cooperatives, yet not as inward-looking production associations but as engaging with civil society to further *Sittlichkeit*. To some extent, the initial view expressed by Neschen is certainly not completely wrong. This is for three reasons:

1. Hegel's view on the importance of property as the foundation of capitalism;
2. Hegel's emphasis that property is a key element of bourgeois society; and
3. Hegel's support for state protection of private property rights.

On the other hand, Hegel's *Philosophy of Right* (1821), according to Ilting (1974:56), states the complete opposite: 'Basically Hegel admits, that provisions relating to private property must be subordinated to the higher spheres of law, a community, and the state.' This is to be understood in Hegel's interest in curbing the free market and 'the cynicism of laissez-faire liberalism'.[435] Hegel being the philosopher of freedom (Franco 1999), many of his key concepts are in fact contradictory to the behaviour of corporate capitalism, markets, and business corporations.[436] These themes are human (not economic) freedom, Hegel's master–slave dialectics, mutual and equal recognition, the 'free will', alienation, the 'world of objects', self-consciousness, self-actualisation, *Geist*, and above all *Sittlichkeit*.[437] All of them challenge business corporations and the way they are governed by corporate management, known as corporate governance. The view of Hegelian philosophy and *Sittlichkeit* on corporate governance is the subject of the next chapter.

# 6
# Corporate Governance and *Sittlichkeit*

*The category of freedom pervades all areas of Hegel's philosophy.*[438]

Business corporations are governed by 'corporate management'. This takes place inside Hegel's 'system of *Sittlichkeit*'. Hence, corporate governance and *Sittlichkeit* are inextricably linked.[439] Therefore, the managerial concept of corporate governance warrants a detailed examination in the light of Hegel's moral philosophy of *Sittlichkeit*.[440] Management and its crypto-scholarly field of management studies commonly see corporate governance as a set of processes, customs, policies, and institutions affecting the way corporations and companies are directed, administered, and controlled.[441] This chapter focuses more on those aspects of corporate governance that are concerned with how corporations are 'administered and controlled' rather than the relationship between corporate boards and shareholders. Corporate control, corporate administration, corporate boards, and shareholder relationships are administered by managers who are paid professionals. As an economic resource, a social class, and as administrators of corporations, these managers often follow their own self-interests, which is not always the same interest as the corporate interest.[442]

In order to prevent managers from making decisions that benefit themselves to the detriment of corporations, a system of checks and balances has been invented.[443] This system is called 'corporate governance'. In the words of Hegelian philosopher and expert on Hegel's writings on *Die Korporation* [the corporation], Wolfgang Kersting (1988:8), corporate governance can be seen as an instrument of internal regulation [*Innensteuerung*]. At a minimum, such an *Innensteuerung* or corporate governance includes a board of directors that hires, fires, and compensates management.[444] In *Sittlichkeit*, the managers of corporate governance are 'members of corporations [that] come together primarily to further their own individual interests (a quite legitimate motive within civil society)'.[445]

With this, Hegelian philosophy points the finger to one of the first problems of corporate governance, namely, the contradiction between managerial 'self-interest' and organisational 'corporate interest'. While textbook ideology on corporate governance and management tells us that these are always the same, reality appears to indicate otherwise.[446] It is endemic – if not systemic – that the interest of CEOs and top-management supersedes corporate interests. The Enron Corporation, the AIG Insurance Corporation, the World.Com Corporation, and Bernie Madoff are only the latest newcomers in a sheer endless list of what Managerialism's ideology labels 'bad apples', indicating that this is not systemic but down to a few bad apples.[447] This endless list of 'bad apples' indicates that the pretended system of 'checks and balances' provides – and this is despite Managerialism's ideology of efficiency – an inefficient system to prevent an ever growing long list of very serious managerial crimes, managerially re-framed as misbehaviours. These misbehaviours encompass a wide variety of corporate activities ranging from minor misdeeds such as faked hotel bills to environmental destruction, white collar crime, and the bankruptcies of entire corporations. The internet site *Wikipedia*, for example, has published an incomplete list of corporate bankruptcies that occurred in spite of – or perhaps because of – 'good' corporate governance as a system of checks and balances.[448]

In other words, what constitutes corporate governance appears not so much to be a well-functioning and efficient system of checks and balances that prevents corporate collapses such as Lehman Brothers, World. Com, Enron, white collar crime, environmental destruction, and the like but a system that produces corporate managers who have successfully isolated themselves from a supposedly efficient system of checks and balances under corporate governance. In sharp contrast to the ideology of corporate checks and balances, *Sittlichkeit* views the role of corporations in the opposite way. It denotes 'the isolated, free individual can be integrated into the harmonious social totality only by identifying with a specific estate [the business estate or business community] and by becoming a member of a corporation'.[449]

Corporate top-management and CEOs are members of corporations. However, top-management and CEOs have successfully isolated themselves from their own middle-management, non-managerial staff, and other stakeholders through a number of ideological instruments starting with the infamous but never existing 'open-door policy'.[450] In reality corporate management has distanced itself from corporations in communicative terms through strict reporting regimes (Klikauer 2008), managerially invented hierarchical structures, power relationships, office locations distant to production sites, outsourcing, and others.

This represents the exact opposite of Hegel's *sittliche* corporation. For Hegel, there should not be any isolation inside corporations. Instead, corporate members – and this includes CEOs – should be 'integrated into the harmonious social totality' (Cullen 1988:28) and into a 'close-knit *sittliche Harmonie*' (Plant 1980:71). In other words, CEOs and other corporate members should be able to 'identify' themselves 'with the harmonious social totality [of] a specific estate', namely, the corporation, and as such anyone should be able to do so simply 'by becoming a member of a corporation' (Cullen 1988:28).

Becoming a member of a well-balanced organisation is designed to compensate for the growing deficit of harmony currently created by corporate governance internally and corporate capitalism externally.[451] Corporate governance should not just have faked corporate mission statements and Orwellian features such as 'open-door policies'. Instead, it should follow an integrative approach moving human beings towards a harmonious organisation. To some extent, this excludes the conversion of market competition into organisational competition as engineered by corporate management and which places employees in a competitive relationship with one another. Corporations should also consciously seek to compensate for a growing deficit of harmony inside capitalist economies. This means that Hegel's *sittliche* corporations are designed to counteract the lack of harmony that exists under capitalist market relationships. In short, *sittliche* corporations should not enhance competitive relationships but create harmony. On the downside, it has been shown that corporations tend to be places where the full extent of competitive relationships exists. This is exposed in the existence of the extreme form of corporate psychopaths and in non-psychopathological but still highly problematic forms of organisational behaviours depicted by corporate management.[452]

For Hegel, corporations are *sittliche* institutions like any other institution in his *System der Sittlichkeit*.[453] As such, they are 'rational social institutions [that] promote collective well-being'.[454] Hence, 'Hegel introduces corporations because he recognises that civil society gives its members the right to form social interest groups to advance jointly their common needs [and] the activity of corporations does comprise a further mode of civil freedom.'[455] Hegel sees corporations as 'one' form of social organisation inside civil society that promotes 'collective well-being', a society's 'common needs', and the mode of 'civil freedom'. This is not economic freedom (free market), business freedom (free exchange of commodities), or managerial freedom (the managerial prerogative) but civic and human freedom. Hegelian philosophy also acknowledges an individual's right of joining a business organisation to 'advance jointly their common needs' and interests as long as they are aligned to *Sittlichkeit*. In sum, Hegel sees corporations as organisations that contribute to the 'common' good of society, not the sectarian needs of shareholders. Hegelian philosophy rejects today's idea of economic rationalism, econometrics, and the neo-liberal view of economics that reduces every eventuality of human life to simple exchange equations while simultaneously eliminating those who are really concerned, namely, human beings:

> According to Hegel, political economy is a human science, not a science that studies impersonal forces or natural laws, but one that takes 'man' as its subject . . . For Hegel, the subject matter of economics is not charts and graphs, but human beings, groups, institutions, and nations. What contemporary economists might learn from Hegel is that the economy is moral, legal, and political – in a word, human.[456]

It appears that the irrational but ideological quest to be seen as 'scientific' has resulted in an artificial objectification of science that has paradoxically eliminated those about whom economic and managerial science was initially concerned, namely, human beings. This quest has de-personalised and de-humanised economic and managerial science. The human subject has been sacrificed in favour of an ideological quest of objectivity and positivism. It appears that the ideological process of 'scientification' – seen as a process that turns management, for example, into the science of management – has been set in motion. As a consequence, Managerialism's prime legitimising agency – management studies – has progressed to an ideological stage where the human subject simply disappears. What is left is pure ideology. The elimination of human beings is damaging to so-called scientific endeavour and is decisively immoral.

Hegelian philosophy would always insist that human beings remain at the centre of management studies, organisational studies, and economics. Hegelian scholars have even argued that his philosophy defines economy not only as a political but more as a social phenomenon. For Hegel, it is a moral–social character that creates organisations such as corporations and their surrounding structure, that is, an economy. Corporations are socially constructed.[457] In Hegel's social and ethical economy, human beings rather than impersonal, de-personalised, and de-humanised mathematical equations take centre stage. But the managerial use of mathematics and numbers is designed to give management the aura of being scientific while simultaneously engineering a highly political enterprise. Managerialism and management studies have furthered this through the use of so-called rational choice models such as the infamous prisoner dilemma. In engineering, managerial, and positivist fashion this serves three functions:

1. It eliminates the human from the managerial equation.
2. It narrows human freedom to the ideology of free choice enshrined in the simplistic notion of an 'A or B' choice. In the words of Greer (1999:558), 'In order to be freely self-determining, an individual human "will" must not choose between arbitrary given ends.' But this is exactly what the managerial prisoner dilemma and management studies' rational choice models demand of individuals.[458]
3. It gives the impression of being technical, value-neutral, objective, natural, and 'scientific'.[459]

Instead of Managerialism's ideology of 'natural' laws which can never exist inside the socially constructed reality of management, human beings remain the key subject in Hegel's concept of *sittliche* corporations. Hegel did not see economics as political economy that links economics to politics; he saw it as a philosopher. In his philosophy, *Sittlichkeit* is communicatively and communally established and, consequently, economics and management always have a social, communicative, and ethical dimension.[460] Hegel's *sittliche* corporation includes the concepts of civil society, community, and *Sittlichkeit*. These are vitally important for *Sittlichkeit* because Hegel's entire system depends on human beings and their integration into a society that has left feudalism behind. Such a society has distinctively modern features, institutions, business organisations, business communities, and a modern social, political, and economic order that places these institutions inside such a society governed by *Sittlichkeit*. In this structure, corporations and the business community are two elements designed to enhance *Sittlichkeit*.

## Hegel and the business community

Together with families and states, the moral task of civil society, economy, and corporations is to integrate societal members into a social and moral order structured through *Sittlichkeit.* Hegel's philosophy comes from a time that can be seen as a gateway between feudalism and modernity. Particularly in Germany, Hegel's 19th-century 'new epoch' [*die neue Zeit*] still carried remnants of the old feudalist regime while already showing features of Enlightenment and modernity. Hegel's 'new epoch' included modern capitalism and modern organisations such as small companies but no business corporations. This might be the very reason why Hegel's original concept of the corporation carried strong connotations to what in the German language is called *Stand.*[461] As Gallagher explains, *Stand* is a word that can be translated by 'status' or 'class', or, in a political–economic context, by 'estate'; Hegel uses this term to cut across all dialectical phases of *Sittlichkeit.* According to Hegel, therefore, the political estates 'still retain in their own function the class distinctions already present in the lower sphere of civil life'.[462] Class distinctions have familial, economic, and political significance.[463] Hegel's corporations related not only to *Stand* but also to four organisational models of his time.[464]

Table 6.1 shows the four terms Hegel uses and their descriptions, explanations, and examples. Hegel's list appears rather inclusive so that most members of a society can be members of Hegel's *sittliche* corporations. But Hegel also excluded some members of civil society from corporate membership. He disqualified those employed in 'agricultural estates . . . and the estate of civil servants'.[465] Hence, 'Hegel admits the incompatibility of a peasantry and nobility with the system of needs'[466] – Hegel's term for the economy.

Nevertheless, in the wake of industrial capitalism many members of the nobility did not survive in their feudalist positions (Moore 1966). In the case of France, for example, Hegel's much admired French Revolution successfully ended the reign of the so-called 'nobility' through the guillotine. In England, on the other hand, the nobility became part of a growing working class but some also became factory owners or were

*Table 6.1* The four institutions reflective of Hegel's corporations

| | **Hegel's German terms** | **Descriptions, explanations, and examples** |
|---|---|---|
| 1 | *Verbände* | Associations, employer federations, political lobbying |
| 2 | *Zünfte* | Guilds, societies |
| 3 | *Gewerbestand* | Business organisations (organisations of internal affairs) |
| 4 | *Berufsgruppen* | Professional associations, e.g. chartered accountants |

employed by companies and corporations. But the feudal to capitalism transition was not a seamless conversion from feudal to capitalist elite. Next to peasants, civil servants, and the nobility, Hegel also excluded the rich from corporate membership. Today, when corporations have amassed stratospheric riches and when hedge-fund managers, corporate bankers, corporate CEOs flaunt their wealth in public, it appears inconceivable that these are to be excluded from corporations.[467] Nevertheless, 'the rich person who remains solely concerned with his own interest . . . does not participate in the recognition that derives from membership in a corporation'.[468] Then, as today, perhaps many of those who are rich and even super-rich do not work in corporations.[469]

Excluding nobility, the rich, and the very rich, Hegel's term 'peasantry' does not relate to today's modern version of commercial farmers working under ROI. Originally, it meant *Stand* or class of a feudal- and soil-based peasantry in the understanding of Moore (1966). They have no place in a modern economy as described by Sir James Steuart and Adam Smith. Modern economies and business corporations are not managed by peasants and nobility. CEOs are not hereditary kings, and top-management is not a medieval court even though it may seem that way to some.[470] In the wake of *The Great Transformation* (Polanyi 1944) class relationships altered completely before, during, and after Hegel. Instead of the two feudal *Stände* or classes of peasants and nobility, Hegel saw a new and fast rising elite based not on land-ownership but on their ability to engage in business.[471] He called these new elites 'business estates' [*der Stand des Gewerbes*]. Rapidly, these business elites became a signifier of capitalist modernity.[472]

Under the ideology of Managerialism, business people – usually in cut-throat competition with each other – like to present themselves as a united front of a so-called 'business community'. This is not like the harmonious idyllic community one imagines but rather corporate leaders finding themselves in a competitive struggle. The harmonious idyllic image of a business community serves ideological functions. Nevertheless, like all good ideologies the Managerialism ideology of a business community also contains an element of reality. Business communities exist when it comes to lobbying against corporate tax rises or an increase in the minimum wage because of a unifying external threat that establishes a necessarily always temporal truce capable of overlayering competition. Business communities also make an appearance when, for example, universities have to be converted from truth-seeking establishments into corporate entities closely linked to the needs of business and corporations so that a business community can take over a science community. Ideologically, terms such as business community quite often imply that there is no diversity of opinion inside such a community.

The ideological term 'community' sets up what Poole (2006) has termed 'Unspeak' – you cannot 'unspeak' community – who would want to be anti-community, non-community, or de-community? This marks the ideological triumph of Managerialism. In Hegelian terms, meanwhile, these business estates are institutional reflections of what Managerialism calls business community. Despite the 'community versus competition' contradictions, business communities – whenever they make an appearance – are part of a modern economy and perhaps even more importantly they are part of a political system. Hegel's business estate has never been a singular unified body. Different business estates contain different institutional setups leading to different forms of corporate governance.[473]

Table 6.2 shows Hegel's original terminology of three areas constituting economic activity. The first column indicates their meaning; the second provides an adaptation to today's economy; and the last illustrates their relevance for corporate governance. In the upper right hand corner the term 'none' indicates that small and medium firms that are involved in craftsmanship generally do not have sophisticated managerial setups like corporate governance. More importantly, however, Hegel saw factory [*Fabrikstand*] and trade [*Handelsstand*] as relevant for corporations.[474] These are the two areas where corporations are formed and corporate governance takes place.

In a certain sense, Hegel's division between *Fabrikstand* and *Handelsstand* carries connotations to Aristotle's understanding of making things and trading them. But referring back to Aristotle comes as no surprise. For Hegel, Aristotle remains 'the only writer who has anything important to say'.[475] The *Fabrikstand* indicates what Aristotle has called those who 'make things' while for Hegel the 'central figure of capitalist development is the *Handelsstand*'[476] reflecting 'those who do' (Aristotle) things. Equipped with Aristotelian philosophy, Hegel saw the *Fabrikstand* as being responsible for producing commercial goods and services and the *Handelsstand* for distributing and financing these commercial goods and services.[477] Not surprisingly, today we find manufacturing corporations dedicated to the former while the stronger finance corporations are dedicated to the latter.

This is followed up in the next column of the table, where Hegelian terminology indicates that corporate governance in the former is dedicated to what today is called operations management while the latter

*Table 6.2* Hegel's three forms of corporate governance

| **Hegel's terms** | **Description** | **Today's Gestalt** | **Today's corporate governance** |
|---|---|---|---|
| *Handwerksstand* craft | Devoted to craftsmanship | Small and medium size businesses | None (limitation of size) |
| *Fabrikstand* factory | Those involved in mass-production in factories | Mass manufacturing, service industry, and knowledge creating firms | Corporate governance dedicated to **Operations Management** to provide commercial commodities and services |
| *Handelsstand* trade | Those engaged in commerce | e.g. banking, insurance, corporate finance, stock exchanges and traders | Corporate governance dedicated to **Marketing and Finance** commercial exchanges, financial services and banking |

is dedicated to marketing and finance. While Hegel's structure appears technical, managerial, and somewhat detailed, it has to be seen in the light of *Sittlichkeit*. In the words of contemporary Irish philosopher Cullen (1988:26), 'Because the business estate [that includes corporations] is essentially devoted to selfish economic pursuits, it stands in special need of moral socialisation.' In other words, Hegel understood that a narrow focus on corporate governance taints the view of those inside the corporation. He was concerned that they lose the overall perspective of *Sittlichkeit*. Therefore, Hegelian philosophy has continuously emphasised that corporations are part of *Sittlichkeit*. They are not to segregate themselves from it by inventing their own *unsittliche* rules and corporate policies, immoral ideologies, narrow purposes, and isolated places.[478]

Nobel Prize winner Milton Friedman (1912–2006) has advocated the exact opposite of Hegel's ideas. Friedman had a unique ability to express the role of corporations in today's society as seen by Managerialism when outlining that corporations are not primarily moral institutions and not set up to engage in morality.[479] This is highly supportive to Managerialism because it enables corporate management to focus on the prime objective of corporations – The Real Bottom Line – and thereby avoids the wasting of time on non-productive activities such as morality. Unsurprisingly, Friedman's statement became one of the most quoted 'CSR → profits' phrases.[480]

Contrary to Hegel's *sittliche* corporations, Friedman's corporations are set up to make profits rather than achieve *Sittlichkeit* (Hegel). According to Friedman and Cohen's (1973) *The Gospel According to the Harvard Business School*, corporations have the one-dimensional goal of The Real Bottom Line. In return, this means that everything that diverts attention away from that is declared unproductive and is exterminated.[481] This signifies two opposing ideologies confronting one another: there is the ideology of shareholder-value, profit-maximisation, and The Real Bottom Line and there is the philosophy of *Sittlichkeit*. This setup positions business corporations against Hegel's *sittliche* corporations.

In the general understanding philosophy includes the concept of 'philo-sophia' seen as the 'love of wisdom' and truth. Nevertheless, the two opposing ends of 'profit versus morality' appear to meet in many human spheres linked to modern society. Among them are market economies and corporations. As a consequence of the one-dimensional Real Bottom Line, neither corporations nor their managers are particularly concerned with philosophy's key interest, namely, truth. In historic terms, the quest for truth has been part of philosophy ever since the Greek mythology of Gods became rational philosophy. Greek *philosophia* represents such a quest for truth. For corporate management, however, truth is only relevant when it is able to increase profits (Friedman), contributes to The Real Bottom Line, and ideologically secures the continued existence of business corporations.[482]

In some cases, corporate managers feel that a quest for truth is a futile enterprise while in other cases they can be 'economic with the truth' when achieving competitive advantages. Nevertheless, the conflict of 'profit versus morality' has been acknowledged in Hegel's *Philosophy of Right* where corporations are positioned. The *Philosophy of Right* makes it clear that 'Hegel sees the *sittliche* corporation as an economic association representing the interests of employers'.[483] But such an interest is linked to the corporation's function as an association [*Zusammenschluß*] for the specific task of socially organised demand-satisfaction.[484] Therefore, corporations should not cut off their social responsibility and instead represent the social truth needed for a healthy society. However, inside Managerialism's paradigm of positivistic science, two elements have been rendered impossible:

1. an acceptance that everything has two sides, that is, Hegel's positives and negatives; and
2. that truth is not a managerially issued truth but carries universal connotations in a Kantian understanding.

Managerialism's one-dimensional view on truth has been supported by positivism, objectivism, and pure science. This means that the Hegelian demand that 'corporations . . . represent the interests of employers' has to be met with the interest of employees as well. Their interest cannot be excluded as management, Managerialism, management studies, management schools, and management textbooks have it. All five have surprisingly little – actually nearly nothing – to say about those 'who are managed', that is, employees, workers, and labour. They are reduced to what Harvard's management writer Magretta (2012:7) calls 'we need other people to perform'. The ideological 'we' means management exclusively; it does not mean 'we' as in employees or all members of a corporation; 'other people' actually means workers – a term painfully avoided and never indexed in a management textbook while 'performance' is the code word for profit.

Neither modern and enlightened thinking as enshrined in the philosopher Immanuel Kant's *Three Critiques* (1781, 1788, 1790) nor eminent management writers themselves such as Morgan (1986, 1993) have been able to challenge Managerialism's main ideology of a one-dimensional take on truth that excludes employees. It indicates that corporate management is only capable of providing a managerial and corporate truth, not a real truth. Contrary to Managerialism's one-dimensional truth there is the philosophical truth. It is imperative to remember that Hegel views philosophy as unique because it only exists of itself – it serves nobody. Corporations, management, and Managerialism represent the very opposite. On this, Hegel noted, 'By declaring the cognition of truth to be a futile endeavour, this self-styled philosophising has reduced all thoughts and all topics to the same level, in other words, to mere opinions and subjective conditions.'[485] This is precisely how management sees ethics – as a matter of mere opinions. But corporate management can never escape from the philosophy of truth. Even when it views 'truth to be a futile endeavour', corporate management has to engage with it and this is in spite of the best ideological efforts of Managerialism to achieve exactly the opposite of Hegelian philosophy. Management views truth as a 'futile endeavour' because it creates discomforting evidence for corporations such as highlighting the immorality of corporations when they are contrasted to the ethical principles of *Sittlichkeit*.

When viewed from Hegel's philosophy, the managerial and the philosophical truth represent two contradictory sets of ideas. One has a 'quest for truth' as its essence while the other pursues a 'quest for profit'. As a result, everything that philosophy does is geared towards truth while everything that corporations do is focused on shareholder-value. This has two structural implications when viewed from, for example, the French philosophical 'knowledge versus power' perspective: one is dialogical while the other is hierarchical.[486] Dialogical structures include mutual and equal recognition while hierarchical configurations are asymmetrical power structures. One is horizontal while the other is vertical. They either exclude recognition altogether, severely damage it, or blatantly de-recognise or misappropriate recognition to serve managerial ends (Anderson 2009). The horizontal recognition is found in philosophy while de- and mis-recognition exist in corporations. Corporate governance frames the de-recognition of employees as human resources, denigrating them to tools, operatives, subordinates, underlings, or assets. The 'people-are-assets' ideology is of particular interest because it appears in the managerial ideology of 'people are our most important assets'. Management equalises human beings to assets, in line with possessions, property, resources, material goods, worldly goods, belongings, and chattels. Simultaneously, the corporate ideology of 'people are our most important asset' is proclaimed. This understanding of language misuse under an 'Organisation of Hypocrisy' can only be possible in Managerialism.[487]

At the same time, management and corporate governance also call human beings simply 'others' through which management achieves organisational outcomes and performance. As such corporate management violates Hegel's notion of a *sittliche* corporation that provides for the livelihood of its members and is capable of recognising individuals as human beings. According to Hegel, 'The member of the corporation does not fear . . . the lack of recognition.'[488] The contradiction of 'corporate de-recognition versus *sittliche* recognition' appears to be the reality in corporations where human beings are de-recognised as 'others' and framed as resources rather than human beings (Bolton & Houlihan 2008). In addition, while Hegelian philosophy denotes that individuals do not 'fear the lack of recognition', some versions of corporate management still reflect Füredi's (2004) *Politics of Fear.*

In managerial regimes it is not totally uncommon that management operates a system called MBF – management by fear.[489] Inevitably, all managerial systems include elements of fear in the case of 'my way or the highway' statements, demotions, the fear of being reprimanded, restructured, 'performance managed out of here', the three-strike rule (1st warning → 2nd warning → 3rd warning = out), disciplinary actions, the composing of so-called 'dirt-files' (Buchanan 2008), and the ultimate fear of being fired. In the Orwellian language of HRM this is framed as 'let go' or 'to seek other opportunities' and constitutes the ultimate fear and de-recognition, namely, the fear of job loss. In addition, workplace bullying, unreasonable workloads, impossible deadlines, negative performance management reviews, and a raft of other managerial techniques exist that show management's 'lack of recognition' towards employees. Meanwhile, *Sittlichkeit* denotes something completely different:

> There is a kind of full recognition in the corporation that makes it like the family, the true recognition and honour owed to its members precisely because of the normative mutuality that the corporation embodies in the shared norms of its practices.[490]

In business corporations, there is no 'full recognition' nor is there 'mutual and equal recognition' but asymmetrical and vertical hierarchies and power relationships between management and non-managerial staff, between and inside top-, middle-, and line-management, and among functional divisions.[491] Even the functional divisions of management have been ranked in accordance to their relevance: 1st = marketing, 2nd = finance, 3rd = operations management, and 4th HRM.

These hierarchical relationships are more often than not based on power rather than the Weberian ideology of bureaucratic functionality as supported by The Servants of Power in management studies.[492] These four managerial functions depict very little synergy with virtually no equilibrium between them. Irrespective of managerial ranking and the contradiction of 'power versus function', all of this destroys Hegel's mutual and equal recognition.[493] In conclusion, the profit-norm and conflicting structures – functionalism versus power – in corporate governance comprehensively annihilate Hegel's ethics of full recognition.

## Moral corporate governance

In sharp contrast to the damaged recognition found inside corporate governance, Hegel's *sittliche* corporations follow a different route when it comes to recognition. According to American philosopher Adriaan Peperzak (2001:472), for example, Hegel's concept of *Sittlichkeit* demands first and foremost mutual and equal recognition between employees and corporate management. In this, corporations are institutions of internal control, steering, and regulation [*ein Instrument der Innensteuerung*].[494] In other words, mutual and equal recognition – *Sittlichkeit*'s core concepts – are also the key to understand management and corporate governance (cf. Schmidt am Busch 2011a). Corporate management has significant moral responsibilities when it comes to *Innensteuerung* or corporate governance. Hegel's *sittliche* corporations are aligned to the ethical concept of *sittliche Innensteuerung*. This leads to the ethical concept of '*sittliche* corporate governance' linked to mutual and equal recognition under *Sittlichkeit*. In order to specify the concept of '*sittliche* corporate governance', the responsibilities and moral configurations of a corporation can be identified as shown in Table 6.3.[495]

Table 6.3 begins with Hegel's key concept, namely, the purpose of the corporation which is to secure the livelihood of its members. As such, *sittliche* corporations take part in the creation of ethical corporate life because they are part of 'ethical life' [*Sittlichkeit*]. If Hegel's *sittliche* corporations are about achieving the self-actualisation of human beings as moral beings, such corporations need to have corporate members. In general, corporations employ individuals through what HRM calls 'recruitment and selection' via labour markets. In other words, business corporations receive their members through a disconnected managerial process called HRM rather than through corporate members themselves which would be the case in Hegel's *sittliche* corporations under '*sittliche* corporate governance'.

*Table 6.3* The corporation and corporate governance

| No. | 75 key elements and functions of a *sittliche* corporation |
|---|---|
| 1. | The purpose of the corporation is to secure the substance of all its members. |
| 2. | The *sittliche* corporation meets its economic goal: stability of living conditions and security of income. |
| 3. | This society is to be stabilised, in his opinion [Hegel] through the formation of corporations. |
| 4. | In corporations, humans are substantially free, i.e. their actions enable them to earn a livelihood, without being subject to economic uncertainties of market movement. |
| 5. | Different people and occupational professions find their living cohesion in a particular organisation or even more specifically (e.g. according to occupational groups) in a sub-organisation such as corporations. |
| 6. | Corporations, as ongoing professional cooperatives, ensure permanency in their members' skills, ability, and professional honour and secure their basic economic needs. |
| 7. | Corporations eliminate an ever increasing mechanisation, routines, and monotony of work (convulsions, i.e. *Zuckungen, Philosophy of Right,* 1821) that result in deskilling under Tayloristic work arrangements that disallow an individual development of skills. |
| 8. | The Hegelian labour market is thus rather strictly regulated through the system of corporations. |
| 9. | Corporate governance would approve and support its members. |
| 10. | It would include the right of wellbeing of all members of a corporation. |
| 11. | It would have respect for their professional and moral standing. |
| 12. | The corporation is every bit as important for the wealthier and more powerful members of the community as it is for medium- and low-income individuals because, although the former are much less materially vulnerable, they are more likely to associate their honour with material success. |
| 13. | In corporations, wealthy property owners lose their arrogance and envy which may influence others while righteousness receives its true recognition and honour. |
| 14. | There is a *sittliche* aspect of being a member of a corporation that determines members' interests and activities directed towards the welfare of their colleagues and the continuation of a corporation. |
| 15. | *Sittlich* is the outcome when all interests are taken into account properly, which implies that corporations are in a position to form a common interest among their members. |
| 16. | Corporations represent an institutionalisation of specific forms of recognition. |
| 17. | Corporate governance should be in the service of public interest. |
| 18. | Corporate governance liberates corporate members from individualistic ways. |
| 19. | There is a collective competence of corporations, to set moral standards for the economic activities of its members. |

(*continued*)

*Table 6.3* (continued)

| No. | 75 key elements and functions of a *sittliche* corporation |
|---|---|
| 20. | Corporations proceed in their moral decision-making according to economic laws. |
| 21. | As a member of a class of a corporation I am able to become aware of claims upon me which restrict my self-seeking and impose upon me some natural-seeming group constrains. |
| 22. | Individuals who join a corporation (employment) or are co-opted by one gain a measure of economic security. |
| 23. | Corporations, however, are limited, partial social units . . . to tame the economy. |
| 24. | A corporation organises the production of usable goods. |
| 25. | The idea of the corporation [as a] voluntary work-related cooperative. |
| 26. | In business-to-business relations, competition among corporations is limited. |
| 27. | There is a corporate distribution of production sites. |
| 28. | For Hegel, the boundaries of a corporative–regulatory economic order of corporations lie where job security of all corporate members is at risk. |
| 29. | The governing collective of a corporation defines market relations of demand and supply. |
| 30. | Corporate members experience two forms of education: schooling in the chosen trade, vocation, or profession; and, more importantly, training in the conduct of the affairs of the corporations. |
| 31. | The individual's experience acquired in corporate life assures a measured social mobility. |
| 32. | Corporations are self-conscious and reflective institutions with self-actualising participants inside a socio-economic order. |
| 33. | Participation of the citizens in the governance of a corporation is an essential ingredient. |
| 34. | Participation in the management of the corporation, in the administration of its affairs, in the decisions of its membership, and in the election of its representatives; hence Hegel would see corporate members as self-law-giving individuals. |
| 35. | The corporation's officers are elected by the membership, the result of the elections are subject to scrutiny by the public authority. |
| 36. | The secondment [or representatives to a parliament] shall be made by the corporation and not by the people. |
| 37. | A corporation is a community with a special purpose. |
| 38. | The corporation regulates all forms of the social intercourse among its members. |
| 39. | Communities of corporate members must retain their corporate and semi-autonomous identities. |
| 40. | Hegel would probably argue that being a member of a corporation adds more to one's life in terms of freedom than it takes away from it. |
| 41. | One's professional identity is in a deep sense part of who one is . . . [this is] embedded in the social structures of the . . . corporation. |

(*continued*)

*Table 6.3* (continued)

| No. | 75 key elements and functions of a *sittliche* corporation |
|---|---|
| 42. | Corporate governance guarantees a concrete solidarity among the 'burghers' (cf. Honneth 2008:6). |
| 43. | A free corporation implied a horizontal mode of association, a principle of sociability and solidarity among workers that reflected the divergent interests of wage-labourers and employers . . . in a form of 'associationism' as the antidote to the atomised individualism of a competitive commercial society. |
| 44. | The corporate spirit contains an uprooting [*Einwurzelung*] of the particular into the universal (Hegel 1821:§289) by unifying both. |
| 45. | A corporation provides for the unselfish purpose of the whole and serves to mediate the purely selfish economic goals of individual members of civil society. |
| 46. | Internally, the social cohesion of corporations is primarily established through a 'shared' set of common values reflecting corporate cohesion. |
| 47. | Corporate governance has to support 'internal corporate solidarity' [*binnenkorporative Solidarität*]. |
| 48. | Inside a corporation's social–cultural sphere, members of a civic community [*Gemeinwesen*] share a corporate spirit of 'being one of us', |
| 49. | Corporations are communities of economic subjects as a conscious association of individuals with similar occupational skills, |
| 50. | Corporations are part of a moral reorganisation of civil society as corporate self-organisation. |
| 51. | Through the corporate-based individual–institution interface, corporate members learn *Sittlichkeit.* |
| 52. | The corporation is a moral self-governing body in civil society. |
| 53. | Generally, the corporation is designed to eliminate the patron–client relationship. |
| 54. | Corporations are introduced through the formula of a return of morality as an immanent fixture of capitalist society. |
| 55. | In corporations, civil society receives a self-governing authority that – in institutional theory – represents the middle between Smith's 'randomness' of market allocation and a quasi-absolute domination through state intervention: corporations eliminate extremes. |
| 56. | By the same token state supervision over corporations ensures that corporations do not ossify [*verknöchern*, Hegel], encapsulate themselves in themselves [*in sich verhausen*, Hegel], and deteriorate into a miserable *Zunftwesen* or guild (Hegel 1821, §255, Zusatz). |
| 57. | Corporations are a means against the despotism and domination of masters and factory owners. |
| 58. | Corporations unify the identity of its members' particular interests with an objective universality of shared interests. |
| 59. | Corporate governance thwarts the misfortunes of the capitalistic market. |
| 60. | Corporations can be understood as internalisation-collectives compensating external-negative results of purely private economic activities through collectively corporate standards. |

(*continued*)

*Table 6.3* (continued)

| No. | 75 key elements and functions of a *sittliche* corporation |
|---|---|
| 61. | An equal distribution of income is more important than the mere level of income. |
| 62. | A corporative organised stability of income supersedes competition. |
| 63. | The purpose of corporate governance is to bring isolated individuals into an economic and ethical order providing a civic community against isolating effects of industrial work. |
| 64. | Working in corporations [is] for Hegel both individually satisfying and socially stabilising. |
| 65. | Corporations prevent their members from the risk of poverty, loss of honour, and isolation from the common cause. |
| 66. | Hegel leaves care of the poor to corporations. |
| 67. | In the corporation poverty loses its arbitrariness as well as its injustice and humiliating character. |
| 68. | When individuals encounter each other in civil society, they accordingly do so as somebody, as particular members of social classes and corporations. |
| 69. | Corporations have a right to establish insurance systems that secure the livelihoods of their members. |
| 70. | Corporations ensure that its members are protected against poverty, illness, and the incapacity for work. |
| 71. | Insofar as corporations protect their members, members have a right to the corporation's help (Hegel 1821:§253). |
| 72. | Corporations offer a place where individuals with their capabilities and skills are recognised, and every person can command the respect due to one in his social position. |
| 73. | Colleagues who share a professional field of knowledge know the skills and efforts one needs in their social sector. They have the skills and competency to assess the relevant qualifications and efforts of their profession comparatively. |
| 74. | Corporations should act as a guard to prevent the civil service from becoming a new aristocracy and a potential tyranny. |
| 75. | Corporations must be given the moral duty to eliminate the corruption of wealth. In corporations, the rich has a true and noble opportunity to acquire to honour . . . here he can use his wealth for the cooperative. |

Unlike the ideological equalisation of commercial and financial markets with labour markets under Managerialism, labour markets are distinctively different.[496] Since Hegel was aware of the negative and pathological impacts of commercial and labour markets on individuals, the Hegelian labour market is strictly regulated through the system of corporations. Hegel's *sittliche* corporations are responsible for regulating labour markets. This means three things for '*sittliche* corporate governance':

1. '*sittliche* corporate governance', corporations, and Managerialism need to reverse their ideological push towards deregulation in favour of regulation;
2. internal labour markets need to be regulated to actively reflect on the parameters set out in *Sittlichkeit*; and
3. externally, corporate governance needs to actively engage with civil society's institutions such as labour markets. These relationships also need to be reflective of *Sittlichkeit*'s mutual recognition (Chitty 2013:686).

This means that today's corporate governance can no longer see itself and its corporations as independent *Robinson Crusoe*-like islands disconnected from civil *society and labour* markets.[497] Instead, it needs to restructure corporations so that they 'are' *sittliche* corporations. Once human beings are employed by corporations through the active interface between *sittliche* corporations and civil society's labour markets and society's regulative institutions, *sittliche* corporate governance approves and supports corporate members including the right of wellbeing of all corporate members. *Sittliche* corporations are places where 'all' members share corporate welfare equally. This means that HRM, for example, is no longer a vertical but a horizontal function moving from the horizontal asymmetry of 'I manage you' to the *sittliche* 'we' of true self-management.[498]

This would involve a re-designing of all current corporate policies so that these no longer award 'managerial perks' to some but not to others. Subsequently, this might even encourage a structural change in the hierarchies as upheld by current corporate management to fully respect the professional and moral standing of corporate members. With that, moral corporate members (Hegel) could (re)-align their lives as corporate members with their professional lives. This means, for example, that professional responsibilities and moral codes would no longer be suppressed by corporate management in favour of the corporate Real Bottom Line. It also means that corporate governance serves *Sittlichkeit* rather than shareholder-value. In short, the more moral imperatives of *Sittlichkeit* take shape [*Gestalt*], the more will the picture of corporate governance as it currently exists start to weaken in favour of '*sittliche* corporate governance'. Eventually, in such a *sittliche* corporation corporate members determine the interests and activities in, at least, three ways:

1. the welfare of their colleagues;
2. the continuation of a corporation; and

3. corporations represent an 'institutionalisation of specific forms of recognition'.[499]

This denotes that the welfare of corporate members is organised by corporate members themselves rather than by management. On the issue of continuation of a corporation, current management thinking as shown, for example, by the *Harvard Business Review* (HBR 2010) coincides with that of '*sittliche* corporate governance' with two exceptions: predominantly, 'existing' (HBR 2010) relates to a corporation rather than to corporate management itself and managerial 'short-termism' (HBR 2010) has to be replaced by 'long-termism' so that a corporation is not sold to the next bidder for handsome managerial payouts, bonuses, golden parachutes, and so on. The third aspect remains significant because business corporations do not represent an 'institutionalisation of specific forms of recognition' as understood by Hegelian philosophy.[500] Hegelian ethics of recognition is about mutual and equal recognition.[501] Recognition is established between two or more equal partners. It carries social and *sittliche*, not individualistic connotations. There is no such thing as one-sided recognition.[502] While recognition might be 'what we owe to each other', Canadian philosopher Charles Taylor puts a higher premium on it, namely, it is 'not just as a courtesy we owe people but is a vital human need'.[503] Overall, '*sittliche* corporate governance' needs to be based on mutual and equal recognition among all corporate members. If corporations seek to be a place for an 'institutionalisation of specific forms of recognition', they need to become *sittliche* corporations.

To achieve that, '*sittliche* corporate governance' needs to liberate corporate members from individualistic ways – the exact opposite of the managerial fostering of hyper-individualism as currently administered by corporate management. It allows individuals to remain inside a *sittliche* community away from 'moral egoism'. In this, the moral goals of individuals are united with the goals of '*sittliche* corporate governance', economic goals of markets, common goals of civil society, and eventually the universal goals of Hegel's 'world spirit'.[504] This leads to a moral corporate life that allows individuals to gain a substantial degree of social–economic harmony and economic security. Simultaneously, it eliminates one of Hegel's most fundamental problems, namely, the arbitrariness or *Willkür* of markets and, as a consequence, managerial decision-making.[505] As a consequence, Hegel's *sittliche* corporations 'tame the economy' by no longer fostering economic arbitrariness and market *Willkür* and they exclude competition for the benefit of profit-making that 'uses' human resources. Instead, a *sittliche* corporation guarantees stable work and income arrangements and regulates economic supply and demand. On the other hand, for-profit corporations are linked to educational institutions that train managers. Management schools – just as business corporations – are exposed to the arbitrariness and *Willkür* of markets. Meanwhile, *sittliche* corporations become educational rather than marketing institutions (Campello 2013:144). This sharply contradicts General Motor's CEO Alfred Sloan's famous statement:

> The point is that General Motors is not in business to make cars, but to make money.

Hence, a *sittliche* management school would no longer exist to 'make money' (Sloan) but to 'educate people'. This is an unthinkable alternative to the rampant Managerialism found in such schools.[506] However, inside such a non-market-driven sphere of education, *sittliche* corporations play a significant role. According to Hegelian ethics, corporate governance – through its links to civil society – establishes two forms of education:

1. schooling in the chosen trade, vocation, and profession; and
2. training in the conduct of the affairs of the corporations.

By the affairs of a *sittliche* corporation, Hegelian ethics does not primarily mean the technicalities, functionalities, and managerial particularities but education has to be understood in the tradition of Aristotle's and Rousseau's educational philosophies. This denotes an education that achieves moral relationships with others in the form of friendship (Aristotle) and a moral participation in the affairs of corporations and civil society.[507] As a consequence, individuals experience social mobility in corporate and societal life. This cannot be reduced to HRM's internal promotions. Instead, it supports mobility in governing the affairs of *sittliche* corporations and civil society. To achieve that, *sittliche* corporations have to establish a self-conscious and reflective union between corporations and society with self-actualising participants inside a socio-economic order (Gallagher 1987:174). Such self-actualising participants are no longer mere economic 'resources' employed by management to increase 'The Corporate Bottom Line'.[508] Instead of the reduction and denigration of human beings to resources and underlings, individuals are participating as corporate citizens in the governance of a corporation. In the words of Heiman (1971:130):

> Participation in the management of the corporation, in the administration of its affairs, in the decisions of its membership, and in the election of its representatives; the corporation's officers are elected by the membership, the result of the elections are subject to scrutiny by the public authority.

This establishes a very different picture to those forms of corporate governance found today. For one, *sittliche* corporate governance is no longer merely an affair of top-management but includes all members of a corporation. Secondly, this introduces one of the most feared words in Managerialism's catalogue of allowable terms: democracy. Hegel's philosophy of *Sittlichkeit* indicates 'the election of representatives' to govern corporations rather than the unilateral and sometimes obscure appointments top-management makes.[509] But there is worse to come for today's business corporations. Hegelian philosophy also suggests that 'elections are subject to scrutiny by the public authority'. Today's corporate governance already includes crypto-democratic 'elections' (sic!) of a board of directors. The format under which this is currently administered might infer connotations of distortions and unfairness. It appears incompatible with any closer electoral examination as, for example, conducted by the 2002 Nobel Peace Prize winner Jimmy Carter setting standards for what can be called 'democratic' (e.g. www.cartercenter.org). In Hegel's *sittliche* corporations these distortions have to be eliminated while participation has to be extended to all corporate members. Finally, corporate elections have to be overseen by public authorities. This might be an unwelcome notion to business corporations that view this as interference and an externality but not so for *sittliche* corporations aligned to *Sittlichkeit*.

Once elected as representatives, these corporate members must retain their corporate and semi-autonomous identities. They are aligned to civil society and *Sittlichkeit* through an awareness that a societal identity is not merely an externality. No longer can the ideology of stakeholders be used to justify cutting corporations off from the moral responsibilities formulated in Hegel's second level of *Sittlichkeit*, namely, civil society. But the semi-autonomous identity of individuals in corporations has another side. This is the balance between corporate and individual identity. 'Hegel would probably argue that being a member of a corporation adds more to one's life in terms of freedom than it takes away from it.'[510] In *Sittlichkeit,* corporate members have an organisational, societal, moral, and individual identity at the same time. This ends Whyte's (1961) *Organisation Men* as a one-dimensional identity that is unilaterally shaped by corporate management and Managerialism. It unifies an individual's organisational identity with a professional identity. 'One's professional identity is in a deep sense part of who one is [and this is] embedded in the social structures of the . . . corporation.'[511] But the shaping of one's identity through Hegel's *sittliche* corporations goes further than that.

Corporate governance also guarantees solidarity among the 'burghers'[512] that is created among corporate members and extends deep into the sphere of civil society. *Sittliche* corporate governance supports what Kersting (1988:9) calls 'internal corporate solidarity' [*binnenkorporative Solidarität*] as an extension towards the *binnenkorporative Solidarität* of civil society. In that way, corporate members can overcome the particular and sectarian interests of corporations and extend their moral interests to a universally shared interest that is organisationally manifested in an organised community of economic subjects as a conscious association with occupational skills. This organised community demands a 'reorganisation of society as corporative self-organisation' inside a *sittlich*–economic constitution of society [*sittliche Wirtschaftsverfassung*]. Inside corporations, the social cohesion establishes a 'shared' set of common values (Schmidt am Busch 2011a). This is not what management studies identify as 'corporate culture' (Buchwalter 2012a:89). Unlike the one-dimensionally created corporate culture of business corporations where the 'shared' is in fact a 'managerially administered' corporate culture, a *sittliche* corporate culture remains an outcome of a shared set of common values established by all corporate members. In that way, 'culture' represents the actual meaning of the term rather than a managerial version of corporate hegemony ideologically re-framed as culture.

The shared universal culture reaches beyond the sectarian, particular, and economic interest of business corporations and thereby 'thwarts the misfortunes of the capitalistic market' (Hegel). To support this is the task of '*sittliche* corporate governance' with the purpose of bringing isolated individuals into the economic, political, and ethical order of *Sittlichkeit.* Inside such a system, corporate members are protected from the risk of poverty, loss of honour, and isolation (Aubenas 2011). Not surprisingly, Hegel leaves care for the isolated poor to corporations because poverty is created not in the spheres of families and states (1 + 3) but in the sphere of civil society (2), economy, and corporations. This indicates that today's corporations would have to radically restructure their present organisational setup so that '*sittliche* corporate governance' is able to establish insurance systems securing the livelihood of corporate members who have a right to the corporation's help (Hegel).

Once corporations are fully established as *sittliche* organisations, individuals encounter each other as members of a *sittliche* order, of a *sittliche* class, and of a *sittliche* corporation. Within the organisational structure of corporate *Sittlichkeit,* corporations remain places where individuals develop their vocational capabilities and skills. These vocational capabilities and skills are officially recognised by *sittliche* corporations. But this is not done through the current managerial setup of HRM but through 'colleagues', that is, co-workers. It moves HRM's asymmetrical and vertical 'I manage you' approach to a horizontal 'colleague to colleague' approach allowing space for Hegel's important ethics of mutual and equal recognition. This 'colleague to colleague' recognition combines the *sittliche* recognition among employees but also recognition of their vocational capabilities and skills. Unlike the non-technical expertise of HRM in most managerial fields ranging from IT, accounting, operations, to many others, Hegel's *sittliche* skill recognition through those 'who share a professional field of knowledge' disallows HRM's performance assessment through outsiders such as HR managers. Instead, it allows performance assessment based on moral and expert knowledge. Such performance assessment and performance management is not based on HRM-ideologies but on vocational capabilities and skills of those who know the skills and efforts one needs in their sector. After all, they have the skills and competency to assess the relevant qualifications and efforts of their profession comparatively.[513] In combining Hegel's mutual and equal recognition with skill recognition and assessment through a 'colleague to colleague' process, corporate members can command respect due to their position in a corporation. Such a form of corporate cohesion also extends beyond the confinements of corporations.

Hegel's *sittliche* corporations act as a safeguard to prevent corporations, corporate governance, and even the 'civil' service from becoming a new aristocracy and potential tyranny. In other words, it is not only the state that supervises corporations as we have seen already but Hegel's *sittliche* corporations that supervise themselves and simultaneously also the states. Hegel's *sittliche* corporations achieve this in two ways:

1. by safeguarding and supervising themselves through corporate members preventing corporate governance from becoming an authoritarian system; and

2. through the relationship between *sittliche* corporations and states. Hegel sees this relationship as reciprocal.

Hegel's *sittliche* corporatio*ns functi*on as supervising institutions towards the state as a system of 'checks and balances'. It is the task of *sittliche* corporations to prevent states and the civil service from becoming new aristocracy and tyranny. *Sittliche* corporations represent the exact opposite of what many business corporations have done throughout centuries starting with the British East India Company, namely, the support of British colonialism, German fascism, Franco's Spain, military dictatorships in Europe, Middle and South America, Africa, the Middle East, and Asia.[514] In *Sittlichkeit,* tyranny is an irrational act. It is contrary to Arendt's (1958) *Human Condition.* But Hegel's moral irrationality also applies to the immorality of the rich. For Hegel the moral 'corruption of wealth' [*Verderben des Reichtums*] can be solved in corporations where wealthy individuals can use their capital for a cooperative. Rather than creating corporate corruption, *sittliche* corporations are a means to avoid it. Only when corporations act in a moral way can they be considered rational. The rational–*Sittlichkeit* link is discussed in the next chapter.

# 7
# Corporate Governance Rationality and Morality

*Hegelian philosophy advocates a transition from human emancipation to political emancipation.*[515]

One of the main moral tasks of a corporation is internal governance [*Innensteuerung*]. Hegel's system of ethical life [*System der Sittlichkeit*] includes *sittliche* corporations and sets out a model that is very different from the business corporation governed and operated under the one-dimensional imperative of The Real Bottom Line.[516] *Sittliche* corporations and business corporations are not the same. It remains imperative to recognise the following: (i) modern Hegelian philosophy that followed Hegel's death has contributed significantly to our understanding of Hegel's *Sittlichkeit* as applied to corporations; (ii) in many ways, this has clarified Hegel's original catalogue that defined *sittliche* corporations; (iii) the current state of research into Hegelian philosophy has exceeded Hegel's own expressions made in his *Philosophy of Right* (1821); and finally, (iv) these new developments together with Hegel's original concept of corporations shape the ethical understanding of corporations and corporate governance.[517] For a start, Hegel was a keen student of British political economy and well informed with regard to the economic developments of industrialism, workshops, companies, firms, and perhaps even the early stage 'corporations' in Britain such as, for example, the British East India Company of 1600. Being a moral philosopher, Hegel did not see modern corporations purely as economic actors. In Hegelian philosophy, corporations – like any other institution or organisation – are seen as rational when they are connected to ethical life [*Sittlichkeit*]. Hence, Hegel's ethics strongly emphasises the social and moral role of corporations and explains the importance Hegel places on corporations as moral actors. Perhaps this sounds rather surprising for today's one-dimensional and, above all, managerially conditioned understanding of business corporations as engineered by Managerialism and corporate mass media.

Hegelian ethics defines the role of corporations as social and moral actors. This creates moral obligations that end the pathologies created by industrial capitalism during Hegel's time as well as modern corporate capitalism. It is the task of Hegel's *sittliche* corporation to prevent inequality in wealth and poverty that, according to Hegel, results in mass pauperisation.[518] The very same is expressed by Adam Smith's 'no linen shirt' statement.[519] Aligned to the Smith–Hegel diagnosis of poverty, Hegel saw corporations as institutions that take part in the creation of poverty but also provide solutions to poverty and mass pauperisation.[520] For Hegel, corporations are institutions that enhance human self-actualisation, self-realisation, *Sittlichkeit*, and above all human freedom. They are institutions that avoid 'moral injuries' [*moralische Verletzungen*] such as 'deception and fraud' ranging from the relative 'harmless' de-recognition [*Verweigerung der Anerkennung*] through 'not-greeting to the stigmatisation of entire groups' of people such as employees and trade unionists.[521] For Hegel, creating moral injuries represents an irrational act.[522] Consequently, only institutions capable of enhancing freedom and *Sittlichkeit* are rational. In the words of Hegelian philosopher Frederick Neuhouser (2011:292), 'Rational social institutions encourage the expression of personal, moral, and social freedom.'[523] In other words, it is the task of corporations and their *Innensteuerung* of corporate governance to encourage the expression of 'personal, moral, and social freedom'. These three freedoms are challenging to today's business corporations.

Table 7.1 indicates that if today's corporations are to be *sittliche* corporations, they must, firstly, recognise the existence of personal, moral, and social freedom; secondly, *sittliche* corporate management goes beyond that by striving towards the actualisation of these three freedoms – making it real; thirdly, corporate governance can never be disconnected from corporate members and both can never be disconnected from *Sittlichkeit*. In short, the Hegelian ethics of self-determination and self-actualisation might be summed up as 'it is the corporate membership that governs corporations and not corporate management that governs corporate members'. This is what German philosopher Bruno Liebrucks (1974:17) calls 'co-determination' [*Mitbestimmung*]. What is set out in Table 7.1 indicates two movements: (i) from business corporations to *sittliche* corporations and (ii) from today's corporate governance to *sittliche*

*Table 7.1* Three freedoms and three challenges

| No. | Form of freedom | Challenges to business corporations |
|---|---|---|
| 1 | **Personal freedom** | The concept of personal freedom challenges the current setup of managerial regimes as much as it challenges management's ideology of the managerial prerogative and the right to manage. It also means the end of Organisation Men (Whyte 1961). |
| 2 | **Moral freedom** | In moral philosophy, moral freedom is inextricably linked to free will and as such challenges the management ideology of handing the free will over to markets.[524] |
| 3 | **Social freedom** | In Hegelian philosophy social freedom does not mean freedom of the individual because freedom always and at the same time means the freedom of others. This challenges corporate management because it grants itself freedom not granted to others inside corporations, namely, middle and lower management, while non-managerial employees are also excluded. |

corporate governance. It also means that *Sittlichkeit* applies to corporations in exactly the same way as it applies to all other institutions and spheres of *Sittlichkeit,* namely, the non-economic part of *sittliche* civil society, family (level 1) and states (level 3).[525]

Civil society and states are to be governed through two moral means: According to Kant, for example, it is the ethics of self-determination; for Hegel, this became self-actualisation. Self-determination and self-actualisation carry strong connotations to what German philosopher Albrecht Wellmer calls *democratic Sittlichkeit.*[526] Not surprisingly, civil society and states are determined and actualised through democracy. As a consequence, '*sittliche* corporate governance' is also to be governed through democracy. Overall, Hegel saw that models of freedom (e.g. Table 7.1) are established in the spheres of civil society, state, and corporations. He envisioned that *Sittlichkeit* established at the first level would have a moral link to corporations denoting a transition from family into civil society in which corporations are located. As such, there are transitional and reciprocal links between family and corporations. Not surprisingly, Hegel noted in his *Philosophy of Right,*[527]

> The corporation is called the second family.

Hegel saw families as a key to corporations and civil society. But he did not mean Managerialism's ideologies such as 'we are all in one boat' and 'the happy corporate family' with the CEO as authoritarian father figure. Business corporations are not families because they are for-profit organisations while families are not. Furthermore, both are not based on the same form of morality. Families exist for mutual and equal recognition based on 'bonds of intimacy' (Hegel) while corporations exist for the achievement of shareholder-value.[528] Corporations exclude mutual and equal recognition and have no bonds of intimacy. Finally, families do not operate with a clear division between shareholders and owners, and between management and non-managerial staff where the latter do the rowing in the 'we are all in one boat' ideology, while others enjoy the upper deck. Managerialism's equalisation of 'family = corporations' represents pure ideology.

For Hegel, however, 'the model for civil society remains the family community [*Gemeinsamkeit und Gemeinwesen*][529] stressing the importance of size and relationship among family members and the spirit of community and togetherness [*Familiengeist and Gemeinschaftsgeist*]. The conversion of a family spirit into a community spirit and a corporate spirit [*Korporationsgeist*][530] means that the moral tasks of families, civil society, and corporations overlap. Hegel saw all three institutions as transmissions towards *Sittlichkeit* based on a rational constitution of civil society and corporations. In Hegelian philosophy, only those institutions that act towards the achievement of *Sittlichkeit* are rational. In return, those institutions that do not strive towards *Sittlichkeit* can be considered irrational.[531] Rational institutions foster an individual's transition from being born into a family towards their transition into a rational, human, and *sittliche* community. In other words, only when corporations are sites for a 'family → society/corporations → state' transition can these be considered rational and ethical. In turn, corporations act irrationally when they hinder the transition from the early family morality to Hegel's higher moralities of the world spirit [*Weltgeist*].

In Hegelian ethics, the equalisation of morality with rationality results from the history of Hegel's philosophy at the crossroad between feudalism's mythical, superstitious, religious, and irrational past and modernity's rationality manifested in Hegel's philosophy.[532] To understand Hegel's rationality, one needs to recall that his historical period was that of pre-Germany where miniature states [*Kleinstaaten*] existed in which a landed, authoritarian, chauvinistic, religious, God-fearing, backward, and extremely anti-democratic nobility still sought to prevent the early signs of rationality and modernity that had already 'infected' substantial sections of Germany's educated elite. The conservative German 'land, soil, and blood' elite worked tirelessly to prevent modern administration, rational democracy, and a capitalist economy (Moore 1966). To some extent, they were brought to backward German miniature states by Napoleon's military victories that Hegel witnessed during his lifetime.[533]

During the early to mid-19th century, pre-German states remained miniature kingdoms – plus Prussia – incapable of an English industrial or a French political revolution. The battle between pre-Enlightenment and Enlightenment was still raging in those asphyxiated miniature kingdoms of the early 19th century. Rationality was seen by German conservatives as a sign of modernity that challenged the old 'God-given' regimes [*von Gottes Gnaden*]. When Hegel used a term such as 'rationality' he formulated a clear challenge to the pre-modern mythical order of Germanic religious irrationality thereby attacking the ruling elite who were at times his employers. In philosophical terms, however, Hegel's 'morality = rationality' equalisation challenged the old 'religion = morality' equation by replacing religion as the sole agency that formulates codes for morality.

Before Hegel, Immanuel Kant formulated rational categorical imperatives for rational morality in his 'groundwork'. Like Kant, Hegel's ethics is a form of rational ethics seeking to achieve *Sittlichkeit* through rational means. The difference between Kant and Hegel is that the former relies on rational law-like categorical imperatives while the latter seeks a rational society with rational institutions. Hegel's philosophy of 'rationality equals morality' means that 'rational institutions are sites for the expression of freedom concerning the way they foster social freedom by providing individuals with particular identities that make social participation both free (un-coerced) and personally satisfying'.[534] The application of Hegelian ethics creates a number of problems for conventional corporate governance: (i) traditionally, corporate governance does not see corporations as 'rational institutions' according to *Sittlichkeit*'s 'rationality equals morality' principle; (ii) corporations have never fostered human freedom, neither internally nor externally; (iii) instead they operate managerial regimes often bordering on fear and creating 'coerced personalities';[535] and most obviously (iv), they remain sites of staunch anti-democracy disallowing corporate members direct participation in corporate affairs and thereby preventing self-determination and self-actualisation (cf. Nussbaum 2010). In contrast, Hegel sees only those institutions as rational that meet four conditions.

Table 7.2 shows four defining characteristics for rational-*sittliche* corporations. Already the first condition constitutes a severe challenge

*Table 7.2* Hegel's four conditions for rational institutions

| **Conditions** | **Identifying elements of moral institution in order to be rational:** |
|---|---|
| Participation | Corporations must be created and operated by all participants. They cannot be created and operated by a disconnected top-down managerial hierarchy in the form of corporate governance. |
| Human freedom | Corporations can never be organised as 'free institutions' supporting human freedom; they remain locked into Fayol's commanding others, delegating tasks to others, and controlling others. |
| Self-actualisation | To be rational institutions, corporations must not only be created by participants but they also must be based on the continuous and uninterrupted self-actualisation of its participants. |
| Rationality & *Sittlichkeit* | To be awarded the Hegelian label 'rational', corporations must not only subscribe to but also be an active expression of *Sittlichkeit*. This means that only those corporations that carry the label 'rational' are moral corporations as defined by *Sittlichkeit*. |

to business corporations because it demands that they are set up and operated by those who are members of such organisations. In Hegelian ethics, this includes corporate governance and non-managerial staff, in business corporations humiliatingly framed as underlings and subordinates. Kant's ethics of self-determination demands the inclusion of corporate members into corporate governance. This is to be seen as inclusive rather than exclusive. The participation of all corporate members determines two issues: corporate members determine themselves – self-determination – and they determine corporate structures such as corporate governance.

In *Sittlichkeit*, these ethical demands take an even more concrete shape in the form of self-actualisation. By self-actualisation, Hegel means that corporations must be the real and factual expression of the actuality of corporate members. The actualisation of members refers to freedom but also relates to what Managerialism calls 'externalities' – those outside of corporations. Hegelian philosophy goes beyond Kantian formalism, self-determination, and categorical imperatives. In Hegelian philosophy, human beings are not seen as individuals but as social beings inside moral institutions. This establishes reciprocal moral responsibilities between human beings and institutions. Today's business corporations struggle with such concepts. Even when discounting democracy, Kant's self-determination and Hegelian self-actualisation remain highly discomforting to them. Modern corporations are run exclusively by upper- and middle-management with total disregard for democracy and the ethical demand for self-actualisation. Corporate anti-democracy is also manifested in management's self-assigned role of commanding others, delegating tasks, and controlling others. All of these have been outlined in the early stage of management and have been practised ever since.

Significantly, Hegelian ethics demands that corporations are set up by 'all' corporate members governed through the full participation of 'all' members. This raises the abhorred spectre of industrial democracy against which corporations, Managerialism, and management studies have spent decades of fighting. For them the rationality of democracy is no rationality at all. Perhaps losing the battle for workplace democracy has been paralleled by a victory of corporations over democracy outside the corporation as issues such as corporate campaign donations, corporate lobbying, and the reduction of democracy to a corporate TV spectacle engineered by corporate mass media shows. Beder has described this takeover as *The Corporate Manipulation of Community Values*.[536] Meanwhile, internally, the anti-democratic ideology of corporations results in non-democratic, non-moral, and non-rational organisations. Hegel's philosophy inextricably links Enlightenment's concept of rationality to morality (Ritter 1974a:222). This might be formulated as 'without rationality no *Sittlichkeit* and without *Sittlichkeit* no rationality'. Nevertheless, modern corporations – under the ideological guidance of Managerialism – operate managerial regimes supported by crypto-scientific management studies that have systematically and deliberately disconnected morality from rationality. Management's denial of the 'rationality equals morality' link of Kantian and Hegelian philosophy and Enlightenment may have three explanations:

(a) it is simply impossible and therefore wrong;
(b) it challenges predominant management ideologies such as Managerialism and therefore threatens those in the position of institutional power, for example, those whom Baritz calls The Servants of Power (1960); and
(c) it is obstructive to the one-dimensional irrationality of profit-maximisation.

As a consequence, once the segregation of rationality and morality had been successfully established, the constitution of business corporations moved from being rational and moral to being irrational and immoral.

But contrary to that, *Sittlichkeit* demands that corporate governance must be an actual expression of the rationality of freedom. However, the managerial framing of human beings as underlings and subordinates is irrational and hardly a feature of freedom. Furthermore, corporate governance needs to foster social freedom. As Hegel says, freedom means to have 'an opportunity to contribute to the actualisation not only of one's own interest but also of another person's freedom'.[537] By this Hegelian philosophy means social and human freedom. *Sittlichkeit* equates 'human' (humanity) and 'personal' (individual) with 'social' freedom (socio-economic institutions). Hegel specifically, clearly, and directly says 'a person's freedom' not corporate (corporations and corporate governance), managerial (managerial regimes), and economic freedom (markets). Nonetheless, he remained concerned with economic freedom based on the 'unfreedom' the market had created in the most advanced economy of his time, namely, the British economy. Hegel's prime objective remains human freedom. As prescribed by *Sittlichkeit*, human freedom always takes priority over all other forms of freedom. One might even argue that Hegel's human freedom can be seen as somewhat of a 'primus inter pares' of economic, corporate, and any other form of freedom including management's self-assigned right to manage.

Hegel's specification of 'providing individuals with particular identities' can never be achieved through the standard, vertical, pyramid-like hierarchies found in every organisational chart of every business corporation. Furthermore, management's obvious contradiction of 'management versus employees' is counterproductive to individuals with moral identities. Finally, being told that one is no longer human but a resource as applied inside managerial regimes is not supportive of 'providing individuals with identities' – resources hardly have identities. While this occurs under corporate governance, HRM ensures that the cold 'human versus resource' contradiction remains invisible to those who are the victims of such an ideology.

Even when one considers a standard managerial definition of corporate governance such as 'corporate governance [is] a system of governing an organisation so that the interests of corporate owners are protected' (Samson & Daft 2012:803), this definition of corporate governance excludes social participation and self-actualisation. This represents a clear case of 'norm versus norm': corporate governance versus social participation/self-actualisation. Once the ideological fog of the managerial definition of corporate governance has been removed what remains is 'a system that protects corporate owners'. But questions such as why do powerful owners of corporations need protection, from whom, and from what remain unasked. Meanwhile corporate governance is not so much about 'protecting owners' but to ensure that The Real Bottom Line is met which translates into ROI for shareholders who are the corporation's owners as the former *Harvard Business Review* editor Magretta[538] has outlined. It is the task of corporate governance to 'faithfully represent the interests of the corporation's owners'. As such, corporate governance focuses on organisational goals, shareholder-value, and profit-maximisation. In sum, corporate governance is not concerned with social participation and self-actualisation but is a non-holistic and highly sectarian affair. It is about 'the battle for corporate control' between owners and management. It is this narrowness that defines corporate governance, not social participation and self-actualisation extended to the whole of a corporation.

## Corporate governance and Hegel's concept of the whole

The exclusion of social participation and self-actualisation is, of course, extended to lower- and middle-management, non-managerial staff, and other so-called stakeholders (trade unions, NGOs, the state, etc.). If, on the other hand, *sittliche* corporations had social participation, they would be free and un-coerced (Hegel). The dark side of corporate pathologies would no longer exist.[539] Above that, *sittliche* corporate governance knows the contradictions between *Sittlichkeit* and functionality, power, common managerial phrases like 'my way or the highway', 'Mushroom Management' and 'FIFO – fit in or f*** off!'.[540] If they did not exist, corporate governance would be able to conduct itself in social participation and in a personally satisfying way. The concept of being 'personally satisfying' is obstructed by the fact that corporate governance is wedged between its task of governing and the stakeholders who own the business. This is attributable to, at least, seven issues.

Table 7.3 outlines some of the reasons why the Hegelian notion of social participation and personally satisfying relationships within corporate governance and between other corporate entities is absent. Internally, corporate governance is not an extension of Hegel's family fostering mutual recognition.[541] Corporate governance hardly resembles family-like institutions because it is not designed to give mutual aid to corporate members, there are no bonds of intimacy and closeness, and there are no natural social relations. In *Sittlichkeit*, however, moral corporations are built as ethical extensions to all three institutions that together create *Sittlichkeit*, namely, families (intimate), civil society (collectivism and community), and state (universal).[542] These three moral

*Table 7.3* Hegel's ethics and the stakeholders of corporate governance

| No. | Corporate governance and its stakeholders |
|---|---|
| 1. | Shareholders (the owners of corporations) |
| 2. | External markets, suppliers (upstream), and customers (downstream) |
| 3. | Organisational demands with regard to functional management: HRM, marketing, operations management, and accounting and finance |
| 4. | Organisational demands with regard to hierarchies: top-management, middle-management, line-management |
| 5. | Organisational demands regarding regional operations and functional divisions (M-form) |
| 6. | Non-managerial staff in the form of employees and their trade unions |
| 7. | External stakeholders: NGOs, states, local communities, etc. |

levels create three moral links to create *Sittlichkeit*. Today's corporations, however, are significantly different. Despite management's ideological rhetoric of 'we are all one big family', Hegel's 'true recognition and honour' does not feature in corporate governance.[543] Instead of being based on Kantian and Hegelian rationality, corporate governance relies on domination where the honour of virtually everyone regarded as non-managerial is reduced to being auxiliaries, appendices, or tools.[544]

Secondly, there is no 'normative mutuality' inside corporate governance as relations between corporate management, shareholders, and employees are not defined by normative mutuality.[545] Instead, these relationships are reflective of Hegel's 'master–slave dialectics' in which one side is reduced to a service in exchange for wages while the other two sides extract surplus-value for shareholder-value with corporate governance providing a 'self-serving' buffer between both.[546] Such an arrangement excludes the rationality of normative mutuality. Thirdly, there are no 'shared norms of its practices inside' a corporation because corporate governance deliberately excludes non-managerial staff from accessing its self-assigned privileges, thereby allowing the managerial 'abuse of organisational perks, favouritism, and nepotism' to flourish.[547] In business corporations, corporate privileges are more often than not limited to those who management writer Magretta (2012:4) calls 'people in positions of institutional power'. In Hegelian ethics, however, privileges are neither self-assigned nor based on power. Instead of being exclusive, *sittliche* privileges are inclusive and exist because of *sittliche* corporate governance. If corporate governance is not part of *Sittlichkeit*, it can neither have nor invent corporate privileges. Meanwhile in the corporate governance of business corporations, privileges occur under headings such as corporate policies, norms, and practices. But when corporate governance develops them, everyone regarded as external to corporate governance is excluded.

As a consequence, corporate governance destroys Hegel's normative mutuality under what is called corporate policies that are invented unilaterally without rationality and mutuality. Instead of the ethics of normative mutuality, non-managerial employees are simply asked to accept the corporate policies of FIFO. This can never create 'shared norms' imperative for a *sittliche* corporation. An organisational culture consisting of managerially induced non-shared norms that intentionally exclude those who are affected from creating such norms annihilates self-determination and self-actualisation. Managerialism's invented ideology of shared norms and organisational culture is designed to increase unquestioned compliance and to make individuals affirm to management's right to manage and the managerial prerogative. Culture is a bottom-up affair of self-actualisation while top-down 'culture' is ideology.

The comprehensive annihilation of normative mutuality under corporate governance has been extended to the individual rational will. Ever since philosophy, humanity, and human beings left the Dark Ages of religious and mythical feudalism, the rational individual will has been part of modernity, Enlightenment, and philosophy. Not surprisingly, the free rational will is a core part of *Sittlichkeit*. In Hegel's concept of an ethical corporation, a corporate member seeks 'the satisfaction of others as well as oneself . . . [In] the corporation . . . rights and welfare are united'.[548] In contrast to *sittliche* corporations, today's corporate governance excludes the mutual satisfaction of one's own will as much as seeking to satisfy the will of others. Will-formation inside current corporate governance can never be rational, based on self-actualisation – it can only be one-dimensional and irrational. With damaged self-actualisation and de-recognition, there is not even a rational 'corporate will', only the will of management. The will of corporate governance is neither free nor can it ever seek the satisfaction of another will because it is directed towards non-human goals and dictated by the non-human and inhuman and (as Hegel would say) *ungeistige* un-spiritual institution of Adam Smith's markets.[549] Internally meanwhile, the damaged will of corporate management is directed towards shareholder-value rather than towards Hegel's 'livelihood, welfare, and happiness of an individual'.[550] Hegel continues with 'individuals come to see how the livelihood, happiness, and legal status of each is interwoven with the livelihood, happiness, and rights of all' (Hegel 1821:§183).

Corporate governance does not foster such a rational understanding. It does not see 'livelihood, happiness, and legal status of each' as relevant to its operations. It does not conceptualise that 'the livelihood, happiness, and rights of all is interwoven with' corporate governance. Instead, employees' livelihood is an externality reduced to wages and salaries that corporate governance sees as a cost-burden. Meanwhile organisational happiness is a term that does not exist in management studies, Managerialism, managerial regimes, management, corporations, and of course corporate governance. Finally, the 'legal status' of human beings is de-recognised through the managerial reframing of them as human resources and their conversion into tools (Buchwalter 2012a:22). This turns them into objects to corporate policies and 'objects of power' (Bauman 1989) with all the pathological consequences one can imagine.

Outside the corporation, Managerialism's ideology of deregulation – read destruction – of labour law has factually reduced the legal status of human beings employed by corporations. Given that Hegelian philosophy determines that 'the sphere of law is the sphere of freedom', the destruction of labour law means the destruction of freedom (Riedel 1974:119). In this sense Managerialism damages people's 'livelihood, happiness, legal status of each' and everyone in civil society. Managerialism and its entourage of managerial economics view livelihood, happiness, and legal status simply as externalities. Similarly, labour law and civil society itself are seen as institutions to be made subservient to corporations so that these 'external' arrangements support The Real Bottom Line.

In other words, corporate governance represents the exact opposite of what Hegelian ethics outlines as 'civil society is a system of complete interdependence' (Cullen 1988:23). There is no 'system of complete interdependence' under corporate governance. Instead, Hegel's dialectical two-way, mutual, and reciprocal interdependence is converted into a one-way street. Managerialism's ideology seeks to make civil society unilaterally dependent on corporations through a process that Habermas calls 'colonisation'.[551] The relationship is not mutual (⇆) but represents the singularity of an asymmetrical power relation: 'corporations → civil society'. Civil society is made submissive, subservient, an auxiliary institution to support corporations.

According to Hegel, societal members are simultaneously corporate members, members of a *sittliche* corporation and the economic sphere. These memberships are reciprocal and mutual relationships. But corporate members are also part of a family and a state (levels 1 + 3 of *Sittlichkeit*). In the words of philosopher Gallagher (1987:174),

> What he does, as corporate member, is solely the corporation; he belongs to the whole which is itself an organ [*Glied*] of the entire society . . . the model of the relationships
>
> 1. family member to the whole family,
> 2. corporate member to the whole corporation, and
> 3. the corporation itself to the state – is that of member to the organic whole in which the individual can be himself only to the extent that he participates in the life of the whole.

In other words, Hegel does not construct an artificial segregation between civil society and corporate governance. There is no schizophrenic split personality into being a morally good and kind family father at night and a corporate raider during the day. Kindness and morality cannot be segregated from believing to be a kind father and a moral person and the immorality of corporate beliefs such as 'in destruction there is opportunity' which describes the frantic buying of gold by commodity traders on 12 September 2001 – the day after September 11th – and the buying of oil shortly before the Iraq invasion in expectation of rising gold and oil prices. While some die – others make money. *Sittlichkeit* renders such managerial ideologies and corporate behaviours irrational. These two examples – gold and oil – are prime examples of the managerial 'Rationality of Irrationality' (Godelier 1966). While society views such behaviour as irrational and immoral, for commodity traders it appears rational. Managerialism discusses the society–corporations interface as stakeholder theory emphasising internal versus external stakeholders. In holistic *Sittlichkeit*, there are no internal–external boundaries and no managerially invented externalities. There are no external stakeholders. Instead, *sittliche* corporations are organic parts [*Glieder*] and living institutions of civil society in which today's strict society–corporate boundaries are merely weak administrative delineations.[552]

In *Sittlichkeit*, there is no clear-cut division between being a member of a family, a corporate member, corporate governance, civil society, and a state. Instead of sharp segregating lines, unity, harmony, and ethical life are established. The ethical engagement between corporate governance, a moral community, civil society, and *Sittlichkeit* means that corporate managers can never insulate themselves from the morality of families, communities, civil society, states, and the universalism of Hegel's world spirit [*Weltgeist*].[553] Corporate governance can never develop a bipolar disorder called MADD as moral attention deficit disorder, moral silence, moral deafness, moral blindness, or moral amnesia.[554] And rational–*sittliche* corporate governance can never disassociate corporate individuals' interest from that of *Sittlichkeit.*

In *Sittlichkeit,* there is no contradiction between the interest of individual managers, management as a group, corporate governance as a sub-group of management, the corporation itself, a local community, civil society, family, the state, and the international community that all resemble Hegel's *Weltgeist.* There is no artificial, illusionary, and largely irrational segregation between management morality, corporate morality, and what management calls 'external' morality (community, civil society, etc.). Instead, *Sittlichkeit* views morality (moral behaviour), ethics (a moral system), and ethical life (Hegel's self-actualisation) as one issue. There is no separating of morality and no relocation or displacement of morality to families, civil society, and states while simultaneously seeking to exclude corporations from moral responsibilities. *Sittlichkeit* remains an issue in all spheres, institutions, and organisations without exception. This is for several reasons. Hegel views corporations as 'an organ [*Glied*] of an entire society'. Hence, corporate governance cannot extract itself from civil society; it cannot view civil society as merely an externality comprising peripheral stakeholders; and it cannot view civil society as an externality.[555]

As such corporate governance 'belongs to the whole' (Hegel) seen as the entirety of *Sittlichkeit.* It is not simply part of a corporation and cannot reduce itself to a neutral-, technical-, or engineering-like function of management that operates exclusively inside corporations and for the sole benefit of shareholders. And, perhaps most importantly, under 21st-century Managerialism, corporate governance cannot relinquish its position of being part of *Sittlichkeit* by having invented CSR.[556] Corporate management views CSR as a function of corporate PR. Not surprisingly, 'most CSR workers in companies sit in the communications and PR departments'.[557] As an ideology, CSR is designed to take care of externalities and is specifically set up to achieve the very opposite of *Sittlichkeit.*

Corporate governance does not mean simply 'to take part' in civil society, states, and a legal system (Benson & Kirsch 2010b). Instead, *sittliche* corporate governance unites the spirit of civil society [*Gemeinschaftsgeist*], state [*Volksgeist*], and legal system [*Rechtsgeist*]. The corporate spirit [*Korporationsgeist ~ esprit de corps*] is a mirror image of *Volksgeist,* and a legal system.[558] In a *sittliche*–legal system, corporations are not mere legal fictions. They cannot exist because human-like rights have been unilaterally given without the self-actualisation of a moral community. Business corporations are not human-like. They reach far beyond their fictitious quasi-legality. In contrast, *sittliche* corporations are the mirror image of a legality found in the principles of *Sittlichkeit.* However, in a highly specified sense, the legal fiction of modern civil codes grants corporations human-like rights. It invented a crypto-legal person. However, in *Sittlichkeit* legal frameworks are always subservient to an ethical whole [*das sittliche Ganze*]. In other words, legal systems that underpin corporations have to be designed to support morality and have to exist in accordance with *Sittlichkeit*'s ethical demand of human self-actualisation that cannot be extended to a socially disconnected business organisation. In contrast, a *sittliche* commercial law supports at least two key principles:

1. the livelihood, for example, income, job security, working conditions, and OHS,[559] and
2. wellbeing, comfort, and happiness of corporate members.

In sharp contrast, corporate laws are not designed to secure the livelihood of individuals. Corporate law is a rather one-dimensional affair supporting business institutions. Strongly supported by Managerialism, corporate lobbyists, for example, work tirelessly to re-frame corporate law in their favour, reduce, and eliminate labour law, consumer safety, and environmental provisions through the ideology of deregulation. This occurs as a contest of 'cost versus livelihood': cost reduction is set against securing the livelihood of employees through decent wages. Secondly, corporate law is not designed to ensure the 'wellbeing, comfort, and happiness' of those employed by corporations. Thirdly, it does not set out to protect the environment and consumers. Under Managerialism's ideology of 'industry self-regulation', this has been handed over to business corporations.[560]

Finally, current corporate laws have not been established on the principles of *Sittlichkeit* but through corporate lobbying such as 'The Best Influence Money Can Buy'.[561] Today's corporate laws have been designed to protect corporations from *Sittlichkeit* and allow them a wide range of activities that impact negatively on its employees, local communities, and the environment. After decades of deregulation, corporate law also assists corporations to create oligopolies, informal, so-called gentleman's agreements, 'breakfast' and more explicit cartels. Corporate law was never designed to achieve *Sittlichkeit.* Its creation violated Hegel's self-actualisation as 'all' affected corporate members were deliberately excluded from direct involvement in the process of law-making. Instead, corporate law – together with the judicial fantasy of 'corporation equals natural person' – has been and is designed to give corporations relatively unhindered powers and to assist them in the creation of what has been termed 'corporate pathologies' or 'The Monstrous Organisation'.[562]

Equipped with the fantasy of possessing a legal foundation, business corporations reflect the Nietzsche-like ethics of 'strong versus weak' in which corporate management is able to impose its managerial will onto all others in and outside the corporation.[563] On the other hand, Hegelian ethics as applied to corporations seeks to prevent this by 'privately owned' but *sittliche* corporations. In addition, they are not part of the states. Hegel did not envision corporations as ruthless enforcing-machines of blind market forces but instead he saw them as scrupulously controlled by states. On corporate governance, Hegel's *Innensteuerung* grants corporate management 'the right to regulate the professional life of their members in relative autonomy' (which is linked to *Sittlichkeit* enshrining the corporate task of preventing . . . poverty [and for that] the corporation's self-regulation includes the right to elect its own board).[564] In sharp contrast to Hegelian forms of participation as self-actualisation, elections to company boards are often mediated, at least partly pre-engineered, and largely conducted by shareholders that are all too often other corporations. Instead of democratic self-actualisation, 'corporate suffrage is reduced to a formal ritual that produces a formal legitimacy'.[565] Hegel's ethics of self-actualisation favours the direct election of corporate management by 'all' those who are governed by it, that is, employees. This is the only way to guarantee self-determination and self-actualisation. In today's version of corporate governance, however, Hegel's ethical demands have only insufficiently become reality as the boards are 'elected' (!) in name only.[566] They are not elected by 'all' corporate members as prescribed in *Sittlichkeit*.

Finally, today's corporations do not include *Sittlichkeit*'s 'unity of rights and welfare' (Bohman 2010) because rights are unilaterally defined as the right of 'management to manage' framed as 'corporate policies'. Rights are not used to create *Sittlichkeit* but to enforce a strict, irrational, immoral, and ideological separation between corporate management and non-managerial staff. Corporate policies assign 'rights' to management and 'responsibilities' to non-managerial staff. The right of corporate management is the right to manage while employees' responsibilities are enforced through rafts of HRM instruments ranging from performance management to the infamous KPIs – key performance indicators. While CEOs are often excluded from the torturous implements of performance management, they are also excluded from KPIs. Their remuneration is often disassociated from corporate-, company-, and share-values.[567] Instead of a Hegelian unification of rights and welfare, managerial rights often terminate privileges for non-managerial employees. Instead of *sittliche* rights as outlined in Hegel's *Philosophy of Right*, corporate governance tends to operate the one-dimensional managerial right to manage. Similarly, social, human, and ethical welfare is largely excluded from corporations. Managerialism views them as externalities. They are assigned to state agencies under Managerialism's ideology of tax-reduction, deregulation, and *The Privatization of Everything*.[568] The outcome is threefold:

1. it converts the concept of general taxation to an 'internal-class-only' mechanism so that the costs of corporate and market pathologies are offloaded onto those affected. These pathologies are to be regulated, administered, and paid for class internally without involving corporations. Simultaneously,
2. market capitalism and corporations are taken out of the picture, totally disassociating them from the pathologies they have created. As a consequence,
3. corporate tax can be reduced to zero. In a true managerial zero-sum game, this will increase profits.

Managerialism's strategy involves a number of complicated chessboard-like moves. But since the 1990s, this has (and will in the future) resulted in tangible outcomes for corporations. Meanwhile, inside corporations, Hegelian welfare is devalued to the simplistic notion of 'wellbeing' and so-called 'wellness programmes', often condensed to subsidised gym-memberships.[569] The silliness of such token schemes is further enhanced by the fact that they are not even designed with the welfare of employees in mind but to sustain a human resource's capability to contribute to profitability under, for example, HRM's 'balanced scorecard'.[570] Nevertheless, it remains HRM's PR task to sell such programmes as corporate welfare under the endlessly rehearsed HRM motto 'people are our most important assets' that equalises humans with 'assets', possessions, property, and chattels (Adonis 2010:18–20). In sum, corporate management circumvents Hegel's notion of a 'unity of rights and welfare' in four ways:

1. corporate programmes are not designed for people but for corporate profitability representing a Kantian 'means' not an 'ends in itself';
2. there is no unity or link between rights and welfare;
3. welfare is not a right under corporate management; and finally,
4. corporate rights and welfare are completely disconnected from *Sittlichkeit*.

Contrary to the views taken up by corporate management, Hegel's point here is that the purpose of a given corporation is universal to the extent that the benefits of membership accrue to all its members; and it is recognised that the individual member 'is actively interested in promoting the . . . aim of that whole'.[571] Firstly, in complete opposition to Hegelian ethics, corporate management does not see corporations as having a universal purpose beyond that of what has been correctly expressed by the former CEO of one of the world's largest corporations – General Motor's CEO Alfred Sloan – 'the point is that General Motors is not in business to make cars, but to make money'.[572] Hence, the purpose of business corporations remains particular and sectarian while Hegel noted that 'the rationality of [*sittliche*] corporations is their factual expression of the common interest of all' and 'it is the corporation spirit acting as a conduit between particularity and universal'.[573] Secondly, for corporate management there is no universal morality from which corporate morality can result (Pogge 2007, 2010). If anything, corporate management tries hard to insulate corporations against the moral values of communities (Henderson 2001). Simultaneously, it is the ideological task of management studies and management ethics to find reasons why moral philosophy does not apply to corporations. Thirdly, unless individuals are part of the inner circle of corporate management, they do not 'accrue benefits' just because of their 'membership' in a corporation. This applies to ordinary and non-managerial corporate members.

Fourthly, corporate governance – and this comes because of the corporate ideology of individuality – does not recognise individual members of a corporation, only the sum-total of their bottom-line contribution as resources. Fifthly, corporate governance does not 'actively promote the interest and aims of the whole'. Instead, it promotes the sectarian interests of corporation → management → top-management → certain groups of managers.[574] The relationship between corporate management and morality has been further highlighted by the German philosopher Kersting when emphasising that

> the corporation is obliged to extend social welfare beyond corporate members. This includes their families which Hegel addressed as a 'second family'. Corporations have to guarantee the subsistence of their members and assure that they receive 'healthy food'. The corporation protects members against the risks associated with free trade. Hegel expected cooperative solidarity inside corporations to compensate for increasing industrialism and the subsequent growth of a lack of harmonisation caused by market society.[575]

Rather than viewing corporate welfare as a cost to be eliminated or restricting it to 'some' corporate members, that is, management, Hegel saw the *sittliche* corporation as achieving the exact opposite. *Sittliche* corporations extend welfare provisions beyond the boundaries of corporations to include the families of corporate members and beyond. *Sittliche* corporations guarantee the subsistence of corporate members. This carries two moral duties: firstly, wages can never be reduced to starvation levels, that is, the working poor should never have come into existence; secondly, and perhaps most problematically for business corporations, this also extends to those business subsidiaries that have been made to appear distant to corporations through outsourcing and the relocation of production to developing countries (Dumenil & Levy 2011). In moral terms, this has achieved what Milgram uncovered as a willingness of perpetrators to act immorally and to confine victims to an abhorrent existence in distant corners of the 'Planet of Slums' that increases with physical distance.[576] It can be summed up in the following formula: the greater the distance between the fashionable and stylish corporate headquarters and outsourced sweatshops, the greater the willingness of management to inflict pain and suffering. It creates the 'Boys with No Names' and management's global sourcing, supply chain management, and global production networks. Suffering in and through corporations is not new.[577] What is new is that these outsourced work regimes are managed by 'distant' corporations. The totality of this represents what Hegel had described as[578]

> a mass of the population is condemned to the stupefying, unhealthy, and insecure labour of the factories, manufacturers, mines and so on . . . this necessity turns into the utmost dismemberment of the will inner, rebellion, and hatred.

Whether working in Adam Smith's 18th-century pin factory, a 19th-century workshop, a 20th-century Tayloristic[579] and Fordist factory, or simply typing numbers into a computerised spread sheet on Microsoft Excel, work still carries elements of 'stupefying' (Hegel) monotony.[580] While many unhealthy forms of work have become an issue of the past, we have not experienced the elimination of unhealthy work.[581] Simultaneously, unhealthy and insecure work has actually increased under Managerialism's push for deregulation, short-term contracts, labour hire firms, outsourcing, franchising, sub-contracting, a general casualisation, and the relentless annihilation of the standard eight-hour-day of permanent employment. All of this causes 'dismemberment of the will, rebellion, and hatred'. So far, Managerialism's ideological offensive combined with the global power of corporate mass media has prevented a turning of Hegel's 'inner' mass-rebellion into 'external' mass-rebellion.

In a *sittliche* corporation, corporate members do not cease to be corporate members when they are no longer part of an individual corporation. This means that welfare provisions reach beyond the employment relationship and the moral responsibility towards others inside civil society. This arrangement might represent a near perfect example of Kant's 'moral duty' because *sittliche* corporations carry moral duties for social welfare that reach out of corporations into civil society establishing mutual moral linkages:

Management ⇄ corporations ⇄ economic sphere ⇄ civil society ⇄ *Sittlichkeit*

Lastly, perhaps more interesting is a corporate assurance of 'healthy food'. During Hegel's 19th century, this was related to malnutrition rather than to what today is advocated as healthy eating in an effort to combat modern health problems such as obesity and heart attacks. Then, as today, *Sittlichkeit* sees corporations as institutions that carry responsibilities for 'healthy food'. In the 21st century, this carries three connotations: (i) food should be nutritious; (ii) a rejection of junk- and fast-food produced by corporations; (iii), corporations refrain from manufacturing and selling unhealthy food (Freudenberg 2012). However, a number of worldwide operative corporations are doing exactly that with 'The McDonald's Corporation' as prime signifier.[582] In *Sittlichkeit*'s understanding of healthy food, the corporate production and sale (e.g. marketing corporations) of junk- and fast-food is highly immoral.

Finally, 'corporate protection against risks associated with free trade' relates to neo-liberalism and its ideological outgrowth of globalisation. Hegel was an ardent opponent of unhindered free markets exposing individuals to arbitrariness [*Willkür*].[583] *Sittlichkeit* does not advocate free markets and it does not deny the existence of pathologies as claimed by Managerialism and 'Corporate Missionaries' (Beder 2006). *Sittlichkeit* indicates that the role of *sittliche* corporations is to protect corporate members from the *Willkür* of the market. Hegel did not view the free market and free trade as ultimate panaceas but as the creator of social and economic illnesses. In other words, corporations are not only the driving force behind corporate globalisation, they are also the creator of global inequalities and pathologies.[584] Hence, they are responsible for counteracting the pathologies of free trade and free markets that affect most negatively those who work for and in corporations, that is, labour.

## Work and labour in Hegel's moral corporation

With rising industrialisation, Hegel – just like Marx (1890) and later Durkheim (1897)[585] – saw that capitalism creates increasing anomies, alienation, and disharmonies caused by markets which remain a continuing feature of capitalism.[586] In his famous master–slave dialectics, Hegel explicitly discusses labour.[587] To compensate for the social illnesses created by markets, Hegel favoured a 'cooperative–corporate solidarity' [*binnenkorporative Solidarität*]. Again, today's business corporations advocate and operate systems that achieve the exact opposite of what *Sittlichkeit* prescribes to be the moral duty of corporations. They employ rafts of HRM experts to ensure that *Sittlichkeit*'s 'cooperative solidarity inside corporations' is destroyed in favour of performance management, individual contracts, competition, individualism, performance-related pay, and so on. Hegel's moral duties of corporations result in severe challenges to business corporations. In most cases, corporations are unwilling to live up to the moral demands enshrined in *Sittlichkeit* or are outright opponents of its principles.

The purpose of a *sittliche* corporation is universal, not particular. It demands that corporations go beyond CSR.[588] But modern corporations do not even extend the ideology of CSR to their own devalued employees who are no more than human resources, assets, and chattel. Management has nullified and deliberately de-recognised human beings through their ideology of human resources.[589] Meanwhile, the ethical meaning of work itself has been negated by denying the importance of work for civil society and human beings as a whole. In the business corporation, work and labour have been reduced to a functionality of corporate management. *Sittlichkeit* outlines the exact opposite. The inclusiveness of labour as *sittliche* human beings and the labour they perform is of fundamental importance in *Sittlichkeit*.[590]

During Hegel's lifetime of rising industrial capitalism, he was well aware of the changing character of the role of labour and work.[591] This became imperative in Hegel's *Sittlichkeit* because of the high currency capitalism placed on work as a constitutive element of economy, civil society, and modernity. For Hegel, work entails six key issues that remain unnoticed by corporate management.[592]

Table 7.4 shows six important elements many of which remain deliberately neglected, un-explored, and intentionally non-applied by

*Table 7.4* Six elements defining work in Hegelian philosophy

| No. | Six characteristics of work as understood in Hegelian philosophy: |
|---|---|
| 1. | Work creates a willingness and a capability to work. |
| 2. | Work creates a framework of continuous and long-term employment. |
| 3. | Work develops an ability to alter nature through the production of goods and services. |
| 4. | Work establishes mutual dependency with others and thereby overcomes the arbitrariness of markets. |
| 5. | Work is an objective activity resulting in the ability of management to exchange worker through worker [substitutability, Hegel's *Ersetzbarkeit*]. |
| 6. | Work creates a set of common skills that can also be replaced. |

management which positions itself against employees, throwing Rawls' (2001:97) famous 'Veil of Ignorance' over those whom Aristotle called 'those who make things' – workers. It remains imperative to understand work in its philosophical nakedness, that is, stripped off all connotations of the present-day experience of Tayloristic–Fordism managerial regimes.[593] What people today experience as work is not the positive event of work as such but managerially organised work inside corporate regimes.[594] In addition, Managerialism has conditioned today's image of work for decades.[595] Once Managerialism's reality-eclipsing fog has been cleared, work assumes a very different position in human society and *Sittlichkeit*. Understanding the real meaning of work today demands the mental capacity to envision individuals as artists and amateurs who work for self-fulfilment and the benefits of society rather than corporate profits in managerial regimes. It means to understand the human and moral value of work. It demands an Orwellian removal of ideological and managerial images to ascertain the purity, morality, and aesthetics of work.[596]

First of all, work creates willingness and a capability to work. The positive and fulfilling experience of non-managerially distorted forms of work is a self-reinforcing mechanism that allows individuals to continue working. Today, one finds positive work outside of managerial regimes and at a secure distance from ROI and The Real Bottom Line. In 21st-century managerial capitalism, positive forms of work are isolated occurrences (e.g. artists). The second element is work's ability to create a framework of continuation and long-termism. This is in sharp contradiction to the managerial drive to alter work from long-term employment to short-term contracting, outsourcing of labour, sub-contracting, and numerous other HRM instruments invented to reduce labour costs.

All of them work favourably towards corporate profits but are damaging to human beings while acting against *Sittlichkeit*.[597]

Hegel's third point is work's capacity to develop human abilities by altering nature through the production of goods and services. This might have been more important during early industrial capitalism as experienced during Hegel's lifetime. The move from 'manufacturing' capitalism towards 'service industry' capitalism has altered the ability of human beings to change 'nature' significantly. But despite the increasingly abstract and symbolic character of work, human beings can still experience work positively. Fourthly, work also establishes mutual dependency through a positive engagement with the work of others, labour itself, and the products that are not exposed to the arbitrariness [*Willkür*] of capitalist markets in the form of a contradiction between commodity and labour markets. On the one hand there is an increasing inter-connectedness of labour with the labour of others through an ever increasing integration of work and company-to-company relations in the form of 'Global Production Networks'.[598] This is accompanied by the ideology of the free – or as Hegel would say *willkürliche* – market (Beder 2006). The *Philosophy of Right* highlights these pathologies of market arbitrariness [*Willkür*]. *Sittliche* corporations are institutions working against *arbitrariness*. In *Sittlichkeit*, the contradictory forces of 'meaningful versus managerial' work can be overcome by structurally enhancing the former while simultaneously reducing the latter. Such a design supports *Sittlichkeit*.

Fifthly, *Sittlichkeit* also rejects the *Willkür* of corporate management as manifested in management's ability to treat labour as exchangeable. Hegel's study of Adam Smith made him aware that capitalist work regimes allow management the exchange of one worker with another. Hegel called this substitutability [*Ersetzbarkeit*]. In any moral philosophy, the managerial idea of human beings being exchangeable and interchangeable is highly problematic. For one, substitutability carries strong connotations to Kant's categorical imperative of 'means versus ends'. Substitutability indicates 'means', not 'ends'. Once human beings are reduced to mere means and resources, they are also reduced to *Ersetzbarkeit*. People become exchangeable and expandable (Schmidt 2007:196). This is extremely damaging to *Sittlichkeit*.

Finally, the managerial idea of exchangeability applies not only to labour and employees, but also to work itself because industrial work creates a set of common skills that can be replaced.[599] This is reflected, for example, in the reduction of education to mere vocational training as conducted by management schools and management studies under the supervision of Managerialism. Its task is to teach functional knowledge to be used inside managerial regimes 'for' The Real Bottom Line to the exclusion of ethics.[600] Degrees and curricula are designed to have high levels of exchange-value. In that way virtually all forms of corporate management in all corporations can use any human resources with a specific set of qualifications as engineered by management schools and training facilities. It renders any manager exchangeable and expandable. On the upside, this increases a human resources' employability while making 'it' – the tool – easily exchangeable. All of this is carried out by management in stark contrast to a *sittliche* understanding of labour and work. The negation of key elements of work and labour is conducted and supported by virtually every institution inside Managerialism's orbit. In sharp contrast to *Sittlichkeit*, corporate management – through corporate policies, for example – can never 'allow [employees to act in] an unselfish point of view in relation to their colleagues'.[601]

In conclusion, *Sittlichkeit* emphasises the positive, human, and moral role of labour and work. It supports work organised for human beings on the principles of *Sittlichkeit* and not for corporate goals. This consists of the inclusion and participation of all corporate members. The *sittliche* treatment of labour and work linked to participation in corporate affairs moves employees beyond the point of selfishness in relation to their colleagues. In other words, what a *sittliche* corporate management engages in is the assistance of employees in creating a work environment that assists workers to develop unselfish relationships to their co-workers, to corporate management, to the corporation, to other economic actors, to civil society, to families and states, and finally to *Sittlichkeit* itself. At present, however, corporate management uses instruments such as, for example, the balanced scorecard system (Kaplan & Norton 1992, 1993, 2004) to achieve the exact opposite of what Hegelian philosophy denotes. Managerialism and corporations cultivate selfishness (management), not unselfishness, (*Sittlichkeit*) even though unselfishness is a key component of *Sittlichkeit* as the next chapter will show.

# 8
# Corporations and *Sittlichkeit*

*Corporations assure the overall context of moral life.*[602]

Hegel's central issue of the *Philosophy of Right* (1821) is *Sittlichkeit* or ethical life, clearly emphasising that corporations are part of *Sittlichkeit.*[603] For Hegel, *Sittlichkeit* represents 'the institutional reality of human selfhood'.[604] When ethical selfhood is applied to business corporations, it becomes apparent that a reversal of much of what is found in today's corporations is required.[605] For example, Hegelian ethics demands a return to a situation where the actuality of ethical life occupies a prime position 'over' business corporations and management. The demand for a turnaround of today's corporations starts with the place where today's corporate managers are trained, namely, business schools.[606] Governed by Managerialism, these business schools are located inside universities. Instead of teaching ethics, the managerial university prefers to train people in vocational and useful knowledge to be used by corporations rather than teaching academic, scholarly, intellectual, and perhaps even critical subjects. Non-revenue-creating academic subjects are often marginalised and excluded. The marginalisation of philosophy in favour of managerial subjects supports a university's economic success, leadership, profit-margins, market share, competitive advantage, wealth accumulation, shareholder-values, profit-maximisation, and so on.[607] This has created serious pathologies 'that can be viewed as misdevelopments [*Fehlentwicklungen*], disorders or social pathologies' according to Hegelian philosopher Axel Honneth.[608] In society, the deliberate decline of ethics in favour of business has led to a class of people who, according to Oscar Wilde (1892),

> know the price of everything and the value of nothing.

Fostered by corporate mass media, the ideology of Managerialism has created a petit-bourgeois mindset of egoistic corporate managers, just as Hegel had predicted. Their actions are defined by selfishness and what Hegelian philosopher Kersting calls 'self-addicted purpose' and it is this *selbstsüchtiger Zweck* that is contradictory to *Sittlichkeit*.[609] Hegel has described this as 'he alone is the only purpose; everything else is nothing to him'.[610] It manifests itself, for example, in Schwartz's (1990) 'Narcissistic Process and Corporate Decay' but the problem of selfishness versus *Sittlichkeit* has more significant implications. Being a philosopher of spirit [*Geist*], Hegel saw another more philosophical and more important conflict, namely, the conflict between *Sittlichkeit*'s ethics of freedom and nature's instincts and desires.[611] Hegel noted in his *Philosophy of Right* that one is unfree when one is 'merely desire-driven'.[612] He calls this 'unfreedom'. Management successfully exploits this. It feasts on individual desires for status, wages, salaries, gratification, bonuses, and petit-bourgeois attitudes. Managerialism's prime writer, found in almost every management textbook, is Frederick Herzberg (1923–2000) who calls the desire for money 'extrinsic rewards' while desire for praise is termed 'intrinsic rewards'.[613] Ever since management's move from 'punishment to reward' regimes, management scavenges on instinctive desires (McGregor 1960, 2006). Management's exploitation of desires has become a largely unchallenged ideology taught at management schools. While Hegelian philosophy sees desire-driven actions as unfreedom, management, meanwhile, systematically fosters them – through, for example, its ingrained system of performance management – for its ends of working exactly in opposition to *Sittlichkeit*.

There are management decisions that are made on desire-driven motives and those that are – more deliberately – made on instrumental rationality such as cost–benefit decisions. The latter are decisions Hegel calls *selbstsüchtiger Zweck* which translates into selfish purpose made by someone who is addicted [*süchtig*] to oneself. These managerial decisions are reflective of *Sophie's Choice*, forcing one to choose between managerially pre-designed options.[614] Managerialism links this to the prisoner dilemma, quasi-scientifically labelled 'rational choice theories'. Both provide management with a conceptual underpinning for *Sophie's Choice*-like manipulations.[615] These manipulations create narrowly defined managerial unfreedoms. They are deliberate distortions of freedom reducing human freedom to pre-conceived choices while Managerialism frames this as 'free' choice.[616] Unlike management's exploitation of instincts and desires, the free choice ideology plays on selfishness assuming that human beings are economic cost–benefit machines (Kaletsky 2009). It represents what Hegel calls *Willkür*, arbitrariness, despotism, and capriciousness. Hence, 'for Hegel freedom unquestionably involves more than man as *homo economicus*, as a maker, buyer, and seller of commodities'.[617]

Neither the concept of a *homo economicus* nor that of a *zoon politikon* has ever questioned the 'exclusive bourgeois/aristocratic right to rule'. This remains one of Hegel's unsolved problems. He knew that a human being is not a *homo economicus*. On the other hand, Hegel relied on the Greek *ζῷον πολιτικόν*, that is, living human beings inside a polis-community.[618] The third element that complicates matters has been Hegel's staunch refusal to 'question the exclusive bourgeois/aristocratic right to rule'. Nonetheless, *Sittlichkeit* combats the petit-bourgeois mindset of egoism, selfishness, managerial ideologies of cost–benefit calculations, the *selbstsüchtige Zweck*, and human beings reduced to *homo economicus*. In the struggle for *Sittlichkeit*, Hegel envisioned an important combatant: corporations [*Korporationen*]. He saw two opposing powers in modern societies.[619]

Figure 8.1 depicts two opposing norms (→←) but with a mediating link between both: the corporation. In many ways, corporations are Hegel's solution for Adam Smith's key problem that not even Smith was able to solve, namely the problematic relationship between market-economic pursuits, such as profits and competition, and society's needs for common goods – the real meaning of 'common'-wealth.[620] Perhaps it even carries connotations to Flügel-Martinsen's 'horizontal socialisation processes' [*horizontale Vergesellschaftungsprozesse*] leading to an entirely different form of today's managerial economy.[621] Hegel never advocated this but he engaged in this dilemma in his *Philosophy of Right*. Unlike Adam Smith's economic and individualistic version of selfishness, for Hegel 'common'-welfare always means 'the welfare of others'.[622] He denotes that an individual's free will has the particular content of welfare. For Hegel, the idea of welfare is 'reflected into . . . the universal element. This moment of universality . . . is the welfare of others.' It creates Hegel's 'ethical universe'.[623]

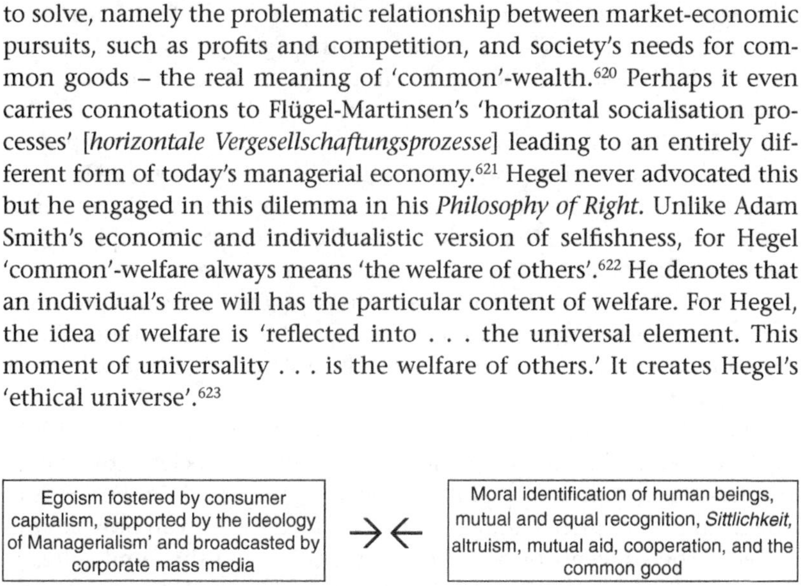


*Figure 8.1* Two opposing norms

But in business corporations, corporate welfare is microscopic, non-universal, and/or reduced to merely a PR exercise while Managerialism's ideology equates 'welfare' with 'costs' that have to be reduced.[624] Hegel's *sittliche* welfare is diametrically opposed to a narrow and self-serving view because *Sittlichkeit* sees welfare as the welfare of others. For today's corporations, however, welfare has no universal content as it has in *Sittlichkeit.* Corporate welfare is not a principle of corporate affairs nor is it a moment of universality. Despite this, *Sittlichkeit* denotes that 'the individual is made to look beyond his self-interest to confront the universal' (Davis 1987:200). Looking beyond self-interest is a key component of *Sittlichkeit* and of a *sittliche* economy.

## Corporate bonds and economic freedom

Explaining the morality of economics, 'Hegel cites the example of *Cicero*, who 'divorced his wife as a business speculation in order to pay his debts with his new wife's dowry'.[625] In *Sittlichkeit,* the reverse has to be the case because of Hegel's dictum that 'family life equals moral life'. Not only is 'the family the immediate moment of the ethical spirit [*sittlicher Geist*]' but the family is also 'the natural sexual attraction transformed into a union on the level of Spirit, into self-conscious love' (Gallagher 1987:167). Hence, in *Sittlichkeit,* an individual finds 'oneself in the family'.[626] This is established through special family bonds and 'the individual experiences as an immediate extension of self and whose subjective bond is love'.[627] These family bonds that Hegel also calls 'blood bonds' are always superior to economic bonds shaped by markets and an 'ethical corporate bond'.[628] In many ways, social, economic, and corporate bonds are very different from family and intimacy bonds. As Hegelian philosopher Cullen (1988:26) explains, 'In the corporation, individuals who share some common economic or vocational bond (members of the various professions, entrepreneurs, tradesmen) come together to form an organisation to represent their common interest.' To understand Hegel's system of bonds three issues are relevant:

Table 8.1 shows three bonds linked to Hegel's three *Sittlichkeit* establishing levels. At the level between family and state, civil society's two subdivisions – the economic and political spheres – are placed. In the words of American philosopher Winfield (1987:38), 'civil society can only be conceived if the concepts of personhood, morality, and the family already lie at hand' (Herrmann-Pillath & Boldyrev 2014:11). With personhood Hegel did not envision Managerialism's ideology of human resources and

*Table 8.1* Three versions of moral bonds

| Bonds | Descriptions |
|---|---|
| Intimacy | The family that provides a 'blood' bond of intimacy as the initial level of an early established morality |
| Sociality | A *sittliche* corporation provides an economic and vocational bond as an extension of *Sittlichkeit*'s first level[629] |
| Universality | The first level (families) and the second level (civil society → social economy → corporations) are linked to the 'universal' bond of the state that provides the final level of morality[630] |

corporate citizens but civil citizens of a polis-community.[631] The ethics of personhood is also alien to corporate marketing that reduces human beings to consumers and shopping units with marketing's task of manipulating consumer habits.[632] Instead of reducing personhood to resources and consumers, *Sittlichkeit* denotes something different, namely, 'personhood is a prerequisite for all further freedoms'.[633] In other words, when corporate management denies personhood – for human resources (internal) and consumers (externally) – they destroy *Sittlichkeit*. While ethical personhood is irrelevant to corporations, personality can be relevant to corporations because it can be manipulated to serve managerial ends. It is the task of organisational psychology and HRM to convert human personality into an organisational personality.[634] This contradicts *Sittlichkeit* and annihilates human personality.[635]

The 'ethical [*sittliche*] dimension of personality reflects an important connection noted by Hegel, namely the link between *ēthos* (custom, way of life) and *ēthikos* (ethical)' (Gallagher 1987:168). For corporate management, there is no personality other than an organisational personality. In this, neither *ēthos* nor *ēthikos* plays any role. The only other role corporations assign to personalities is the externality of a consuming person. But *Sittlichkeit* does not see civil society as a place where human-to-human relationships and people's attitudes are defined by marketing. Instead, it 'means a *sittliche* life, as Hegel describes it that is at once familial, economic, and political with no actual priority awarded to any of these dimensions' (Gallagher 1987:163). Hegel's three moral spheres contain not only three different 'bonds' as outlined above but also three different versions of freedom. Being a philosopher of freedom, Hegel envisioned three 'bonds' linked to three freedoms:

Table 8.2 shows the three levels of *Sittlichkeit* with the first being family love and family ties. They form the initial morality defined by intimacy and blood relations. These personal bonds lead to personal freedom that establishes personhood and represents an initial bond of mutual and equal recognition. Perhaps the second level is the most problematic in Hegelian ethics. It is governed by economic bonds that are in conflict with the social bonds of civil society. Unlike families, the sphere of civil society is split into two contradictory parts:

1. in the non-economic part of civil society social bonds are established through mutual and equal recognition; and
2. in the economic part with corporations, these bonds are somewhat damaged and/or harder to establish because of competition between economic agents.

This results in a damaged version of freedom that has been ideologically framed as 'economic freedom' reflecting Hegel's arbitrariness and capriciousness [*Willkür*]. At the final level, Hegel's concept of bonds is somewhat of a cumulative element of two earlier bonds, namely family- and social bonds leading to personal- and economic freedom. It is imperative to remember that Hegel did not see freedom narrowly confined to individual choices as pretended in Managerialism's prisoner dilemma and its rational choice model. Instead, he saw 'freedom as man's telos'.[636] Hegelian ethics would call Managerialism's choice model *Willkür*. This has two implications:

1. Hegel's freedom is not libertarianism's freedom that eliminates institutions. Instead, *Sittlichkeit* relies on institutions.
2. Hegel does not advocate a laissez-faire economy. He strongly favours socially created ethical institutions.

These institutions (1 and 2) must fulfil several moral criteria. They must be established and run by those involved in these institutions and they must be part of *Sittlichkeit*. For Hegel, there is a fundamental contradiction

*Table 8.2* Three moral bonds and three freedoms

| Moral institutions | | Types of moral bonds | | Types of freedom |
|---|---|---|---|---|
| Family | → | Blood and intimate bonds | → | Personal freedom |
| Civil society, economic & corporations | → | Social and economic bonds | → | Social and economic freedom |
| State | → | Universal bonds | → | Universal freedom |

between institutions that are not created and run by participants – such as business corporations – and institutions mirroring *Sittlichkeit*. Hence, in his *Philosophy of Right* (1821) Hegel notes, 'the highest form of freedom for individuals is "being with oneself" in social institutions' (Wood 2011:306). This means that individuals can reach the highest form of freedom inside a *sittliche* corporation if they are with 'themselves' in an institution that is created and operated by corporate members fulfilling Hegelian self-actualisation and 'collective self-determination of social human beings [working towards] the historic emancipation of mankind'.[637] But these moral and self-actualised corporations remain just one institution inside *Sittlichkeit* and they are not even the dominant institutions of civil society. The relationship between states, civil society (corporations), and families in Hegel's philosophy has been expressed by Winfield in the following way:[638]

> As Hegel suggests, if the state were to allow for no civil society to realise the reciprocal pursuit of individual interests, state rule would stand in irreconcilable opposition to the interests of citizens. Instead of securing the totality of freedom, the state would then exclude a whole dimension of their autonomy and so forfeit its own legitimacy. Therefore, Hegel concludes, there should be a civil society to provide the sphere of freedom for the reciprocal realisation of individual interests.

The task of a *sittliche* state is to guarantee a functioning civil society in which individuals are free to pursue their interests linked to *Sittlichkeit*, a common interest, and Rousseau's *volonté générale* (Gilbert 2013:215). But civil society – including economics and corporations – is also the place where citizens deal with several contradictions, such as 'individual versus collective' and 'competition versus solidarity'.[639] Hegel calls the latter 'solidarity of social groups' [*Gruppensolidarität*].[640] This cannot be achieved inside families and states because of the narrowness of family bonds and the administrative universalism of states. As problematic as the ethical universal state is, states are forced to support economy and corporations (Kervégan 2008:243). This results in problems because it creates poverty and unlike business corporations 'Hegel was deeply troubled by poverty'.[641] But Hegelian philosophy also includes one further complexity, namely, the dialectics between 'state ⇆ corporation'. Constructed as checks and balances, *Sittlichkeit* also includes a 'corporation-to-state' relationship. In the words of Kersting (1988:10), 'Hegel awards the corporations the role of being . . .

the moral root of the state.'[642] For Hegel, this constitutes two institutional dilemmas associated with the complexity of corporations inside civil society and states, testifying to the difficulties associated with the three levels of *Sittlichkeit*.

At each level, Hegel envisioned a different type of bond and freedom. As a 'philosopher of freedom', he links moral bonds to types of freedom (Neuhouser 2011:289). At the first level, individual and personal freedom is established and subsequently extended to civil society once individuals graduate beyond the realm of families. Hegel calls freedom in civil society social–economic freedom. 'The concept of freedom is developed among a dialectical path parallel to that of *Sittlichkeit*, and therefore parallel to the economy.[643] But freedom also extends from family to civil society and corporations and from there it enters into a state, establishing universal freedom. In *Sittlichkeit*, 'we achieve freedom when we devote ourselves to a rational end beyond our own self-interest' (Wood 2011:304). Meanwhile,

- in families, the interest of the family supersedes self-interest;
- in society, the common interest of civil society supersedes selfishness; and
- in states, the universal interest of humanity supersedes egoism/individualism.

This represents an ascending scale of increasing freedom in *Sittlichkeit*.[644] The ascendancy is shown in 'the progressive development of the familial, economic and political aspects of *Sittlichkeit*'.[645] Hegel's socio-economic bonds create ethical behaviour at the level of corporations. Here, a common, social–economic, and vocational bond overcomes the destructiveness of economic competition. It battles Schumpeter's creative destruction [*schöpferische Zerstörung*, 1942], avoiding pathological consequences that flow from the destructiveness of competition.[646] The institutional arrangement to combat the negative consequences of competition is found in an extended organisational form of the moral corporation that goes beyond business corporations. Hegel envisioned a moral corporation consisting of members of various professions, entrepreneurs, and tradesmen who came together to form an organisation representing their common interest. It is through this common interest that Hegel's *sittliche* corporation provides an organisational tool to reduce competition in favour of the common interest, solidarity, morality, 'human sanctity, and dignity'.[647]

Hegel noted in his *Philosophy of Right*, 'The sanctity of . . . the dignity of corporate membership [*die Ehre der Korporation*] is a fixed point [*Moment*] in which the unorganised atoms [*die Desorganisation*] of civil society revolve.'[648] A moral corporation remains an institution 'that frees the individual from its atomistic isolation'.[649] This is essential because 'the principle of isolated individuality [contains] the principle of violence'.[650] Hegelian philosopher Honneth has outlined the purpose of Managerialism's ideology of individualism to perfection when noting that 'as an isolated subject, a human being is cut off in all its reflexive freedom from the external world of social agencies and institutions'.[651] Hegel would disagree with business corporations reframing human beings into isolated resources with no sanctity and no dignity other than the final insult of 'people are our most important assets' in Managerialism's 'people equals resource/chattels' equation. Instead, he sees corporations as places where human life – not merely existence – translates into human dignity.[652]

But a prevailing negative image of corporations in the mind of the general public continues despite the best and well-financed efforts of corporations, corporate mass media, and Managerialism.[653] The rather negative image of corporations might have been eliminated if today's corporations were indeed not institutions in 'which the unorganised atoms [*die Desorganisation*] of civil society' could actually find a place that overcomes, not enhances the atomisation and fragmentation [Hegel's *Zerrissenheit*] of civil society. Ending this remains the focus of *Sittlichkeit* through its insistence that individual freedom can never exist without social freedom. Hegel's overriding purpose, however, was to find a solution to 'the problem of man's (sic!) social and cultural fragmentation' (Davis 1987:185). While Hegel thought that moral corporations are a valuable contributor towards *Sittlichkeit*, today's corporations appear to move in the opposite direction creating atomised human resources.

Like Émile Durkheim's 'Anomie' (1858–1917) many years later, Hegel worryingly foresaw an atomisation of society into unorganised atoms.[654] This only sharpened after 20th-century consumer capitalism replaced 19th-century liberal capitalism, leading to a reversal of Karl Marx's prediction. Consumer capitalism infected a once revolutionary working class of 19th-century liberal capitalism with petit-bourgeois attitudes such as individualism, competition, petty-ownership, egoism, selfishness, and 'the economist model of economic man as a free-floating, self-directing atom'.[655] These attitudes have been nurtured by Managerialism colonising virtually all sections of the lifeworld since the mid-20th century. To some extent, Hegel foresaw these developments because 'he was avowedly hostile to and fearful of the consequences of the selfish motivations of bourgeois materialism'.[656] This is easy to understand given Hegel's *Phenomenology of the Geist* (spirit). Mass-consumerism, marketing gimmicks, Packard's *Hidden Persuaders*,[657] psychological manipulation of consumer choices, a petit-bourgeois selfish mindset, relentless mass advertising on radio, newspapers, magazines, billboards, TV, internet, product placement in movies, and so on are designed to manipulate people's *Geist*.

Hence, 20th-century consumer capitalism marches on: first, in the form of an 'Affluent Society', and today with 'Affluenza' where affluence has become an influenza, creating the pandemic of the socio-pathological illness of 'Affluenza' – rampant consumerism enshrined in the famous words 'we buy things we don't need with money we don't have to impress people we don't like'.[658] But Managerialism has even managed to convert Hegel's original concept of ownership – a minimum of possessions are essential for freedom – into two equations: 'owning things = good' and 'owning more things = better'. It has also invented a third equation, namely, that owning 'consumer goods' equals 'corporate ownership of other corporations'. Both are not the equivalent to human freedom nor are they equal as Hegelian philosophy has extensively made clear.[659] Under corporate capitalism, Hegel's ownership exists mainly in two highly separated forms even though Managerialism seeks to pretend they are exactly the same to ideologically protect corporate ownership:

1. corporate ownership: shareholder ownership of corporations and
2. private possessions: consumptive commodities established through *Geist*-destroying mindless consumerism

Above that, Hegel's critique of stratospheric disparities between rich (corporate ownership) and poor (cheap consumer possessions) continue to be reality.[660] These are the consequences when Managerialism merges corporate ownership (shareholding) with private possessions (consumer commodities) so that the separation of both becomes eclipsed by an ideology. The ideology capable of achieving this is the ideology of the free market in which consumers hunt cheap consumer possessions while in the other market corporations compete with other corporations. But the relationship of corporations to markets is often ideological rather than factual as former *Harvard Business Review* editor Magretta (2012:81) explained:

> Truth be told, the competition every manager longs for is a lot closer to Microsoft's end of the spectrum than it is to the dairy farmers'. All the talk about the virtues of competition notwithstanding, the aim of business strategy is to move an enterprise away from perfect competition and in the direction of monopoly.

Corporate management is well aware that markets are not good for them. Hence, the ideology of Managerialism is paralleled by a never-ending quest for what management studies calls 'strategic management' to give corporations a competitive advantage. The task of strategic management is the pursuit of monopolies that exterminate the much acclaimed 'free market' as much as possible, thereby rendering 'the free market' a pure ideology. But Managerialism's ideology of 'a perfect equilibrium' in markets also dims their understanding that markets 'systematically generate a class of the poor who are forced out of the market and are thus unable to participate' (Maker 1987:9). Not surprisingly, 'the free market for Hegel is not a problem-solver . . . but a sphere that creates problems'.[661] A key problem – monopolistic structures – appears when too many corporations are forced out of the market. Everyone is needed as a consumer. Everyone has been a consumer without exception. Without *Geist*-numbing consumerism, there is no consumer capitalism and perhaps there are no corporations either. In other words, anaesthetising the mind of people is a necessary condition of corporate capitalism. In Drucker's 'ruthless game' of corporate capitalism, consumers have to be mindless and they can be attracted away from competing corporations but they must remain inside consumer capitalism.

In sum, what corporate management sees is not civil society but markets with people as mindless [*geistlose*] shopping units. Corporations avoid focusing on inequalities and poverty as Hegel did. For corporations, markets represent opportunities to sustain and increase market-shares. This is the key to what strategic management calls 'the positioning school' and what is called 'defender, prospector, analyser, and reactor' corporations.[662] The positioning school of strategic competition has reduced the main problem of Hegel to 'a seemingly mindless game of chance at which any donkey could win provided only that he be ruthless'.[663] Management tools like the defender–prospector–analyser–reactor model, the positioning school, the SWOT analysis, and many others deliberately exclude morality.[664] Morality and *Sittlichkeit*, if considered at all, play a distant, remote, and unimportant role as a sideshow. It is equally likely that Managerialism and corporations deliberately engineer MADD – moral attention deficit disorder. The Bermuda Triangle of Managerialism successfully sinks all pathological effects of their actions, models, concepts, and ideologies. Nevertheless, they constitute one of the main problems of Hegel's philosophy: poverty. Once the problem is returned to those that create poverty – corporate capitalism and corporations – and examined from the standpoint of *Sittlichkeit*, the dilemma of corporations and Managerialism emerges.

But this is also the point of one of Hegelian philosophy's greatest failings. It is imperative to recognise that 'herein lies Hegel's dilemma: he acknowledged that the dialectic of bourgeois society necessarily and inevitably created wealth and poverty, but he refused to leap beyond the boundaries and limits of that society'.[665] While acknowledging the pathologies created by corporations and corporate capitalism, Hegelian philosophy remains committed to capitalism, markets, and moral corporations.

However, Hegel considers what corporate management deliberately excludes, namely, the social, economic, political, and psychological impact of their activities. Today's corporate management is not concerned with questions such as 'how poverty is to be abolished [nevertheless this remains] one of the most disturbing problems which agitates modern society' (Herzog 2011:153). Perhaps this is precisely the reason why Hegelian philosophy is so important and why it is so persistently excluded from management textbooks.[666] Hegelian ethics refocuses our attention on questions of management that its 'offsider' management studies never discuss. According to *Sittlichkeit*, this is exactly where corporations have a role to play. Although 'the corporation is not directly intended to alleviate poverty, it has the welfare of its members as one of its conscious aims, providing them with the security and stability of occupation that prevents them from joining the ranks of the poor'.[667] Hence, far from being cut off, an issue of MADD, a simple externality, 'routine PR and corporate spin', or the current managerial fashion of CSR, Hegelian ethics points the finger at the direct link between corporations and poverty.[668] This is the unavoidable consequence of being part of corporate capitalism. In *Sittlichkeit*, preventing poverty is an integral part of a *sittliche* corporation. The ideological triage of management, management studies, and Managerialism cannot treat poverty: this is shown by Rawls' (2001:97) 'Veil of Ignorance'; shelving it away; and the fact that poverty is not a PR–CSR exercise.[669] Despite Hegel's idea that corporations have the task to prevent poverty, *Sittlichkeit* would not advocate this to be a corporation's 'main' task. According to Hegel, corporations are 'not directly intended' for that. In turn, they are 'indirectly' intended to alleviate poverty as part of their moral duty of caring for corporate members and the corporations–society link of *Sittlichkeit*. Nevertheless, their moral duty has two implications:[670]

1. Corporations have a 'moral duty' to keep the welfare of its members as one of its conscious aims. This reaches beyond Kant's moral duty and beyond the idea that the alleviation of poverty is 'just one' of many corporate aims. In *Sittlichkeit*, this is a vital part and one of the strongest reasons justifying the existence of corporations. Most importantly, poverty elimination remains a 'conscious aim' of corporations, not merely a sideshow or a spin-off (Bourdieu & Accardo 1999).
2. Corporations are responsible for security and stability of occupation. But this also means that occupations can change – as they do – during a process that creates new occupations while eliminating older ones (e.g. from blacksmith to CNC). The dying and creating of different occupations has been a feature of capitalism. Occupational transitions will occur in many areas (Reich 1992; Smith 2010). The key to understand *Sittlichkeit* is 'how' this is managed.

In short, human beings are not merely resources that can be fired under management's cost-cutting drive that often provides no more than the ideology for managerial arbitrariness [*Willkür*]. Furthermore, Hegel's *sittliche* corporation prevents corporate members from joining the ranks of the poor. And this, of course, includes the 'Boys with No Names' labouring away in invisible sweatshops semi-owned by corporations.[671] The immorality of geographical distancing between corporate headquarters and sweatshops is illuminated when exposed to the work of American psychologist Milgram who found that 'the willingness to inflict pain on others increases with distance'.[672] The 'corporate headquarter-to-sweatshop' distance indicates increased immoral behaviour while simultaneously making it easier for corporations to keep themselves safe from the consequences of their immoralities. Meanwhile, 'corporate' mass media do the utmost to eclipse the link between 'corporate distance and the willingness to inflict pain' in favour of TV sequels such as *American Idol* rather than 'Boys with No Names'.

Today's producers – those who Aristotle referred to as 'those who make things', that is, employees – have been rendered invisible. During his historical period, Hegel's producers [*Produzenten*] – those who actually produced something through labour – where still understood in Aristotle's terms as 'those who really make things', that is, labourers and workers. These producers play an important role in Hegel's self-actualisation. In Hegelian philosophy 'these producers [workers] together with consumers determine the policies of a general opinion' (Kersting 1988L:4). Today, this is no longer the case because the place where Hegel's general opinion was formed – the public sphere – has been successfully colonised by corporate mass media.[673] The public sphere of Hegel's 18th and 19th century has been effectively taken over, leading to a distorted image of reality.[674] Inside the colonised ex-public sphere, individuals can no longer engage in shaping Rousseau's general will and Hegel's general opinion. As a result, corporate mass media's colonisation has destroyed the open public sphere so that a link between corporations and poverty can no longer be formed. It created what German philosopher Adorno (1944) calls

> there is no way of living a false life correctly.

The power of corporate mass media has largely eclipsed the fact that we live among the ranks of the poor who have been confined to the distant corners of the 'Planet of Slums'.[675] Globalisation has been successfully disassociated from global slums. The shiny corporate headquarters of corporate management are made to appear disconnected from the 'Boys with No Names' who nobody knows any longer.[676] The triage of (i) corporate takeover of the public sphere, (ii) the power of corporate mass media, and (iii) the ideological offensives of Managerialism even allowed this cover-up to be labelled CSR.[677]

Rather than representing *Sittlichkeit*, business corporations have created the exact opposite in the form of economic inequalities and social pathologies. They do not see themselves as part of society but as purely economic, technical, engineering-like, and managerial institutions independent of civil society and *Sittlichkeit*. Not surprisingly, their prime ideological support mechanism of management studies is inward- (managerial) rather than outward- (societal) looking. It has management and corporations focus with very occasional, ideological, pre-framed, and highly conditioned excursions into externalities, a managerial term describing everything external to corporations. When management studies include externalities, it is exclusively from the standpoint of Managerialism while simultaneously claiming to be value-free and standpoint-less.[678] It comes as no surprise that business corporations see themselves separated from Hegel's three organisational levels of *Sittlichkeit*.

Corporations have invented their own managerial form of internal corporate governance rather than a '*sittliche*–ethical' form of governance adhering to *Sittlichkeit*. Beyond that, they view externalities such as states and their regulative power as unwarranted and intrusive. Hegelian ethics has noticed that corporations 'see the state as an alien power intent on restricting their freedom'.[679] Historically, Hegel's predictions on business corporations, business, and economics direct our attention to corporate management that views states with suspicion, as alien, interfering, and dispensable. This explains two things:

1. the intense ideological fight of corporations and Managerialism against state regulation under the banner of deregulation and industry self-regulation, the code word of managerial non-regulation; and
2. the presence of highly limited levels of direct state control over corporations based on deliberately engineered declining state regulations.

Managerialism's largely unchallenged ideology that state influence has to be curbed is a widely held view among corporate managers (Drucker 2010:9–16). However, Hegelian ethics opposes such a standpoint because Hegel's concept of corporations supervised by states is not the simplistic managerial zero-sum game of 'state versus corporation'. Instead, 'a properly supervised system of corporations need not place crippling restrictions on the freedom of business'.[680] Unlike Karl Marx (1818–1883), Hegel did not advocate the abolition of corporations and capitalism in favour of state-socialism[681] but perhaps opted for something similar to a socialisation of corporations. In fact, Hegel was against crippling restrictions on the freedom of business.[682] But he would reject Herr von Hayek's political catechism of neo-liberalism and free marketers.[683]

Finally, Hegel was not a communist because he unrepentantly favoured capital, commercial property, and corporations. And his ethics was not anarchistic because of his strong support for a robust authoritative state. In today's political categories, Hegel might be labelled somewhat of a liberal democrat in the US tradition (civil rights and freedom) and a social-democrat in the continental European tradition (state powers to curb markets and social welfare).[684] Most obviously, Hegel did not advocate the annihilation of corporations. He was against stiff state regulations so as not to suffocate them. Instead of Managerialism's 'them versus us' view of 'state versus corporation', Hegel's *sittliche* state is to 'properly supervise' corporations. He specifically supported 'the freedom of businesses'. But Managerialism has altered the Hegelian arrangement between 'properly supervised corporations' and 'the freedom of businesses' in favour of the latter. This shift in favour of business corporations marks the decline in spirit [*Geist*] as an unavoidable consequence.

## From corporate spirit to universal spirit

One of the key problems of Hegelian philosophy that arises with state-supervised corporations is that of 'spirit versus spirit', 'corporate spirit versus universal spirit', and '*Korporationsgeist* versus *Weltgeist*' – Hegel's term of a universal spirit. This means, first of all, that Managerialism's ideology of 'state suffocating corporations' is not supported by the highly limited powers of direct control that states have over corporations. In addition, there is next to no democratic control over corporations from the inside where corporations remain democratic exclusion zones. For example, terms such as 'industrial democracy', for example, have been successfully deleted from human vocabulary.[685] With this, corporate management has been able to insulate itself against *Sittlichkeit*. Hence, 'there ought to be a civil society to provide the sphere of freedom for the reciprocal realisation of independent interests'.[686] But the formulas of business corporations are 'civil society equals consumers' and 'freedom equals business freedom'. In management's quest for The Real Bottom Line, the Hegelian concept of 'an institutional dependence of the corporations on the larger whole' (Bohman 2010:445) does not exist. For corporations, the larger whole – ethical community, civic society, and *Sittlichkeit* – mostly comes in two rather narrow versions:

1. external stakeholders: such as suppliers, customers, banks (warranted), states, trade unions, and NGOs (unwarranted) and
2. internal stakeholders: employees (cost factor), workplace trade union representation and European-style works councils (to be avoided).[687]

In other words, corporations do not see themselves as an organic entity [*organisches Glied*] of *Sittlichkeit* but perceive non-corporate institutions merely as external stakeholders, unwarranted, and as threats. In short, business corporations view these moral institutions exclusive rather than inclusive. This view prevents Hegel's mutual and equal recognition which is a precursor to *Sittlichkeit*.[688] Rather than being part of civil society, states, and *Sittlichkeit*, corporations have installed two layers of protection against them, namely, the ideology of stakeholders to protect them against civil society and deregulation directed against states. Instead of operating protective armours, *Sittlichkeit* is rather different in relation to civil society and states. It does not want corporations to have protective shielding against civil society, NGOs, trade unions, and states. Instead, Hegelian philosophy sees corporations and corporate members as active and organic parts of *Sittlichkeit* unifying corporate and universal spirit [*Korporations- und Weltgeist*]. In other words, corporate membership [*Korporationsgeist*] produces four kinds of 'from–to' relationships:

1. **From particular interests to universal interests**
   In the words of Hegelian philosopher Gallagher (1987:174), 'The corporation is an important transition point; it is here that one's particular interest becomes self-consciously the interest of the whole.'[689] This issues a few challenges to business corporations because they do not see themselves as transition points. By this Hegel meant the transition of the *Geist* as moral consciousness from a family spirit [*Familiengeist*] to communal spirit [*Gemeinschaftsgeist*] to state/universal spirit [*Weltgeist*]. On this transitional trajectory, *sittliche* corporations are important gateways for one's *Geist*.
2. **From corporate spirit to the spirit of *Sittlichkeit***
   On the ascendancy of family to universal spirit, corporations are important. Together with the community spirit of civil society, their corporate spirit [*Korporationsgeist*] is a precursor to *Sittlichkeit*.[690] Until now, no corporation has ever seen itself in such a role. Corporate members of *sittliche* corporations see themselves as transiting from a corporate to a universal sprit. They realise that the particularity of corporate interests can never be subordinate to *Sittlichkeit*'s universal interests. This is the moral development of the *Geist*, self-consciousness, spirit, and morality. Simultaneously, all this also means a corporate interest in social and economic wellbeing universally applied.
3. **From corporations to civil society**
   The interest in social and economic wellbeing signifies that *sittliche* corporations occupy a unique role in civil society because it is 'through the corporation [that] citizens address... the problems of their society' (Wallace 1999:431). Rather than creating problems, *sittliche* corporations are institutions through which individuals can address problems.[691] This creates a totally different picture of today's corporations. Corporations can no longer be seen as pure business organisations serving shareholder interest and following markets nailed to a

never-ending treadmill of profits. Instead, *sittliche* corporations unify the corporate spirit with Hegel's universal *Weltgeist*. Current business corporations need to be reconfigured to become gateways between civil society and economic systems within *Sittlichkeit* valuing ethical life over economic affairs. Finally, corporations can no longer cut themselves off from social wellbeing reduced to economic egoism, moral selfishness, and The Real Bottom Line.

4. **From corporations to states**
Instead of Managerialism's drive to cut social welfare provisions, *sittliche* corporations work towards the exact opposite (Dumenil & Levy 2011). According to Greer (1999:575), 'The corporations . . . are institutions rooted in civil society that prepares us for life in the state.' Corporations connect corporate to non-corporate members of the non-economic sphere of civil society. This also includes a 'society → state' link. The corporate spirit of corporate members prepares them for a 'life in the state'. For Hegel, life in the state is the higher good compared to life in corporations. The universal spirit [*Weltgeist*] always supersedes the corporate spirit [*Korporationsgeist*]. It is the moral duty of corporations to prepare its members for a life of higher morality. Inside corporations, corporate members need to achieve a transition from a corporate and particular interest to the social interests of civil society and eventually to the universal interests of the state.

But today's corporations are still asphyxiated inside highly particular self-interests cutting off vital parts of *Sittlichkeit*. Hegelian philosophy establishes these essential parts. This is reflected, for example, in Hegel's concept of particular interests that become self-consciously the interest of the whole. This denotes the exact opposite of what business corporations do. Hegel did not mean to enhance any highly particular, self-interested, narrow version of The Real Bottom Line excluding social, economic, and moral wellbeing. For example, in *Sittlichkeit* it is nonsensical to argue that corporate CSR provides a service to communities and thereby automatically and self-consciously [represents] the interest of the whole. They do not. If corporations do this, they would refrain from viewing those institutions outside of corporations, such as family, civil society, and state as mere externalities ideologically re-framed as stakeholders. Corporations would also avoid narrowing the interest of the whole to The Real Bottom Line while CSR would be obsolete. CSR and The Real Bottom Line can never represent Hegel's *Weltgeist*. In sum, business corporations do not fail only *Sittlichkeit*, they actively work against it.

Nevertheless, *Sittlichkeit* also advocates that 'corporations must ultimately be subordinated to the higher interest of the state' (Cullen 1988:32). Despite the managerial ideologies of externalities, there are substantial corporation–society/state relationships. They continue notwithstanding the best efforts of Managerialism.[692] All non-corporate institutions and corporations exist inside *Sittlichkeit* and the state. States hold a somewhat unique position. Despite Managerialism's idea of a footloose corporation, corporations are inextricably linked to states in which they 'have to' reside (Derudder et al. 2012). So far, business corporations have not managed to escape from that. Hegel's *Philosophy of Right* (1821) favours the state as the ultimate guarantor of ethical corporate behaviour for three reasons:

1. **Trusting corporations**
   Quite correctly, Hegel did not trust corporations to be moral actors because of their addiction to The Real Bottom Line. Perhaps Hegel trusted corporate self-regulation like society trusts murderers to regulate themselves. He knew that the imperatives of the much acclaimed 'competitive advantage'[693] run counter to *Sittlichkeit* in a struggle of 'competition versus morality'. Hegel might also not have trusted corporate mission statements on ethics, corporate ethical codes, and CSR. They have, collectively, shown that they are not able to lock corporations inside the parameters of *Sittlichkeit* (Smale 2006).
2. **The power of corporations**
   Hegel did not view the power of families strong enough to ensure that business corporations behave morally. This has two implications: in sociology's 'agency versus structure', Hegelian ethics favours 'structure', organisations, and institutions over individual 'actors' (Giddens 1979). *Sittlichkeit* does not see individual managers (agency) capable of imposing morality on organisational profit demands. The reverse has been the case. Hegelian thinking correctly foreshadowed that management training does not lead to Aristotelian virtue ethics, Hegel's self-reflective, critical, and cultural education.[694]
3. **The power of civil society**
   Finally, Hegel did not see that society's non-managerial institutions are capable of ensuring corporate moral behaviour. Hegelian ethics foreshadows that eventually corporations would become more powerful than any other societal institution including civil society itself. This became reality during the 20th century for, perhaps, five reasons: (i) the

successful destruction of trade unions disabled a force that was, at least partially, able to prevent corporations from disconnecting themselves from *Sittlichkeit*; (ii) NGOs have been unable to fill the 'representation gap' opened up by the annihilation of trade unions (Heery 2009); (iii) a decline of 'public' broadcasting accompanied by a rise of corporate mass media enhancing the power of corporations;[695] (iv) the increasing managerialisation of public administration, the privatisation of schools, universities, hospitals, and rafts of other institutions inside the sphere of civil society have enhanced the power of corporations and its ideology enshrined in Managerialism; and finally, (v) the deregulation of labour law has successfully removed and/or weakened controlling agencies such as consumer protection authorities, and labour regulation institutions.[696]

If corporations seek to be moral entities of community and society, *Sittlichkeit* suggests the following: 'Hegel describes the process of realisation of the community as "government", by which he means the collective self-government by which the community manages its affairs.'[697] This denotes 'collective positive freedom as the membership in a social whole' (Herzog 2011:202). Corporations have used terms such as CSR and corporate citizenship to create the impression of being morally responsible members of a community for ideological reasons.[698] But once exposed to *Sittlichkeit*, it becomes clear that business corporations run into several serious problems: corporations are not interested in a community that is self-actualised. They do not actualise themselves in a community. This is despite ideologies such as corporate culture, mission statements, core values, and being a stakeholder. In the end, corporations remain committed to the very reason for their existence: profits. The former CEO of General Motors – Sloan – worded this even better by saying 'GM existed, not to make motor cars, but to make money'.[699]

Secondly, corporations see themselves as business entities devoted to Nobel Prize winner Milton Friedman's statement: 'The Social Responsibility of Business is to Increase its Profits'. Inside corporations this becomes a game-plan just as Peter Drucker noted: business is a 'mindless donkey game'.[700] But Drucker's 'mindless donkey game' impacts on people. Business corporations equate people to resources 'because of' (!) the ideology of corporate citizenship. Externally people cannot be just people as they are useless to corporations unless they are converted into consumers. However, *sittliche* corporations demand something completely different to the corporate resource/consumer conversion of people. For Hegel, 'membership in a corporation is an essential feature of membership in civil society' (Wood 2011:303). This carries, at least, three meanings:

1. **Membership**
   Hegel's term membership is not to be seen as reflective of today's asymmetrical employment relationship established between two non-equals. This is, for example, depicted during job interviews when corporate management with institutional power meets a job applicant with virtually no power.[701] This is for two reasons: the cost of 'getting a job' versus the cost of 'not getting a job' is significantly higher for job applicants; the cost of a managerial choice between applicants (A or B) is next to zero for corporate management.[702] In other words, those who are nervous during job interviews are not managers but applicants. Despite the managerial ideology of 'corporate members', the reality of employment relationships – even at its entry point – is inherently asymmetrical. It is not based on membership but on 'institutional power' (Magretta 2012:4). In contrast, Hegel's term 'membership' carries two connotations: (i) voluntarism and (ii) non-profit. In the corporate setting neither one exists.
2. **Bonds and *Geist***
   Membership is an essential feature of civil society and corporations. Hegel views the link between membership and institutions entirely different from the way business corporations perceive it. The ethics of mutuality and social bonds of civil society flow into corporations. The determining factor for *Sittlichkeit* is the flow of bonds of intimacy (family) → social bonds (society) → universal bonds (state) and back into smaller and more particular entities, for example, corporations. Hegel's ethics denotes that the stronger and more determining social and universal bonds of larger societal entities (society and states) shape the morality of those institutions that exist inside larger structures (Horowitz 1966:11). This demands corporate affairs to mirror those inside civil society and states. As Hegel would say, the moral *Geist* flows from state [*Staatsgeist*] and civil society [*Gemeinschaftsgeist*] back into corporations [*Korporationsgeist*].
3. **Collective self-government**
   *Sittlichkeit*'s understanding of government is not reflected in the managerial term corporate governance because corporate governance is not defined by collective self-government or self-actualisation (Hegel) in which 'all' members participate. Corporations manage their affairs neither in the spirit of a community, a collective, nor in that of universality. Instead, corporate governance is unilaterally

> assigned to top-management that, through layers of functional, divisional, lower-, middle-, and line-management, and so on, manages corporate affairs. In sum, when corporations are measured against Hegel's membership, bonds, spirit [*Geist*], self-actualisation, and collective self-government, corporate ideologies evaporate into thin air.

The three meanings noted above (—1–3) impact negatively on collective self-government and on collective ends. 'Each function [of a corporation is designed to] foster amongst its members a distinctive kind of particular identity that makes it possible for them to subordinate their purely private (egoistic) interest to collective ends and to do so willingly.'[703] Such a distinctive kind of particular identity runs contrary to being a human resource.[704] More important, however, are two additional points: Firstly, private, particular, and egoistic corporate interests are subordinate to collective ends. This denotes the reversal of what is found in business corporations. Secondly, the above Hegelian notion also conveys that corporations 'do so willingly'. In *Sittlichkeit*, no external forces such as states, trade unions, NGOs, and local communities can compel corporations to act morally – they act willingly. Equally, no internal forces, such as shareholders and employees, can force corporations to act morally. It is exactly this willingness to act morally that make corporations institutions of *Sittlichkeit*.

This is supported through the ethical notion that 'through the corporation, citizens regain a connection with the whole understood as national consciousness' (Nakano 2004:46) and the perspective that 'the corporation is the crucial middle term permitting the isolated self-seeking individual to initiate the process of integration into the community as a whole'.[705] However, business corporations create isolated and 'atomised' (Hegel) human resources using ideologies such as PRP (performance-related pay), individual bargaining, competition, highly individualised promotions often constructed as a zero-sum games that enhance employee competition, individual employment contracts, balanced scorecards, and so on.[706] As a result one does not find ethical civic citizens in corporations but highly conformist 'Organisation Men'.[707] These deformed resources are not 'integrated' and 'connected with the whole' of a *sittliche* community. Hegelian philosopher Honneth (2008b) identifies three reasons for this:

1. a growing part of the population is struggling to have access to opportunities of subsistence-assuring forms of employment,

2. a second section of society performs work activities unprotected by law under highly deregulated conditions, and
3. a third section is currently experiencing the rapid de-professionalisation and de-'companisation' (*Entbetrieblichung*, e.g. outsourcing and franchising) of their formerly more secure occupations.

External to companies these developments are supported and legitimised through Managerialism. Internally, they are encapsulated inside managerial regimes creating corporate cultures designed to support corporate particularities engineered against an ethical and universal community spirit [*Gemeinschaftsgeist*]. Today's corporate human resources – rather than Hegel's *sittliche* citizens – are engineered through HRM instruments.[708] In sum, not even Managerialism's myth of corporate citizenship that devalues human beings is able to eclipse corporate non-*Sittlichkeit*.

Hegel's 'larger whole of a *sittliche* society' includes ethical values such as fairness and justice and 'what [kind of corporations] . . . a just society should have'.[709] His *sittliche* corporations are guided by those moral imperatives that define the whole with justice being one of *Sittlichkeit*'s defining elements. 'Hegel regards economic activities [as conducted by corporations] as part of normative social relations and economic relations as the matter of justice in society.'[710] This is what Hegelian philosopher Kersting (1988L:5) called 'an effective and dense code of social norms'. Hegel's *sittliche* corporations are part of 'normative social relations' and of a normative social code. *Sittliche* corporations are not based on managerial relations. Instead, corporate behaviour is a matter of social relations, normative codes, justice, and *Sittlichkeit*. However, these *sittliche* principles exist in sharp contradiction to corporate management.

In contrast to *sittliche* corporations, business corporations do not exist for justice. Their main activity is not directed towards what American philosopher John Rawls (1921–2002) called 'Justice as Fairness'. Neither is it directed towards Hegel's understanding of corporate justice inside *Sittlichkeit*. For one, the hierarchical and asymmetrical power relations that define business corporations disallow the treatment of everyone with fairness.[711] Hence, a moral issue such as wage justice, for example, cannot exist in corporations. But it can exist in *sittliche* corporations as German philosopher Schmidt am Busch (2011:86) has outlined, 'Hegel implicitly upholds the following two theses: as a member of a functioning corporation a bourgeois [owner] is not interested in attaining an ever increasing level of (a) personal consumption and (b) personal income.' In other words, a citoyen governing – rather than bourgeois owning – a *sittliche* corporation also establishes wage justice because corporate intentions follow *sittliche* goals rather than 'personal consumption and income' as it is the case with bourgeois-owners and corporate shareholders fostering injustices amongst corporate members in favour of profits.[712] This also creates injustices and alienation among corporate members. Similar to Rawlsian justice as fairness, *Sittlichkeit* includes justice as non-alienation. Not surprisingly, once viewed from *Sittlichkeit*,[713]

> the most important solution for alienation Hegel considers is the corporation [because] the corporation reintegrates individuals in civil society, protects them against contingencies and educates them. Through the corporation, individuals recover mutual recognition and the sense of belonging to a community. It is not only an economic and social but also an ethical entity which can remedy the alienation generated by overproduction . . . Hegel thinks that the corporation provides the moment of mutual recognition and restrains the unlimited and self-defeating movement of capitalism.

Rather than being the solution to the ethical problem of alienation, business corporations continue to produce alienation.[714] If corporations were aligned to *Sittlichkeit*, they needed to undertake serious steps away from alienation and towards morality. When Hegel thought of corporations as institutions to 'moralise capital' [*Versittlichung des Kapitals*], *sittliche* corporations represent exactly that. In sum, *sittliche* corporations fulfil four tasks. They

1. are moral coordinators between individuals and society;
2. are self-regulated with the participation of all corporate members;
3. encourage the self-actualisation of corporate members; and
4. create and enhance moral knowledge.

This results in three moral challenges for business corporations and their economic affairs: 'firstly, that the economy be made a sphere of right offering everyone the full array of commodity relations; second, that civil authority regulate the economy to guarantee all their exercise of economic freedom; third, that government act to prevent economic power and interest from obstructing political freedom' (Winfield 1987:63). All this can only occur inside but not above, outside, or against *Sittlichkeit*.

The disassociation of business corporations from *Sittlichkeit* leads to what Hegelian philosopher Kersting (1988:9) calls 'demoralification'

[*Entsittlichung*]. Business corporations are demoralising [*entsittlichende*] institutions departing significantly from *Sittlichkeit*. This can be summed up in four points: business corporations do not offer 'everyone' the full array of wealth and commodity relations because corporate capitalism is marginalising and excluding, for example, the absolute and relative poor as well as the growing number of working poor while simultaneously weakening Hegel's civic *sittliche* institutions.[715] Managerialism's ideological programme has been successful in diminishing the role of civic authorities in favour of 'industry self-regulation' and deregulation. Today's authorities are no longer in a position to guarantee the exercise of economic freedom either between corporations and small and medium firms or between corporations and individuals as, for example, the 'McLibel Case' has shown.[716] Equally, state governments are no longer in a position to prevent corporate-economic power from obstructing political freedom. Corporate mass media have become too powerful and governments are too dependent on them. They are today's true gatekeepers that provide and deny access to the public sphere during publicised spectacles called elections, exhibited on TV under the motto 'if it's not on TV – it does not exist'.[717] These four points sharply contradict the role of moral corporations inside *Sittlichkeit*. Ultimately, Hegel's *sittliche* corporation has the essential duty of raising the vision of those engaged in today's isolating corporations above purely economic matters to affairs of a public and *sittliche* character. In contrast to the current ideological and narrow content of managerial corporate culture, the cultivation of an Aristotelian–Rousseau–Hegelian moral-public character is one of the key moral duties of *sittliche* corporations. This represents a clear-cut contradiction between two versions of corporations: profit-making and *sittliche* corporations. The final chapter will discuss this – very Hegelian – contradiction.

# 9
# Conclusion: The Moral Corporation

*The corporation represents the socialisation of a torn-to-parts and disintegrated bourgeois society.*[718]

This chapter draws several conclusions covering all previous chapters and discusses the contradiction resulting from an application of Hegel's *Sittlichkeit* to business corporations. It is a dilemma of two diverging norms: business corporations versus *sittliche* corporations. Hegel outlined *sittliche* corporations in his *Philosophy of Right* (1821) and *Phenomenology* (1807) after having initially drawn up rudimentary parameters for *Sittlichkeit* in the *System of Ethical Life*.[719] Hegel's 'critical humanism'[720] developed into a comprehensive 'system of *Sittlichkeit*' inside which corporations represent one form of moral life. For Hegel, moral life denotes that 'the supreme purpose of man is to be moral' (Dickey 1987:192). But he also used the term *Sittlichkeit* to differentiate his social, collective, and institutional form of ethics from Kant's individualistic formalism. In contrast to Kant, Hegel's moral life [*Sittlichkeit*] is about creating morality, not abstract formulas. It does not exclude people from the process of creating *sittliche* norms. In *Sittlichkeit*, people create institutions for moral life and in that way *Sittlichkeit* fulfils Hegel's self-actualisation by establishing moral rules that are created and carried out by those to whom they apply. This is not a mere utopian request for human freedom. Hegelian institutions are institutions of freedom: 'This is not about the principles of a possible freedom, but about the concrete freedom of the people in his society.'[721]

The emphasis on the creation of moral rules led Hegel to the use of the term *Sittlichkeit* rather than morality and ethics. It differentiates his *Sittlichkeit* from Kantian and many other moral philosophies. *Sittliche* corporations are moral institutions of *Sittlichkeit*, corporations that represent moral life in the spirit of *Sittlichkeit*. Unlike morality's formal rules such as those developed by Kant, Hegel emphasised moral 'life' as a form of actualising *Sittlichkeit*. Hence, *Sittlichkeit*'s closest approximation in English is moral life. Given its power, many Hegelian and Neo-Hegelian philosophers have discussed, interpreted, clarified, and examined the term *Sittlichkeit*. The interpretations of Hegel's corporations and *Sittlichkeit* have been based on Hegel's original passages that defined corporations in the *Philosophy of Right* (1821).[722]

According to Hegel, the description of the 'business class' is being 'concentrated on the particular' (Schmidt 2007:262). By this Hegel meant that businesses represent the particular, sectarian, and, above all, 'non-universal' but economic interest of, for example, corporate shareholder-value, profit-maximisation, ROI, and The Real Bottom Line. To achieve this, Hegel thought that 'corporations are especially appropriate'. They comprise members of civil society that are – by virtue of their own particular skill – also corporate members. This reinforces the moral corporation–society interface but also carries connotations of not letting corporations out of sight. Hence, the respect that members of corporations command is due to their corporate–societal dual-membership. Individual corporate members have 'the right of exercising one's skill [which] is made rational in the corporation'.

But perhaps the most valuable statement is Hegel's concept 'as the family was the first, so the corporation is the second ethical root of the state'. This assigns corporations a definite place inside *Sittlichkeit* – after families and before the state – and links corporations to families as well as to states. The position of corporations has been outlined briefly by Hegel but also in some of his other writings related to his corporations as well as in recent Hegel interpretations that have led to a substantial volume of literature on Hegelian corporations. Never has Hegel's concept of *sittliche* corporations been brought into direct contact with business corporations. No book has ever contrasted Hegel's *sittliche* corporations with business corporations in a 'norm versus norm' project that compares the moral norms of *sittliche* corporations to those of business corporations. This is despite the fact that the history of Hegelian ethics in corporations and the history of corporations – that resulted in what we know to be business corporations today – have run parallel to each other.

The outcome has been two totally separated streams of literature. On the one hand, there is the literature on *Sittlichkeit*. On the other, there is also an extensive body of literature on business corporations. The problem is that, until today, both have never met. While this might appear astonishing, the following issues are perhaps even more surprising. Since Hegel wrote and eventually published the *Philosophy of Right*, roughly two hundred years have passed. During this period, business corporations were created and numerous academics and scholars in management/economics and moral philosophy have written an endless number of books and articles on this. On the one hand, there are studies on Hegelian philosophy – his morality, *Sittlichkeit*, corporations, and so on – while on the other there are studies on management, Managerialism, management ethics, corporations, corporate management, business, economics, CSR, and so on. Both sets have produced volumes of writing. But nobody has ever considered that there could be a link between Hegel's *Sittlichkeit* – that specifically discusses corporations – and business corporations as we know them today. In other words, it has taken roughly 200 years for the first discussion on the link between Hegel's *Sittlichkeit* and the business corporation to occur.

But there is another shortcoming. It does not so much concern management ethics because of its ideological character but it concerns Hegelian scholarship. In the *Philosophy of Right, Sittlichkeit* makes it abundantly obvious that inside *Sittlichkeit* everyone and every socially constructed institution – including business corporations – are part of *Sittlichkeit*. There is no exception. Therefore all of Hegel's *sittliche* parameters also apply to business corporations. Nevertheless, there has been an astounding and perhaps comprehensive failure of Hegelian scholarship during the last 150+ years to consider the link between *Sittlichkeit* and business corporations. In addition, one of philosophy's most important shortcomings has been noted by Hegel himself – Hegelian philosophy enforces it on anyone writing in the area of philosophy, moral philosophy, ethics, and management ethics. It applies to the subject at hand just as much as it does to the self and remains perhaps the key deficit of philosophy from which not even Hegel's own philosophy can escape. Hegel noted this philosophical dilemma right at the beginning of his *Philosophy of Right*. It represents one of his most famous quotes:

> The Owl of Minerva takes flight only as the dusk begins to fall.

The quote above is part of the *Philosophy of Right*'s Preface where the relevant section reads:

> Philosophy always arrives too late to do any such teaching. As the thought of the world, philosophy appears only in the period after

> actuality has been achieved and has completed its formative process. The lesson of the concept, which necessarily is also taught by history, is that only in the ripeness of actuality does the ideal appear over against the real, and that only then does this ideal comprehend this same real world in its substance and build it up for itself into the configuration of an intellectual realm. When philosophy paints its grey in grey, then a configuration of life has grown old, and cannot be rejuvenated by this grey in grey, but only understood; the Owl of Minerva takes flight only as the dusk begins to fall.[723]

Hegelian philosophy denotes that philosophy and ethics, including a discussion on *Sittlichkeit* of business corporations, always arrives at the scene too late. But this immediately creates yet another dilemma: Hegel's ethics of corporations does not follow his own 'Owl of the Minerva' dictum. Hegel wrote his ethics of corporations 'before' almost all of those corporations that are known to us had been initiated. In other words, there is certainly a contradiction between

1. Hegel's philosophy of the Owl of Minerva always arriving too late at the scene;
2. his own writings on corporations; and
3. the factual and historical creation of nearly all modern corporations during the later period of the 19th and throughout the 20th century.[724]

Hegel's *Philosophy of Right* was published during the early 19th century and discusses *sittliche* corporations 'before' modern corporations existed while most of the latter were obviously established 'after' that period. It is imperative to remember that Hegel's *sittliche* corporation – albeit a business – is formed on *Sittlichkeit* of the corporative–economic constitution. These corporations were social and ethical institutions, more than they were business institutions. Nevertheless, Hegel's very own Owl of Minerva that always arrives too late at the scene' did not arrive too late in this instance. What historically occurred was the very opposite – it arrived early enough or perhaps even too early.

In any case, Hegel's *Sittlichkeit* of corporations had zero impact on today's business corporations. They developed completely independent of *Sittlichkeit* to become profit-determined, market-driven, and shareholder-focused business organisations dedicated to ROI, The Real Bottom Line, and depicting all the pathological hallmarks experienced throughout the history of corporations. Today, these business corporations appear to manifest the very opposite of *Sittlichkeit*. The factual domination of business corporations over Hegel's *sittliche* corporations may have four possible explanations.

Table 9.1 shows four possible reasons for the parallel appearance of Hegel's *sittliche* corporations and the rise of business corporations. To various degrees, all four reasons outlined above might have contributed to the non-recognition of Hegelian ethics by management writers and particularly writers in the vicinity of management ethics. The most likely reason for never engaging with *Sittlichkeit* and *sittliche* corporations might be found in options 3+4, in other words, the blissful ignorance[725] (3) and ideology (4) displayed in management studies, and Managerialism. Equally, it might reside in the fact that no social actor has been powerful enough to ensure that corporations develop within *Sittlichkeit* (4). This may have been further exacerbated by a limited mental incapacity of management writers to understand Hegelian ethics and/or by a deliberate choice to treat Hegelian ethics with blissful ignorance. In philosophical terms, this could be a conscious or unconscious reflection of *Pascal's Wager* that states, 'stick with what you know and you will be rewarded'. For Pascal rewards came from God.

Meanwhile, Managerialism's The Servants of Power, the ideologues of intrinsic and extrinsic rewards, come from an unquestioning subscription of Managerialism as a kind of 'Going with the Flow' inside managerial universities.[726] More often than not this leads to so-called successful careers, corporate research grants, promotions, conference attendance, reduction of teaching, publications in so-called 'top' journals measured on their submissiveness to Managerialism, consultancy fees provided by corporations, and so on. It provides for a comfortable life inside the managerial paradigm in the form of an ideological motivation of present management writers to 'think inside the box'. It establishes a comfort-zone inside which management ethics has its assigned playground at which it can play 'at will' without bothering corporations. This also avoids even the slightest thought that may challenge the all-prevailing, ideological, and one-dimensional paradigm of Managerialism.[727] The Servants of Power have signed a Faustian-pact with Managerialism. The inner workings of Faust's devilish pact have been outlined by Hegel's contemporary, the novelist Johann Wolfgang von Goethe.[728]

Through their overwhelming power, business corporations developed impervious to notions of morality and Hegelian *Sittlichkeit* throughout their existence. Already in the 19th century, corporations had established one of the most relevant successes with, as corporations call it, an 'externality', namely, the state, when they received recognition for the invented legal fiction of being a 'natural' person 'that' (!) could buy and

*Table 9.1* Hegel and the modern corporations: two movements

| | Options | Explanations |
|---|---|---|
| 1 | Hegel was wrong | Hegel was simply wrong – the Owl of Minerva does 'not' always arrive too late at the scene[729] |
| 2 | Segregation | Two themes that run parallel: Managerialism versus philosophy, German idealism versus Anglo-Saxon empiricism, philosophical texts versus managerial texts, philosophically trained versus managerially trained academics, management studies and business schools versus scholars in philosophy departments |
| 3 | Incomprehension and ideology | Writers of management, management history, ethics, corporations, and corporate governance stayed clear of Hegel's moral philosophy for, at least, three reasons:<br>• perhaps there is an insufficient mental capability to understand Hegelian philosophy;<br>• management ethics stays within their ideological paradigm of three to four so-called 'key themes of management ethics' limited to virtue ethics, Kantian ethics, utilitarianism, and perhaps Rawlsian justice theories[730] asphyxiated in Pascal's Wager-like belief-system,[731] and<br>• they deliberately ignored Hegelian ethics for ideological reasons in order not to uncover discomforting evidence challenging the one-dimensional profit orientation and pathological behaviour of business corporations. |
| 4 | Knowledge and power | Perhaps one of the best explanations comes from one of Hegel's more outstanding students, the Left Hegelian Karl Marx. Marx might have been correct and the problem really lies in what Marx had noted in his thesis eleven: 'philosophers have hitherto only interpreted the world in various ways; the point is to change it' and in Hegel's own words, 'freedom as the ideal of that which is original and natural, does not exist as original or natural. Rather it must be sought out and won'.[732] Hence Hegel's and Marx' ethics demand acting in favour of *sittliche* corporations. This is something avoided by management ethics, management writers, and, above all, by Managerialism. |

sell property and commercial goods.[733] This provided corporations with a legal-operative frame, followed by the subsequent invention of the ideology of 'corporate personhood'.[734] Even to the non-philosophically trained eye it might appear obvious that 'corporate personhood' is an oxymoron riddled with contradictions.[735] Firstly, there is the nonsensical equation of 'corporation equals person' when common sense tells us that corporations are not persons. But common sense is not so common when it comes to the legal justification of a misleading mirage. Nevertheless, it marks the equalisation of two non-equals. Secondly, a philosophical definition of personhood has next to nothing to do with the legal fiction of corporate personhood.

After corporations were furnished with what the legal system had dutifully supplied but what remains philosophical nonsense and a moral obscenity, they moved on. Soon, they invented the ideology of Managerialism securing corporations against the externality of society and even ethics while *sittliche* corporations represented the opposite. With the generous assistance of management studies and The Servants of Power, Managerialism was able to convert moral philosophy into management ethics, adjusting the former to Managerialism's ideological demands. In business schools, Managerialism shelves a much reduced and often distorted version of 'moral philosophy' – now called 'corporate social responsibility' – into a secure box labelled 'management ethics'. This box is placed in a safe distance from so-called 'core' management subjects such as accounting, marketing, HRM, and operations management – receiving the label 'elective' with the hidden transcript 'not relevant'. Meanwhile management writers submissively contributed to the rise of business corporations and Managerialism.

Simultaneously, they reduced ethics to an appendage of Managerialism, incorporating it into the corporate framework to make corporations appear moral. This is a clean-cut application of Rosenfeld et al.'s *Impression Management* (1995). Managerialism's agenda excluded Hegelian ethics because the main premises of *Sittlichkeit* – human freedom, mutual and equal recognition, non-alienation, no poverty, *Sittlichkeit*, and so on – fit even less to Managerialism than many other forms of moral philosophy. So far no *Servant of Power* has endeavoured to adjust Hegel's *Sittlichkeit* to Managerialism. Perhaps there was no need to do so because The Servants of Power established a useful crypto-morality for corporations. It might simply be a question of 'why bother with Hegel when your prime objective is not knowledge-creation but ideological support for management and corporations'. In the ideological orbit of managerial quasi-ethics, *Sittlichkeit* would unnecessarily complicate matters. It is a great virtue of ideology that simplicity adds strength as expressed in Managerialism's favourite: 'KISS = keep it simple, stupid!' Keeping Hegelian ethics out adds value to the ideology of Managerialism.

The exact opposite has been discussed in the proceeding chapters where Hegelian ethics is not adjusted to suit Managerialism and business corporations; no ideological standpoint is taken; Hegelian ethics does not remain inside the box of management ethics; instead, it challenges business corporations when corporate norms are contradictory to *Sittlichkeit.* Hence, the previous chapters represent a thoroughly Hegelian project constructed as a three-stage approach highlighting contradictions between two norms: the moral norms of Hegel's *sittliche* corporations and the business norms of modern corporations. This can be shown as a three-stage process.

In this book the three steps outlined in Table 9.2 have been completed through an examination of Hegel's original and authentic texts and his writings on corporations. They presented a close approximation to Hegel's original version of truth. This included substantial writings on Hegel's *sittliche* corporations by Hegelian and Neo-Hegelian philosophers during the roughly 180 years since Hegel's death.[736] These were applied to business corporations in a 'norm versus norm' approach, namely, Hegel's 'ethical norms versus business norms'. The outcome of this approach is found in the preceding eight chapters.

One conclusion is that business corporations do not represent *sittliche* corporations. Historically, this pathological misdevelopment [*pathologische Fehlentwicklung*] has occurred because of either corporate strength or the impotence of virtually all non-corporate actors and institutions of *Sittlichkeit* (family, institutions of civil society, and states including legislative, executive, and judicial) in keeping corporations within *Sittlichkeit.*[737] This failure begins with the initial level of *Sittlichkeit,* namely, the family. But families have never been strong enough to impact positively on the historical development of business corporations, curbing unethical and

*Table 9.2* Hegelian dialectics and corporations

| Stages | Dialectics | Application |
|---|---|---|
| 1 | Thesis | Presents Hegel's original and Hegelian concepts of a *sittliche* corporation |
| 2 | Anti-thesis | This is contrasted to the norms of business corporations |
| 3 | Synthesis | Creates thorough reflections on business corporations from the standpoint of *Sittlichkeit* |

pathological corporate behaviours (Benson 2012). Similarly, virtually all other non-corporate actors inside *Sittlichkeit*'s level of civil society have failed to keep business corporations inside *Sittlichkeit*.

Hegel developed a solution to the pathologies created by business corporations in the form of extravagance and wealth paralleled by poverty and *Pöbel* [rubble]. His solution was the state. Today, states have comprehensively failed to ensure that corporations remain inside *Sittlichkeit*. But the complete failure of all three levels to keep business corporations inside *Sittlichkeit* includes not only institutions and organisations. When viewed from the sociological perspective of 'actors versus structure', the failure also extends to actors (Giddens 1979). No individual actor has been able to secure corporations inside *Sittlichkeit*. On the other hand, it is next to impossible to locate the failure exclusively inside *Sittlichkeit*'s structure for two reasons:

1. Hegel was not able to place all actors, institutions, and organisations against the business corporation and the economic sphere because many of those did not come to light during Hegel's lifetime. What he saw was a rising and increasingly powerful state that – if governed by people under Rousseau's 'general will' – should have been able to control corporations; and
2. Hegel's *Sittlichkeit* quite correctly described and predicted one of the foremost unsolvable dilemmas of modern society and corporate capitalism, namely, the dilemma of 'ethics versus profits'.

Hegel was simply not in a position to anticipate the *Colossus of the Corporation* (Beatty 2001), the *Corporation's Pathological Pursuit of Profit and Power* (Achbar & Abbott 2003), the *Leviathans of Multinational Corporations* (Chandler & Mazlish 2005), and the *Organizational Pathologies* (Samuel 2010) that business corporations have created since the mid-19th century. Despite the invasiveness and high visibility of corporate power, the reason for the comprehensive failure of modern moral philosophers – including Hegel experts – to contrast business corporations to *Sittlichkeit* rests, most likely, on the fact that Hegel's 19th-century corporations were constructed very differently from what business corporations have become today. Bringing together *Sittlichkeit* and business corporations is justified in the very Hegelian fact that both are part of *Sittlichkeit*. In *Sittlichkeit*, corporations are institutional parts of the ethics of moral life.

However, Hegel's original concept of the *sittliche* corporation carried strong connotations to an institution that carried very limited links with business corporations, namely, 'associations' [*Verbände*]. Perhaps a useful description of how Hegel might have seen a *Verband* comes from one of Germany's main apologists, legitimising writer, and proponent of the 'Wilhelminian Empire, Industrialisation, and Capitalism' (Marcuse 1964), namely, Max Weber (1924). He described Verbände as

> the pure end-rational association, a case of agreement as to a continuing course of action oriented purely to the promotion of specific outer interests, economic or other, of its members; the value-rational association motivated by inner interests, for example, the rational sect, if it does not cultivate emotional and affective interests, but seeks only to serve a 'cause.' This last case, to be sure, seldom occurs in anything approaching the pure type.[738]

When seen from the German thinking on *Verbände*, business corporations have very little in common with such associations. This might explain why the disassociation between both has occurred. Nevertheless, *Sittlichkeit* sees *sittliche* corporations, *Verbände*, associations, and business corporations as part of a modern economy. They are part of what Hegel called 'business estates' [*Der Stand des Gewerbes*]. Today, Managerialism has re-labelled it as a business community. The term community has been misappropriated by Managerialism in a highly ideological way because it carries metaphoric connotations to a harmonious community. Meanwhile in the non-ideological business reality, corporate-to-corporate relationships are defined by the brutality of cold and rather disharmonious market relationships.[739] Based on his awareness and study of Scottish and British political economy, Hegel foresaw the pathological consequences of competition among businesses. For him, the business corporation remains part of *Sittlichkeit*, civil society, and economy. In short, corporations are industrial actors and as such part of the sphere of the political economy and *Sittlichkeit*.

Unlike *sittliche* corporations, modern corporations differ significantly from *Sittlichkeit*. The ethics that defines *sittliche* corporations is a result of cooperation, mutual and equal recognition, self-actualisation, and mutual benefits. These are based on blood- and social relationships at the family and civic levels, representing civil and human rights, democracy, citizen-to-citizen, and citizen-to-state relationships.[740] However, modern corporations have followed a different mode as they do not create mutuality, social benefits, and equal recognition but competition and profits. Once viewed from the standpoint of Hegel's *Sittlichkeit*, a corporation remains 'the odd one out'. The essence of the corporation is not cooperation but competitive market relationships. At the dawn of industrialism, Hegel saw two main 'misdevelopments' [*Fehlentwicklungen*] associated with economics, industrial capitalism, markets, and corporations, namely, an ever widening gap between rich and poor and the creation of a disenfranchised, marginalised, atomised, and alienated underclass. He called them *Pöbel* or rubble.[741] Hegel's rubble carries connotations to Adam Smith's (1759, 1776) notion of the shabby, worn-out and torn 'linen shirt which makes it impossible to appear in public without shame'. Perhaps Smith's description gave the astute student of British economic theory, Karl Marx, the metaphor of a torn shirt or rag [*Lumpen*] that proletarians were forced to wear. To avoid workers from becoming *Lumpenproletariat* or *Pöbel*, Hegelian philosophy argues

> that the capitalistic laisser aller, laisser faire creates worse monopolies than the ancient guilds, and that an economy driven by the market alone is a true plague. Corporations are needed to prevent temporary over-employment and an excess of unskilled and cheap labour.[742]

Today, many of these unskilled and underpaid labourers, called the working poor, are forced to the edges of the market and suffer a marginalised existence (Fields 2012). Hegel saw that free markets create monopolies which lead to poverty and social pathologies of 'plague'-like proportions.[743] To prevent that, *sittliche* corporations remain deeply embedded in *Sittlichkeit*. As such, they are institutions that counteract the pathological tendencies created by market competition. But this can only be achieved if corporations are constructed as *sittliche* corporations. Hence, there is a moral demand to re-position business corporations inside *Sittlichkeit* in order to become *sittliche* corporations. Only then will they be able to develop into *sittliche* institutions capable of enhancing society in which ethical life rather than competition can flourish.

To achieve this, corporate governance needs to be radically re-shaped so that it represents something distinctively different from its current format.[744] These rules can establish a mechanism for re-positioning business corporations back into *Sittlichkeit*. The position of *sittliche* corporations is shown in Figure 9.1.

Figure 9.1 shows the position of *sittliche* corporations inside *Sittlichkeit*. In this system, a *sittliche* spirit [*Geist*] develops, at first, in families [*Familiengeist*] in order to turn into a civil society oriented in community-minded spirit [*Gemeinschaftsgeist*] which eventually leads to a universal ethical spirit [*Weltgeist – sittliche Welt*].[745] In this structural ascendancy from intimate to universal ethics and bonds, Hegel envisioned civil society as a

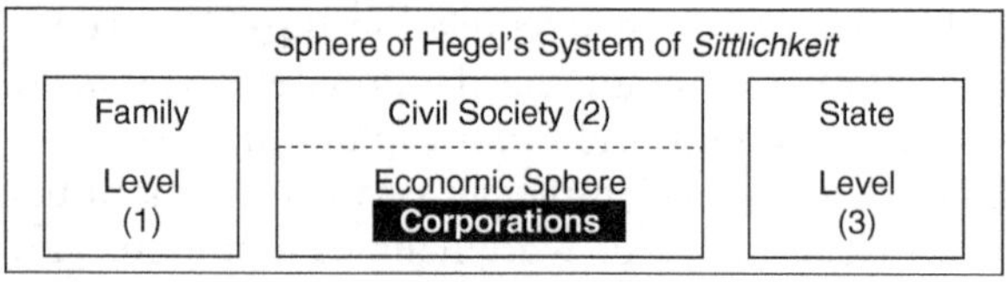


*Figure 9.1* The position of the moral corporation

transition sphere for a spirit that is designed to become a universal-ethical spirit. *Sittliche* corporations are institutions that transform individualistic family spirits into universal-ethical spirits [*Weltgeist*]. They are part of a transition from a rather narrow-minded family spirit towards a universal spirit [*Weltgeist*]. According to Hegelian ethics, this transition defines the lives of individuals, starting with the experience of morality and intimacy in family life and ending with an awareness of an abstract universal spirit [*Weltgeist*]. Individuals remain part of a *family-Geist* just as much as they are part of Hegel's *Weltgeist*.[746] A refined picture of such Hegelian ascendancy of moral development is depicted in Table 9.3.

Table 9.3 shows the ascending development of a moral *Geist*/spirit in seven stages from its earliest manifestations as an individual-sprit that becomes a family spirit when individuals experience families as the first social unit beyond the self. The next transition from family to community spirit occurs at the interface between family and other social networks such as peers, groups, and bands of friends. This establishes a community spirit that moves on to become a more socially oriented spirit when experiencing larger networks existing beyond family and friends, namely, society – Hegel's civil society. At this level, individuals experience society's civic and economic side in the form of work, employment, and managerial regimes. This takes place in firms, companies, and corporations. From there, a corporate spirit develops and moves towards the morality of the next larger unit, namely, the state. Hegelian ethics did not differentiate between the morality of states and higher levels such as the universality of international institutions.[747] It is precisely because 'Hegelian ideas cannot be divorced from his time' (Burbidge 1988:viii) that Hegel was unable to foretell functioning international organisations (GATT, UN, WHO, ITF, IMF, etc.). Nevertheless, Hegel's universal *Sittlichkeit* includes what Hegelian philosopher Buchwalter (2012) calls an 'international we'.[748]

Hegel's lifetime experience was the conservative and backward regionalism of miniature states [*Kleinstaaten*] pre-dating German unification.[749]

*Table 9.3* Morality, *Geist*, and bonds of corporations

| **Levels** | **1 →** | **2 →** | **3 →** | **4 →** | **5 →** | **6 →** | **7 →** |
|---|---|---|---|---|---|---|---|
| Of morality | Individual | Family | Community | Civil society | Corporation | State | Universal |
| | → | → | → | → | → | → | → |
| Of spirit of *Geist* | Individual spirit *Personalgeist* | Family spirit *Familiengeist* | Community spirit *Gemeinschaftsgeist* | Societal spirit *Gesellschaftsgeist* | Corporate spirit *Korporationsgeist* | State spirit *Staatsgeist* | Universal spirit *Weltgeist* |
| | → | → | → | → | → | → | → |
| Of bonds | Self, mind–body | Intimacy and kinship | Reciprocity of groups | Support and mutuality | Solidarity | Law and order | Human rights |

With a life in different pre-German mini-states, Hegel saw a unified state as an improvement. But he appeared unable to envision supranational configurations of international organisations like the UN. Consequently, he only foresaw one universal level of morality represented in the highest organisation human beings had developed during the 19th century: the state. Nevertheless, Hegel's *Weltgeist* indicates his awareness that there is something beyond the state. Overall, however, Table 9.3 represents a structure in which a person goes through several stages of moral development which starts with rather individual and perhaps ego-centred morality, moves on towards the family to enter into groups/peers and eventually society, leading to universal morality. This marks a scale of morality that depicts the movement from individualist to universal morality. In sum, Hegel's system of *Sittlichkeit* represents an expanding level of consciousness and morality that might be pictured as a fountain-like shape.

Figure 9.2 shows the ascendancy of human morality from a relatively simple individualistic level to a universal and more abstract level. Hegel's development of morality describes an intimate perspective (self and family) to become a social perspective of community and civil society, eventually leading to an abstract universal level of global and international ethics. Such a moral development can be summed up in the words of Bauhaus architect Walter Gropius (1883–1969): 'A human mind is like an umbrella – it functions best when open.' It depicts an increased awareness and recognition of ever larger institutions accompanied by even more abstract levels of moral understanding. In conclusion, Hegel's stages of moral development reflect two things: the human ability to understand more abstract institutions and the ability to comprehend even more complex moral and social structures. This carries connotations to the overall moral development of human beings.

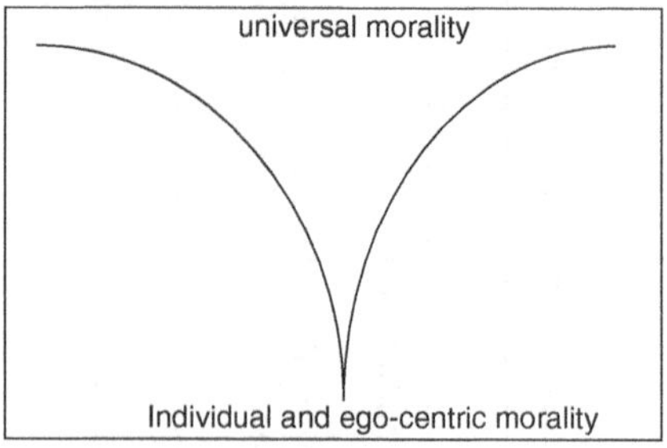


*Figure 9.2* The fountain of moral development

## The morality of Hegel and Kohlberg

The ascending level of moral awareness reflects an increase in intellectual openness and mental capacity that is paralleled by the development of the human brain. The brain develops parallel to the increasing experience of larger societal structures. This leads to the psychological–moral concept of an increased capacity of human cognition that is linked to two elements: (i) an increase in brain development that is connected to (ii) the development of cognitive and moral understanding. This has been empirically supported by the work of Swiss psychologist and philosopher Jean Piaget (1896–1980). Piaget developed a three-stage model of 'pre-operational', 'concrete operational', and 'formal operational' stages of human cognitive development (Piaget 1928, 1932, 1951). It means that the development of human beings allows for increased cognitive abilities and an improved ability to recognise complex social and moral structures. Recognising oneself as a moral entity, a family as a moral institution, groups of friends as moral actors, society as a moral collective, and eventually the universality of universal human rights are all vital components in the development of human beings and human morality. The moral development of human beings recognising other human beings inside social settings is 'a vital human need' (Taylor 1994). The recognition of other human beings, social structures, and complex moralities is fundamental to Hegelian philosophy.[750]

The suggestion of an increased awareness of morality and a rising level of abstractness in the form of a 'family-to-universality' development is strongly supported by Hegelian philosophy that places high significance on the human ability to recognise complex social and moral structures. Young individuals are able to recognise themselves at first, family later, and civil society, state, and international institutions after that. Eventually, this will lead to the recognition of universal, global, and international morality. This is shown in *Sittlichkeit*'s three-stage 'family → society → state' concept which has been expanded in Table 9.3. Hegel's developmental perspective of human ethics expands as individuals experience larger social formations. His 19th-century human conceptions of ethics developed from 'individual → family → universal'. Piaget's early 20th-century work on human cognition supports this. Yet, both their works have also been empirically supported through field studies undertaken during the late 20th century. American ethicists and psychologist Lawrence Kohlberg's (1927–1987) longitudinal experiments linked his empirical findings to moral philosophy.[751] Compared to Hegel, Kohlberg developed a more fine-tuned model of human morality.

Like the ascending stages of Hegel's *Sittlichkeit* and Piaget's operational cognition, Kohlberg's sophisticated instruments concern human morality. His model consists of seven stages:[752]

Table 9.4 shows Kohlberg's moral orientations and Hegel's *Sittlichkeit* – both ascend towards universal ethics. However, there is also one decisive difference. There is one aspect that neither Hegel nor Piaget had included while Kohlberg did. The crucial difference between Hegel/Piaget and Kohlberg is Kohlberg's seventh stage defined as morality 'beyond humanity'. By this, Kohlberg meant a broadening of morality from human beings to non-human life, that is, plants and animals encompassing *environmental ethics*.[753] *Sittlichkeit* deals predominantly with human beings. Kohlberg's inclusion covers environmental ethics that has become more prominent in the field of moral philosophy during the 21st century. Kohlberg's seven stages cover the complete set of human moralities. In some way, his seventh stage of environmental ethics adds to Hegel's *Sittlichkeit*; both models are ascending; both develop from the individual towards the universal and both are complementary to each other. In Hegelian terms, Kohlberg's stages 1 to 2 mirror Hegel's family morality and *Familiengeist*; Kohlberg's stages 3 to 5 mirror Hegel's concept of civil society as *Gemeinschaftsgeist*; while Hegel's universal morality [Hegel's *Weltgeist*] mirrors Kohlberg's stages 6 and 7 because both – Hegel and Kohlberg – see them as universal stages of morality.

*Table 9.4* Kohlberg's seven stages of morality

| No. | Kohlberg's moral orientations | Hegel's *Sittlichkeit* |
|---|---|---|
| 1. | Obedience and avoidance of punishment | Family |
| 2. | Personal benefits and rewards and getting a good deal for oneself | Family |
| 3. | Conforming to social expectations and gaining approval | Family/society |
| 4. | Protecting law and order and maintaining the existing system of official social arrangements | Civic society |
| 5. | Promoting justice and welfare within a wider community as defined in open and reasonable debate | Civic society |
| 6. | Defending everyone's right to justice and welfare, universally applied | Universal |
| 7. | Respecting the cosmos as an integral whole and an openness extending well beyond humanity | Global |

*Sittlichkeit* starts with families. Similarly, Kohlberg's model starts with young family members who show somewhat instinctive responses to an early stage of what Kohlberg terms 'obedience and avoidance of punishment' and being 'ruled by fear' (Kojève 1996:56; O'Neill 1996:9). Inside families, however, young individuals soon learn to differentiate between punishment and rewards and between themselves and family members. This development leads to stage 2 in which a selfish morality of 'personal benefits and rewards and getting a good deal for oneself' dominates. Sociologists call this 'egocentric' while in moral philosophy it is termed moral egoism.[754] Hegel's and Kohlberg's 'families-to-society' gateway is manifested by a lessening of family ties and paralleled by a growing importance of relationships with peers, groups, friends, and social networks. The next level indicates recognition of more abstract social structures. In families – perhaps even more so in social groupings – Kohlberg's morality of 'conforming to social expectations and gaining approval' becomes relevant.

The moral base of civil society is, however, manifested in stage 4 where Kohlberg's morality of 'protecting law and order and maintaining the existing system of official social arrangements' develops. Hegel's community spirit [*Gemeinschaftsgeist*] underwrites a society's moral order and legal system.[755] But this is only one aspect of Kohlberg's morality and Hegel's community spirit and civil society. The second dimension of Kohlberg's and Hegel's society represents an even more mature form of morality. This is civil society's concept of 'promoting justice and welfare within a wider community as defined in open and reasonable debate' (e.g. Habermas 1997). In Kohlberg's terminology, Hegel's civil society expresses 'social expectations' (stage 3), 'law and order' (stage 4), and 'justice and welfare' (stage 5). Kohlberg's late 20th-century model provides a more sophisticated notion that enhances Hegel's early 19th-century concept of civil society. But Hegel and Kohlberg also reach beyond civil society and both models provide institutions for that. Hegel's ethical universality, for example, is expressed in Kohlberg's sixth and seventh stages. Kohlberg's sixth stage is about 'defending everyone's right to justice and welfare, universally applied' while stage 7 concerns 'respecting the cosmos as an integral whole & an openness extending well beyond humanity'.

With the exception of Kohlberg's seventh stage of environmental ethics, Hegel's *Sittlichkeit* covers six of Kohlberg's stages. By inference, however, Hegel's model can be extended to Kohlberg's seventh stage of environmental ethics. There is no ethical and philosophical reason why plant and animal life as well as environmental ethics cannot be part of *Sittlichkeit.* It comes as no surprise that in the 150 years between Hegel and Kohlberg, not only sociology, psychology, and philosophy have improved but the human awareness of the fact that ethics cannot avoid the moral questions connected to the non-human world of plant and animal life has also improved.[756]

Nevertheless, the two institutions that are at the centre of Hegel's discussion are *sittliche* corporations and business corporations and these are located at different levels of morality when measured against Kohlberg's model. In Hegel's model of *Sittlichkeit,* however, both versions of corporations are located in the sphere of civil society as corporations are neither families nor states. In Kohlberg's model, both corporations leave their assigned place as indicated in Figure 9.3. The morality of Hegel's *sittliche* corporations and business corporations is not reflective of their socio-economic place – of civil society (Hegel) – when viewed from Kohlberg's perspective. Hegel's *sittliche* corporations and business corporations take sharply different turns when measured against Kohlberg's stages of morality. This can be shown as in Figure 9.3.

Figure 9.3 shows the places of business corporations and Hegel's *sittliche* corporations along Kohlberg's continuum of morality. The morality of business corporations is reflective of Kohlberg's stages 1 and 2 while the morality of Hegel's *sittliche* corporations is reflective of stages 3–7. Business corporations operate with the moral instruments of stages 1 (obedience) and 2 (selfishness). These are reflective of Hegel's family morality and Kohlberg's infantile relationships. For example, business corporations operate a double system of internal/external 'obedience'. Externally, there are three forces: strict obedience to markets; powerful competitors, and regulative states;[757] internally, corporate management demands total 'obedience to personal authority' (Locke 1996:19) because management consists of 'people in positions of institutional power'.[758] Corporate regimes demand strict obedience from individuals who are no longer human beings but human resources. Management *expects them to be* conformist and obedient 'Organisation Men'.[759] In historical terms, today's obedient human resources existed under strict punishment regimes during the 18th and 19th century when early corporations, factories, and the

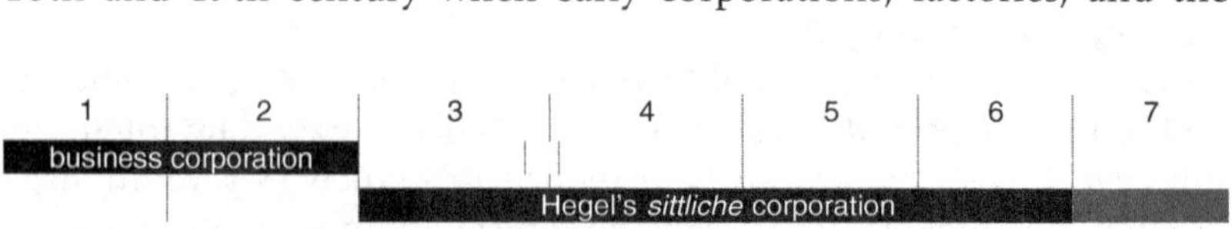


*Figure 9.3* Two corporations and two moralities

infamous *Satanic Mills* were run by factory management that relied on the overseer's whip to get their way.[760]

While the overseer's whip has been instrumental for management during the 18th and 19th centuries, during the 20th century management changed its tune. This marked the only significant change. It marked a move from managerial regimes using punishment towards managerial regimes that rely more on rewards. The significance of the 'punishment → rewards' change has been expressed in what the managerial Servants of Power have termed 'Theory X' (punishment) and 'Theory Y' (rewards).[761] In terms of morality, the 'punishment → reward' or 'X → Y' shift signifies a minor move from Kohlberg's 1 → 2: from obedience and punishment to 'personal benefits & rewards and getting a good deal for oneself'. It marks a feature of infantile morality (Kohlberg) also found in Hegelian families.

Nevertheless, this shift also depicts a level of morality that has been carried over into civil society. There are remnants of child-like behaviours signifying a failure to develop to a moral stage reflective of a person that has matured. This is exhibited by individuals who have, in moral terms, failed to graduate beyond the individualist level of selfishness and moral egoism. Moral maturity beyond individualism, selfishness, narcissistic addictions, 'addiction to profit' [*Sucht des Gewinns*], 'self-addiction' [*Selbstsucht*], and moral egoism, however, is essential for families, civil society, and *Sittlichkeit*.[762] Mature adults reach beyond what Kohlberg has described as 'getting a good deal for oneself' that is reflective of Hegel's lower margins of families and Kohlberg's level 2. Nevertheless, Hegel's *Selbstsucht* and Kohlberg's 'getting a good deal for oneself' signify the most serious shift that corporations and management have undertaken since their inception. It is the move from Kohlberg's level 1 (Theory X = punishment) to 2 (Theory Y = rewards). Virtually everything corporations do is for their own benefit. Corporate ideologues have skilfully linked individualism to an invented corporate belief-system of having 'some kind of internal moral compass' to 'do the right thing' (Holzer 2010:127). Corporate ideologies such as these serve three purposes:

1. they individualise ethics away from moral concepts such as *Sittlichkeit*;
2. they reduce abstraction to the simplicity of corporate ideology – KISS = 'keep it simple, stupid!'; and
3. they hide corporate immoralities behind the veil of 'do the right thing' which means one thing for management (profit-maximisation and getting a good deal) and another for everybody else.[763]

To a minor extent, business corporations also represent Kohlberg's morality of level 3, namely, 'conforming to social expectations and gaining approval'. In Hegelian philosophy, this marks the gateway between family and civil society; in business corporations there is no gateway. Internally, corporations impose conformity by enforcing a one-dimensional managerial version of what management calls 'corporate culture'. It is geared towards conforming to 'managerial' expectations in the form of the infamous KPIs, performance management, and rafts of other HRM tools. This is not at all related to conforming to 'social' expectations and gaining approval from society. Hegel's civil society represents merely an externality to business corporations. They do not seek to conform to social expectations, nor to those of society or employees for three reasons:

1. business corporations view social expectations of employees and society as largely irrelevant to managerial expectations, that is, The Real Bottom Line;
2. management's invention of a one-dimensional corporate culture is designed neither to create nor to satisfy social expectations. Instead, it is invented and enforced to sustain managerial regimes needed for managerial outcomes, that is, shareholder-value, and profit-maximisation; and
3. business corporations do not depend on gaining approval from civil society and employees. The only approval business corporations really need is shareholder and legal approval.

This locks business corporations firmly at Kohlberg's moral levels 1 and 2. It depicts a pre-family/family-like morality. Higher up the scale, the threshold between Kohlberg's moralities of stages 3 and 4 represents the entrance to what Hegel calls civil society. Business corporations can never pass this threshold. Higher levels of morality are simply closed off to them (cf. Figure 9.3). Simultaneously, Hegel's *sittliche* corporations are starting to take shape at the advanced levels of morality. The way Hegel designed *sittliche* corporations allows them to accomplish Kohlberg's moral task of 'protecting law and order and maintaining the existing system of official social arrangements'. In sharp contrast, business corporations neither protect law and order nor do they maintain the existing system of official social arrangements. Instead, they only adhere to law and order when forced to. Corporate PR sells this to the public as being a good corporate citizen and as CSR. The outstanding success of corporate ideologies such as corporate citizen and CSR has been exemplified by the corporations of the tobacco industry as noted by academics:[764]

> In the twentieth century, there were 100 million tobacco-related deaths, and it is anticipated that as many as 1 billion people will die from tobacco in the current century. The majority of these deaths will be in the developing world, where tobacco companies work hard to limit controls on tobacco sales, surround smoking with images of glamour and modernity, and target youth.

It has been said that Nazi Germany's war machine, in which German corporations purchased Jewish slave-labour from the SS[765] for a fixed price in a programme called 'death by labour' [*Vernichtung durch Arbeit*],[766] with death and concentration camps with hideous inscriptions such as 'labour makes you free' [*Arbeit macht frei*], a race-war of total annihilation against Eastern Europe, Gestapo torture, the mass executions of the *Einsatzgruppen*, and so on, amounted to roughly 60 million deaths.[767] Today's tobacco corporations measure up to that. Simultaneously, they pretend to be good corporate citizens with CSR in law-abiding corporations. Fittingly, they can claim to operate within the parameters of the law just as the *Harvard Business School*'s 'Ethical Leader's Decision Tree' (Bagley 2003) outlines. At the same time, Managerialism seeks to change 'law and order' in their favour through ideologies such as deregulation, privatisation, less state interference and control, less red tape, and more industry self-regulation which ideally translates into no regulation.[768] At the same time, business corporations do not seek to 'preserve the existing system of official social arrangements' but to convert every eventuality of human life into commercial- and market-driven exchanges. This has been framed as 'reform', a term that does not carry any connotation to Martin Luther's meaning of forward-looking improvements and the reformation of a corrupt church. Business corporations seek to transform the 'existing system of official social arrangements' into a system of managerial exchanges. This would annihilate Hegel's *Sittlichkeit*.

Business corporations are totally incapable of reaching the true home of civil society: Hegel's *Sittlichkeit* which in Kohlbergian terms represents stage 5 – 'promoting justice and welfare within a wider community as defined in open and reasonable debate'. Business corporations do neither.[769] An 'open and reasonable debate' is Kohlberg's terminology for democracy. Business corporations are not democratic institutions. Instead, they are staunchly anti-democratic internally and/or they have even established a record of fighting against democracy.[770] On the other side, Hegel's *sittliche* corporations are specifically designed to 'promote justice and welfare within a wider community as defined in open and reasonable debate'. But they are more than that. *Sittliche* corporations have the task of 'defending everyone's right to justice and welfare, universally applied' as outlined in Kohlberg's stage 6 and Hegel's universalism [*Weltgeist*]. Business corporations view this as not related to them. They have also been working actively against it. Instead of Hegelian moral universalism, business corporations claim four functions to be universal. The universal right

1. of corporations to exist and to do business;
2. of three institutions (management, managerial regimes, and Managerialism);
3. of the 'right to manage' (Harris 1982); and
4. of markets, market economies, and corporate capitalism.

While these are all highly particular, sectarian, and purely managerial goals, Managerialism seeks to make us believe these are universal. Of course, all of this does not include Kohlberg's moral stage of 'respecting the cosmos . . . beyond humanity'. While environmental ethics represents the highest level of Kohlbergian morality, it remains relatively untouched by Hegel's *Sittlichkeit* which does not directly extend to the non-human world even though Hegel talks of a *sittliche Kosmos* (Horstmann 1974:282). However, *sittliche* corporations are well equipped to achieve Kohlberg's highest level of morality.[771] This is the advantage of practising the kinds of moralities that have been located at levels 3 to 6. In Hegelian terms, this means that *sittliche* corporations represent the morality of civil society (3–5) and of universalism (6). Therefore, they are equipped to apply the moralities of these stages to the non-human world of environmental ethics (7). By contrast, business corporations need to leave the lowest levels of morality (1–2) and enter into the pre-societal level of family morality in order to advance to moralities of civil society (3–5). They would still need to undertake one more step to enter into Hegel's universal level. Only then could the morality of the non-human world of environmental ethics be applied to business corporations. They could no longer operate the Orwellian conversion of 'natural' into 'business' environment. Simultaneously, sustainability would no longer mean Managerialism's 'sustainability of a corporation when facing increased competition' but sustainability in the true understanding of the word. Such a move to environmental ethics would represent a significantly longer stretch for business corporations compared to *sittliche* corporations.

Compared to the blatant fostering of unbridled consumerism by business corporations, the task of a *sittliche* corporation would be to overcome such 'unbridled consumerism'.[772] In other words, if individuals were recognised by corporate members, such individuals would not have to strive for false recognition through conspicuous consumption. Unlike the life in *sittliche* corporations, existence in business corporations is reminiscent of Adorno's 'there is no way of living a false life correctly'. Instead, moral life in *sittliche* corporations goes beyond pure self-interest striving for a common aim. Such corporations also recognise the need for care for those corporate members who have fallen into distress. This is aligned to individuals becoming engaged in 'their' *sittliche* corporation. When performing these tasks, corporate members take into account wider – social and political – considerations rather than considerations of private business. They act collectively rather than individually. When configurations of such a membership-driven *sittliche* corporation (Herzog 2011:187) are viewed from the perspective of Kohlberg's moral stages, the following emerges:

1. **Professionalism**
   *Sittliche* corporations are professional institutions – not purely business organisations defined by The Real Bottom Line. While business organisations are located at the moral level of selfishness, professional institutions depict a level of morality that goes beyond that. Professional institutions portray moralities beyond individualism (2) depicting Hegel's *Gemeinschaftsgeist* (3), order and law (4).
2. **State supervision**
   To be supervised by states means that the morality of corporations is also supervised by states. In other words, states that represent universal *Sittlichkeit* ensure that corporations are also actual expressions of universal *Sittlichkeit* (6).
3. **Overcome risks**
   One of the main aims assigned to corporations is their ability to fight against the *Willkür*, arbitrariness, and risks of markets which Hegelian ethics associates with the creation of *Pöbel*, poverty, the poor, and the working poor. The elimination of these reflects Kohlberg's stage 5 as it depicts the moral level of 'promoting justice & welfare within a wider community' (5).

4. **Consumerism**
   The moral task of 'overcoming unbridled consumerism' is a clear reflection of going beyond individualism, selfishness, and consumerism. In that, *sittliche* corporations seek to foster human goals rather than consumerism, individualism, and selfishness as fostered by corporations and Managerialism. Such non-consumerist but human and moral goals are reflective of Kohlberg's stage 5 (5).
5. **Recognition**
   Hegel's key concept of recognition means that individuals are recognised by other corporate members. According to Taylor (1994), recognition is 'a vital human need'. For mutual and equal recognition Hegelian philosophy demands 'others' as recognition can never be an individual but is, in fact, a social act. The moral concept of recognition depends on the social (3) and a moral order (4). Corporations based on the Kohlbergian principles of stages 5 and 6 (open debate, social welfare, democracy, and universalism) would be highly favourable to Hegel's ethics of recognition (3–6).
6. **Democracy**
   The Hegelian moral concept that 'individuals become engaged in the running of the corporation and its internal politics' is reflected in Kohlberg's stage 5 that supports 'open and reasonable debate' (5).
7. **Wider political considerations**
   The concept of corporate members taking wider considerations into account carries strong connotations of Kohlberg's political sphere (5 and 6). It rejects corporations as selfish institutions with a narrow interest. Instead, it echoes Aristotle's *polis* and Rousseau's 'general will' [*volonté générale*]. This is found in Hegel's civil society and Kohlberg's 'open and reasonable debate within a wider community' (5) universally applied (6). In sum, corporations are not simply organisations for ROI but engage in wider considerations (5 and 6).
8. **Collectivism**
   Finally, the moral concept of acting collectively rather than individually mirrors community, corporate, and universal spirit. It is a clear-cut rejection of individualism while relating to virtually every form of moral spirit beyond the corporate selfishness exhibited by business corporations. In Kohlberg's language, collectivism of a community and universal spirit (3–6) can be extended to a holistic spirit that goes beyond humanity (7). Hegelian morality of collectivism represents (3–6) a possible extension to environmental ethics (7).

When exposed to Kohlberg's moral stages, *sittliche* corporations show to an overwhelming degree that they are located at stages 3 to 6 with the possible inclusion of stage 7. The overall conclusion from measuring *sittliche* corporations against Kohlberg's moral stages is that *sittliche* corporations clearly represent higher levels of morality compared to business corporations. The brief elaboration of bringing *sittliche* corporations and business corporations in line with Kohlberg's seven moral stages shows that *sittliche* corporations far outstrip business corporations when it comes to morality (Kohlberg) and *Sittlichkeit* (Hegel). But this still raises three final questions:

1. firstly, why has the business corporation developed into an institution that displays low morality when measured against Kohlberg's moral stages?;
2. secondly, why did Hegel's *sittliche* corporations not become the model for business corporations?; and
3. finally, how can business corporations become *sittliche* corporations according to Hegel's system of *Sittlichkeit*?

The answer to these three questions is to be found in a – yet to be written – book because the scope of this book was to elaborate Hegel's system of *Sittlichkeit* and the place of corporations inside this system. It remains imperative to remember that Hegel was a philosopher of freedom who would always contrast the relative unfreedom of the daily existence of working people in business corporations to his most profound concept, that of freedom:[773]

> The fact that a person has a free will makes freedom a quality of what it means to be human. The renunciation of freedom means to waiver that you are human.

# Notes

## 1 Introduction: Hegel's Philosophy of Corporations

1 Hinchman (1984:230).
2 Taylor (1975:29); Peperzak (1991:240); Riedel (2011:59); Žižek (2014:91ff.).
3 Gallagher (1987:179); Harding (2003).
4 Bowie (1999); Sison (2008).
5 Peperzak (1991:237ff.); Schmidt (2007); Hutchings (2015:4f.); Gilbert (2013:81); Ritter (1970:322ff.); Giusti (1987:32); Campello (2013, 2013a); Göhler (1974:356).
6 Ritter (1974a:227); Lübbe (1962:38); Hösle (1987:540); Schmidt (2007); Edmundts & Horstmann (2002:101); Siep (2007:25); Buchwalter (2013:99); Moser (2003:20); Gilbert (2013:175, 177ff.); Campello (2013a:240); Niji (2014:288–295); Rettig (2014:92).
7 Schecter (2013:40); Ilting (1974:64); Ritter (1974:153); Buchwalter (2012a:51); Benhabib (1981:160); Honneth (2011:10).
8 Klikauer (2012); Magretta (2012:196); Locke (1996:1); MacIntyre (1970:5).
9 Hutchings (2015:11).
10 Dickey (1987:213); Hemming (2014:1); Riedel (1974d:815ff.); Žižek (2014:30); Herrmann-Pillath & Boldyrev (2014:21f.).
11 Heiman (1971:111); Bobbio (1974:97); Riedel (1977:244–247); Nusser (1981:560); Ottmann (1981:374); Giusti (1987:300ff.); Maker (1987:24); Winfield (1987:56); Seymour-Smith (1998); Schmidt am Busch (2002:148); Mesch (2005:360); Ross (2008b:47); Nahm (2008:257); Herzog (2011, 2013).
12 http://plato.stanford.edu/entries/original-position/#VeiIgn
13 Hartman (1996); Gabor (2000); Boatright (2009); Koslowski (2010); Shaw & Barry (2010); Wicks et al. (2010); De Cremer & Tenbrunsel (2011); Mele (2011); Jackson (2011); Painter-Morland & ten Bos (2011); Sandbu (2011); Shaw (2011); Tsoukas & Chia (2011); Carroll & Buchholtz (2012); Crane & Matten (2012); Jennings (2012); Johnson (2012); Ferrell et al. (2013); Giacalone & Promislo (2013); Donaldson & Werhane (2008:347).
14 Miles & Snow (1978:20–23); Miles & Snow (1978:20–23).
15 Rawls (1972, 2001); Klikauer (2012).
16 Rawls (1972:132; 1980:522).
17 Ritter (1970:333); Giusti (1987:242).
18 Niji (2014:288–295); Pfreundschuh (1977); Gibson-Graham et al. (2013); Sitrin & Azzellini (2014); Jossa (2014); Hecker (2014); Counihan & Siniscalchi (2014); Kaswan (2014); Gilbert (2013).
19 Trevino & Nelson (2011); Shaw & Barry (2010).
20 Giusti (1987:12); Göhler (1974:475).
21 Riedel (1977); Fulda (1992).
22 Pöggeler (1961:256); Taylor (1975:127ff.); Seymour-Smith (1998); Marx (1996:37); Gabler (1843).
23 Schmidt (2007:32); Mesch (2005:358); Pinkard (2001:82).
24 Rawls (2001); Fischer (2012:75f.); Priddat (1990:241); Herrmann-Pillath & Boldyrev (2014:9); Glockner (1965:177); Cole (2004:580).

25 Loomis (2015); Thibodeau & Freier (2014); Lussier & Sherman (2014); Urban (2014); McKenna & Feingold (2014); Haerens & Zott (2014); Chorafas (2014); Beachler & Shevory (2014).
26 Scott (1997:15ff.); Zeitlin (1974); Gilbert (2013:9).
27 Davis (1917); Berle & Means (1933); Abbott (1936); McLaughlin (1940); Burnham (1945); Drucker (1946); Zeitlin (1974); Conard (1976); Hessen (1979); Prahalad & Hamel (1990); Marchand (1991); Korton (1995); Chandler & Mazlish (2005).
28 money.cnn.com/magazines/fortune/fortune_archive/2005/08/08/8267642/index.htm; www.client9themovie.com/; wikipedia.org/wiki/Client_9...; Shelp & Ehrbar (2009).
29 Gilbert (2013:chs 9–11); Gibson-Graham et al. (2013).
30 MacIntyre (1970:9).
31 These will dutifully be noted as 'a publisher's request'; Urban (2014:3).
32 Glockner (1965:420).
33 Ferrarin (2011:435); Gilbert (2013:185).
34 Ferrarin (2011:435); Herrmann-Pillath & Boldyrev (2014:2).
35 Gilbert (2013:252).
36 DeVos (2006:94); Pöggeler (1961:258); Hegel (1805/06a); Gabler (1843:106); Göhler (1974:201–336); Habermas (1974:790); Taylor (1975:130); Fink (1977); Bondeli (1998:161); Ritter (1974b:154); Fulda (2001:176); Priddat (2001:45, 49); Edmundts & Horstmann (2002:37ff. & 49); Ottow (2001:474); Höfler (2009); Zambrana (2012); Escalante (2012:24); Hutchings (2015:3).
37 Kelly (1969:349); Schmidt (2007:35f.); Escalante (2012:17); Žižek (2012: 137ff.).
38 Gottfried Wilhelm Leibniz (1646–1716); Johann Christian Friedrich Hölderlin (1770–1843); Friedrich Wilhelm Joseph Schelling (1775–1854); Johann Gottlieb Fichte (1762–1814); Jean-Jacques Rousseau (1712–1778); Immanuel Kant (1724–1804); Pippin (2010:71); Honneth (2007a); Holz (1968); Kelly (1969:3–8); Rockmore (1997:2f.); Kelly (1969:8f., 336).
39 Herzog (2011:60; 2013).
40 Aristotle (384BC–322BC); Pöggeler (1961:262); Pinkard (2001:73, 75).
41 Rockmore (1997:1); Christensen (1986).
42 Henrich (1971:160); Horowitz (1966:5); Henrich (1971:212); Pöggeler (1961:268); Gilbert (2013:93); Ilting (1974a:759ff.); Herrmann-Pillath & Boldyrev (2014:26).
43 Habermas (1988:20); Sarakinsky (1992:7, 8, 21); Rölli (2013); Kiesch (2002:15); Sinderbrink (2007:1, 4); Speight (2008:2); Jameson (2010:4); Pippin (2010:280); Zambrana (2012:277); Henrich (1971:188); Glockner (1965:422); McKenna (2011:155); Kelly (1969:10, 309); Kelly (1969:304, 332); Dickey (1987:vii); Purtschert (2008:923). Rockmore (1997:6); Church (2008); Schmidt (2007:52).
44 Žižek (2014:100).
45 Heinrich Heine (1797–1856); Hennig (2014:3); Hösle (1987:1).
46 Marcuse (1941:56); Pippin (2010:195); Lübbe (1962:30); Ilting (1974:52); Drydyk (1986:99); Edmundts & Horstmann (2002:13); Römpp (2008:7); Lamb (1988:5); Dickey (1987:232); Schmidt (2007:84, 151); Cole (2004:577); Moyar (2013:600); Gilbert (2013:1).
47 Inwood (1992); Magee (2011); Bobbio (1974:86).

48 Marcuse (1941:169); Pippin (2010:26); Priddat (1990:121).
49 Pöggeler (1961:256); Cole (2004:579); Wildt (2005:461); Jameson (2010:78); Pinkard (2014:195); Marcuse (1941:162); Taylor (1975:133); Kelly (1969:2, 20); Riedel (1974a:266); Edmundts & Horstmann (2002:9); Koslowski (2008:107).
50 Hennig (2014:2); Khurana (2013); Taylor (1975:551).
51 Kersting (1988L:6);Horowitz (1966:7); Gilbert (2013:23); Liebrucks (1974:24); Horowitz (1966); Priddat (2001:48); Flügel-Martinsen (2009:560); O'Connor (2012); Macdonald (2012:128); Buchwalter (2013:113).
52 Mortiz (1839); Knox (1940); Horowitz (1966:5); Ilting (1973:142); Horstmann (1974:276); Maihofer (1974:362); Riedel (1974:9); Villey (1974:138); Baum (1978:194); D'Hondt (1988); Benhabib (1981:154); Edmundts & Horstmann (2002:15–31); Lübbe (1962:41).
53 Taylor (1975:13); Rosenzweig (1974); Gilbert (2013:6); Hutchings (2015); Taylor (1975:548).
54 Cole (2004:587); Moore (1966); Herrmann-Pillath & Boldyrev (2014:22); Lübbe (1962:41).
55 Lukács (1974:752); Schmidt (2007:16); Kervégan (2008); Hettling (1990); Taylor (1975:73).
56 Kelly (1969:331); Koslowski (2008:98).
57 Horkheimer (1972:13); Westphal (2012:171); Breckman (2001:544, 557); Breckman (2001); Hemming (2014:9).
58 Löwith (1962:13); Lübbe (1962:29).
59 Siep (1979:146); Escalante (2012:46).
60 Kervégan (2008:223); Riedel (1969:78); Hinchman (1984:222); Carré (2013:313); Hennig (2014:5); Lübbe (1967:348); Seissl (2013); Ritter (1957); Fetscher (1973:XII).
61 Locke (2011); Locke & Spender (2011); Klikauer (2013); Jaros (2014); Clegg (2014).
62 Baritz (1960); Brief (2000).
63 Ritter (1974b:1026ff.); Seymour-Smith (1998).
64 Moser (2003); Löwith (1962); Lübbe (1962); Honneth (2014:1).
65 wikipedia.org/wiki/Junghegelianer; wikipedia.org/wiki/Althegelianer; Hoffheimer (1995:v, 8); Lübbe (1967:241); Riedel (1981:238); Moser (2003:48, 60, 70); Marcuse (1941:251); Ritter (1970:327); Taylor (1975:537); Pinkard (2014:195); Priddat (1990:201); Kiesch (2002:15); Gilbert (2013:162); Moser (2003:35, 38, 50ff.); Dieter Henrich (1971:215) 'letter-disciple of Hegel' (Bauman 1987).
66 Comte (1853); MacIntyre (1970:8).
67 Cole (2004:577); Cole (2004:598ff.); Gilbert (2013:10).
68 Belmonte (2002); Greer (1999); Honneth (2007); Marcuse (1964); Nancy (2002); Schweppenhäuser (1970); Tassone (2005); Žižek (1993); Buchwalter (1991:258); Edmundts & Horstmann (2002:64).
69 Taylor (1975:134); Žižek (2012:195).
70 Macdonald (2012:127); Ballard (1955); Dutta (2012:7ff.); McKenna (2011).
71 Taylor (1975:545).
72 Hoffheimer (1995:10).
73 Pöggeler (1961:289); Horowitz (1966:14); Moore (1966); Bloch (1962:168); Nusser (1970); Nederman (1987:500); 'D'Hondt (1988); Breckman (2001:557); Edmundts & Horstmann (2002:10); Schmidt (2007:17); Kervégan (2008:223); Houlgate (2009); Comay (2011).

74 Römpp (2008:200); Kojève (1947).
75 Dutta (2012:8); Bondeli (1998:153); Hutchings (2015:2).
76 Locke (1996:3); Hayek (1944).
77 Buchwalter (1991:260); Wischke (1993:3).
78 Marcuse (1941:326); Engels (1892); Henrich (1971:7); Horkheimer (1972); Althaus (2000); Lenz (2007:5); Breckman (2001:545); Eduard Gans (1797–1839), wikipedia.org/wiki/Eduard_Gans; Löwith (1962:2); Žižek (2012:237).
79 Henrich (1971:7).
80 Klikauer (2007:65); Edmundts & Horstmann (2002:40).
81 Gilbert (2013:172).
82 Drydyk (1986:110); Kant Trilogy of Critiques (1781, 1788, 1790).
83 Adorno (1944); Adorno & Horkheimer (1944); Searle (1996); Klikauer (2007:35, 67f.); Locke (2011).
84 Berle & Means (1933).
85 Hegel (1807); Macdonald (2012:126); Gabler (1843:106).
86 Sayama (2004:128).
87 Zeitlin (1974:1073ff.); Marglin (1974); Locke (1996); Hemming (2014:1).
88 Magretta (2012); Klikauer (2007, 2008).
89 Gilbert (2013:178).
90 Gibson-Graham et al. (2013); Gilbert (2013:214).
91 French (1979:215); Bakan (2004); Achbar & Abbott (2003); Mander (2001); Clements (2011:127ff.).
92 Locke (1996:20ff.); Abelshauser (2014:3).
93 Herrmann-Pillath & Boldyrev (2014:29); Gilbert (2013:1); Gibson-Graham et al. (2013); Priddat (1990:98); Koslowski (2008:90); Ashton (1999:7); Hemming (2014:8).
94 Scholem & Adorno (1994); Finlayson (2002); Delanty (2004); Foster (2007); Freyenhagen (2011); en.wikipedia.org/wiki/Ineffability
95 Löwith (1962:9).
96 Schmidt (2007:33, 63f., 259); Dubsky (1970:408); Hösle (1987:369); Escalante (2012:12); Marcuse (1974:668).
97 Priddat (1990:12); Hegel (1821).
98 Hösle (1987:1).
99 Schmidt (2007); Fichte (1798); Riedel (1969:80); Siep (1979:157, 174); Goh (2012:2ff.). Siep (1979:200).
100 Herzog (2011, 2013); Mandell (2002); Dickey (1987:186ff.); Hinchman (1984:223).
101 Maker (1987:16); Hegel (1821); Wallace (1999:427); Dickey (1987:192); Ottow (2001:471); Arndt (1985:99); Riedel (1974c:816); Lübbe (1962:30); Habermas (1974:810); Lukács (1974:702f., 772); Riedel (1974c:815, 819); Göhler (1974:536); Rosenzweig (1974:629); Riedel (1974d:819); Siep (1979:153); Winfield (1987:32); Kersting (1988:2); Priddat (1990:1, 9, 11); Wallace (1999:427); Edmundts & Horstmann (2002:102); Schmidt (2007:19); Herzog (2011:75); Schmidt am Busch (2011a:218); Westphal (2012:158).
102 Hegel mentions Adam Smith only twice (Priddat 1990:22).
103 Campello (2013:115).
104 Watson (2003).
105 Friedman (1970); Korton (1995); Locke (1996); Chomsky (1999); Soederberg (2010).

106 Garsten & Hernes (2009:5); French (1979:207).
107 Herzog (2011); Breckman (2001:547).
108 Honneth (2007:4); Escalante (2012:150ff.); Honneth (1995).
109 Kersting (1988:3); Samuel (2010).
110 Samuel (2010) & Honneth (2007:4); Gilbert (2013:162).
111 Zoglfagharieh (2009:7); Gallagher (1987:173).
112 Neuhouser (2011:287); Hinchman (1984:226).
113 Honneth (1995); Anderson (2009); Barshack (2010); Bohman (2010); Brink (2010); Buchwalter (2012); Chitty (2013); Quante (2013); Laitinen (2014); Escalante (2012:30, 38).
114 Priddat (1990:184); Siep (2008:5); Giusti (1987:262).
115 Gellerman (1989:74); Gray et al. (2005).
116 Gabler (1843:146); Pinkard (2014:211).
117 Eckl (2013:403).

## 2 Modern Corporations and Hegel's Ethical Corporation

118 Fatton (1986:586); Knox (1940); Hegel (1798–9).
119 Sayama (2004).
120 Magretta (2012); Nederman (1987:510f.).
121 Chitty (2013:688); Klikauer (2013).
122 Patten (1995:577).
123 Stillman (1980:103); Honneth (2005:96); Ottow (2001:470); Eckl (2013:405).
124 Gilbert (2013:79).
125 Adorno (1944); (Brink 2010); Gilbert (2013:180).
126 Schmidt (2007:168); Voswinkel (2001).
127 Schmidt (2007); Lübbe (1962:31); Steer (2013:204); Sayama (2004:118); Herrmann-Pillath & Boldyrev (2014).
128 Hinchman (1984:257).
129 Priddat (1990:9); Giusti (1987:302).
130 Treptow(1972:77); Plant(1980:74); Eecke(1980:98f.); Priddat(1990:194–218); Sayama (2004:177).
131 www.corporations.org/system/top100.html and dstevenwhite.com/2011/08/14/the-top-175-global-economic-entities-2010/
132 Klikauer (2013); Herrmann-Pillath & Boldyrev (2014).
133 Morgan (1986, 1993); Adler (2014).
134 Toews (1980:45); Knowles (1983:61); Fatton (1986); Nederman (1987); Greer (1999:574); Wallace (1999:431); Merrill (2000); Norris (2004:412); Neschen (2008:205–209).
135 Ross (2008b:47); Heiman (1971:111).
136 Neschen (2008); Herzog (2013); Gilbert (2013).
137 Heiman (1971:125); Rowland (2006: 81ff., 90).
138 Bakan (2004:16); Marchand (1998).
139 Eduard Gans, 1797–1839 (wikipedia.org/wiki/Eduard_Gans); Breckman (2001:554); Chriss (2012); Riedel (1981:234–268); Hemming (2014:9); Hoffheimer (1995:v, x).
140 Peperzak (2001:469–474); Hubig (2001); Heiman (1971).
141 Koslowski (2008:102); Riedel (1977:250); Ottow (2001:467).

142 Niji (2014:288).
143 Schmidt am Busch (2002:143); Hegel's *Philosophy of Right* (1821:§187).
144 Sayama (2004:27).
145 Peperzak (2001:471); Heiman (1971:116); Gilbert (2013:220ff.).
146 Kersting (1988:9).
147 Giusti (1987:279).
148 Menke (1992:79); Smith (1759); Riedel (1969:76f.); Winfield (1984); Kersting (1988L:28); Greer (1999:564); Sayama (2004:96); Herzog (2011:76); Greer (1999:552); Plant (1980:59); Dickey (1987:213f.).
149 Plant (1980:86); Bakan (2004); Schrijvers (2004); Bolchover (2005); Jackall (1988, 2006); Punch (2008); Adonis (2010).
150 Riedel (1969:77f.).
151 Png (2012:242ff.); Bertram (2008:885).
152 Plant (1980:70); Priddat (1990:12, 14); Lakebrink (1964); Kliger (2014).
153 Herzog (2011:76; 2013); Eecke (1980:99).
154 www.iep.utm.edu/hegelsoc; Ross (2008b:50); Gallagher (1987:174); Hutchings (2015:8).
155 Gottfried Wilhelm Leibniz (1646–1716); Gabler (1843:202).
156 Rowland (2006); Hubig (2001); Kliger (2014); Seissl (2013:10).
157 Schmidt am Busch (2002:138); www.nybooks.com
158 Heiman (1971:123); *Philosophy of Right* (1821:§251); Herrmann-Pillath & Boldyrev (2014:28).
159 Lexicon.ft.com/; ifc.org/ifcext/corporategovernance; Clarke & Branson (2012); Samson & Daft (2012:730); Williams & Zumbansen (2011); Peet (2003).
160 Dickey (1987:212); Taylor (1975:31); Gilbert (2013:56).
161 Priddat (1990:41); Moyar (2013:587).
162 Rowland (2006:xi); Dorary (1988).
163 Baritz (1960); Brief (2000); Trevino et al. (2000); Babiak & Hare (2006:xiii, ix); Rowland (2006:54, 151ff.).
164 Klikauer (2010); Bird & Waters (1989); Bird (1996); Rowland (2006:xiii); Locke (2011); Taylor (1975:5).
165 Bakan (2004); Nakano (2004:45); Bose & Lyons (2010).
166 Greer (1999:556); Edmundts & Horstmann (2002:62f.); Gilbert (2013:3); Bordignon (2013); Žižek (2014:15).
167 Marglin (1974); Marchand (1998); Locke (1996); Locke & Spender (2011).
168 Korton (1995); Rowland (2006:91); Soederberg (2010).
169 Jacoby (1977); Bird & Waters (1989); Bird (1996); Bauman & Donsikis (2013).
170 Westphal (2002:307); Chitty (2013:686).
171 Winfield (2011:233); Drucker (1971); Neuhouser (2011:283); Herzog (2011).
172 Ross (2008b:57); Winfield (1984, 1987).
173 Lakebrink (1964:185); Dutta (2012:1); Pinkard (2014:198).
174 Korsgaard (1996); O'Connor (2012:1); Apel (1980:24).
175 Rae (2012); Hubig (2001); Taylor (1975:131); Marx (1996:37); Quante (2013); Pinkard (2014:23); Žižek (2012:198).
176 Riedel (1981:250).
177 Holz (1968); Ottmann (1981:365); Siep (1979:162;2008); Speight (2008:42); Aching (2012); Gilbert (2013:105); Habermas (1974:814); Taylor (1975:561).

178 Rockmore (1997:4); Gloy (1985:190); Schmidt (2007:209); Bertram (2008:880, 886); Purtschert (2008:926); Zurn (2005:378); Pippin (2010); Ritter Herrschaft (1974b:1084ff., 1088ff.); Seissl (2013:10).
179 Siep (1979:252); Gilbert (2013:105); Hösle (1987:378); Escalante (2012:25); Campello (2013:20).
180 Jameson (2010:54); Pöggeler (1961:285).
181 Schmidt (2007:23); Purtschert (2008:927); Semler (1989, 1993, 2004).
182 Edmundts & Horstmann (2002:100); Riedel (1977:250).
183 Holz (1968:10); Hegel (1996:30); Lenz (2007:3); Kelly (1969:12, 21, 333ff.); Ottmann (1981:375ff.); Gloy (1985); Lamb (1988:10ff.); Redding (1996:123ff.); Rockmore (1997:63f.); Römpp (2008:72); Nahm (2008:199); Jameson (2010:88); Schmidt am Busch (2010:191); Pippin (2010:61).
184 Blake (1804); Dickens (1853); Engels (1892).
185 Priddat (1990:173).
186 Benson (1977); Clegg (1989); Morgan (1986, 1993); Buchanan & Badham (2008).
187 Hegel (1807); Siep (1979:155); Taylor (1994); Honneth (1995); Zurn (2005); López (2013); Quante (2013); Escalante (2012:30).
188 *Philosophy of Right* (1821:§253).
189 Bolchover (2005); Fatton (1986:583); Kervégan (2008:224).
190 Habermas (1974:791); Honneth (1997:26).
191 Quante (2013); Giusti (1987:246).
192 Honneth (1995); Habermas (1988).

## 3 The Morality of Management Studies

193 Locke & Spender (2011:187); Klikauer (2014).
194 Bird & Waters (1989); Perlmutter (1997); Harding (2003); Locke (2011).
195 Taylor (1911); Fayol (1916); Locke (1996:19); Lipietz (2013:129); Klikauer (2013).
196 Bowles & Gintis (1976); Cohen (1973); Locke (2011).
197 Göhler (1974:337ff.); Glockner (1965:423, 424); Dickey (1987:208).
198 Klikauer (2007:76–96, 2011, 2013, 2015).
199 Apel (1980:248); Kemple (2007); Locke & Spender (2011); Locke (2011:99); Dickey (1987:227); Kervégan (2008:226); Palmer (2006:556); Willmott (2011).
200 Hegel as quoted in Dickey (1987:219).
201 Marcuse (1966); Voswinkel (2001:18).
202 Wiltermuth & Flynn (2013); Neumann & Morgenstern (1944); Abella (2008); Locke (1996:100, 108); Klikauer (2007:128–142); Ellison (2006:5ff.); Nowak & Highfield (2011); Klikauer (2012a).
203 Burley & Hoedeman (2011); www.corporateeurope.org/lobbycracy; Clements (2011:2); Priddat (1990:281).
204 Drucker (1971:50f.); Zeitlin (1974:1074); Enteman (1993); Rees & Rodley (1995); Pena (2001); Kasser (2002); Saunders (2006); Locke (2011).
205 Benson & Kirsch (2010b:459); McKenna (2006); Foster (2010); Holzer (2010:1).

206 Chomsky (1991); Beder (2000a, 2006); Aspromourgos (2012); Locke & Spender (2011).
207 Benson & Kirsch (2010b:475); Goldhagen (1996); www.buynothingday.co.uk; Popper (1945).
208 Lindstrom (2008); Eckhardt et al. (2013).
209 Benson & Krisch (2010a); Foster (2010); Holzer (2010:2).
210 Chomsky (1999); Beder (2000); Goldsmith & Mander (2001); O'Connell (2005); Dehesa (2006); Monbiot (2008); Timmerman (2009); Schmidt am Busch (2011a:37); Luntz (2007).
211 Lukács (1974:712); Hegel (1821); Honneth (2008b:335); Hegel (1807, 1821).
212 Zengotita (2005); Dickens (1853); Žižek (2014:30, 40); Locke (1996); Morgan (1986, 1993).
213 Fayol (1916); Magretta (2012:4); Klikauer (2013).
214 Baritz (1960); Brief (2000); Löwith (1962:35).
215 Klikauer (2007:144); Locke (2011:95); Klikauer (2013).
216 Soderbergh (2000:74); Clements (2011:79ff.); Lukács (1974:752).
217 Zeitlin (1974:1073ff.); Marglin (1974); Jackson (1986); Locke (1996).
218 Magretta (2012); Klikauer (2007, 2008); Pinkard (2014:197); Zeitlin (1974:1096).
219 French (1979:215); Clements (2011:127ff.); Bird & Waters (1989:82); Bakan (2004); Achbar & Abbott (2003); Mander (2001); Stohl & Grillot (2009); Bridge & Le Billon (2012).
220 Göhler (1974:13–102); Landau (1974:181); Kaletsky (2009:151); Maker (1987:4); Kersting (1988:2, 1988L); Cristi (1989:725); Lukács (1996); Dickey (1987:221).
221 Soderbergh (2000); Korton (1995); Utting (2003:2f.); Palazzo & Richter (2005); Buchwalter (2012a:22).
222 Garsten & Hernes (2009:5); French (1979:207); Scherer & Palazzo (2007).
223 Quinn (1953:1); Petit (1961:98); Silk & Vogel (1976:238); Djelic & Vranceanu (2009).
224 Hoffman & Moore (1982:299); Drucker (1981:18, 34); Carr (1968:148); Cohen (1973).
225 Groucho Marx's quote is from Henriques (2007:19); Gupta (2010); Apel (1964).
226 Benson & Kirsch (2010b:466); Palazzo & Richter (2005:393); Einstein (2012).
227 Klikauer (2011); Benson & Kirsch (2010b:476).
228 Riedel (1974c:835); Riley (2001:124).
229 Younge (2007:18); O'Neill (1996:12); Kojève (1996:53).
230 Zambrana (2012:277); Apel (1980:248).
231 Greer (1999:557); Glockner (1965:419ff.).
232 Herzog (2011:66, 2013); Horowitz (1966:9); Klikauer (2012:89ff.); Falke (2008:37); Gottschlich (2009:152); Liebrucks (1974:27); Lukács (1974:704f.).
233 Buchwalter (2012a:206); Klikauer (2012:105ff.); Pöggeler (1961:285); Kojève (1996:52); Purtschert (2008:929); Hegel (1821:§261/409); Kervégan (2008:237).
234 Stillman (1980:114); Hegel (1821); O'Neill (1996:10); Hyppolite (1996:74ff.); Hinchman (1984:258); Honneth (1997); Mesch (2005:349); Siep (2008); Buchwalter (2012a:207); Klikauer (2010:5).

235 Römpp (2008:43); Plant (1980:59).
236 Eecke (1980:94); Penolidis (2009:116f.); Höfler (2009:246);Kojève (1996:49); Siep (2007:28); Gilbert (2013:156).
237 Horstmann (1974:283); Schmidt (2007:75); Gabler (1843:160); O'Neill (1996:8).
238 http://www.marxists.org/reference/archive/marcuse/works/reason/marcuse2.htm
239 http://en.wikipedia.org/wiki/Norman_E._Bowie; Klikauer (2010:5, 231); Kiechel (2010).
240 Hegel (1821:254); Lukács (1974:738).
241 Mumby (1997); Gramsci (1971).
242 Perlmutter (1997); Harding (2003); Klikauer (2007:90); Jobrack (2011).
243 Galbraith (1958); Levitt (1958); March & Simon (1958); Baritz (1960); Petit (1961); Whyte (1961); Blauner (1964); Braverman (1974); Marglin (1974); Bowles & Gintis (1976); Zimbalist (1975); Cleckley (1976); Gorz (1982); Goldman & van Houten (1977); Mant (1977); Davis & Silk (1978); Edwards (1979); Offe & Wiesenthal (1980); Burawoy (1979, 1985); Bramel & Friend (1981); Clegg (1981); Hochschield (1983); Murphy (1993); Triado (1984); Putterman (1986); Toffler (1990); Hyman (1987); Jackall (1988, 2006); Schwartz (1990); Enteman (1993); Kleinberg Neimark (1995); Abrahamson (1996); Locke (1996); Punch (1996, 2001, 2008); Cullen (1988); Chomsky (1999); Brief (2000); Beder (2000, 2006); Beder et al. (2009); Mander (2001); Melman (2001); Pena (2001); Brunsson (2002); Klein (2000); Kasser (2002); Magretta (2012); Parker (2002); Schweickart (2002); Morse (2004); Schrijvers (2004, 2005); Bakan (2004); Thompson (2004); Younge (2007); Bolchover (2005); Bogle (2005); Gantman (2005); Lindstrom (2005, 2008); Maier (2005); Tuckman (2005); Babiak & Hare (2006); Boddy (2006); Gautrey & Phipps (2006); Henriques (2007); Buchanan & Badham (2008); Abella (2008); Kohut (2008); Theodosius (2008); Adamson (2009); Daniel (2009); Diefenbach (2009); Fleming & Zyglidopoulos (2009); McQueen (2009); Oade (2009); Gautié & Schmitt (2010); Johnsen (2010); Kothari (2010); Shaw & Barry (2010); Thompson & Smith (2010); Einarsen (2011). On textbooks, see: Harding (2003); Klikauer (2007: 216f.).
244 D'Hondt (1988); Taylor (1975).
245 Lozano (2003:46f.); Warren et al. (2011); Ilting (1975:52ff.).
246 Bakken (2009:12); Magretta (2012); Harding (2003); Perlmutter (1997); Kreitner (2009); Jones & George (2011); Akers (1989); Gellerman (1993).
247 Giddens (1979); Sample et al. (2004:213–276).
248 Gabor (2000); Donaldson & Werhane (2008); Boatright (2009); Shaw & Barry (2010); Wicks et al. (2010); Mele (2011); Jackson (2011); Sandbu (2011); Shaw (2011); Carroll & Buchholtz (2012); Crane & Matten (2012); Johnson (2012); Ferrell et al. (2013); Gabor (2000).
249 Taylor (1911); Fayol (1916).
250 Samson & Daft (2012, 2012a); Perlmutter (1997); Harding (2003); Jobrack (2011).
251 Baritz (1960); Kohn (1999:19, 24–26); Lemov (2006); Klikauer (2007:76–96); Roethlinsberger (1943:180); Karlins & Andrews (1972:6); Powers & Vogel (1980); Scherer & Palazzo (2007).

## 4 Corporations and Hegel's Ethical Institutions

252 Rousseau as quoted by Riley (2001:124).

253 Hegel (1821); Horowitz (1966:11); Kelly (1969:348); Cullen (1988:22); Greer (1999:561); Ross (2008b:50); Römpp (2008:199, 204f., 226); Herzog (2011:70); O'Connor (2012:4); Gilbert (2013:11); Hutchings (2015:5).

254 Siep (1979:270, 2008:6); Schmidt (2007:172); Blaschke (1974:316, 321); DeVos (2006); Honneth (2011:50); Siep (1979:158); Ashton (1999:4); Hemming (2014:5); Hutchings (2015:7).

255 Blaschke (1974:327); Honneth (1997); Siep (1979:241, 2008); Honneth (2005:113ff.); Schmidt (2007:72); Schmidt (2007:74); Siep (2007:29).

256 Taylor (1994:26); Lukács (1974:741); Honneth (1997); Schmidt am Busch (2011:64); Wildt (2005:472); Martineau et al. (2012:2); Quante (2013).

257 Hegel (1821); Vartenberg (1981:175); Schmidt (2007:50); Ross (2008a, 2008b:51); Römpp (2008:210); Heiman (1971:124); Wischke (1993:3).

258 http://en.wikipedia.org/wiki/Timeline_of_human_evolution; Kropotkin (1902); Axelrod (1984, 1997); Honneth (1997:27); Krebs (2008, 2011); Nowak & Highfield (2011); Klikauer (2012a); Westphal (2012:160).

259 Spencer (1880); Darwin (1871); Axelrod (1984, 1997); Krebs (2008, 2011).

260 Fatton (1986:583); Habermas (1974:790); Mesch (2005:354); Hegel (1821:§36).

261 Riedel (1969:76); Blaschke (1974:319); Riedel (1974b:124); Riedel (1974a:248ff.); Horstmann (1974:280); Göhler (1974a:354); Siep (1979:201); Jackson (1986:140ff.); Priddat (1990:33); Villey (1974:140); Gilbert (2013:143f.); Hemming (2014:12).

262 Ottow (2001:472); Steer (2013:204); Nederman (1987:512); Priddat (1990:33); Maihofer (1974); Riedel (1977); Honneth (1997:30); O'Connor (2012:11); Gilbert (2013:188); Heiman (1971:129); Ross (2008a, 2008b:51); Baum (1978:176); Kastner (2008); Ross (2008b:49); Kervégan (2008:231); Ottow (2001:472); Lukács (1974:764); Purtschert (2010:1040); Gilbert (2013:206); Riley (2001:124); Moyar (2013:603); Siep (2004:24); Gilbert (2013:12).

263 Heiman (1971:123); Greer (1999:561); Krebs (2011); Nowak & Highfield (2011); Schmidt am Busch (2011:64); Hyppolite (1996:75); Barshack (2010:164); Bose (2010); Buchwalter (2012a:54); Liebrucks (1974:44); Hyppolite (1996:78f.).

264 Buchwalter (2013:100); Gilbert (2013:58).

265 Priddat (1990:218); Westphal (2002:311); Gilbert (2013:182).

266 Schmidt am Busch (2011:65); Siep (2008:3); Schweppenhäuser (1993:137).

267 Rowland (2006:55); Magretta (2012:129–140); Kropotkin (1902); Bernstein (2010); Krebs (2011); Nowak & Highfield (2011); Porter (1979, 1980, 1985, 1986, 1998, 1998a); Riley (2001:126).

268 Herzog (2011:78); Bohnert & Bohnert (1981); Priddat (1990:219).

269 Lukács (1974:748); Flügel-Martinsen (2009:571).

270 Lukács (1974:708); Priddat (1990:56, 193).

271 Westphal (2002:309); Priddat (1990:39, 57, 232); Stillman (1980:114); Horowitz (1966:12); O'Neill (1996:3).

272 Fatton (1986:588); Priddat (1990:36); Höfler (2009:248); Clements (2011); Schmidt (2007:259).

273 Hegel (1807); Fatton (1986:588); Lukács (1974:705); Schmidt am Busch (2002:139, 2011a:261). Ritter (1974:157); Stewart (2012); Priddat (1990:148); Scott (1997).

274 German Idealism (www.iep.utm.edu & plato.stanford.edu); DeVos (1996:108); Höfler (2009:248); Schmidt (2007:150).
275 Wellmer (1999:296); Hinchman (1984:217); Edmundts & Horstmann (2002:52); Westphal (2002:315); Honneth (2005:96f.); Rössler (2005:401); Schmidt am Busch (2002:131); Gilbert (2013:9).
276 Schmidt (2007:169f.); Wischke (1993:30).
277 Hegel (1807); Schmidt am Busch (2011a:200); Ottmann (1981:376).
278 Hegel (Zusatz zu §14, in: Priddat 1990:168); Cootner (1964); Liebrucks (1974:39); Priddat (1990:62); Taleb (2005); Honneth (2007a:3); Westphal (2012:168).
279 Hobbes (1651); Buchwalter (2012a:201).
280 Stillman (1980:104); Hegel (1805/06); Ritter (1974a:217); Blaschke (1974:313); Pereboom (2004); Searle (2007); Schmidt am Busch (2011a:155); Goh (2012).
281 Cullen (1988:22); Hegel (1821:§289R); Riedel (1974a:248); Fatton (1986:583); Winfield (1987:39); Cristi (1989:725); Winfield (1984); Mesch (2005:357); Löwith (1962:21).
282 Kohlberg (1958, 1971, 1973, 1981, 1984); Kohlberg & Kramer (1969); Klikauer (2010:126–169, 2012).
283 Menke (1992:81); Hutchings (2015:4).
284 Hegel (1807); Lukács (1974, 1996); Edmundts & Horstmann (2002:51); Schmidt am Busch (2001:189).
285 Dickey (1987:211); Burris (1988); Bewes (2002); Honneth (2005, 2008a); Hall (2011).
286 Fatton (1986:58); Plant (1980:74); Priddat (1990:23–25); Herzog (2011a:845).
287 Fatton (1986:580); Magee (2011:64).
288 Samuel (2010:4); Stillman (1980:113); Honneth (1997:31).
289 Benson & Kirsch (2010a:463); Galtung (1969).
290 Honneth (1997:34); Nederman (1987:512).
291 Maker (1987:17); Buchwalter (2012a:22).
292 Cristi (1989:737); Priddat (1990:311).
293 Maker (1987:11); Kersting (1988:9).
294 Rawls (1972, 1980, 1993, 1999, 2001); Clark & Gintis (1978); McCarthy (1994); Maffettone (2010); Priddat (1990:34).
295 Westphal (2012:158); Hinchman (1984:218); Dickey (1987:216); Patten (1995); Schneidereit (2011:11); Gilbert (2013:259); Kersting (1988:4); Edmundts & Horstmann (2002:98) www.rg.mpg.de/de/forschung/policey-wissenschaft/; Schmidt am Busch (2011a:227f.); Priddat (1990:218); Siep (1979:217).
296 Maker (1987:25); Winfield (1987:33, 37); Gallagher (1987:170, 177, 179); Hegel (1821:145, 265); Liebrucks (1974:13).
297 Maker (1987:25); Siep (1979:252).
298 Gloy (1985:196); Siep (2008:2).
299 Kaplan & Norton (1992, 1993, 2004); Alexander (2011); Selekman (1959:54).
300 Cullen (1988:23); Plant (1980:70).
301 Hegel (1821:125 as quoted in: Gallagher 1987:171).
302 Styron (1979); Magretta (2012:1); Eckl (2013:395).
303 Riedel (1974a:267); Priddat (1990:109); Aguilar & Herod (2006); Ross (2009); Kalleberg (2011); Tangian (2011); Jones (2011); Buchwalter (2013:108).
304 Honneth (2007:4); Foster (2010:97).

305 Pilapil (2011:84); Henrich (1971:204); Villey (1974:139); Westphal (1993:114); Greer (1999:567); Babiak & Hare (2006:xiv); Honneth (2007:4); Schmidt am Busch (2011:63; 2011a:201); Gilbert (2013:166ff.).
306 Hegel (1821, quoted from Sarakinsky 1992:17); Knowles (1983:61); Patten (1995:576).
307 Habermas (1988); Chomsky (1991); Beder (2006); Huff (2011).
308 Hegel (1821); Priddat (1990:49f., 55, 192); Henrich (1971:204); Maker (1987:18, 26); Westphal (1993:113); Schmidt (2007:169); Neuhouser (2011:287); Schmidt am Busch (2011a:201); Gilbert (2013:162).
309 Quoted from Neuhouser (2011:287).
310 Lindstrom (2008); Davis (2007); USA (2007); Timmerman (2009); Sheth (2010); Watkins (2011); Voiculescu & Yanacopulos (2011).
311 Sheth (2010); Pogge (2007, 2010).
312 Herzog (2011:150); Herzog (2013).
313 Hegel (1807); O'Neill (1996:16); Anderson (2009).
314 Bohman (2010:444); Drydyk (1986:120); Nederman (1987:515); Westphal (1993:112); Ross (2008b:51f.); Schmidt am Busch (2011:83); Ottow (2001:743).
315 Piven & Clowad (1971); Wisdom (1993); Drydyk (1986:120); Frank (2005); Honneth (2008:6); Cohen & Winston (2010); Ehrenreich (2011).
316 Riedel (1974a:258); Gloy (1985:190); Priddat (1990:30); Dickey (1987:223); Kervégan (2008:236); Chitty (2013).
317 Schmidt am Busch (2011a:1); Purtschert (2008:929); Aching (2012); Magretta (2012); Samuel (2010:159); Adorno (1944); Anderson (2009); Brink (2010); Hegel (1807); Schmidt am Busch (2011a:227); Priddat (1990:60); Gaston & Khalid (2010).
318 Hegel (1821§244A); Stillman (1980:113); Baum (1978:193); Priddat (1990:174); Koslowski (2008:103).
319 Heiman (1971:121); Henrich (1971:204); Riedel (1977:248); Plant (1980:84); Stillman (1980:113); Vartenberg (1981:176); Drydyk (1986:114); Fatton (1986:590); Cullen (1988:34); Kersting (1988L:27); Cristi (1989:730); Westphal (1993:113); Greer (1999:569); Breckman (2001:550); Nakano (2004:42); Norris (2004:412); Herzog (2011:79, 154).
320 Hegel (1821:§244); Herzog (2011:154); Priddat (1990:127f.).
321 Westphal (2012:164); en.wikipedia.org/wiki/Poverty_threshold
322 Hegel (1821:§252R); Westphal (1993:112); Cullen (1988:36).
323 Ehrenreich (2011); EWCO (2010); Tangian (2009); Lingafelter (2005).
324 Magretta (2012:27); Benson & Kirsch (2010a:462); Plant (1980:75).
325 Magretta (2012:1); Priddat (1990:129).
326 Zeitlin (1974:1097); Mander (2001); Pereboom (2004).
327 Hegel (1821); Schmidt am Busch (2011:72f.).
328 Magretta (2012:78); Priddat (1990:153f.).

## 5 The Morality of Corporate Relationships

329 Rousseau as quoted by Riley (2001:130).
330 Bertram (2008:895).
331 www.infed.org/thinkers/adorno_on_education; Macdonald (2011); Adorno (1944); Habermas (1974:800).

332 Schecter (2010); Levitt (1958:42); Brennan et al. (1961:8); Baum (1978:185); Petrick & Quinn (1997:45); Brenner & Molander (1977:69); Brennan et al. (1961:163); Brenner & Molander (1977:59); Bolchover (2005:2); Schecter (2010).
333 Hegel (1807); Peddle (2000:117); Taylor (1975:570).
334 Landau (1974:177); Baum (1978:182); Kojève (1996:58); Flügel-Martinsen (2009:566); Goh (2012).
335 Abrahamson (1996); Prahalad & Hamel (1990).
336 Godelier (1966); Brunsson (1985); Priddat (1990:58, 208).
337 Lukács (1974:694); Priddat (1990:29); Hemming (2014:3).
338 Hyman (1987); Knights & Morgan (1991); Kerfoot & Knights (1993); Shrivastava (1986); Diefenbach (2007, 2009).
339 Jacoby (1977); Bird & Waters (1989); Bird (1996); Samuel (2010); Holzer (2010:1).
340 Priddat (1990:14); Schneidereit (2011:118).
341 Baillargeon (2013); Klikauer (2014c).
342 Riley (2001:136); Honneth (2007:4); Carré (2013:312ff.); Foster (2010:97).
343 Hennig (2014:1); Lübbe (1967:245ff.); Peperzak (1991:256); Göhler (1974:470); Göhler (1974:476); Nederman (1987:514); Lübbe (1967:240).
344 Hegel (1821); Greis (1995); Ross (2008b:52).
345 Henrich (1971:203); Kelly (1969:323ff.); Jackson (1986:141); Schmidt am Busch (2011a:171ff.); Gilbert (2013:3).
346 Chandler (1962); Gabor (2000); Lazonick (2013).
347 Buchwalter (2012a:56, 85); Horowitz (1966:21); Gilbert(2013:77); Taylor (1975:540).
348 Campello (2013:78); Mead (1934); Sallaz (2013); Scott (1997); Erickson (2009); Drucker (1946); Rothkopf (2012); Boggs (2012).
349 Holzer (2010:13); Tugendhat (1871:131); Hegelian philosophy advocates the opposite: 'it is a methodological necessity for Hegel to position the law above the economy' (es ist für Hegel eine methodologische Notwendigkeit gewesen, das Recht höher zu stellen als die Ökonomie, Lukács 1974:742).
350 Brunsson (2002); Holzer (2010:129).
351 Burley & Hoedeman (2011); www.corporatewatch.org; www.corporateeurope.org
352 Ottow (2001:474); Hinchman (1984:232).
353 Fatton (1986:594); Patten (1995:577); Hegel (I Zusatz zu § 236, in: Priddat 1990:113).
354 Heiman (1971:126); Horowitz (1966:17); Ross (2008b:54); Hegel (1821:§270); Davis (1987:198); Schmidt (2007:133).
355 Hegel (1821); Herzog (2011:83, 2013).
356 Magretta (2012:81); en.wikipedia.org/wiki/Warren_Buffett
357 As seen in, for example, the movie films such as *Metropolis* and *Blade Runner* en.wikipedia.org/wiki/Metropolis_(film) and en.wikipedia.org/wiki/Blade_Runner
358 Crompton (2008); Kerbo (2012); Doob (2013); Schmidt (2007:59).
359 Hobbes (1651); Lukács (1974:698); Schneidereit (2011:114).
360 Plant (1980:77); Baum (1978:184); Hegel (1821:§189); Cristi (1989:725); Schmidt (2007:53); Wiltermuth & Flynn (2013).
361 Priddat (1990:262); Schmidt (2007:25); Ottow (2001:470).

362 Benson & Kirsch (2010a:460); Shah (2006); Samuel (2010); Magretta (2012: 127); http://motherjones.com/politics/1977/09/pinto-madness; (Birsch & Fielder 1994; en.wikipedia.org/wiki/Ford_Pinto).
363 Hegel (1821:§185, 243, 244).
364 Wallace (1999:429); Khurana (2013).
365 Winfield (1987:57); Gilbert (2013:194ff.); Hoffheimer (1995:1ff., 60f.).
366 Korsgaard (1986, 1996); Axinn (1971).
367 Weaver et al. (1999:283); Campello (2013:23).
368 Engels (1892); Durkheim (1893, 1912, 1983); Dahrendorf (1959); Thompson (1963); Hobsbawm (1968); Göhler (1974:348); Lasch (1977); Humphries (2010); Schmidt am Busch (2002:145); Nederman (1987:512).
369 Adriaan Peperzak (2001:470); Hutchings (2015:4). Hegel (1821, as quoted in Schmidt am Busch 2011a:236); Priddat (1990:84); Dickey (1987:211).
370 Maker (1987:19); Lasch (1977); Priddat (1990:188).
371 Friedrich Engels (1892); Eagleton (2011:9); Durkheim (1983, 1893, 1897, 1912).
372 Engels (1892); Lasch (1977).
373 Neschen (2008:26); Lukács (1974:689–758); Edmundts & Horstmann (2002:94); Dickey (1987:211); Houlgate (2010:297f.).
374 Neschen (2008); Gilbert (2013:219); Moser (2003:19); Pinkard (2014:227).
375 Buchwalter (2012a:15); Horowitz (1966:28); Horstmann (1974:281); Schmidt (2007:229); Priddat (1990:42); Flügel-Martinsen (2009:569).
376 http://en.wikipedia.org/wiki/Gross_national_happiness
377 Priddat (1990:36); Schneidereit (2011:120); Eckl (2013:407); Klikauer (2013b); Gilbert (2013:166).
378 Hegel (1821); Henrich (1971:204); Vartenberg (1981:176); Priddat (1990:66f.); Honneth (2008:4); en.wikipedia.org/wiki/Gini_coefficient; Benhabib (1981: 158); Schmidt am Busch (2002:145); Hegel (1821:§244).
379 Plant (1980:83); Hösle (1987:539); Ruda (2011); Hennig (2014:20); Klikauer (2013b).
380 Buchwalter (2012a:86); Gilbert (2013:94).
381 Westphal (1992:34–35); Riedel (1974a:269); Samuel (2010:159); Sutherland (1949); Gilbert (2013:165).
382 Nederman (1987:514); Sayama (2004).
383 www.usatoday.com; money.cnn.com; en.wikipedia.org/wiki/Dennis_Kozlowski; abcnews.go.com/Primetime/story?id=132070&page=1; Stillman (1980:112); Bryce (2002); Gray et al. (2005); Rowland (2006); Kothari (2010); Samuel (2010:85–114); Priddat (1990:232).
384 Lukács (1996); Sayama (2004).
385 www.poverty.com
386 http://en.wikipedia.org/wiki/Gini_coefficient
387 Rowland (2006:134ff.); Packer (2011:29); Hacker & Pierson (2010).
388 Priddat (1990:34, 73, 172); Jackson (1986:142); Bertram (2008:879); Quante (2013); Honneth (1995); Anderson (2009); Schmidt am Busch (2011:64).
389 Neschen (2008:40); Patten (1995, 1999); Schmidt (2007:138).
390 Cohen & Winston (2010); Nederman (1987:517).
391 Antonio (1981); Eagleton (2011); Pinkard (2014:195, 204).
392 Alan Patten (1995:577); Priddat (1990:20).
393 Lukács (1974:739); Stillman (1980:103); Patten (1995); Cole (2004:584ff.); Schmidt (2007:182); Tonn (2004); Eckl (2013:405).

394 en.wikipedia.org/wiki/Poverty
395 http://en.wikipedia.org/wiki/Poverty_threshold
396 Landau (1974:179); Hamilton & Dennis (2005); Hirata (2011).
397 Shleifer & Vishny (1986); Holderness & Sheehan (1988); López et al. (1999); Bakan (2004); Rehbein et al. (2012).
398 Maker (1987:5); Kojève (1996:56f.); Herzog (2011:79); Hösle (1987:377); Gilbert (2013:40–44).
399 Marglin (1974); Locke (1996); Magretta (2012).
400 Siep (1979:147); Gilbert (2013:179).
401 Hegel (1821:§253R, as quoted in Cullen 1988:27); Stillman (1980:112); Cristi (1989:730); Fatton (1986:590); Northouse (2011); Schmidt am Busch (2011a:248–250); Priddat (1990:32, 73, 83, 124fd.).
402 abcnews.go.com/Primetime/story?id=132070&page=1; usatoday.com...tyco; abc.net.au...1360571; Hegel (1821§247); money.cnn.com...tyco; wikipedia ... Kozlowski; Bryce (2002); Gray et al. (2005); Rowland (2006); Kothari (2010); Liebrucks (1974:42); Priddat (1990:65); Niji (2014:289); Honneth (2011:12); Schmidt am Busch (2002:144).
403 Galbraith (1958); Dahrendorf (1959); Gorz (1982).
404 Hamilton & Dennis (2005); Galbraith (1958).
405 Hegel (1821 as quoted in Plant 1980:82).
406 Hegel (1821:§185, as quoted by Herzog 2011:79).
407 Westphal (2012:162f.); Hegel (1821:§§250–256).
408 Zengotita (2005); Westphal (2002:318); Gilbert (2013:162).
409 Brecht & Ottwald (1932); Marcuse (1966); Gorz (1982).
410 Plant (1980:81); Eecke (1980:91, 95f.); Marcuse (1974:683); Gilbert (2013:183, 268ff.); Honneth (2014).
411 Tocqueville (1835); Dryzek (1996); Canfora (2006); Giusti (1987:307ff.).
412 Elster (1998); Freeman (2000); Gastil & Levine (2006); Gutmann & Thompson (2004); Parkinson & Mansbridge (2012); Ugarriza & Caluwaerts (2014).
413 Klikauer (2010:155); Ross (2008b:49); Foster (2010); Benson & Kirsch (2010a).
414 Westphal (2012:168); Ottow (2001:470); Hegel (1821:§234); Hinchman (1984240); Lübbe (1962:35); Hösle (1987:488); Siep (1979:288); Hegel (1821:§35); Hemming (2014:4); Gilbert (2013:110–113); Ritter (1970:329).
415 Habermas (1988); Klikauer (2008); Riedel (1974a:254); Priddat (1990:27); Siep (1979:162).
416 Riley (2001:132); Rosenow (1992); Lukács (1974:740); Riedel (1974c:824); Priddat (1990:268).
417 Hegel (1821); Henrich (1971:204).
418 Hegel (1805/06).
419 Sarakinsky (1992:7); Riedel (1974:825).
420 Cootner (1964); Taleb (2005); Priddat (1990:82); Nederman (1987:512).
421 Hegel (1807); Holz (1968); Purtschert (2008:927); Vartenberg (1981:175).
422 Cootner (1964); Taleb (2005); Johnsen (2010:181); Klikauer (2010:151); Chevalier-Roignant et al. (2011).
423 Hegel (1807); Priddat (1990:130); Ottmann (1981:373).
424 Alexander (2011); Kaplan and Norton (1992, 1993, 2004); Honneth (2007a:4).
425 Nowak & Highfield (2011); Klikauer (2012a).
426 Berger & Luckmann (1967); Searle (1996); Löwith (1962:30).

427 Gallagher (1987:170); Bobbio (1974:100); Riedel (1974a:264); Kersting (1988L:3&8); Cristi (1989:725); Priddat (1990:13, 57); Wallace (1999:428); Buchwalter (2012a:88f.); Hegel (1821, as quoted in Kersting 1988L:6).
428 Herzog (2011:78); Herzog (2013).
429 Schrijvers (2004); Samuel (2010).
430 Habermas (1974:811); Priddat (1990:58).
431 Fatton (1986:580f.); Gilbert (2013:215).
432 Niji (2014:2291).
433 Schmidt am Busch (2011:248); Giusti (1987:302).
434 Lehmbruch & Schmitter (1982); Williamson (1985); Vliet van (2011); Schneidereit (2011:117).
435 Neschen (2008:279); Hösle (1987:553).
436 Mander (2001); Nader (2011); Rushkoff (2011).
437 Bewes (2002); Lukács (1974:697); Riedel (1969:89); Dubsky (1970:433).

## 6 Corporate Governance and *Sittlichkeit*

438 Horowitz (1966:7).
439 Coffee (2006); Sayama (2004:120).
440 Brink (2010); Felo (2011); Rossouw (2011).
441 Useem (1990); Felo (2011:281); Rossouw (2011); Williams & Zumbansen (2011); Padgett (2012).
442 Stillman (1980:112); Bryce (2002); Gray et al. (2005); Rowland (2006); Kothari (2010); Samuel (2010:85–114).
443 Freeman (1984); Sternberg (1997); Bonnafous-Boucher & Porcher (2010); Holzer (2010); Solomon (2010); Samson & Daft (2012:184ff.); Clarke & Branson (2012).
444 lexicon.ft.com/; ifc.org/ifcext/corporategovernance; Clarke & Branson (2012).
445 Cullen (1988:27); Kersting (1988:9); Ferrara (1993); Riedel (1981:245).
446 Schwartz (1990); Schrijvers (2004); Samuel (2010).
447 www.usatoday.com; money.cnn.com; wikipedia.org/wiki/Dennis_Kozlowski; en.wikipedia.org/wiki/Corporate_crime.abcnews.go.com; Bryce (2002); Gray et al. (2005); Rowland (2006); Kothari (2010).
448 Punch (1996, 2008); Benson & Kirsch (2010a:463–465); Gaines-Ross (2008); Shah (2006); Samuel (2010:101ff.); Benson & Kirsch (2010:461, 481); wikipedia.org/wiki/List_of_business_failures
449 Cullen (1988:28); Eecke (1980:97); Hutchings (2015:9); Schmidt (2007:36); Hinchman (1984:226); Scott (1997); Eckl (2013:408); MacIntyre (1970:17).
450 Lee (1988); Moore (1989).
451 Herzog (2011:80); Steuart (1770); Sayama (2004:172); Herrmann-Pillath & Boldyrev (2014:158).
452 Whyte (1961); Nader (1967); Zeitlin (1974); Clinard (1983); Crittenden (1984); Jackall (1988, 2006); Schwartz (1990); Bird (1996); Punch (1996); Chomsky (1999); Brief (2000); Mander (2001); Parker (2002); Achbar & Abbott (2003); Watson (2003); Bakan (2004); Schrijvers (2004, 2005); Bolchover (2005); Babiak & Hare (2006); Saunders (2006); Leap (2007); Minkes & Minkes (2008); Punch (2008); Croall (2009); Adonis (2010); Johnsen (2010); Samuel (2010); Soederberg (2010); Watkins (2011); Voiculescu & Yanacopulos (2011).

453 Ilting (1974a:766ff.); Herrmann-Pillath & Boldyrev (2014:27).
454 Neuhouser (2011:291); Honneth (2011:56); Campello (2013:119ff.); Herrmann-Pillath & Boldyrev (2014:165).
455 Winfield (1987:59f.); Winfield (1984).
456 Gallagher (1987:172, 180); Plant (1980:59); Gallagher (1987:180).
457 Berger & Luckmann (1967); Searle (1996).
458 Kastner (2008:80); Campello (2013:139).
459 Klikauer (2008:96ff.); Gottschlich (2009).
460 Kervégan (2008:231); Habermas (1997); Klikauer (2007, 2008).
461 Priddat (1990:12, 272); Lübbe (1967:244); Peperzak (1991:272); Campello (2013:240); Riedel (1981:244).
462 Gallagher (1987:172f.); Hegel (1821); Giusti (1987:272); Rosenzweig (1974:639).
463 Fatton (1986:579); Breckman (2001:549); Kauffmann (2009).
464 Kersting (1988L:20); Hennig (2014:19); Abelshauser (2014:1); Carré (2013:315); Sayama (2004:240); Rosenzweig (1974:632).
465 Schmidt am Busch (2002:130; 2011:79); Priddat (1990:274); Göhler (1974:456, 571).
466 Winfield (1987:54); Kersting (1988L:11); Herzog (2011:76); Schmidt am Busch (2011a:227, 234); Sayama (2004:125).
467 Riedel (1974a:267); Hegel (1821:§243, §244, §243, §244).
468 Stillman (1980:113); Hegel (1821:§254, 255); Quante (2013); Siep (1979:249).
469 www.forbes.com/billionaires
470 Schrijvers (2004); Bolchover (2005); Congdon (2011); Harms & Spain (2015).
471 Priddat (1990:272); Riedel (1977:243); Schmidt (2007:235); Ottow (2001:473).
472 Schmidt (2007:235ff.); Siep (2008:5); Houlgate (2009:275); Breckman (2001:546).
473 Hegel (1821:§204, as quoted from Cullen 1988:29); Davis (1987:199); Kersting (1988:3; 1988L:12, 20); Gilbert (2013:172); Göhler (1974:398ff.).
474 Schneidereit (2011:115); Hösle (1987:545).
475 Ferrarin (2011:433); Houlgate (2009); Priddat (1990:200).
476 Lukács (1974:709f.); Sayama (2004:240).
477 Lukács (1974:712); Schmidt am Busch (2002:138).
478 Janis (1982, 1985); Herrmann-Pillath & Boldyrev (2014:164).
479 Marglin (1974); Locke (1996); Mander (2001); Bakan (2004); Rowland (2006:102); Locke & Spender (2011); Jobrack (2011).
480 Friedman (1970); Schwartz & Salia (2012); Dickey (1987:217); Adorno (1944).
481 Mander (2001); Benson & Kirsch (2010b).
482 Magretta (2012:129–140); Rowland (2006:58); Kreitner (2009); Jones & George (2011).
483 Cullen (1988:26); Herrmann-Pillath & Boldyrev (2014:164ff., 193).
484 Edmundts & Horstmann (2002:103).
485 Hegel (1821); Nakano (2004:35).
486 Foucault (1980); Townley (1993); Baudrillard (1994); Klikauer (2007, 2008).
487 Adonis (2010); Williams & Zumbansen (2011); Klikauer (2007, 2008); Cole (2004:584ff.); Eckl (2013:405f.); Brunsson (2002); Huzzard & Östergren (2002); Foote (2001).
488 Bohman (2010:445); Greis (1995).
489 Schrijvers (2004); Svendsen (2008); Klikauer (2012); Virilio (2012).

490 Bohman (2010:445); Ross (2008b:54); Schmidt am Busch (2011:72); Buchwalter (2012a:93).
491 Hegel (1807); Honneth (1995); Anderson (2009).
492 Marcuse (1964); Clegg (1989); Jackson (1986:147ff.); Schrijvers (2004).
493 Clegg (1989); Mumby (2001); McCally (2002); Buchanan & Badham (2008).
494 Kersting (1988:8); Seissl (2013:9).
495 Abelshauser (2014:2); Ashton (1999:4f.); Boggs (2012); Bohler (2009:229); Bondeli (1998:154); Braverman (1974); Breckman (2001:551ff.); Brooks (2013:124); Buchwalter (2012a:30, 100, 105, 109); Buchwalter (2013:11, 110f.); Campello (2013:134, 140); Carré (2013:316); Clegg (1971); Burnier (1980); Comack (2012); Cullen (1988:24); Eckl (2005:172f.); Eisenstadt & Roniger (1980); Escalante (2012:38); Fišera (1978); Fraser (2010); Galin (1978); Gallagher (1987:174); Gilbert (2013:178ff., 182, 188f.); Giusti (1987:303–309); Gorter (2007); Gramsci (1969); Greer (1999:570); Grzybowski (1957); Habermas 2010:343); Hegel (1821:§142); Heiman (1971:3f., 9, 130); Herrmann-Pillath & Boldyrev (2014:12, 24, 160f.); Herzog (2011:82, 112f., 181, 188); Hinchman (1984:230–232); Holmstrom (1989); Honneth (2008b:334f., 338); Honneth (2011:12f., 54f.); Honneth (2014:223–253); Hösle (1987:375, 553); Hutchings (2015:8); Kastner (2008:80f.); Kastner (2008:81); Kersting (1988:9); Kervégan (2008:235); Kliger (2014); Klikauer (2014); Kolaja (1965); Lübbe (1967:243); Lucardie (2014); Moser (2003:43, 170); Musch (2011:1); Nederman (1987:512ff.); Ness & Azzellini (2011); Niji (2014:285–294); Ottow (2001:472ff.); Pannokoek (2010); Pinkard (2014:225); Plant (1980:80); Poguntke (1987); Prescott & Rothwell (2012); Priddat (1990:18, 122, 131, 137, 190, 194, 197, 199, 200ff., 206–209, 214f., 218, 227, 234–239, 273); Raden (1968); Riedel (1974a:265, 268); Riedel (1977:247); Riedel (1981:247, 250); Ritter (1970:322); Ross (2008b:53); Rothkopf (2012); Rowland (2006:98); Sayama (2004:199, 228); Schmidt (2007:17, 259); Schmidt am Busch (2001:754ff.; 2011:80, 82; 2011a:21, 23, 235, 239, 242ff.); Schmitter & Lehmbruch (1979); Shipway (1988); Siep (1979:149); Sirianni (1982); Sitton (1987:86); Smith (1985); Sturmthal (1964); Taylor (1975:139); Vishnu (1984); Wallace (1999:431); wikipedia.org/wiki/Eduard_Gans
496 Offe & Wiesenthal (1980); Smith (2010).
497 Defoe (1719); Taylor (1975:541); Riedel (1974a:248); Quante (2013).
498 McGregor (1960, 2006); Azevedo & Gitahy (2010).
499 Schmidt am Busch (2011a:23, 242).
500 Honneth (1995); Anderson (2009); Chitty (2013); Quante (2013); Schmidt am Busch (2013); Renault (2013).
501 Kropotkin (1902); Nowak & Highfield (2011).
502 Ikäheimo & Laitinen (2010:38); Honneth (2011:337).
503 Taylor (1994:26).
504 Riedel (1981:240); Buchwalter (2012); Dames (2011); Zambrana (2012).
505 Cootner (1964); Hyman (1987); Taleb (2005); Ariely (2010); Hemming (2014:4); Sayama (2004:172, 175).
506 Locke & Spender (2011); Klikauer (2013); Anteby (2013).
507 Rousseau (1755); Freire (1970, 2000); Priddat (1990:96).
508 Estes (1996); Pearson (2011); Magretta (2012).
509 As Selekman (1959:43); Clegg (1989); Schrijvers (2004); Buchanan & Badham (2008); Klikauer (2013); Gilbert (2013:184).

510 Herzog (2011:188; 2013).
511 Herzog (2011:113; 2013).
512 Honneth (2008:6); Rousseau (1755); Rosenow (1992).
513 Schmidt am Busch (2011a:239); Prahalad & Hamel (1990:3f.).
514 Boorstein (1977); Estes (1996); Pilger (2001); Nicosia & Huener (2004); Bakan (2004); Clements (2011).

## 7 Corporate Governance Rationality and Morality

515 A 'human emancipation' to 'political emancipation' (Horowitz 1966:6); see also Hegelian philosopher Eduard Gans on 'one can deny or postpone the emancipation for a time, but one cannot avoid its inevitable result' (Hoffheimer 1995:8).
516 Magretta (2012:129–140); Estes (1996); Einstein (2012); http://hbr.org
517 Heiman (1971); Peperzak (2001); Neschen (2008); Ferrarin (2011).
518 Herzog (2011:80; 2013); Pinkard (2001:75).
519 Aubenas (2011); Gilbert (2013:176); Priddat (1990:39); www.worldhunger.org
520 Gilbert (2013:176); Carré (2013:315).
521 Honneth (1997:34); Sartre (1996:89); Mesch (2005:352).
522 Moggach & Lledman (1997:541).
523 Honneth (2011:59); Althusser (1997:90); Herrmann-Pillath & Boldyrev (2014:157).
524 Buchwalter (2012a:22); Campello (2013:109); Sayama (2004:171); Brooks (2013).
525 Gilbert (2013:180); Göhler (1974:526).
526 As quoted in Buchwalter (2012a:87); Wellmer (1991, 1993); Westphal (2012:155); Lukács (1974:752).
527 Hegel (1821:252); Gallagher (1987:173); Davis (1987:205); Hösle (1987:553); Nederman (1987:514); Kersting (1988L:37); Greis (1995); Breckman (2001:553); Nakano (2004:45); Peperzak (2001:472); Herzog (2011:82, 153; 2013); Westphal (2012:155); Schmidt am Busch (2011:81; 2011a:236); Ottow (2001:473).
528 Wildt (2005:473); Quante (2013).
529 Hegel (1807, 272; PR, 163 170, 252, 303); Gallagher (1987:170); Ilting (1974:63); Ritter (1970:333).
530 Baum (1978:189); Katz (1994); Miller (1984); McKee (2014).
531 Schmidt (2007:125); Carré (2013:315).
532 Descartes (1596–1650), Leibniz (1646–1716), Rousseau (1712–1778) and Kant (1724–1804); Houlgate (2009).
533 D'Hondt (1988); Comay (2011).
534 Neuhouser (2011:292); Eecke (1980:94); Westphal (2012:154).
535 Monk (1997); Füredi (2004); Svendsen (2008); Virilio (2012).
536 Gore (2007); Beder (2006); Estes (1996); Lindstrom (2008); Foster (2010); Einstein (2012).
537 As quoted in Wallace (1999:424).
538 All quotes in this paragraph are from: Magretta (2012:31, 129–140; 2012:31; 2012:32).

539 Schwartz (1990); Jackall (1988, 2006); Brunsson (2002); Achbar & Abbott (2003); Bunting (2004); Schrijvers (2004, 2005); Bolchover (2005); Babiak & Hare (2006); Adonis (2010); Soederberg (2010).
540 Weber (1924); Clegg (1981, 1989); wikipedia.org/wiki/Mushroom_management
541 Kohlberg (1958, 1971, 1973, 1981, 1984); Kohlberg & Kramer (1969); Adelman (1980:127); Klikauer (2010:126–169; 2012).
542 Ritter (1970:330); Carré (2013:317); Althusser (1997:21).
543 Bohman (2010:445); Gilbert (2013:170); Herzog (2011a:848).
544 Nahm (2008:160ff.); Gilbert (2013:65).
545 Bohman (2010:445); Ritter (1970:346).
546 Kojève (1947); Holz (1968); Althusser (1997:117f.); Hyppolite (1996:83f.).
547 Bird & Waters (1989:77); Bohman (2010:445).
548 Hegel (1821); Peddle (2000:126).
549 Sandel (1998); Boltanski & Chiapello (2005).
550 Westphal (2002:318); Gilbert (2013:162).
551 en.wikipedia.org/wiki/Lifeworld; Husserl (1936); Habermas (1997); Hyder & Rheinberger (2010);
552 Eecke (1980:92); Fulda (2001:178).
553 Beadle & Moore (2011:105); MacIntyre (1970).
554 Jacoby (1977, 1997); Bird & Waters (1989:79); Bird (1996); Klikauer (2010:2, 109).
555 http://en.wikipedia.org/wiki/Externality; http://www.corporatewatch.org/?lid=2670
556 Holzer (2010:3); wikipedia.org/wiki/Nestl%C3%A9_boycott; www.ibfan.org/fact-nestle.html; Benson & Kirsch (2010a:480); Gaines-Ross (2008); Plesch & Blankenburg (2008); Corporatewatch (2012).
557 Corporatewatch (2012); www.corporatewatch.org; www.corpwatch.org/; www.aflcio.org/Corporate-Watch
558 Buchwalter (2012a:95); Bobbio (1974:85); Ritter (1974b:154–206).
559 Priddat (1990:48); Moser (2003:20); Dickey (1987:182); Habermas (2010:344).
560 Bakan (2004); Bernstein (2010); Corporatewatch (2012:3).
561 newint.org/features/2011/01/01/10-worst-corporate-lobbyists
562 Thanem (2011); Watson (1997).
563 Machiavelli (1532); Hobbes (1651); Nietzsche (1880, 1883); Klikauer (2010:178).
564 Peperzak (2001:470–471); Ross (2008b:53); Herzog (2011:150); Gilbert (2013:130); Casuso (2013:31–75).
565 Eecke (1980:96); Bakan (2004).
566 http://www.icahnreport.com/report/2008/06/corporate-board.html
567 Townley (2005); Rowland (2006); Kothari (2010); Kramar et al. (2011).
568 Mandell (2002); Wahl (2011); Rowland (2006:101).
569 Arnold & Randal (2010:433, 483); (Magretta 2012:31).
570 Kaplan & Norton (1992, 1993, 2004); Townley (2005); Alexander (2011).
571 Hegel (1821§253R as quoted in Cullen 1988:27).
572 Leonard & Weber (1970); Farber (2002:59); Klikauer (2013b).
573 Priddat (1990:28); Flügel-Martinsen (2009:571); Siep (1979:292); Hutchings (2015:8).
574 Schrijvers (2004); Achbar & Abbott (2003); Samuel (2010).
575 Kersting (1988L:37); Plant (1980:60).
576 Milgram (1963, 1973, 1973, 1974, 1992); Blass (1991, 2002).

577 Sheth (2010); Rossington (2014).
578 As quoted from Plant (1980:79, Hegel XI, S. 251, in: Priddat 1990:123); Cristi (1989:730, 737); Benhabib (1981:157).
579 Taylor (1911); analytictech.com/mb021/taylor; Riedel (1981:251).
580 Priddat (1990:56); Gilbert (2013:177); Dubsky (1970:428); Sayama (2004:146, 225); Riedel (1969:94); Riedel (1974d:832); Arndt 1985:114); Schmidt (2007:60, 196).
581 Haigh (2006); McQueen (2009); Salvendy (2012); Siep (1979:260).
582 Armstrong & Loach (1997); Burley & Hoedeman (2011); O'Brian (2012); www.huffingtonpost.com
583 Cootner (1964); Nusser (1981:556); Taleb (2005); Ariely (2010); Cristi (1989:725); Priddat (1990:29); Edmundts & Horstmann (2002:97).
584 Human Development Report (1999); http://hdr.undp.org/en/content/human-development-report-1999; Sayama (2004:228).
585 Marx (1890); Durkheim (1897); Dubsky (1970:410); Göhler (1974:483ff.).
586 Marx (1890); Engels (1892); Thompson (1963); Hobsbawm (1968); Sennett & Cobb (1972); Dickey (1987:254ff.); Kojève (1996:55); Habermas (1996); Ashton (1999:6); Sennett (2006, 2012); Vallas (2011); Priddat (1990:34); Rössler (2005:389ff.).
587 Hegel (1807); Dubsky (1970:408ff.); Habermas (1974:8006); Lukács (1974:698); Riedel (1974b:113); Adelman (1980:126ff.); Sayama (2004:151f.); Sichler (2010); Arndt (1985:99); Schmidt (2007:190); Cole (2004:581ff., 593); López (2013); Žižek (2014:30).
588 Raman & Lipschutz (2010); Henderson (2001:30f.).
589 Locke (1996); Magretta (2012).
590 Hemming (2014:2); Sayama (2004:143); Ilting (1974:71).
591 Dickey (1987:253); Engels (1892); Thompson (1963); Hobsbawm (1968); Sheehan (1973); Eeckhout (2009); Dubofsky & Dulles (2010).
592 Kersting (1988L:7); Klikauer (2007); Smith (2010); Bolton (2012).
593 Hegel (I, §197, in: Priddat 1990:204); Schmidt (2007:195); Smith (2010); Riedel (1969:88).
594 Ottow (2001:473); Riedel (1981:250).
595 Zengotita (2005); Klikauer (2013).
596 Adorno (1944); Brink (2010); Freyenhagen (2011, 2013).
597 Negray (2012); Gottfried (2012).
598 Coe et al. (2008); Henderson et al. (2002).
599 Braverman (1974); Smith (2010).
600 Bird & Waters, (1989:78); Campello (2013:23).
601 Wallace (1999:431); Reidel (1974d:828).

## 8 Corporations and *Sittlichkeit*

602 'Korporationen sind für den sittlichen Gesamtzusammenhang' (Flügel-Martinsen 2009:571).
603 Giusti (1987:300ff.); Niji (2014:292).
604 Ritter (1974a:234); O'Connor (2012).
605 Gallagher (1987:159); Römpp (2008:221).
606 Locke (2011); Augier & March (2011).
607 Prahalad & Hamel (1990); Allen et al. (2013); Klikauer (2013b); Gilbert (2013:52); Nowak & Highfield (2011).

608 Honneth (2007:4, 8); Riedel (1969:79); Honneth (2007a:8); Foster (2010:97); Barnes (2006); Suarez-Villa (2012); Robinson (2014).
609 Kersting (1988L:2); Treptow (1972:36ff.).
610 'Hegel (1821:§182Z, quoted from Kersting 1988L:2).
611 Treptow (1972:11); Westphal (2012:161); Zambrana (2012:277).
612 Wallace (1999:424); Abelshauser (2014:1).
613 Herzberg, et al. (1959); Herzberg (1966, 2011); Ewen et al. (1966); Wildt (2005:463); Dickey (1987:248).
614 Styron (1979); Klikauer (2010:116, 142); Bauman (1989); Katz (2006).
615 Styron (1979); Nowak & Highfield (2011); on Willkür, see: Gallagher (1987:170); Hemming (2014:4).
616 Bird & Waters (1989:74); Priddat (1990:48).
617 Maker (1987:12); Kersting (1988L:5); Wallace (1999:428); Bertram (2008:883).
618 Buchwalter (2012a:20); Ilting (1974:61, 64); Ritter (1974a:227); Riedel (1974c:835); Höfler (2009:252); Peperzak (1991:251); Sayama (2004:95).
619 Herrmann-Pillath & Boldyrev (2014:16); Nowak & Highfield (2011); Klikauer (2012a); Moyar (2013:588).
620 Westphal (2002:315); Abelshauser (2014:2).
621 Flügel-Martinsen (2009:371); Png (2012).
622 Hegel (III, S. 192, in: Priddat 1990:53).
623 Hegel (1821:125 as quoted in: Gallagher 1987:171); Kersting (1988:5); Priddat (1990:19); Riedel (1981:248); Hennig (2014:20); Ottow (2001:470); Herzog (2011:194); Schweppenhäuser (1993:135); Gilbert (2013:164).
624 Roelofs (2003); Magretta (2012); Klikauer (2013).
625 Hegel (1821:180) as quoted in: Gallagher 1987:165).
626 Knowles (1983:423); Giusti (1987:271).
627 Greer (1999:561); Habermas (1974:789); Bertram (2008:878); Escalante (2012:42).
628 Quoted in Cristi (1989:730); Dickey (1987:214).
629 Kohlberg (1958, 1971, 1973, 1981, 1984); Kohlberg & Kramer (1969); Klikauer (2010:126–169).
630 Wood (2011:303); Williams (2011:396); Dorary (1988); Hegel (1801); Taylor (1975:67); Sayama (2004:100).
631 Buchwalter (2012a:54); Liebrucks (1974:45); Escalante (2012:26).
632 Kersting (1988L:4); Hösle (1987:541).
633 Winfield (1987:38); Winfield (1984); Bose (2010).
634 Whyte (1961); Levine (2012:288); Sayama (2004:152).
635 Göhler (1974:539); Klikauer (2013).
636 Maker (1987:13); Horowitz (1966).
637 Translated from Schmidt (2007:64); Buchwalter (2012a:11).
638 Winfield (1987:39); Giusti (1987:300).
639 Priddat (1990:289); Hinchman (1984:221).
640 Kersting (1988L:13); Campello (2013:138).
641 Westphal (2002:318); Ashton (1999:6); Klikauer (2013b).
642 Kersting (1988:10); Schmidt am Busch (2002:131); Niji (2014:290).
643 Gallagher (1987:175); Apel (1964).
644 Kohlberg (1958, 1971, 1973, 1981, 1984); Kohlberg & Kramer (1969); Klikauer (2010:126–169; 2012, 2014c).
645 Gallagher (1987:175); Breckman (2001:562).

646 Magretta (2012:79); Hayek (1944); Porter (1985); Stengel (2011); O'Connor (2012:11).
647 Bolton (2012); Koslowski (2008:102).
648 Hegel (1821:§255R, quoted in: Cullen 1988:26); Kersting (1988L:2); Norris (2004:414); Göhler (1974a:356); O'Connor (2012:7).
649 Kersting (1988:4; 1988L:12); Ilting (1974:59); Herzog (2011:89, 93, 97).
650 Liebrucks (1974:45); Honneth (2011:50).
651 Honneth (2011:50); Siep (1979:190).
652 Bolton (2012); Holzer (2010).
653 Martin (2004); Cohen (2005); Croteau & Hoynes (2006); Kumar (2007); McChesney (2008); Fortner & Fackler (2011).
654 Durkheim (1893, 1897); Sennett & Cobb (1972).
655 Maker (1987:14); Dickey (1987:243).
656 Fatton (1986:582); Kemple (2007); Pinkard (2014:195).
657 Packard (1959); Lindstrom (2005, 2008).
658 Mills (1951); Galbraith (1958); http://en.wikipedia.org/wiki/Growth_Fetish; Hamilton & Dennis (2005).
659 Soederberg (2010); Maker (1987:11); Hegel (1821:§194 as quoted by Kersting (1988L:5); Schmidt (2007:161).
660 WWW.Unicef.ORG; Singer (1972); Pogge (2007, 2010); Pogge & Horton (2008).
661 Herzog (2011:87); Herzog (2013).
662 Miles & Snow (1978); Ghoshal (2005); Mintzberg et al. (2009); Samson & Daft (2012a, 2012b).
663 Peter Drucker as quoted in Magretta (2012:1).
664 http://en.wikipedia.org/wiki/SWOT_analysis
665 Fatton (1986:581); Treptow (1972:11); Giusti (1987:279); Honneth (2014:9); Carré (2013:315); Klikauer (2013b).
666 Gabor (2000); Donaldson & Werhane (2008); Donaldson & Werhane (2008:347); Boatright (2009); Shaw & Barry (2010); Wicks et al. (2010); Mele (2011); Jackson (2011); Sandbu (2011); Shaw (2011); Carroll & Buchholtz (2012); Ferrell et al. (2013).
667 Davis (1987:205); Aguilar & Herod (2006).
668 Jacoby (1977, 1997); Foster (2010:97–99).
669 Henderson (2001); Capaldi (2005); Benson & Kirsch (2010a, 2010b); Raman & Lipschutz (2010).
670 http://plato.stanford.edu/entries/kant-moral/
671 Blass (2002); Sheth (2010); Dumenil & Levy (2011).
672 Hampden-Turner (1970:126); Bauman (1989:155; 2000:27); Blass (1991:400, 407); Katz (2006).
673 Habermas (1988); Herman & Chomsky (1988).
674 Habermas (1997); Enzensberger (1974); Habermas (1988); Chomsky (1991); Martin (2004); Cohen (2005); Croteau & Hoynes (2006); Bennett (2007); Kumar (2007); McChesney (2008); Rosoff et al. (2009); Morgan (2010); Huff (2011); Fortner & Fackler (2011).
675 Davis (2007); Bourdieu & Accardo (1999).
676 Singer (1972); Senigaglia (2013).
677 Abrahamson (1996); Benson & Kirsch (2010b).
678 Achbar & Abbott (2003); oecd.org/glossary

679 Cullen (1988:23); Bernstein (2010).
680 Cullen (1988:26); Treptow (1972:196); Lukács (1974:729).
681 Lukács (1974:704); Edmundts & Horstmann (2002:103).
682 http://www.transparency.org; www.corporatewatch.org; www.corpwatch.org, etc.; Surowieki (2013).
683 Hayek (1944, 1960, 1978) and Milton Friedman (1970).
684 Anderson (2001); Drydyk (1986); Feola (2010); Smith (1989a, 1989b); Winfield (1983); Schmidt am Busch (2002:157).
685 Locke (2011); Zengotita (2005); Steer (2013:206).
686 Hunt (1988:71); O'Neill (1996:10).
687 Kreitner (2009:42); Selekman (1959:54, 58).
688 Honneth (1995); Anderson (2009).
689 Hegel (I, Zusatz zu §15, in: Priddat (1990:103); Gadamer (1996:149ff.); Carré (2013:316).
690 Kersting (1988:9); Cristi (1989:730); Kohlberg (1958, 1971, 1973, 1981, 1984); Kohlberg & Kramer (1969); Klikauer (2012).
691 Saunders (2006); Johnsen (2010); Samuel (2010).
692 Sondergergh (2000); Klikauer (2013).
693 Porter (1985); Magretta (2012); Pinto (2016); Barney (2015); Gamble (2015); Noe et al. (2015).
694 Lübbe (1962:38); Siep (2008:4); Herrmann-Pillath & Boldyrev (2014:165); Klikauer (2014); Chomsky (1999:99ff.); Ashton (1999:4); López (2013).
695 Martin (2004); Cohen (2005); Croteau & Hoynes (2006); Kumar (2007); McChesney (2008); Fortner & Fackler (2011); Straubhaar et al. (2011).
696 Mandell (2002); Neuhouser (2011:292).
697 Quoted in Menke (1992:78).
698 Rosenfeld et al. (1995); Benson & Kirsch (2010b).
699 Farber (2002:59); Achbar & Abbott (2003); Simon et al. (2006).
700 Magretta (2012:1); Chevalier-Roignant et. al. (2011).
701 Braverman (1974); Hyman (1979, 1989); Offe & Wiesenthal (1980); Magretta (2012); Gall (2012); Gall et al. (2012); Gross (2012); Upchurch (2012); Jessop (2012).
702 Jackson et al. (2012); Poundstone (2012).
703 Neuhouser (2011:292); Lübbe (1962:30).
704 Bolton & Houlihan (2008); Bolton (2012); Klikauer (2014c).
705 Cullen (1988:36); Honneth (2008b:334).
706 Kaplan & Norton (1992, 1993, 2004); Paauwe (2009).
707 Whyte (1961); Bird & Waters (1989:76).
708 Klikauer (2007:194; 2008:128; 2010:39, 84).
709 Winfield (1987:32); Landau (1974:185); Winfield (1984).
710 Nakano (2004:37); Rawls (1972, 1980, 1993, 1999, 2001); Clark & Gintis (1978); McCarthy (1994); Maffettone (2010); Klikauer (2010:130–132, 155f., 265f.).
711 Wood (1972); Husamim (1978); Zimmerman (1981); Jackall (1988, 2006); Achbar & Abbott (2003); Schrijvers (2004); Bolchover (2005); Adonis (2010); Katz-Fishman & Scott (2012); Heiman (1971:130).
712 Priddat (1990:282); Lübbe (1962:38).
713 Quoted from Nakano (2004:43f.); Drydyk (1986:120); Schmidt am Busch (2011:79); Hegel (1821:§201).

714 Coser (2012:242); Rae (2012); Göhler (1974:544); Rosenzweig (1974:631).
715 Foster (1998); Shipler (2005); Thompson (2010); Gilabert (2012).
716 McDonald's Corporation v Steel & Morris (wikipedia.org/wiki/McLibel_Case).
717 Habermas (1988, 2006); Herman & Chomsky (1988); Chomsky (1991); Greenwald (2004); Luntz (2007); Gore (2007); Graber (2012); Mirkinson (2012); Duignan (2013); www.outfoxed.org

## 9 Conclusion: The Moral Corporation

718 Translated from Hegelian philosopher Riedel (1977:250), original text: 'die Korporation ist die Vergesellschaftung der zerrissenen Theile und Desintegration der bürgerlichen Gesellschaft'.
719 Hegel (1803/04); Fulda (1966); Westphal (2012:157); Schmidt (2007:33); Hinchman (1984:230).
720 Dickey (1987:193); Bové (1986); Sturm et al. (1999); Lupton (2014).
721 Liebrucks (1974:35); Fritzman (2012); Hinchman (1984:258).
722 Hegel (1821, Part II on Civil Society, Section §250–256), www.marxists.org/reference/archive/hegel/works/pr/prconten.htm
723 Buchwalter (2012a:14); Liebrucks (1974:22); Ilting (1974:73); Bloch (1962:167).
724 Davis (1917); Beatty (2001); Chandler & Mazlish (2005); Giroux & Pollock (2010); Hunt & Lautzenheiser (2011).
725 http://en.wiktionary.org/wiki/ignorance_is_bliss; Rawls (1972:97).
726 Baritz (1960); Brief (2000); Herzberg (1966, 2011); Smith (2010).
727 Ward (1924); Kearns (2007); Donaldson & Werhane (2008); Jobrack (2011).
728 Johann Wolfgang von Goethe (1749–1832); Thomas Mann (1948).
729 On the other hand, there is the dictum of Canadian philosopher John Burbidge that philosophy 'cannot foretell the future' (1988:viii).
730 Rawls (1972, 1980, 1993, 1999, 2001); Clark & Gintis (1978); McCarthy (1994); Maffettone (2010).
731 Pascal (1660); Krailsheimer (1980); Bourdieu (2000).
732 Hegel's *Phenomenology* (1807:40–41) as quoted in: Gallagher (1987:181).
733 wikipedia.org/wiki/Corporate_personhood; Schmidt (2007:164).
734 Hamilton (1938); McLaughlin (1940); McCurdy (1975); Phillips et al. (2004); Gore (2007); Ritz (2007); Laufer (2008); Magnuson (2008); Friedrichs (2009); Hartmann (2010).
735 Benson & Kirsch (2010a); Foster (2010).
736 D'Hondt (1988); Schmidt (2007:121); Žižek (2012).
737 Honneth (2007:4); Schmidt (2007:245); Foster (2010:97); Kervégan (2008:227).
738 www.ne.jp/asahi/moriyuki/abukuma/weber/method/basic/basic_concept_frame.html
739 Quittner & Slatalla (1998); Schrijvers (2004).
740 Schmidt (2007:263); Gilbert (2013:58).
741 Dickey (1987:206); Ruda (2011); Campello (2013:141).
742 Peperzak (2001:471); Dickey (1987:206).
743 Peperzak (2011:471); Anderson (1993:141ff.); Davis (2007); Aguilar & Herod (2006).
744 Deetz (1992); Klikauer (2010:193–216); industrialdemocracy.org

745 Riedel (1974b:109); Gottschlich (2009:166); Patten (1995:594).
746 http://www.hegel.net/en/eb1911.htm#3; Kantian philosophy and Pogge (2007) and Pogge & Horton (2008); Hutchings (2010).
747 D'Hondt (1988); Buchwalter (2012, 2012a).
748 Hutchings (2010); Freeman (2011); Gilabert (2012).
749 D'Hondt (1988); Priddat (1990:80).
750 Taylor (1994); Honneth (1995); Anderson (2009).
751 Klikauer (2012, 2014a, 2014c).
752 Kohlberg (1958, 1971, 1973, 1981, 1984); Kohlberg & Kramer (1969); Klikauer (2010:126–169, 2012, 2013a, 2013c).
753 Singer (1978, 1990, 2000, 2007); Bookchin (1962, 1982, 1990, 1995, 2001); Hawken (1993); Keller (2010); Klikauer (2010:126–169); Newell (2012); Magnuson (2013); Thiele (2013); Radkau (2013).
754 http://en.wikipedia.org/wiki/Egocentrism
755 Priddat (1990:41); Schmidt (2007:126).
756 Houlgate (1998); Stone (2005); http://ndpr.nd.edu/
757 Smith (1776); Miles & Snow (1978); Porter (1985); Milgram (1963, 1972, 1973, 1974, 1992); Blass (1991, 2002); Bernstein (2010); Herzog (2011).
758 Magretta (2012:4); in Hegelian terms this means 'es stehen sich zwei lebendige Individuen gegenüber, die aber nicht die gleiche Macht haben' (there are two opposite living individuals, but they do not have the same power) (Escalante 2012:25); i.e. the institutional power of management (Magretta 2012).
759 Whyte (1961); Bolton & Houlihan (2008); Hinchman (1984:255).
760 Engels (1892); Thompson (1963); Hobsbawm (1968); Priddat (1990:91); Eeckhout (2009); Humphries (2010).
761 McGregor (1960, 2006).
762 Riedel (1974a:264); Kropotkin (1902); Axelrod (1984, 1997); Krebs (2008, 2011); Nowak & Highfield (2011); Schmidt am Busch (2011a:227).
763 Harding (2003); Jobrack (2011); Beardwell & Claydon (2011); Belcourt et al. (2011); Jackson et al. (2012); Kramar et al. (2011); Macky (2008); Patrick et al. (2011); Schrijvers (2004).
764 Benson & Kirsch (2010a:468); Gaines-Ross (2008) www.who.int; Smale (2006:2).
765 https://en.wikipedia.org/wiki/Schutzstaffel; Rhodes (2010).
766 en.wikipedia.org/wiki/Extermination_through_labor; Levi (1959); Bauman (1989); Todorov (1996).
767 http://www.theawfultruth.com/salbmw/; Rummel (1994); Goldhagen (1996, 2009); Snyder (2010).
768 Hayek (1944); www.abc.net.au/lateline/content/2012
769 Deetz (1992); Habermas (1997); Watson (2003); Mumby (1997, 2001); Beder (2000, 2006); Poole (2006); Klikauer (2007, 2008).
770 Wilson (1974); Deetz (1992); Ritz (2001); Hoopes (2011).
771 Samuel (2010:8); wikipedia.org/wiki/Sustainability
772 Herzog (2011:187); Herzog (2013).
773 Riedel (1974b:113); Honneth's (2011:47ff.).

# Bibliography


Abbott, C. C. 1936. *The Rise of the Business Corporation*, Ann Arbor: Edwards Brothers, Inc., Lithoprinters.

Abella, A. 2008. *Soldiers of Reason: The RAND Corporation and the Rise of the American Empire*, New York: Harcourt.

Abelshauser, W. 2014. Kartelle in der deutschen Wirtschaftskultur, guest presentation for Das Kartellverbot in *der Sozialen Marktwirtschaft*, 8 April 2014, Düsseldorf: European Trust Institute (www.eu-trust.org/download/2014/140408); 7 pages.

Abrahamson, E. 1996. Management Fashion, *Academy of Management Review*, vol. 21, no. 1, pp. 254–285.

Achbar, M. & Abbott, J. 2003. *The Corporation: The Pathological Pursuit of Profit and Power* (DVD 145 min.), Toronto: Big Picture Media Corporation.

Aching, G. 2012. The Slave's Work: Reading Slavery through Hegel's Master-Slave Dialectic, *PMLA (The Modern Language Association of America)*, vol. 127, no. 4, pp. 912–917.

Adamson, M. 2009. The Human Capital Strategy, *Ephemera* (e-journal: www.ephemera.org), vol. 9, no. 4, pp. 271–284.

Adelman, H. 1980. Of Human Bondage: Labour, Bondage, and Freedom in the Phenomenology, in: Verene, D. P. (ed.) *Hegel's Social and Political Thought – The Philosophy of Objective Spirit*, Sussex: Harvester Press.

Adler, P. S. (ed.) 2014. *Oxford Handbook of Sociology, Social Theory and Organization Studies. Contemporary Currents*, Corby: Oxford University Press.

Adonis, J. 2010. *Corporate Punishment – Smashing the Management Clichés for Leaders in a New World*, Milton: Wiley.

Adorno, T. W. 1944. *Minima Moralia – Reflections from the Damaged Life*, Dennis Redmond (2005) translation: http://www.efn.org/~dredmond/MinimaMoralia.html

Adorno, T. W. 1971. *Erziehung zur Mündigkeit* [*Education to Maturity*], Frankfurt: Suhrkamp Publishing.

Adorno, T. W. & Horkheimer, M. 1944. *The Culture Industry: Enlightenment as Mass Deception*, Transcribed by Andy Blunden 1998; proofed and corrected February 2005, web download, November 2005.

Aguilar, L. L. M. & Herod, A. (eds.) 2006. *The Dirty Work of Neoliberalism: Cleaners in the Global Economy*, Malden: Blackwell.

Akers, J. F. 1989. Ethics and Competitiveness – Putting First Things First, *MIT Sloan Management Review*, vol. 30, no. 2, pp. 69–79.

Alexander, J. 2011. *Performance and Power*, Oxford: Polity Press.

Allen, W. et al. 2013. *Managerial Economics: Theory, Applications, and Cases* (8th ed.), New York: W.W. Norton & Company.

Althaus, H. 2000. *Hegel – An Intellectual Biography*, Cambridge: Polity Press.

Althusser, L. 1997. *The Spectre of Hegel – Early Writings*, London: Verso.

Alvesson, M. 2002. *Understanding Organisational Culture*, London: Sage.

Anderson, E. 1993. *Values in Ethics and Economics*, Cambridge: Harvard University Press.

Anderson, J. 2001. Hegel's Implicit View on How to Solve the Problem of Poverty, in: Williams, R. (ed.) *Beyond Liberalism and Communitarism: Essays on Hegel's "Philosophy of Right"*, New York: Sunny Press.
Anderson, S. S. C. 2009. *Hegel's Theory of Recognition – From Oppression to Ethical Liberal Modernity*, London: Continuum.
Anteby, M. 2013. *Manufacturing Morals: The Values of Silence in Business School Education*, Chicago: University of Chicago Press.
Antonio, R. J. 1981. Immanent Critique as the Core of Critical Theory: Its Origins and Developments in Hegel, Marx and Contemporary Thought, *British Journal of Sociology*, vol. 32, no. 3, pp. 330–345.
Antoniou, A-S. & Cooper, G. 2011. *New Directions in Organisational Psychology and Behavioural Medicine*, Farnham Surrey: Ashgate.
Apel, K. O. 1964. Reflexion und Materielle Praxis – Zur erkenntnisantroposlogischen Begründung der Dialektik zwischen Hegel und Marx [Reflection and Material Practice – On the Insightfulness of Anthropological Reasoning of Dialectic between Hegel and Marx], *Hegel-Studien Beiheft 1* (Heidelberger Hegel-Tage 1962 – Vorträge und Dokumente), Bonn: Bouvier Press.
Apel, K. O. 1980. *Towards a Transformation of Philosophy*, London: Routledge.
Arendt, H. 1958. *The Human Condition*, Chicago: Chicago University Press.
Ariely, D. 2010. Good Decisions. Bad Outcomes, *Harvard Business Review*, 1 December 2010, 9 pages.
Armstrong, F. & Loach, K. 1997. *McLible* (TV documentary), London: BBC2.
Armstrong, M. 2012. *Armstrong's Handbook of HRM Practice* (12th ed.), London & Philadelphia: Kogan Page.
Arndt, A. 1985. Zur Herkunft und Funktion des Arbeitsbegriffs in Hegels Geistesphilosophie [On the Origins and Funciton of Labour in Hegel's Philosophy of the Spirit], *Archiv für Begriffsgeschichte*, vol. 29, pp. 99–115.
Arnold, J. & Randal, R. 2010. *Work Psychology – Understanding Human Behaviour in the Workplace* (5th ed.), London: Prentice-Hall.
Ashton, P. 1999. Hegel and Labour, in: *The Legacy of Hegel Seminar, Melbourne: University of Melbourne* (Seminar February 1999: www.marxist.org).
Aspromourgos, T. 2012. The Managerialist University: An Economic Interpretation, *Australian University Review*, vol. 54, no. 2, pp. 44–49.
Aubenas, F. 2011. *The Night Cleaner*, Oxford: Polity Press.
Augier, M. & March, J. G. 2011. *The Roots, Rituals, and Rhetorics of Change: North American Business Schools after the Second World War*, Stanford: Stanford Business Books.
Axelrod, R. 1984. *The Evolution of Cooperation*, New York: Basic Books.
Axelrod, R. 1997. *The Complexity of Cooperation: Agent-Based Models of Competition and Collaboration*, Princeton: Princeton University Press.
Axinn, S. 1971. Kant, Authority, and the French Revolution, *Journal of the History of Ideas*, vol. 32, no. 3, pp. 423–432.
Azevedo, A. & Gitahy, L. 2010. The Cooperative Movement, Self-Management, and Competitiveness: The Case of Mondragon Corporatcion Cooperativa, *Working USA – A Journal of Labor and Society*, vol. 13, no. 1, pp. 5–29.
Babiak, P. & Hare, R. D. 2006. *Snakes in Suits: When Psychopaths Go to Work*, New York: Regan Books.
Bagley, C. E. 2003. The Ethical Leader's Decision Tree, *Harvard Business Review*, February, p. 19.
Baillargeon, N. 2013. *Order without Power*, New York: Seven Stories Press.

Bakan, J. 2004. *The Corporation – The Pathological Pursuit of Profit and Power*, London: Free Press.

Bakken, T. 2009. Risk, Responsibility and Conscience, in: Garsten, C. & Hernes, T. (eds.) *Ethical Dilemmas in Management*, London: Routledge.

Ballard, E. G. 1955. On the Nature and Use of Dialectic, *Philosophy of Science*, vol. 22, no. 3, pp. 205–213.

Baritz, L. 1960. *The Servants of Power. A History of the Use of Social Science in American Industry*, Middletown: Wesleyan University Press.

Barnes, P. 2006. *Capitalism 3.0: A Guide to Reclaiming the Commons*, San Francisco: Berrett-Koehler Publishers.

Barney, J. B. 2015. *Strategic Management and Competitive Advantage: Concepts and Cases* (5th ed.), Boston: Pearson.

Barshack, L. 2010. '…That All Members Should be Loved in the Same Way…', in: von den Brink, B. & Owen, D. (eds.) *Recognition and Power – Axel Honneth and the Tradition of Critical Social Theory*, Cambridge: Cambridge University Press.

Baudrillard, J. 1994. *Simulacra and Simulation*, Ann Arbor: University of Michigan Press.

Baum, M. 1978. Gemeinwohl und allgemeiner Wille in Hegels Rechtsphilosophie [Welfare and General Will in Hegels' *Philosophy of Right*], *Archiv für Geschichte der Philosophie*, vol. 60, no. 2, pp. 175–198.

Bauman, Z. 1987. *Legislators and Interpreters: On Modernity, Post-Modernity, and Intellectuals*, Cambridge: Polity Press.

Bauman, Z. 1989. *Modernity and the Holocaust*, Oxford: Blackwell.

Bauman, Z. 2000. *Liquid Modernity*, Cambridge: Polity Press.

Bauman, Z. & Donsikis, L. 2013. *Moral Blindness*, Oxford: Polity Press.

Beachler, D. W. & Shevory, T. 2014. *When Good Companies Go Bad: 100 Corporate Miscalculations and Misdeeds*, Santa Barbara: ABC-CLIO.

Beadle, R. & Moore, G. 2011. MacIntyre, Neo-Aristotlianism and Organisation Theory, in: Tsoukas, H. & Chia, R. (eds.) *Philosophy and Organisation Theory*, Bingley: Emerald Publishing.

Beardwell, J. & Claydon, T. 2011. *Human Resource Management: A Contemporary Approach*, London: Financial Times Press.

Beatty, J. (ed.) 2001. *Colossus: How the Corporation Changed America*, New York: Broadway Books.

Beder, S. 2000. *Global Spin: The Corporate Assault on Environmentalism*, Melbourne: Scribe Publications.

Beder, S. 2000a. *Selling Work Ethics – From Puritan Pulpit to Corporate PR*, London: Zed Books.

Beder, S. 2006. *Free Market Missionaries – The Corporate Manipulation of Community Values*, London: Earthscan Press.

Beder, S., Varney, W. & Gosden, R. 2009. *This Little Kiddy Went to Market: The Corporate Capture of Childhood*, Sydney: UNSW Press.

Belcourt, M., Bohlander, G. & Snell, S. 2011. *Managing Human Resources – Canadian Edition* (6th ed.), Scarborough: Nelson Learning.

Belmonte, N. 2002. Evolving Negativity: From Hegel to Derrida, *Philosophy and Social Criticism*, vol. 28, no. 1, pp. 18–58.

Benhabib, S. 1981. The Logic of Civil Society: A Reconsideration of Hegel and Marx, *Philosophy & Social Criticism*, vol. 8, no. 2, pp. 151–166.

Benhabib, S. 1985. The Generalised and the Concrete Other: The Kohlberg-Gilligan Controvers and Feminist Theory, *Praxis International*, no. 4, pp. 402–424.

Bennett, W. L. 2007. *News: The Politics of Illusion* (7th ed.), New York: Pearson Longman.
Benson, K. J. 1977. Organizations: A Dialectical View, *Administrative Science Quarterly*, vol. 22, no. 1, pp. 1–21.
Benson, P. 2012. *Tobacco Capitalism: Growers, Migrant Workers, and the Changing Face of Global Industry*, Princeton: Princeton University Press.
Benson, P. & Kirsch, S. 2010a. Corporate Oxymorons, *Dialectical Anthropology*, no. 34, pp. 45–48.
Benson, P. & Kirsch, S. 2010b. Capitalism and the Politics of Resignation, *Current Anthropology*, vol. 51, no. 4, pp. 459–486.
Berger, P. & Luckmann, T. 1967. *The Social Construction of Reality*, New York: Garden City.
Berle, A. A. & Means, G. C. 1933. *The Modern Corporation and Private Property*, New York: Macmillan.
Berlin, I. 1969. Two Concepts of Liberty, in: Berlin, I. (ed.) *Four Essays on Liberty*, London: Oxford University Press.
Bernstein, J. M. 2010. Hegel on Wall Street, *New York Times*, New York, 3 October 2010, http://opinionator.blogs.nytimes.com/2010/10/03/hegel-on-wall-street/
Bertram, G. W. 2008. Hegel und die Frage der Intersubjektivität – Die Phänomenologie des Geistes als Explikation der sozialen Strukturen der Rationalität [Hegel and the Question of Intersubjectivity – The Phenomenology of Spirit as an Explication of the Social Structures of Rationality], *Deutsche Zeitschrift für Philosophie*, vol. 56, no. 6, pp. 877–898.
Bewes, T. 2002. *Reification, or The Anxiety of Late Capitalism*, London: Verso.
Bird, F. B. 1996. *The Muted Conscience – Moral Silence and the Practice of Ethics in Business*, Westport: Quorum Books.
Bird, F. B. & Waters, J. A. 1989. The Moral Muteness of Managers, *California Management Review*, vol. 32, no. 1, pp. 73–88.
Birsch, D. & Fielder, J. H. (eds.) 1994. *The Ford Pinto Case: A Study in Applied Ethics, Business, and Technology*, Albany: State University of New York Press.
Blake, W. 1804. *Jerusalem – The Emanation of the Giant Albion* (edited with an introduction and notes by Morton D. Paley), London & Princeton: William Blake Trust/Princeton University Press (1991).
Blaschke, S. 1974. Natürliche Sittlichkeit und bürgerliche Gesellschaft. Hegels Konstruktion der Familie als sittliche Intimität im entsittlichten Leben [Natural Morality and Civil Society. Hegel's Construction of the Family as a Moral Intimacy in a De-moralised Life], in: Riedel, M. (ed.) *Materialien zu Hegel's Rechtsphilosophie* [*Resources to Hegel's Philosophy of Right*], vol. 2, Frankfurt: Suhrkamp Press.
Blass, T. 1991. Understanding Behavior in the Milgram Obedience Experiment: The Role of Personality, Situations, and their Interactions, *Journal of Personality and Social Psychology*, vol. 60, no. 3, pp. 398–413.
Blass, T. 2002. The Man Who Shocked the World, *Psychology Today*, March/April, pp. 68–74.
Blauner, R. 1964. *Alienation and Freedom – The Factory Worker and His Industry*, Chicago: Chicago University Press.
Bloch, E. 1962. Hegel und die Anamnesis, *Hegel-Studien Beiheft 1* (Heidelberger Hegel-Tage 1962 – Vorträge und Dokumente), Bonn: Bouvier Press.
Boatright, J. R. 2009. *Ethics and the Conduct of Business* (6th ed.), London: Pearson.

Bobbio, N. 1974. Hegel und die Naturrechtslehre [Hegel and the Philosophy of Nature], in: Riedel, M. (ed.) *Materialien zu Hegel's Rechtsphilosophie* [*Resources to Hegel's Philosophy of Right*], vol. 2, Frankfurt: Suhrkamp Press.
Boddy, C. R. 2006. The Dark Side of Management Decisions: Organisational Psychopaths, *Management Decisions*, vol. 44, no. 10, pp. 1461–1475.
Boggs, C. 2012. *Empire Versus Democracy: The Triumph of Corporate and Military Power*, London: Routledge.
Bogle, J. C. 2005. *The Battle for the Soul of Capitalism*, New Haven: Yale University Press.
Bohler, K. F. 2009. Berufsethische Elemente von Professionalität in der Jugendhilfe, in: Becker-Lenz, R. (ed.) *Berufsethische Elemente von Professionalität in der Jugendhilfe*, Wiesbaden: VS Verlag für Sozialwissenschaften Press.
Bohman, J. 2010. Is Hegel a Republican? Pippin, Recognition, and Domination in the Philosophy of Right, *Inquiry*, vol. 53, no. 5, pp. 435–449.
Bohnert, Jo. & Bohnert, Jü. 1981. Hegels Darstellung der bürgerlichen Gesellschaft im Naturrechtsaufsatz von 1802, *Zeitschrift für philosophische Forschung* [*Journal of Philosophical Research*], vol. 35, no. 3/4, special issue for Hegel's 150th anniversary [Zum 150. Todestag von Georg Friedrich Wilhelm Hegel], pp. 531–551.
Bolchover, D. 2005. *The Living Dead – Switched off Zoned Out, The Shocking Truth about Office Life*, Chichester: Capstone Press.
Boltanski, L. & Chiapello, E. 2005. *The New Spirit of Capitalism* (transl. by Gregory Elliott), London: Verso.
Bolton, S. 2012. *Dimensions of Dignity at Work*, London: Routledge.
Bolton, S. C. & Houlihan, M. (eds.) 2008. *Searching for the Human in Human Resource Management*, Basingstoke: Palgrave.
Bondeli, M. 1998. Zur Friedensstiftenden Funktion der Vernunft bei Kant und Hegel [On Kant's and Hegel's Peace Establishing Function of Reason], *Hegel-Studien*, vol. 33, pp. 153–175.
Bonnafous-Boucher, M. & Porcher, S. 2010. Towards a Stakeholder Society: Stakeholder Theory vs. Theory of Civil Society, *European Journal of Management*, vol. 7, no. 4, pp. 205–216.
Bookchin, M. 1962. *Our Synthetic Environment*, New York: Knopf.
Bookchin, M. 1982. *The Ecology of Freedom: The Emergence and Dissolution of Hierarchy*, Palo Alto: Cheshire Books.
Bookchin, M. 1990. *The Philosophy of Social Ecology: Essays on Dialectical Naturalism*, Montréal: Black Rose Books.
Bookchin, M. 1995. *Re-Enchanting Humanity: A Defense of the Human Spirit against Antihumanism, Misanthropy, Mysticism, and Primitivism*, London: Cassell.
Bookchin, M. 2001. What is Social Ecology?, in: Boylan, M. (ed.) *Environmental Ethics*, New Jersey: Prentice Hall.
Bookchin, M. & Foreman, D. 1991. *Defending the Earth*, New York: Black Rose Books.
Boorstein, E. 1977. *Allende's Chile: An Inside View*, New York: International Publishers.
Bordignon, M. 2013. Contradiction or Not-contradiction? This is the Problem, in: Arndt, M. (ed.) *Hegel-Jahrbuch 2013*, Berlin: deGruyter Press, pp. 163–170.
Bose, P. 2010. General Electric, Corporate Personhood, and the Emergence of the Professional Manager, in: Bose, P. & Lyons, L. E. (eds.) *Cultural Critique and the Global Corporation*, Bloomington: Indiana University Press.
Bose, P. & Lyons, L. E. (eds.) 2010. *Cultural Critique and the Global Corporation*, Bloomington: Indiana University Press.

Bourdieu, P. 2000. *Pascalian Meditations*, Cambridge: Cambridge University Press.
Bourdieu, P. & Accardo, A. 1999. *The Weight of the World: Social Suffering in Contemporary Society*, Cambridge: Polity Press.
Bové, P. A. 1986. *Intellectuals in Power: A Genealogy of Critical Humanism*, New York: Columbia University Press.
Bowie, N. E. 1999. *Business Ethics – A Kantian Perspective*, Oxford: Blackwell.
Bowles, S. & Gintis, H. 1976. *Schooling in Capitalist America: Educational Reform and the Contradictions of Economic Life*, New York: Basic Books.
Bramel, C. & Friend, R. 1981. Hawthorne, The Myth of the Docile Worker, and Class Bias in Psychology, *American Psychologist*, vol. 36, no. 8, pp. 867–878.
Braverman, H. 1974. *Labor and Monopoly Capital – The Degradation of Work in the Twentieth Century*, New York: Monthly Review Press.
Brecht, B. & Ottwald, E. 1932. *Kuhle Wampe Oder: To Whom Does the World Belong?* (*Wem gehört die Welt?*), Movie Release Date: 23 April 1933 (USA).
Breckman, W. 2001. Eduard Gans and the Crisis of Hegelianism, *Journal of the History of Ideas*, vol. 62, no. 3, pp. 543–564.
Brennan, J. J., Valtz, J. J., Shallenberger, J. B. & Stanton, V. P. 1961. How Ethical Are Businessmen?, *Harvard Business Review*, (July–August), pp. 6–16 & 158–176.
Brenner, S. N. & Molander, E. A. 1977. Is the Ethics of Business Changing?, *Harvard Business Review*, (January–February), pp. 57–71.
Bridge, G. & Le Billon, P. 2012. *Oil*, Oxford: Polity Press.
Brief, A. 2000. Still Servants of Power, *Journal of Management Inquiry*, vol. 9, no. 4, pp. 342–351.
Brink, B. v. d. 2010. Damaged Life – Power and Recognition in Adorno's Ethics, in: von den Brink, B. & Owen, D. (eds.) *Recognition and Power – Axel Honneth and the Tradition of Critical Social Theory*, Cambridge: Cambridge University Press.
Brooks, T. 2013. *Hegel's Political Philosophy – A Systematic Reading of the Philosophy of Right* (2nd ed.), Edinburgh: Edinburgh University Press.
Brunsson, N. 1985. *The Irrational Organisation*, New York: John Wiley & Sons.
Brunsson, N. 2002. *The Organisation of Hypocrisy – Talk, Decisions and Actions in Organisations* (2nd ed.), Abingdon: Marston Books.
Bryce, R. 2002. *Pipe Dreams – Greed, Ego, and the Death of Enron* (Performance Review Committee), New York: Public Affairs Press.
Buchanan, D. A. 2008. You Stab My Back, I'll Stab Yours: Management Experience and Perceptions of Organization Political Behaviour, *British Journal of Management*, vol. 19, no. 1, pp. 49–64.
Buchanan, D. & Badham, R. 2008. *Power, Politics, and Organisational Change* (2nd ed.), London: Sage.
Buchwalter, A. 1991. Hegel, Marx, and the Concept of Immanent Critique, *Journal of the History of Philosophy*, vol. 29, no. 2, pp. 253–279.
Buchwalter, A. 2012. Hegel, Global Justice, and Mutual Recognition, *Studies in Global Justice*, vol. 10, pp. 211–232.
Buchwalter, A. 2012a. *Dialectics, Politics, and the Contemporary Value of Hegel's Practical Philosophy*, London: Routledge.
Buchwalter, A. 2013. Hegel, Human Rights, and Political Membership, *Hegel-Bulletin*, vol. 34, no. 1, pp. 98–119.
Bunting, M. 2004. *Willing Slaves – How the Overwork Culture Is Ruling Our Lives*, London: Harper Collins Publishers.

Burawoy, M. 1979. *Manufacturing Consent: Changes in the Labor Process under Monopoly Capitalism*, Chicago: University of Chicago Press.

Burawoy, M. 1985. *The Politics of Production*, London: Verso.

Burbidge, J. 1988. Introduction: Jacques D'Hondt's Hegel, in: D'Hondt, J. (ed.) *Hegel and his Time*, Peterborough: Broadview Press.

Burley, H. & Hoedeman, O. 2011. The Best Influence Money can Buy: Presenting the 10 Worst Corporate Lobbyists, *New Internationalist*, January–February [www.newint.com.au/].

Burnham, J. 1945. *The Managerial Revolution*, Harmondsworth: Pengiun Books.

Burnier, M. 1980. *FIAT: conseils ouvriers et syndicat: Turin 1918–1980*, Paris: Éditions ouvrières.

Burris, V. 1988. Reification: A Marxist Perspective, *California Sociologist*, vol. 10, no. 1, pp. 22–43.

Campello, F. 2013. Die Natur der Sittlichkeit - Grundlage einer Theorie der Institutionen nach Hegel [The Nature of Sittlichkeit - Foundations for an Institutional Theory According to Hegel], PhD Dissertation at the Institute of Philosophy at Frankfurt University, 29 January 2013, 186 pages.

Campello, F. 2013a. Leidenschaften und Interessen: Hegel und die kritische Begründung der politischen Ökonomie [Passion and Interest: Hegel's Critical Foundations of Political Economy], *Capa*, vol. 1, no. 1, pp. 226–253 (periodicos.unb.br).

Canfora, L. 2006. *Democracy in Europe – A History of an Ideology*, London: Blackwell.

Capaldi, N. 2005. Corporate Social Responsibility and the Bottom Line, *International Journal of Social Economics*, vol. 32, no. 5, pp. 408–423.

Carr, A. Z. 1968. Is Business Bluffing Ethics?, *Harvard Business Review*, (January–February), pp. 143–153.

Carré, L. 2013. Die Sozialpathologien der Moderne - Hegel und Durkheim im Vergleich, in: Arndt, M. (ed.) *Hegel-Jahrbuch 2013*, Berlin: deGruyter Press, pp. 312–317.

Carroll, A. B. & Buchholtz, A. K. 2012. *Business & Society: Ethics, Sustainability, and Stakeholder Management* (8th ed.), Mason: South-Western, Cengage Learning.

Cascio, W. F. 2000. *Costing Human Resources: The Financial Impact of Behavior in Organizations* (4th ed.), Cincinnati: South-Western College Pub.

Casuso, G. 2013. *Dimensionen der Exklusion: sozialphilosophische Beiträge zu Demokratie und Macht* [*Dimensions of Exclusion: Social-Philosophical Contributions on Democracy and Power*], Freiburg: Alber Verlag (Alber Press).

Chandler, A. 1962. *Strategy and Structure*, Cambridge: MIT Press.

Chandler, A. D. & Mazlish, B. (eds.) 2005. *Leviathans: Multinational Corporations and the New Global History*, Cambridge: Cambridge University Press.

Chevalier-Roignant, B., Trigeorgis, L. & Dixit, A. K. 2011. *Competitive Strategy: Options and Games*, Cambridge: MIT Press.

Chitty, A. 2013. Recognition and Property in Hegel and Early Marx, *Ethical Theory and Moral Practice*, vol. 16, no. 4, pp. 685–697.

Chomsky, N. 1957. *Syntactic Structures*, The Hague: Mouton Press.

Chomsky, N. 1991. *Media Control – The Spectacular Achievements of Propaganda* (2nd ed.), New York: Seven Stories Press.

Chomsky, N. 1999. *Profit over People: Neoliberalism and Global Order*, New York: Seven Stories Press.

Chorafas, D. N. 2014. *Business Efficiency and Ethics: Values and Strategic Decision-making*, New York: Palgrave.

Chriss, J. J. 2012. *Social Control – An Introduction* (2nd ed.), Oxford: Polity Press.

Christensen, D. E. 1986. Kant and Hegel, *Review of Metaphysics*, vol. 40, no. 2, pp. 339–363.

Church, J. 2008. Review of Dean Moyar and Michael Quante's Hegel's Hegel's *Phenomenology* of Spirit: A Critical Guide, in: *Philosophical Reviews*, http://ndpr.nd.edu/recent-reviews/

Clark, B. & Gintis, H. 1978. Rawlsian Justice and Economic Systems, *Philosophy and Public Affairs*, vol. 7, no. 4, pp. 302–325.

Clarke, T. & Branson, D. (eds.) 2012. *The Sage Handbook of Corporate Governance*, Thousand Oaks: Sage.

Cleckley, H. 1976. *The Mask of Sanity – An Attempt to Clarify Some Issues about the So-called Psychopathic Personality*, Saint Louis: The C V Mosby Company.

Clegg, I. 1971. *Workers' Self-management in Algeria*, New York: Monthy Review Press.

Clegg, S. 1981. Organization and Control, *Administrative Science Quarterly*, vol. 26, no. 4, pp. 545–562.

Clegg, S. 1989. *Frameworks of Power*, London: Sage.

Clegg, S. 2014. Managerialism: Born in the USA, *Academy of Management Review*, vol. 39, no. 4, pp. 566–585.

Clements, J. D. 2011. *Corporations are not People: Why They have More Rights Than You Do and What You can Do About It*, San Francisco: Berrett-Koehler Publishers.

Clinard, M. B. 1983. *Corporate Ethics and Crime: The Role of Middle Management*, Beverly Hills: Sage Publications.

Coe, N. M., Dicken, P. & Hess, M. 2008. Introduction: Global Production Networks – Debates and Challenges, *Journal of Economic Geography*, vol. 8, no. 3, pp. 267–269.

Coffee, J. C. 2006. *Gatekeepers: The Professions and Corporate Governance*, Oxford: Oxford University Press.

Cohen, E. D. 2005. *News Incorporated: Corporate Media Ownership and Its Threat to Democracy*, Amherst: Prometheus Books.

Cohen, L. & Winston, J. 2010. *What's the Matter with Kansas?* (a film, 1 videodisc, 90 min.): sd., col.; 4 ¾ cm), Chicago: Tallgrass Productions.

Cohen, P. 1973. *The Gospel According to the Harvard Business School*, Garden City: Doubleday.

Cole, A. 2004. What Hegel's Master/Salve Dialectics Really Means, *Journal of Medieval and Early Modern Studies*, vol. 34, no. 3, pp. 577–610.

Comack, M. 2012. *Wild Socialism: Workers Councils in Revolutionary Berlin, 1918–21*, Lanham: University Press of America.

Comay, R. 2011. *Mourning Sickness – Hegel and the French Revolution*, Stanford: Stanford University Press.

Comte, A. 1853. *Essential Writings on Positivism* (original translation by Harriet Martineau, 1853), reprint 1975 by New York: Harper.

Conard, A. F. 1976. *Corporations in Perspective*, Mineola: Foundation Press.

Congdon, T. 2011. *Money in a Free Society: Keynes, Friedman, and the New Crisis in Capitalism*, New York: Encounter Books.

Cootner, P. H. (ed.) 1964. *The Random Character of Stock Market Prices*, Cambridge: MIT Press.

Corporatewatch. 2012. *The Arguments Against CSR*, London: Corporate Watch, website, accessed: 17 May 2012 (http://www.corporatewatch.org/?lid=2670).

Coser, L. A. 2012. *The Idea of Social Structure: Papers in Honor of Robert K. Merton*, New Brunswick: Transaction Publishers.

Counihan, C. & Siniscalchi, V. (eds.) 2014. *Food Activism: Agency, Democracy and Economy*, London: Bloomsbury.

Crane, A. & Matten, D. 2012. *New Directions in Business Ethics*, Thousand Oaks: Sage Publications.

Cristi, F. R. 1989. Hegel's Conservative Liberalism, *Canadian Journal of Political Science*, vol. 22, no. 4, pp. 717–738.

Crittenden, A. 1984. The Age of 'Me-First' Management, *The New York Times* (Late Edition, East Coast), New York, 19 August 1984, p. A.1.

Croall, H. (ed.) 2009. *Corporate Crime* (Three-Volume Set), London: Sage.

Crompton, R. 2008. *Class and Stratification* (3rd ed.), Cambridge: Polity Press.

Croteau, D. & Hoynes, D. W. 2006. *The Business of Media: Corporate Media and the Public Interest*, Thousand Oaks: Pine Forge Press.

Cullen, B. 1988. The Mediating Role of Estates and Corporations in Hegel's Theory of Political Representation, in: Cullen, B. (ed.) *Hegel Today*, Aldershot: Avebury Press.

Cullen, D. 1997. Maslow, Monekys, and Motivational Theory, *Organization*, vol. 4, no. 3, pp. 355–373.

D'Hondt, J. 1988. *Hegel and his Time*, Peterborough: Broadview Press.

Dahrendorf, R. 1959. *Class and Class Conflict in Industrial Society*, Stanford: Stanford University Press.

Dames, N. 2011. On Hegel, History, and Reading as if for Life: Response, *Victorian Studies*, vol. 53, no. 3, pp. 437–444.

Daniel, T. A. 2009. *Stop Bullying at Work: Strategies and Tools for HR and Legal Professionals*, Alexandria: Society for Human Resource Management.

Darwin, C. 1871. *The Decent of Man, and Selection in Relation to Sex* (2nd ed.), London: John Murray.

Davis, J. S. 1917. *Essays in the Earlier History of American Corporations*, Cambridge: Harvard University Press.

Davis, M. 2007. *Planet of Slums*, London: Verso.

Davis, R. E. 1987. Property and Labour in Hegel's Concept of Freedom, in: Maker, W. (ed.) *Hegel on Economics and Freedom*, Macon: Mercer University Press.

Davis, H. & Silk, A. 1978. *Behavioral and Management Science in Marketing*, New York: Ronald Press.

De Cremer, D. & Tenbrunsel, E. (eds.) 2011. *Behavioral Business Ethics: Shaping an Emerging Field*, New York: Routledge.

Deetz, S. 1992. *Democracy in an Age of Corporate Colonization*, Albany: State University of New York Press.

Defoe, D. 1719. *Robinson Crusoe*, London: Penguin Classics (2003).

Dehesa, G. 2006. *Winners and Losers in Globalisation*, Oxford: Blackwell Press.

Delanty, G. 2004. *Theodor W. Adorno – Four-Volume Set*, London: Sage Press.

Derudder, B. et al. (eds.) 2012. *International Handbook of Globalization and World Cities*, Cheltenham: Edward Elgar.

DeVos, L. 1996. Hegels Enzyklopädie 1827 und 1830: Die Offenheit des Systems? [Hegel's Encyclopedia and the Open System], *Hegel-Studien*, vol. 31, Hamburg: Felix Meiner Press.

DeVos, L. 2006. Institution Familie – Die Ermöglichung einer nicht-individualistischen Freiheit [The Family Institutions – The Ability of Non-individualistic Freedom], *Hegel-Studien*, vol. 41, Hamburg: Felix Meiner Press.
Dickens, C. 1853. *Bleak House* (published monthly: March 1852–September 1853), London: Bradbury & Evans (London Penguin Classics, 2003).
Dickey, L. 1987. *Hegel – Religion, Economics, and the Politics of Spirit 1770–1807*, Cambridge: Cambridge University Press.
Diefenbach, T. 2007. The Managerialistic Ideology of Organisational Change Management, *Journal of Organizational Change Management*, vol. 20, no. 1, pp. 126–144.
Diefenbach, T. 2009. *Management and the Dominance of Managers: An Inquiry Into Why and How Managers Rule our Organisations*, New York: Routledge.
Djelic, M-L. & Vranceanu, R. (eds.) 2009. *Moral Foundations of Management Knowledge*, Cheltenham: Edward Elgar.
Donaldson, T. & Werhane, P. H. 2008. *Ethical Issues in Business: A Philosophical Approach*, Upper Saddle River: Pearson/Prentice Hall.
Doob, C. B. 2013. *Social Inequality and Social Stratification in US Society*, Upper Saddle River: Pearson.
Dorary, B. 1988. *From Taylorism to Fordism – A Rational Madness*, London: Free Association Books.
Drucker, P. F. 1946. *Concept of the Corporation*, New York: John Day Co.
Drucker, P. F. 1971. The New Markets and the New Capitalism, in: Bell, D. & Kristol, I. (eds.) *Capitalism Today*, New York: Basic Books.
Drucker, P. F. 1981. What is Business Ethics, *The Public Interest*, vol. 63 (Spring), pp. 18–36.
Drucker, P. F. 2010. *The Drucker Lectures: Essential Lessons on Management, Society, and Economy* (ed. by Rick Wartzman), New York: McGraw-Hill.
Drydyk, J. 1986. Hegel's Politics: Liberal or Democratic?, *Canadian Journal of Philosophy*, vol. 16, no. 1, pp. 99–122.
Dryzek, J. 1996. *Democracy in Capitalist Times – Ideals, Limits, and Struggles*, Oxford: Oxford University Press.
Dubofsky, M. & Dulles, R. 2010. *Labor in America: A History* (8th ed.), Wheeling: Harlan Davidson.
Dubsky, I. 1970. Hegels Arbeitsbegriff und die idealisitische Dialektik, in: Fetscher, I. (ed.) *Hegel in der Sicht der neueren Forschung* [*Hegel from the Perspective of New Research*], Darmstadt: Wissenschaftliche Buchgesellschaft.
Duignan, B. (ed.) 2013. *Political Parties, Interest Groups, and Elections*, New York: Britannica Educational Publishing.
Dumenil, G. & Levy, D. 2011. *The Crisis of Neoliberalism*, Cambridge: Harvard University Press.
Durkheim, E. 1893. *The Division of Labor in Society*, New York: Free Press (1933).
Durkheim, E. 1897. *Suicide: A Study in Sociology*, New York: The Free Press (1951).
Durkheim, E. 1912. *The Elementary Forms of Religious Life*, translated by Karen E. Fields (1995), New York: Free Press.
Durkheim, E. 1983. Professional Ethics and Civic Morals, in: Baumrin, B. & Freedman, B. (eds.) *Moral Responsibility and the Professions*, New York: Haven Publications.
Dutta, D. K. 2012. Firms in Turbulent Environments and the Competition-Cooperation Paradox: Insights from Hegel's Dialectic, *International Journal of Management Concepts and Philosophy*, vol. 6, no. 4, pp. 280–297.

Eagleton, T. 2011. *Why Marx Was Right*, New Haven: Yale University Press.

Eckhardt, G. M., Dholakia, N. & Varman, R. 2013. Ideology for the 10 Billion: Introduction to Globalization of Marketing Ideology, *Journal of Macromarketing*, vol. 33, no. 1, pp. 7–12.

Eckl, A. 2005. Der Begriff des Eigentums in der Rechtsphilosophy Hegels [The Concept of Property in Hegel's Philosophy of Right], in: Eckl, A. & Ludwig, B. (eds.) *Was ist Eigentum? Philosophische Eigentumstheorien von Platon bis Habermas*, München: Beck Press.

Eckl, A. 2013. Kant and Hegel on Property, in: Luetge, C. (ed.) *Handbook of the Philosophical Foundations of Business Ethics*, Heidelberg: Springer Press.

Edmundts, D. & Horstmann, R-P. 2002. *G. W. F. Hegel – Eine Einführung* [*Hegel and Introduction*], Stuttgart: Reclam-Press.

Edwards, R. 1979. *Contested Terrain*, London: Heinemann.

Eecke ver, W. 1980. Relation Between Economics and Politics in Hegel, in: Verene, D. P. (ed.) *Hegel's Social and Political Thought – The Philosophy of Objective Spirit*, Sussex: Harvester Press.

Eeckhout, P. (ed.) 2009. *Supervision and Authority in Industry: Western European Experiences*, New York: Berghahn Books.

Ehrenreich, B. 2011. *Nickel and Dimed: On (not) Getting by in America*, New York: Picador.

Einarsen, S. (eds.) 2011. *Bullying and Harassment in the Workplace: Developments in Theory, Research, and Practice*, Boca Raton: CRC Press.

Einstein, M. 2012. *Compassion, Inc.: How Corporate America Blurs the Line between What We Buy, Who We are, and Those We Help*, Berkeley: University of California Press.

Eisenstadt, S. N. & Roniger, L. 1980. Patron – Client Relations as a Model of Structuring Social Exchange, *Comparative Studies in Society & History*, vol. 22, no. 1, pp. 42–77.

Ellison, G. 2006. Bounded Rationality in Industrial Organization, in: Blundell, R., Newey, K. W. & Persson, T. (eds.) *Advances in Economics and Econometrics: Theory and Applications, Ninth World Congress*, Cambridge: Cambridge University Press (Internet download: www.hss.caltech.edu).

Elster, J. (ed.) 1998. *Deliberative Democracy*, Cambridge: Cambridge University Press.

Engels, F. 1892. *The Condition of the Working Class in Britain in 1844*, London: Allen & Unwin (reprint 1952).

Enteman, W. F. 1993. *Managerialism: The Emergence of a New Ideology*, Madison: University of Wisconsin Press.

Enzensberger, H. G. 1974. *The Affirmation Industry – On Literature, Politics, and the Media*, New York (1974): Continuum Book, The Seabury Press.

Erickson, M. 2009. *Business and Society*, Oxford: Polity Press.

Escalante, M. S. 2012. *Intersubjektivität und Anerkennung – Hegels Ansatz (1802–07) und seine kritische Auslegung bei Honneth (1992)* [*Inter-subjectivity and Recognition – Hegel's Concept and Honneth's Critical Interpretation*], Frankfurt: Peter Lang.

Estes, R. 1996. *Tyranny of the Bottom Line: Why Corporations Make Good People Do Bad Things*, San Francisco: Berrett-Koehler Publishers.

EWCO. 2010. *Flexible Forms of Work: 'Very Atypical' Contractual Arrangements*, Dublin: European Working Conditions Observatory Report, March 2010, 40 pages.

Ewen, R. B., Smith, P. C. & Hulin, C. L. 1966. An Empirical Test of the Herzberg Two-Factor Theory, *Journal of Applied Psychology*, vol. 50, no. 6, pp. 544–550.

Falke, G. 2008. Anerkennung – Da lacht Hegel [Recognition – Hegel's Laughter], *Frankfurter Allgemeine Zeitung*, no. 287 (8 December 2008), p. 37.

Farber, D. 2002. *Sloan Rules: Alfred P. Sloan and the Triumph of General Motors*, Chicago: University of Chicago Press.

Fatton. R. 1986. Hegel and the Riddle of Poverty: The Limits of Bourgeois Political Economy, *History of Political Economy*, vol. 16, no. 4, pp. 579–600.

Fayol, H. 1916. *Managerialism Industrielle et Generale* (Industrial and General Managerialism), London: Sir I. Pitman & Sons Ltd. (1930).

Feinberg, J. 2007. Psychological Egoism, in: Shafer-Landau, R. (ed.) *Ethical Theory – An Anthology*, Oxford: Blackwell.

Felo, A. J. 2011. Corporate Governance and Business Ethics, in: Brink, A. (ed.) *Corporate Governance and Business Ethics*, Series: Ethical Economy, vol. 39, New York: Springer Press.

Feola, M. 2010. Truth and Illusion in the Philosophy of Right: Hegel and Liberalism, *Philosophy and Social Criticism*, vol. 36, no. 5, pp. 567–585.

Ferrara, A. 1993. *Modernity and Authenticity: A Study in the Social and Ethical Thought of Jean-Jacques Rousseau*, Albany: State University of New York Press.

Ferrarin, A. 2011. Hegel's Aristotle: Philosophy and Its Time, in: Houlgate, S. & Baur, M. (eds.) *A Companion to Hegel*, Oxford: Blackwell.

Ferrell, O. C., Fraedrich, J. & Ferrell, L. 2013. *Business Ethics: Ethical Decision Making and Cases* (9th ed.), Mason: Cengage Press.

Fetscher, I. 1973. Preface, in: Fetscher, I. (ed.) *Hegel in der Sicht der neueren Forschung* [*Hegel from the Perspective of New Research*], Darmstadt: Wissenschaftliche Buchgesellschaft.

Fichte, J. G. 1798. *The System of Ethics* (translated & edited by D. Breazeale & G. Zöller, 2005), Cambridge: Cambridge University Press.

Fields, G. S. 2012. *Working Hard, Working Poor: A Global Journey*, New York: Oxford University Press.

Fink, E. 1977. *Hegel: phänomenologische Interpretation der "Phänomenologie des Geistes* [*Hegel: Phenomenological Interpretation of Phenomenology of Spirit*] (republished in 2012), Frankfurt: Klostermann Publisher.

Finlayson, J. G. 2002. Adorno on the Ethical and the Ineffable, *European Journal of Philosophy*, vol. 10, no. 1, pp. 1–25.

Fischer, G. 2012. Aufstieg und Absturz der deutschen Philosophie [Rise and Decline of German Philosophy], *Professorenforum*, vol. 13, no. 1, pp. 72–81.

Fišera, V. (ed.) 1978. *Workers' Councils in Czechoslovakia, 1968–9: Documents and Essays*, London: Allison & Busby.

Flach, W. 1971. Hegels Bestimmung des Verhältnisses von Freiheit und Gleichheit [Hegel's Definition of the Relationship between Liberty and Equality], *Archiv für Rechts- und Sozialphilosophie*, vol. 57, no. 4, pp. 549–557.

Fleming, P. & Zyglidopoulos, S. C. 2009. *Charting Corporate Corruption: Agency, Structure, and Escalation*, Cheltenham: Edward Elgar.

Flügel-Martinsen, O. 2009. Befragung der Freiheit – Freiheit der Befragung [Questions of Freedom – Freedom of Questioning], *Leviathan*, vol. 37, no. 4, pp. 559–574.

Flynn, J. 2014. System and Lifeworld in Habermas' Theory of Democracy, *Philosophy & Social Criticism*, online before publication.

Foote, D. 2001. The Question of Ethical Hypocrisy in Human Resource Management in the UK and Irish Charity Sectors, *Journal of Business Ethics*, vol. 34, no. 1, pp. 25–38.

Fortner, R. S. & Fackler, P. M. (eds.) 2011. *The Handbook of Global Communication and Media Ethics*, Chichester: Wiley-Blackwell.
Foster, J. E. 1998. Absolute versus Relative Poverty, *American Economic Review*, vol. 88, no. 2, pp. 335–341.
Foster, R. 2007. *Adorno: The Recovery of Experience*, Albany: State University of New York Press.
Foster, R. J. 2010. Corporate Oxymorons and the Anthropology of Corporations, *Dialectical Anthropology*, vol. 1, no. 34, pp. 95–102.
Foucault, M. 1970. *The Order of Things: An Archaeology of the Human Sciences*, London: Tavistock Publications.
Foucault, M. 1980. *Power/Knowledge: Selected Interviews and Other Writings 1972/1977* (edited & translated by Colin Gordon), Brighton: Harvester Press.
Foucault, M. 1995. *Discipline and Punish: The Birth of the Prison*, New York: Vintage Books.
Franco, P. 1999. *Hegel's Philosophy of Freedom*, New Haven: Yale University Press.
Frank, T. 2005. *What's the Matter with Kansas?: How Conservatives won the Heart of America*, New York: Henry Holt.
Fraser, D. 2010. Deskilling: A New Discourse and Some New Evidence, *Economic and Labour Relations Review*, vol. 21, no. 2, pp. 51–74.
Freeman, M. 2011. *Human Rights* (2nd ed.), Oxford: Polity Press.
Freeman, R. E. 1984. *Strategic Management: A Stakeholder Approach*. Boston: Pitman.
Freeman, S. 2000. Deliberative Democracy: A Sympathetic Comment, *Philosophy & Public Affairs*, vol. 29, no. 4, pp. 371–418.
Freire, P. 1970. *Pedagogy of the Oppressed* (transl. by Myra Bergman Ramos), New York: Continuum.
Freire, P. 2000. *Pedagogy of the Oppressed* (30th anniversary edition), New York: Continuum.
French, P. A. 1979. The Corporation as a Moral Person, *American Philosophical Quarterly*, vol. 16, no. 3, pp. 207–215.
Freudenberg, N. 2012. The Manufacture of Lifestyle: The Role of Corporations in Unhealthy Living, *Journal of Public Health Policy* (advance online publication 19 January 2012; www.palgrave-journals.com/jphp/journal/vaop/ncurrent/abs/jphp201160a).
Freyenhagen, F. 2011. Adorno's Ethics without the Ineffable, *Telos*, no. 155, pp. 127–149.
Freyenhagen, F. 2013. *Adorno's Practical Philosophy: Living Less Wrongly*, New York: Cambridge University Press.
Friedman, M. 1970. The Social Responsibility of Business is to Increase its Profits, *The New York Magazine*, 13 September 1970.
Friedrichs, D. O. 2009. *Corporate Personhood and Corporate Decision Making. Trusted Criminals: White Collar Crime in Contemporary Society*, Mason: South-Western-Cengage Learning.
Fritzman, J. M. 2012. *Hegel*, Oxford: Polity Press.
Fromm, E. 1995. *To have or to be?*, London: Abacus.
Fulda, H. F. 1966. Zur Logik der Phänomenologies von 1807 [On the Logic of the *Phenomenology* 1807], *Hegel-Studien*, Beiheft 3, Bonn: Bouvier Press.
Fulda, H. F. 1992. Die Entwicklung des Begriffs in Hegels Rechtsphilosophie [The Development of the Concept in Hegel's 'Philosophy of Right'], in: Angehrn, E. (ed.) *Dialektischer Negativismus: Michael Theunissen zum 60. Geburtstag* [*Dialectical Negativism*], Frankfurt: Suhrkamp Press.

Fulda, H. F. 2001. Hegels Betriff des Absoluten Geistes [Hegel's Concept of the Absolute Spirit], *Hegel-Studien* (*Hegel-Studies*, ed. by Jaeschke & Siep), vol. 36, Hamburg: Meiner Press.

Füredi, F. 2004. *Politics of Fear*, London: Continuum.

Gabler, G. A. 1843. *Die Hegelsche Philosophie – Beiträge zu ihrer richtigen Beurteilung und Würdigung* [*Hegelian Philosophy – Contributions to Its Proper Evaluation and Assessment*], Berlin: Duncker Press (Bayerische Staatsbibliothek Internet download: www.bsb-muenchen-digital.de).

Gabor, A. 2000. *The Capitalist Philosophers*, New York: Time Books/Random House.

Gadamer, H. H. 1966. Die Verkehrte Welt [The World Upside Down], *Hegel-Studien*, Beiheft 3, Bonn: Bouvier Press.

Gadamer, H. H. 1996. Hegel's Dialectic of Self-Consciousness, in: O'Neill, J. (ed.) *Hegel's Dialectic of Desire and Recognition – Texts and Commentary*, Albany: State University of New York Press.

Gaines-Ross, L. 2008. *Corporate Reputation: 12 Steps to Safeguarding and Recovering Reputation*, Hoboken: Wiley.

Galbraith, J. K. 1958. *The Affluent Society*, Boston: Houghton Mifflin.

Galin, A. 1978. *Workers Participation in Management in Israel: Successes and Failures*, Geneva: International Institute for Labour Studies.

Gall, G. 2012. Richard Hyman: An Assessment of his Industrial Relations: A Marxist Introduction, *Capital & Class*, vol. 36, no. 1, pp. 135–149.

Gall, G., Wilkinson, A. & Hurd, R. 2012. *The International Handbook of Labour Unions: Responses to Neo-liberalism*, Cheltenham: Edward Elgar.

Gallagher, S. 1987. Interdependence and Freedom in Hegel's Economics, in: Maker, W. (ed.) *Hegel on Economics and Freedom*, Macon: Mercer University Press.

Galtung, J. 1969. Violence, Peace, and Peace Research, *Journal of Peace Research*, vol. 6, no. 3, pp. 167–191.

Gamble, J. 2015. *Essentials of Strategic Management: The Quest for Competitive Advantage* (4th ed.), New York: McGraw-Hill Education.

Gantman, E. R. 2005. *Capitalism, Social Privilege, and Managerial Ideologies*, Farnham: Ashgate.

Garsten, C. & Hernes, T. 2009. Introduction – Dilemmas of Ethical Organizing, in: Garsten, C. & Hernes, T. (eds.) *Ethical Dilemmas in Management*, London: Routledge.

Gastil, J. & Levine, P. (eds.) 2006. *The Deliberative Democracy Handbook: Strategies for Effective Civic Engagement in the Twenty-First Century*, Burlington: Ashgate.

Gaston, N. & Khalid, A. N. 2010. *Globalization and Economic Integration: Winners and Losers in the Asia-Pacific*, Cheltenham: Edward Elgar.

Gautié, J. & Schmitt, J. 2010. *Low-Wage Work in the Wealthy World*, New York: Russell Sage Foundation.

Gautrey, C. & Phipps, M. 2006. *21 Dirty Tricks at Work*, New York: MJF Books/Fine Communications.

Geis, G. 2011. *White-Collar and Corporate Crime: A Documentary and Reference Guide*, Santa Barbara: Greenwood.

Gellerman, S. W. 1993. Why 'Good' Managers Make Bad Ethical Choices, in: Chryssides, G. D. & Kaler, J. H. (eds.) *An Introduction to Business Ethics*, London: International Thomson Business Press.

Ghoshal, S. 2005. Bad Management Theories Are Destroying Good Management Practices, *Academy of Management Learning & Education*, vol. 4, no. 1, pp. 75–91.

Giacalone, R. A. & Promislo, M. D. (eds.) 2013. *Handbook of Unethical Work Behavior: Implications for Individual Well-Being*, Armonk: M.E. Sharpe.

Gibson-Graham, J. K., Cameron, J. & Healy, S. 2013. *Take Back the Economy: An Ethical Guide for Transforming Our Communities*, Minneapolis: University of Minnesota Press.

Giddens, A. 1979. *Central Problems in Social Theory: Action, Structure and Contradictions in Social Analysis*, Berkeley: University of California Press.

Gilabert, P. 2012. *From Global Poverty to Global Equality: A Philosophical Exploration*, Oxford: Oxford University Press.

Gilbert, B. 2013. *The Vitality of Contradiction: Hegel, Politics, and the Dialectic of Liberal-Capitalism*, Montréal: McGill-Queen's University Press.

Giroux, H. A. & Pollock, G. 2010. *The Mouse that Roared: Disney and the End of Innocence* (2nd student ed.), Lanham: Rowman & Littlefield Publishers.

Giusti, M. A. 1987. *Hegel's Kritik der Modernen Welt* [*Hegel's Critique of the Modern World*], Würzburg: Königsheusen und Neumann Press.

Glockner, H. 1965. Beiträge zum Verständnis und zur Kritik Hegels sowie zur Umgestaltung sein Geisteswelt [Contributions to the Understanding and Critique of Hegel and his Transformation of the World Spirit], *Hegel-Studien – Beiheft 2*, Bonn: Bouvier Press.

Gloy, K. 1985. Bemerkungen zum Kapitel. Herrschaft und Knechtschaft. in Hegels Phanomenologie des Geistes, *Zeitschrift für philosophische Forschung*, vol. 39, no. 2, pp. 187–213.

Godelier, M. 1966. *Rationality and Irrationality in Economics*, New York: Monthly Review Press.

Goh, K-H. 2012. Between Determinism and Indeterminism: The Freedom of Choice in Fichte's Das System der Sittenlehre, *European Journal of Philosophy* (online before publication).

Göhler, G. (ed.) 1974. *Georg Wilhelm Friedrich Hegel – Frühe Politische Systeme* [*Hegel's Early Political Systems*], Frankfurt: Ullstein Press.

Göhler, G. 1974a. Dialektik und Politik in Hegels frühen politischen Systemen. Kommentar und Analysen [Dialectic in Hegel's Early Political and Political Systems – Comment and Analysis], in: Göhler, G. (ed.) *Georg Wilhelm Friedrich Hegel – Frühe politische Systeme* [*G W F Hegel – Early Political Systems*], Frankfurt: Uhlstein Press.

Goldhagen, D. J. 1996. *Hitler's Willing Executioners: Ordinary Germans and the Holocaust*, New York: Knopf & Random House.

Goldhagen, D. J. 2009. *Worse Than War – Genocide, Eliminationism, and the Ongoing Assault on Humanity*, New York: Perseus Books.

Goldman, P. & van Houten, D. R. 1977. Managerial Strategies and the Worker: A Marxist Analysis of Bureaucracy, *Sociological Quarterly*, vol. 18, no. 1, pp. 108–125.

Goldsmith, E. & Mander, J. (eds.) 2001. *The Case Against the Global Economy – And for a Turn towards Localisation*, London: Earthscan Press.

Gore, A. 2007. *The Assault on Reason*, London: Bloomsbury.

Gorter, H. 2007. *Non-leninist Marxism: Writings on the Workers Councils*, St Petersburg (FL): Red and Black Publishers.

Gorz, A. 1982. *Farewell to the Working Class – An Essay on Post-Industrial Socialism*, London: South End Press.

Gottfried, H. 2012. *Gender, Work, and Economy*, Oxford: Polity Press.

Gottschlich, M. 2009. Technische Wissenschaftlichkeit und Entfremdung – Die beobachtende Vernunft in Hegels Phänomenologie des Geistes, *Hegel-Studien – Beiheft 50*, Hamburg: Felix Meidner Press.

Graber, D. 2012. *On Media: Making Sense of Politics*, Boulder: Paradigm Publishers.

Gramsci, A. 1969. *Soviets in Italy*, Nottingham: Institute for Workers' Control.

Gramsci, A. 1971. *Selections from the Prison Notebooks of Antonio Gramsci* (transl. by Quintin Hoare and Geoffrey Nowell Smith), New York: International Publishers & Antonio Gramsci's *Prison Notebooks*, vols. 1–2 (1992–2007), Columbia University Press.

Gray, K. L., Frieder, L. A. & Clark, G. W. 2005. *Corporate Scandals: The Many Faces of Greed – The Great Heist, Financial Bubbles and the Absence of Virtue*, St. Paul: Paragon House.

Greenwald, R. 2004. *Outfoxed: Rupert Murdoch's War on Journalism* (DVD documentary, 78 mins), MoveOn.org-Brave New Films, Release date: 13 July 2004.

Greer, M. R. 1999. Individuality and the Economic Order in Hegel's Philosophy of Right, *European Journal of the History of Economic Thought*, vol. 6, no. 4, pp. 552–580.

Greis, F. 1995. Bürgerliche Gesellschaft zwischen Verstandesstaat und Sittlichkeit: Untersuchungen zur Rechtsphilsophie Hegels [Bourgeois Society between the Rational State and *Sittlichkeit*: Inquiries into Hegel's *Philosophy of Right*], Master Theses (Diplomarbeit: Professor Anzenbacher), Mainz: Johannes Gutenberg University, Faculty of Catholic Theology.

Gross, J. A. 2012. The Human Rights Movement at U.S. Workplaces: Challenges and Changes, *Industrial and Labor Relations Review*, vol. 65, no. 1, pp. 3–16.

Grzybowski, K. 1957. Polish Workers' Councils, *Journal of Central European Affairs*, vol. 17, no. 3, pp. 272–286.

Gupta, A. D. (ed.) 2010. *Ethics, Business, and Society: Managing Responsibly*, Thousand Oaks: Response Books.

Gutmann, A. & Thompson, D. 2004. *Why Deliberative Democracy?*, Princeton: Princeton University Press.

Habermas, J. 1974. Arbeit und Interaction [Labour and Interaction], in: Göhler, G. (ed.) *Georg Wilhelm Friedrich Hegel – Frühe politische Systeme* [*G W F Hegel – Early Political Systems*], Frankfurt: Uhlstein Press.

Habermas, J. 1988. *Structural Transformation of the Public Sphere*, Cambridge: MIT Press (reprint 2006).

Habermas, J. 1996. Labour and Interaction: Remarks on Hegel's Jen Philosophy of Mind, in: O'Neill, J. (ed.) *Hegel's Dialectic of Desire and Recognition – Texts and Commentary*, Albany: State University of New York Press.

Habermas, J. 1997. *The Theory of Communicative Action: Reason and the Rationalisation of Society*, Vols. I & II (reprint), Cambridge: Polity Press.

Habermas, J. 2006. *Political Communication in Media Society*, Key Note at the 56th Annual Conference of the International Communication Association, Dresden (Germany), 19–23 June 2006.

Habermas, J. 2010. Das Konzept der Menschenwürde und die realistische Utopie der Menschenrechte [The Concept of Human Dignity and the Realistic Utopia of Human Rights], *Deutsche Zeitschrift für Philosophie*, vol. 58, no. 3, pp. 343–357.

Hacker, S. J. & Pierson, P. 2010. *Winner-Take-All Politics: How Washington Made the Rich Richer-and Turned Its Back on the Middle Class*, New York: Simon & Schuster.

Haerens, M. & Zott, L. M. 2014. *Corporate Social Responsibility*, Detroit: Greenhaven Press.
Haigh, G. 2006. *Asbestos House: The Secret History of James Hardie Industries*, Melbourne: Scribe.
Hall, T. 2011. Reification, Materialism, and Praxis: Adorno's Critique of Lukács, *Telos*, no. 155, pp. 61–82.
Hamilton, C. & Dennis, R. 2005. *Affluenza – When Too Much is Never Enough*, Sydney: Allen & Unwin.
Hamilton, W. H. 1938. *The Path of Due Process of Law. Ethics*, vol. 48, no. 3, pp. 269–296.
Hampden-Turner, C. M. 1970. *Radical Man*, London: Duckworth.
Hancock, P. & Tyler, M. 2002. Managing Subjectivity and the Dialectics of Self-Consciousness: Hegel and Organisational Theory, *Organization*, vol. 8, no. 4, pp. 565–585.
Harding, N. 2003. *The Social Construction of Management – Texts and Identities*, London: Routledge.
Harms, P. D. & Spain, S. M. 2015. Beyond the Bright Side: Dark Personality at Work, *Applied Psychology*, vol. 64, no. 1, pp. 15–24.
Harris, H. J. 1982. *The Right to Manage: Industrial Relations Policies of American Business in the 1940s*, Madison: University of Wisconsin Press.
Hartman, E. 1996. *Organizational Ethics and the Good Life*, New York: Oxford University Press.
Hartmann, T. 2010. *Unequal Protection: How Corporations Became "People" – And How You Can Fight Back*. San Francisco: Berrett-Koehler.
Hawken, P. 1993. *The Ecology of Commerce – A Declaration of Sustainability*, London: Phoenix.
Hayek, F. A. 1944. *The Road to Serfdom*, London: Routledge.
Hayek, F. A. 1960. *The Constitution of Liberty*, London: Routledge.
Hayek, F. A. 1978. *Liberalism* in his *New Studies in Philosophy, Politics, Economics and the History of Ideas*, London: Routledge.
HBR. 2010. The Management Tip – Three Tips for Achieving Short-Term Career Goals, *Harvard Business Review*, 23 July 2010, http://hbr.org/tip/2010/07/23/three-tips-for-achieving-short-term-career-goals
Hecker, G. F. 2014. *Bandera Electric Cooperative Inc.: Enhancing Quality of Life for 75 Years*, Virginia Beach: The Donning Company Publishers.
Heery, E. 2009. The Representation Gap and the Future of Worker Representation, *Industrial Relations Journal* (Special Issue: Special Tribute Issue to Brian Towers), vol. 40, no. 4, pp. 324–336.
Hegel, G. W. F. 1796. Erstes Systemprogramm des Deutschen Idealismus (First System Programme of German Idealism), in: Hoffmeister, J. (ed.) *Dokumente zu Hegels Entwicklung* (Documents of Hegel's Development), Stuttgart: Fr. Fromanns Press (1936).
Hegel, G. W. F. 1801. *Differenz des Fichteschen und Schellingschen Systems der Philosophie* (Difference of Fichte's and Schelling's System of Philosophy), in: Dietzsch, S. (ed.) *Differenz des Fichteschen und Schellingschen Systems der Philosophie*, Westberlin: Verlag das Europäische Buch (1986).
Hegel, G. W. F. 1803/04. *System of Ethical Life* (edited and translated by T. M. Knox, 1979), Albany: State University of New York Press. marxist.org/reference/hegel

Hegel, G. W. F. 1805/06. *Lectures on the History of Philosophy* (three volumes; transl. by E. Haldane & F. H. Simson), New York: Humanities Press (1968).

Hegel, G. W. F. 1805/06a. *Jena Philosophie des Geistes* [*Jena Philosophy of the Spirit*] (transl. by L. Rauch, 1983). *Hegel and the Human Spirit*, Detroit: Wayne State University Press.

Hegel, G. W. F. 1807. *The Phenomenology of Mind/Spirit*, Mineola: Dover Publications (2003); also: projekt.gutenberg.de/hegel/phaenom/phaenom; Phenomenology of Spirit, in: McNeill, W. & Feldman, K. (eds.) 1998. *Continental Philosophy – An Anthology*, Oxford: Blackwell.

Hegel, G. W. F. 1812–1816. *Science of Logic* (transl. A. V. Miller), London: G. Allen & Unwin (1969); *also known as: The Encyclopedia of the Philosophical Sciences or Enzyclopädie der philosophischen Wissenschaften im Grundrisse.*

Hegel, G. W. F. 1821. *The Philosophy of Right* [*Grundlinien der Philosophie des Rechts*] (translated with notes by T. M. Knox, 1965), Oxford: Clarendon Press. Excerpt, in: McNeill, W. & Feldman, K. (eds.) 1998. *Continental Philosophy – An Anthology*, Oxford: Blackwell & also: www.marxists.org & libcom.org/library/philosophy-right-hegel

Hegel, G. W. F. 1996. Lordship and Bondage, in: O'Neill, J. (ed.) *Hegel's Dialectic of Desire and Recognition – Texts and Commentary*, Albany: State University of New York Press.

Heiman, G. 1971. The Source and Significance of Hegel's Corporate Doctrine, in: Pelczynski, Z. A. (ed.) *Hegel's Political Philosophy – Problems and Perspectives*, Cambridge: Cambridge University Press.

Hemming, L. P. 2014. Hegel: Reproduction as Production, *Theoria & Praxis*, vol. 1, no. 2, pp. 1–13.

Henderson, D. 2001. The Case Against 'Corporate Social Responsibility', *Policy*, vol. 17, no. 2, pp. 28–32 (www.cis.org.au/images/stories/policy-magazine).

Henderson, J., Dicken, P., Hess, M., Coe, N. & Yeung, H. W. C. 2002. Global Production Networks and the Analysis of Economic Development, *Review of International Political Economy*, vol. 9, no. 3, pp. 436–464.

Hennig, E. 2014. *"Ich Will" – Hegel's Darstellung der Differenz der alten und der modenen Welt* [*Hegel and the Difference between the Old and the Modern World*], U3L-Ringvorlesung (Frankfurt University): Sommer-Semester 2014, download: eike-hennig.de/aktuell/Hegel%20Ringvorlesung%20Vortrag.pdf; 30 pages.

Henrich, D. 1971. *Hegel im Kontext* [*Hegel in Context*] (1st new edition, 2010), Frankfurt: Suhrkamp Press.

Henriques, A. 2007. *Corporate Truth – The Limits to Transparency*, London: Earthscan.

Herman, E. S. & Chomsky, N. 1988. *Manufacturing Consent: The Political Economy of the Mass Media*, New York: Pantheon Books.

Herrmann-Pillath, C. & Boldyrev, I. A. 2014. *Hegel, Institutions, and Economics: Performing the Social*, London: Routledge.

Herzberg, F. 1966. *Work and the Nature of Man*, Cleveland: World Publishing.

Herzberg, F. 2011. One More Time: How Do You Motivate Employees?, in: HBR (ed.) *HBR's 10 Must Reads – On Managing People*, Cambridge: Harvard Business School Press.

Herzberg, F., Mausner, B. & Snyderman, B. B. 1959. *The Motivation to Work*, New York: John Wiley.

Herzog, L. 2011. *Inventing the Market. Smith, Hegel, and Political Theory*, DPhil Thesis at New College, Oxford University (unpublished theses).

Herzog, L. 2011a. Wer sind wir, wenn wir arbeiten? Soziale Identität im Markt bei Smith und Hegel [Who are We When We Work? Social Identity at Smith and Hegel], *Deutsche Zeitschrift für Philosophie*, vol. 59, no. 6, pp. 835–852.

Herzog, L. 2013. *Inventing the Market: Smith, Hegel, and Political Theory*, Oxford: Oxford University Press.

Hess, M. 1845. Die Letzten Philsophen [The Last Philosophers], in: Löwith, K. (ed.) 1962. *Die Hegelsche Linke* [*The Left Hegelians*], Stuttgart: Friedrich Frommann Press.

Hessen, R. 1979. *In Defense of the Corporation*, Stanford: Hoover Institution Press & Stanford University.

Hettling, M. 1990. *Reform ohne Revolution: Bürgertum, Bürokratie und kommunale Selbstverwaltung in Württemberg von 1800 bis 1850* [*Reform without Revolution: Civil Society, Bureaucracy, and Communal Self-government in Württemberg between 1800 and 1850*], Göttingen: Vandenhoeck & Ruprecht Press.

Hinchman, L. P. 1984. *Hegel's Critique of the Enlightenment*, Tampa: University of South Florida Press.

Hirata, J. 2011. *Happiness, Ethics and Economics*, London: Routledge.

Hobbes, T. 1651. *Leviathan*, London: Dent.

Hobsbawm, E. J. 1968. *Industry and Empire: An Economic History of Britain since 1750*, London: Weidenfeld & Nicolson (rev. ed. New York: New Press, 1999).

Hoffheimer, M. H. 1995. *Eduard Gans and the Hegelian Philosophy of Law*, Dordrecht: Kluwer Academic Publishers.

Hoffman, M. W. & Moore, J. M. 1982. What is Business Ethics? A Reply to Peter Drucker, *Journal of Business Ethics*, vol. 1, no. 4, pp. 293–300.

Hochschild, A. R. 1983. *The Managed Heart: Commercialization of Human Feeling*, Berkeley: University of California Press

Höfler, M. 2009. Der wahre Geist – Die Sittlichkeit und ihre Auflösung in den Rechtszustand [The True Spirit – Sittlichkeit and their Resolution in the Legal Status], *Hegel-Studien – Beiheft 50*, Hamburg: Felix Meidner Press.

Holderness, C. G. & Sheehan, D. P. 1988. The Role of Majority Shareholders in Publicly Held Corporations: An Exploratory Analysis, *Journal of Financial Economics*, vol. 20, pp. 317–346.

Holmstrom, M. 1989. *Industrial Democracy in Italy: Workers Co-ops and the Self-management Debate*, Aldershot: Avebury.

Holz, H. H. 1968. *Herr und Knecht bei Leibniz und Hegel: Zur Interpretation der Klassengesellschaft* [*Master and Servant in Leibniz and Hegel – An Interpretation of Class Society*], Neuwied: Luchterhand Press.

Holzer, B. 2010. *Moralizing the Corporation: Transnational Activism and Corporate Accountability*, Cheltenham: Edward Elgar.

Honneth, A. 1995. *The Struggle for Recognition – The Moral Grammar of Social Conflicts*, Cambridge: Polity Press.

Honneth, A. 1997. Anerkennung und moralische Verpflichtung, *Zeitschrift für philosophische Forschung*, vol. 51, no. 1, pp. 25–41.

Honneth, A. 2005. Reification: A Recognition-Theoretical View, *Tanner Lectures on Human Values*, Berkeley: University of California, 14–16 March 2005.

Honneth, A. 2007. The Work of Negativity: A Psychoanalytical Revision of the Theory of Recognition, in: Deranty, J-P., Petherbridge, D., Rundell, J. &

Sinderbink, R. (eds.) *Recognition, Work, Politics – New Directions in French Critical Theory*, Ldeiden: Brill Press.

Honneth, A. 2007a. Gerechtigkeit und kommunikative Freiheit. Überlegungen im Anschluss an Hegel [Justice and Communicative Freedom – Further Reflections on Hegel], *Eurozine-Journal*, http://www.eurozine.com/articles/2007-01-17-honneth-de.html

Honneth, A. 2008. Über Arbeit. Tun und Lassen [On Work – Doing and Not Doing], *Polar-Online Magazine* (www.polar-zeitschrift.de), vol. 4/2008, pp. 1–7.

Honneth, A. 2008a. *Reification: A New Look*, Oxford: Oxford University Press.

Honneth, A. 2008b. Arbeit und Annerkennung – Versuch einer Neubestimmung [Labour and Recognition – A Re-examination], *Deutsche Zeitschrift für Philosophie*, vol. 56, no. 3, pp. 327–341.

Honneth, A. 2011. *Das Recht auf Freiheit – Grundriss einer demokratischen Sittlichkeit* [*The Right to Freedom – Outline of a Democratic Morality*, German Leseproble www.suhrkamp.de], Frankfurt: Suhrkamp Press.

Honneth, A. 2014. *Freedom's Right – The Social Foundations of Democratic Life*, New York: Columbia University Press.

Hoopes, J. 2011. *Corporate Dreams: Big Business in American Democracy from the Great Depression to the Great Recession*, New Brunswick: Rutgers University Press.

Horkheimer, M. 1972. *Critical Theory – Selected Essays* (transl. by M. J. O'Connell et al.), New York: Herder.

Horowitz, I. L. 1966. The Hegelian Concept of Political Freedom, *Journal of Politics*, vol. 28, no. 1, pp. 3–28.

Horstmann, R. P. 1974. Über die Rolle der bürgerlichen Gesellschaft in Hegels politischer Philosophie [On the Role of Civil Society in Hegel's Political Philosophy], in: Riedel, M. (ed.) *Materialien zu Hegel's Rechtsphilosophie* [*Resources to Hegel's Philosophy of Right*], vol. 2, Frankfurt: Suhrkamp Press.

Hösle, V. 1987. *Hegels System – Der Idealismus der Subjektivität und das Problem der Intersubjektivität, Band 1: Systementwicklung und Logik* [*Hegel's System – Idealism and Subjectivity and the Problem of Inter-subjectivity, vol. 1: Development of the System and Logic*] & *Band 2: Philosophie der Natur und des Geistes* [*Philosophy of Nature and Spirit*], Hamburg: Felix Meidner Press.

Houlgate, S. (ed.) 1998. *Hegel and the Philosophy of Nature*, Albany: State University of New York Press.

Houlgate, S. 2009. Phänomenologie, Philosophie und Geschichte: Zu Hegels Deutung der französischen Revolution [Phenomenology, Philosophy and history: On Hegel's Interpretation of the French Revolution], *Hegel-Studien – Beiheft 50*, Hamburg: Felix Meidner Press.

Houlgate, S. 2010. Logic, Spirit, and Freedom in the State: Appreciative and Critical Thoughts on Adriaan Peperzak's Modenr Freedom, *Continental Philosophy Review*, vol. 43, no. 2, pp. 293–305.

Houlgate, S. 2011. G.W.F Hegel: An Introduction to His Life and Thought, in: Houlgate, S. & Baur, M (eds.) *The Blackwell Companion to Hegel*, Oxford: Wiley-Blackwell.

Hubig, C. 2001. Macht und Dynamik der Technik – Hegel's verborgene Technikphilosophie [Power and Dynamics of Technology – Hegel's Hidden Philosophy of Technology], in: Bubner, R. (ed.) *Die Weltgeschichte – Das Weltgericht?* [*World History – World Court?*], Stuttgart Hegel-Congress 1999, Stuttgart: Klett-Cotta Press.

Huff, M. 2011. *Censored 2012: Sourcebook for the Media Revolution: The Top Censored Stories and Media Analysis of 2010–2011*, New York: Seven Stories.

Humphries, J. 2010. *Childhood and Child Labour in the British Industrial Revolution*, Cambridge: Cambridge University Press.

Hunt, E. K. & Lautzenheiser, M. 2011. *History of Economic Thought: A Critical Perspective* (3rd ed.), Armonk: M.E. Sharpe.

Hunt, G. 1988. Hegel and Economic Science, in: Cullen, B. (ed.) *Hegel Today*, Aldershot: Avebury Press.

Husamim, Z. I. 1978. Marx on Distributive Justice, *Philosophy & Public Affairs*, vol. 8, no. 1, pp. 27–64.

Husserl, E. 1936. *The Crisis of European Sciences and Transcendental Phenomenology; An Introduction to Phenomenological Philosophy* (transl. by David Carr, 1970), Evanston: Northwestern University Press.

Hutchings, K. 2010. *Global Ethics: An Introduction*, Cambridge: Polity Press.

Hutchings, K. 2015. Hegel, Georg Wilhelm Friedrich (1770–1831), in: Gibbons, M. T. (ed.) *Encyclopaedia of Political Thought*, Milton: John Wiley.

Huzzard, T. & Östergren, K. 2002. When Norms Collide: Learning under Organizational Hypocrisy, *British Journal of Management*, vol. 13, no. S2, pp. S47–S59.

Hyder, D. & Rheinberger, J. (eds.) 2010. *Science and the Life-World: Essays on Husserl's Crisis of European Sciences*, Stanford: Stanford University Press.

Hyman, R. 1979. *Industrial Relations*, London: Macmillan.

Hyman, R. 1987. Strategy or Structure, *Work, Employment & Society*, vol. 1, no. 1, pp. 25–55.

Hyman, R. 1989. *The Political Economy of Industrial Relations*, London: Macmillan.

Hyppolite, J. 1996. Self-Consciousness and Life: The Independence of Self-Consciousness, in: O'Neill, J. (ed.) *Hegel's Dialectic of Desire and Recognition – Texts and Commentary*, Albany: State University of New York Press.

Ikäheimo, H. & Laitinen, A. 2010. Analyzing Recognition: Identification, Acknowledgement, and Recognitive Attitudes towards Persons, in: Brink, B. v-d & Owen, D. (eds.) *Recognition and Power – Axel Honneth and the Tradition of Critical Social Theory*, Cambridge: Cambridge University Press.

Ilting, H-K. 1973. Die Sprache der Revolution [The Language of Revolution], *Der Spiegel*, no. 13, pp. 142–145.

Ilting, H-K. 1974. Die Struktur der Hegelschen Rechtsphilosophie [The Structure of Hegel's Philosophy of Right], in: Riedel, M. (ed.) *Materialien zu Hegel's Rechtsphilosophie* [*Resources to Hegel's Philosophy of Right*], vol. 2, Frankfurt: Suhrkamp Press.

Ilting, H-K. 1974a. Hegels Auseinandersetzung mit der aristotelischen Politik [Hegel's Debate of Aristotle's Politics], in: Göhler, G. (ed.) *Georg Wilhelm Friedrich Hegel – Frühe Politische Systeme* [*Hegel's Early Political Systems*], Frankfurt: Ullstein Press.

Ilting, H-K. 1975. *Die Struktur der Hegelschen Rechtsphilosophie* [*The Structure of Hegel's Philosophy of Right*], Frankfurt: Suhrkamp Press.

Inwood, M. 1992. *The Hegel Dictionary*, Oxford: Blackwell Press.

Jackall, R. 1988. *Moral Mazes – The World of Corporate Managers*, Oxford: Oxford University Press.

Jackall, R. 2006. *Moral Mazes – The World of Corporate Managers* (20th anniversary edition), Oxford: Oxford University Press.

Jackson, M. W. 1986. Bureaucracy in Hegel's Political Theory, *Administration & Society*, vol. 18, no. 2, pp. 139–157.

Jackson, S. E., Schuler, R. S. & Werner, S. 2012. *Managing Human Resources* (11th ed.), Mason: South Western Cengage Learning.

Jackson, T. 2011. *International Management Ethics*, Cambridge: Cambridge University Press.

Jacoby, R. 1977. *Social Amnesia: A Critique of Conformist Psychology from Adler to Laing*, Hassocks: Harvester Press.

Jacoby, R. 1997. *Social Amnesia – A Critique of Contemporary Psychology*, London: Transaction Publishers.

Jameson, F. 2010. *The Hegel Variations – On the Phenomenology of Spirit*, London: Verso.

Janis, I. L. 1982. *Groupthink*, Boston: Houghton Mifflin Press.

Janis, I. L. 1985. *Victims of Groupthinking*, Boston: Houghton Mifflin Press.

Jaros, S. 2014. Managerialism – Book Review on Klikauer's Managerialism, *Management Learning*, vol. 45, no. 2, pp. 238–242.

Jennings, M. M. 2012. *Business Ethics: Case Studies and Selected Readings* (7th ed.), Mason: South-Western, Cengage Learning.

Jessop, B. 2012. Marxist Approach to Power, in: Amenta, E., Nash, K. & Scott, A. (eds.) *The Wiley-Blackwell Companion to Political Sociology*, Oxford: Blackwell Publisher.

Jobrack, B. 2011. *Tyranny of the Textbook: An Insider Exposes how Educational Materials undermine Reforms*, Lanham: Rowman & Littlefield Publishers.

Johnsen, R. 2010. 'Is Your Manager a Psychopath? … Are You?' The Human-Animal Divide at Work, in: Muhr, S. L., Sorensen, B. M. & Vallentin, S. (eds.) *Ethics and Organisational Practice*, Cheltenham: Edward Elgar.

Johnson, E. G. 2012. *Organisational Ethics – A Practical Approach* (2nd ed.), Thousand Oaks: Sage.

Jones, G. R. & George, J. M. 2011. *Essentials of Contemporary Management* (4th ed.), New York: McGraw-Hill.

Jones, O. 2011. *Chavs: The Demonization of the Working Class*, London: Verso.

Jossa, B. 2014. *Producer Cooperatives as a New Mode of Production*, London: Routledge.

Kaletsky, A. 2009. Goodbye, Homo Economicus, *Real-World Economics Review*, issue no. 50, pp. 151–156 (www.paecon.net/PAEReview/issue50/Kaletsky50.pdf).

Kalleberg, A. L. 2011. *Good Jobs, Bad Jobs: The Rise of Polarized and Precarious Employment Systems in the United States, 1970s to 2000s*, New York: Russell Sage Foundation.

Kant, I. 1781. Critique of Pure Reason, in: McNeill, W. & Feldman, K. (eds.), 1998. *Continental Philosophy – An Anthology*, Oxford: Blackwell.

Kant, I. 1785. *Groundwork of the Metaphysics of Morals* (translated and edited by Mary Gregor and Jens Timmermann; with an introduction by Christine M. Korsgaard, 2012), Cambridge: Cambridge University Press.

Kant, I. 1788. *The Critique of Practical Reason*, eBooks, Project Gutenberg.

Kant, I. 1790. *Critique of Judgement*, Indianapolis (1987): Hackett Publishing Co.

Kaplan, R. S. & Norton, D. P. 1992. The Balanced Scorecard: Measures that Drive Performance, *Harvard Business Review*, January–February, pp. 71–80.

Kaplan, R. S. & Norton, D. P. 1993. Putting the Balanced Scorecard to Work, *Harvard Business Review*, September–October, pp. 2–16.

Kaplan, R. S. & Norton, D. P. 2004. The Strategy Map: Guide to Aligning Intangible Assets. *Strategy & Leadership*, vol. 32, no. 5, pp. 10–17.

Karlins, M. & Andrews, L. M. 1972. *Man Controlled – Readings in the Psychology of Behavior Control*, New York: The Free Press.

Kasser, T. 2002. *The High Price of Materialism*, Cambridge: Bradford Books/MIT Press.

Kastner, H. 2008. Noch Einmal: Die Einstellung des Monarchen – oder Hegels "versteckte" Demokratietheorie [Once More: The Attitude of the Monarch – Or Hegel's Hidden Theory of Democracy], *Hegel-Studien* (*Hegel-Studies*, ed. by Jaeschke & Siep), vol. 43, Hamburg: Meiner Press.

Kaswan, M. J. 2014. *Happiness, Democracy, and the Cooperative Movement: The Radical Utilitarianism of William Thompson*, Albany: State University of New York Press.

Katz, D. R. 1994. *Just Do It: The Nike Spirit in the Corporate World*, New York: Random House.

Katz, E. (ed.) 2006. *Death by Design: Science, Technology, and Engineering in Nazi Germany*, New York: Pearson Longman.

Katz-Fishman, W. & Scott, J. 2012. Wage Labor, in: *Wiley-Blackwell Encyclopedia of Globalization*, http://onlinelibrary.wiley.com/book/10.1002/9780470670590 (published online: 29 February 2012).

Kauffmann, E. 2009. The Political Writings of Max Weber: The Challenge of Freedom, *Max Weber Studies*, vol. 9, no. 1–2, pp. 143–163.

Kearns, P. 2007. *The Value Motive: The Only Alternative to the Profit Motive*, Hoboken: John Wiley.

Keller, D. R. (ed.) 2010. *Environmental Ethics – The Big Questions*, Oxford: Blackwell.

Kelly, G. A. 1969. *Idealism, Politics, and History – Sources of Hegelian Thought*, Cambridge: Cambridge University Press.

Kemple, T. M. 2007. Spirits of Late Capitalism, *Theory, Culture & Society*, vol. 24, no. 3, pp. 147–159.

Kerbo, H. R. 2012. *Social Stratification and Inequality: Class Conflict in Historical, Comparative, and Global Perspective* (8th ed.), New York: McGraw-Hill.

Kerfoot, D. & Knights, D. 1993. Management, Masculinity and Manipulation: From Paternalism to Corporate Strategy in Financial Services in Britain, *Journal of Management Studies*, vol. 30, no. 4, pp. 659–677.

Kersting, W. 1988. *Polizei und Korporation in Hegels Darstellung der burgerlichen Gesellschaft* [*Police and Corporation in Hegel's View of the Bourgeois Society*], Hegel-Jahrbuch (Hegel-Yearbook), pp. 373–382, original pre-submission manuscript forwarded: 14 February 2012, 10 pages.

Kersting, W. 1988L. *Polizei und Korporation in Hegels Darstellung der burgerlichen Gesellschaft*, Kiel: Public Lecture, Private Corespondence (email: 14 February 2012).

Kervégan, J. F. 2008. Jenseits der Democratie [Beyond Democracy], *Deutsche Zeitschrift für Philosophie*, vol. 56, no. 2, pp. 223–243.

Khurana, T. (ed.) 2013. *The Freedom of Life – Hegelian Perspectives: Freiheit und Gesetz III* [*Freedom and Law III*], Berlin: August Press.

Kiechel, W. 2010. *The Lords of Strategy: The Secret Intellectual History of the New Corporate World*, Boston: Harvard Business Press.

Kieran, M. 1997. *Media Ethics: A Philosophical Approach*, Westport: Praeger.

Kiesch, P. 2002. *Über Karl Marx – "Zur Kritik der Hegelschen Rechtsphilosophy"* [*On Karl Marx – A Critique of Hegel's Philosophy of Right*], Munich: Grin Press.

Killian, R. A. 1976. *Human Resource Management: An ROI Approach*, New York: AMACOM.
Klein, N. 2000. *No Logo: Taking Aim at the Brand Bullies*, New York: Picador.
Kleinberg Neimark, M. 1995. The Selling of Ethics – The Ethics of Business Meets the Business of Ethics, *Accounting, Auditing & Accountability Journal*, vol. 8, no. 3, pp. 81–96.
Kliger, I. 2014. Hegel's Political Philosophy and the Social Imaginary of Early Russian Realism, *Studies in East European Thought* (published online: 15 March 2014), pp. 1–11.
Klikauer, T. 2007. *Communication and Management at Work*, Basingstoke: Palgrave.
Klikauer, T. 2008. *Management Communication – Communicative Ethics and Action*, Basingstoke: Palgrave.
Klikauer, T. 2010. *Critical Management Ethics*, Basingstoke: Palgrave.
Klikauer, T. 2011. Management and Emancipation – Two Opposing Ideas: The Oxford Handbook of Critical Management Studies, *International Journal of Social Economics*, vol. 38, no. 6, pp. 573–580.
Klikauer, T. 2012. *Seven Management Moralities*, Basingstoke: Palgrave.
Klikauer, T. 2012a. Evolution, Altruism, and Human Behaviour, *Organization*, vol. 19, no. 6, pp. 939–940.
Klikauer, T. 2013. *Managerialism – Critique of an Ideology*, Basingstoke: Palgrave.
Klikauer, T. 2013a. Companioning Hegel, *The Owl of Minerva*, vol. 44, no. 1/2, pp. 154–168.
Klikauer, T. 2013b. Hegel on Profits, Poverty, and Politics, *Radical Philosophy Review*, vol. 16, no. 3, pp. 789–799.
Klikauer, T. 2014. Emancipatory Education – A Review Essay, *Australian University Review*, vol. 56, no. 1, pp. 91–96.
Klikauer, T. 2014a. Human Resource Management & Kohlberg's Scale of Moral Development, *Philosophy of Management*, vol. 13, no. 1, pp. 73–95.
Klikauer, T. 2014b. Hierarchy in Organisations, *International Journal of Social Economics*, vol. 41, no. 8, pp. 714–719.
Klikauer, T. 2014c. *Seven Human Resource Management Moralities*, Basingstoke: Palgrave.
Klikauer, T. 2015. Critical Management Studies and Critical Theory: A Review, *Capital & Class*, vol. 39, no. 2, pp. 197–220.
Knights, D. & Morgan, G. 1991. Corporate Strategy, Organizations, and Subjectivity: A Critique, *Organization Studies*, vol. 12, no. 2, pp. 251–273.
Knowles, D. 1983. Hegel on Property and Personality, *The Philosophical Quarterly*, vol. 33, no. 130, pp. 45–62.
Knox, T. M. 1940. Hegel and Prussianism, *Philosophy*, vol. 15, no. 57, pp. 51–63.
Kohlberg, L. 1958. *The Development of Modes of Thinking and Choices in Years 10 to 16*, PhD Thesis at the University of Chicago (San Francisco: Harper & Row, 1981).
Kohlberg, L. 1971. From Is to Ought, in: Mishel, T. (ed.) *Cognitive Development and Epistemology*, New York: Academic Press.
Kohlberg, L. 1973. The Claim to Moral Adequacy of a Highest Stage of Moral Judgement, *The Journal of Philosophy*, vol. 70, no. 18, pp. 630–646.
Kohlberg, L. 1981 & 1984. *Essays on Moral Development* (vols. 1 & 2), San Francisco: Harper & Row.
Kohlberg, L. & Kramer, R. 1969. Continuities and Discontinuities in Child and Adult Moral Development, *Human Development*, vol. 12, pp. 93–120.

Kohn, A. 1999. *Punished By Rewards: The Trouble with Gold Stars, Incentive Plans, A's, Praise, and Other Bribes*, Boston: Houghton-Mifflin.

Kohut, M. R. 2008. *The Complete Guide to Understanding, Controlling, and Stopping Bullies & Bullying at Work: A Complete Guide for Managers, Supervisors, and Co-Workers*, Ocala: Atlantic Publishing Group.

Kojève, A. 1947. *Introduction to the Reading of Hegel*, Ithaca (1969): New York: Basic Books and Cornell University Press (1986).

Kojève, A. 1996. Desire and Work in the Master and Slave, in: O'Neill, J. (ed.) *Hegel's Dialectic of Desire and Recognition – Texts and Commentary*, Albany: State University of New York Press.

Kolaja, J. T. 1965. *Workers' Councils: The Yugoslav Experience*, London: Tavistock Publications.

Korsgaard, C. M. 1986. The Right to Lie: Kant on Dealing with Evil, *Philosophy & Public Affairs*, vol. 15, no. 4, pp. 325–349.

Korsgaard, C. M. 1996. *Creating the Kingdom of Ends*, Cambridge: Cambridge University Press.

Korton, D. C. 1995. *When Corporations Rule the World*, West Hartford: Kumarian Press.

Koslowski, P. (ed.) 2010. *Elements of a Philosophy of Management and Organization*, Heidelberg: Springer.

Koslowski, S. 2008. Hegel als Theoretiker der bürgerlichen Gesellschaft und des modernen Staates? [Hegel as a Theoretician of Bourgeois Society and the Modern State?], *Archiv für Rechts- und Sozialphilosophie*, vol. 94, no. 1, pp. 86–110.

Kothari, V. B. 2010. *Executive Greed: Examining Business Failures that Contributed to the Economic Crisis*, Basingstoke: Palgrave Macmillan.

Krailsheimer, A. 1980. *Pascal*, Oxford: Oxford University Press.

Kramar, R., Bartram, T. & DeCieri, H. (eds.) 2011. *Human Resource Management in Australia* (4th ed.), Sydney: McGrath-Hill.

Kramar, R., Bartram, T. & DeCieri, H. (eds.) 2014. *Human Resource Management in Australia* (5th ed.), Sydney: McGrath-Hill.

Krebs, D. L. 2008. Morality: An Evolutionary Account, *Perspectives on Psychological Science*, vol. 3, no. 3, pp. 149–172.

Krebs, D. L. 2011. *The Origins of Morality: An Evolutionary Account*, Oxford: Oxford University Press.

Kreitner, R. 2009. *Management* (11th ed.), Boston: Houghton Mifflin Harcourt Publishing.

Kropotkin, P. A. 1902. *Mutual Aid, A Factor of Evolution* (foreword by A. Montagu, *The Struggle for Existence* by T. H. Huxley, new introd. for Garland ed. by E. Kingston-Mann), New York: Garland Pub. (1955 & 1972).

Kumar, D. 2007. *Outside the Box: Corporate Media, Globalization, and the UPS Strike*, Urbana: University of Illinois Press.

Laitinen, A. 2014. Collective Intentionality and Recognition from Others (pp. 213–227), in: Konzelmann, Z., Schmid, A. & Bernhard, H. (eds.) *Institutions, Emotions, and Group Agents – Studies in the Philosophy of Sociality*, vol. 2, Heidelberg: Springer.

Lakebrink, B. 1964. Freiheit und Notwendigkeit in Hegels Philosophie [Freedom and Necessity in Hegel's Philosophy], *Hegel-Studien Beiheft 1* (Heidelberger Hegel-Tage 1962 – Vorträge und Dokumente), Bonn: Bouvier Press.

Lamb, D. 1988. Teleology and Hegel's Dialectic of History, in: Cullen, B. (ed.) *Hegel Today*, Aldershot: Avebury Press.

Landau, P. 1974. Hegels Begründung des Vertragrechts [Hegel's Reasoning for Contractual Law], in: Riedel, M. (ed.) *Materialien zu Hegel's Rechtsphilosophie* [*Resources to Hegel's Philosophy of Right*], vol. 2, Frankfurt: Suhrkamp Press.

Lasch, C. 1977. *Haven in a Heartless World: The Family Besieged*, New York: Basic Books.

Laufer, W. S. 2008. *Recognizing Pershonhood. Corporate Bodies and Guilty Minds: The Failure of Corporate Criminal Liability*. Chicago: University of Chicago Press.

Lazonick, W. 2013. Alfred Chandler's Managerial Revolution, in: *Oxford Handbook of Management Theorists*, Oxford: Oxford University Press.

Leap, T. 2007. *Dishonest Dollars: The Dynamics of White-Collar Crime*, Cornell: Cornell University Press.

Lee, A. 1988. *Call me Roger*, Chicago: Contemporary Books.

Lehmbruch, G. & Schmitter, P. C. 1982. *Patterns of Corporatist Policy-Making*, London: Sage Publications.

Lemov, R. 2006. *World as Laboratory – Experiments with Mice, Mazes and Men*, New York: Hill and Wang.

Lenz, K. 2007. *Georg Wilhelm Friedrich Hegels Begriff von "Selbständigkeit und Unselbständigkeit des Selbstbewustseins" bzw. "Herrschaft und Knechtschaft"* [*Hegel's Concept of Self-determination and Non-self-determination of Self-consciousness or Master and Servant*], Munich: Grin Press.

Leonard, W. N. & Weber, M. G. 1970. Automakers and Dealers: A Study of Criminogenic Market Forces, *Law & Society Review*, vol. 4, no. 3, pp. 407–424.

Levi, P. 1959. *If this is a Man*, New York: Orion Press.

Levine, N. 2012. *Marx's Discourse with Hegel*, Basingstoke: Palgrave.

Levitt, T. 1958. The Dangers of Social Responsibility, *Harvard Business Review*, September–October, pp. 41–50.

Liebrucks, B. 1974. Recht, Moralität und *Sittlichkeit* bei Hegel [Right, Morality, and *Sittlichkeit* in Hegel], in: Riedel, M. (ed.) *Materialien zu Hegel's Rechtsphilosophie* [*Resources to Hegel's Philosophy of Right*], vol. 2, Frankfurt: Suhrkamp Press.

Lindstrom, M. 2005. *Brand Sense: Build Powerful Brands through Touch, Taste, Smell, Sight, and Sound*, New York: Free Press.

Lindstrom, M. 2008. *Buyology: Truth and Lies about Why We Buy*, New York: Doubleday.

Lingafelter, T. 2005. Low Wage Workers and High Housing Costs, *Labor Studies Journal*, vol. 30, no. 2, pp. 41–60.

Lipietz, A. 2013. Fears and Hopes: The Crisis of the Liberal-Productivist Model and Its Green Alternative, *Capital & Class*, vol. 37, no. 1, pp. 127–141.

Locke, R. R. 1996. *The Collapse of the American Management Mystique*, New York: Oxford University Press.

Locke, R. R. 2011. Reform of Financial Education in US Business Schools: An Historian's View, *Real-World Economic Review*, issue no. 58 (www.paecon.net/PAEReview).

Locke, R. R. & Spender, J. C. 2011. *Confronting Managerialism: How the Business Elite and Their Schools Threw Our Lives out of Balance*, London: Zed Books.

Loomis, E. 2015. *Out of Sight: The Long and Disturbing Story of Corporations Outsourcing Catastrophe*, New York: New Press.

Lozano, J. M. 2003. An Approach to Business Ethics, *Ethical Perspectives*, vol. 10, no. 1, pp. 46–65.

López, A. J. 2013. Occupying Reality: Fanon Reading Hegel, *South Atlantic Quarterly*, vol. 112, no. 1, pp. 71–78.

López de Silanes, F., La Porta, R. & Shleifer, A. 1999. Corporate Ownership Around the World, *Journal of Finance*, vol. 54, no. 2, pp. 471–517.

Löwith, K. 1962. *Die Hegelsche Linke* [*The Left Hegelians*], Stuttgart: Friedrich Frommann Press.

Lübbe, H. 1962. *Die Hegelsche Rechte* [*Conservative Hegelianism*], Stuttgart: Friedrich Frommann Press.

Lübbe, H. 1967. Hegels Kritik der politisierten Gesellschaft [Hegel's Critique on a Politicised Society], *Schweizer Monatshefte*, vol. 47, no. 3, pp. 237–251.

Lucardie, P. 2014. *Democratic Extremism in Theory and Practice: All Power to the People*, London: Routledge.

Lukács, G. 1948. Der junge Hegel – Über die Beziehung von Dialektik und Ökonomie (The Young Hegel – On the Relationship between Dialectics and Economy) (vol. 8 of Lukács works) Neuwied: Luchterhand Press; The Young Hegel: Studies in the Relations between Dialectics and Economics (translated from the German by Rodney Livingstone), London: Merlin Press (1975).

Lukács, G. 1974. *Hegels objektiver Idealismus und die Ökonomie* [Hegel's Objective Idealism and Economics], in: Göhler, G. (ed.) *Georg Wilhelm Friedrich Hegel – Frühe politische Systeme* [*G W F Hegel – Early Political Systems*], Frankfurt: Uhlstein Press.

Lukács, G. 1996. Hegel's Economics During the Jena Period, in: O'Neill, J. (ed.) *Hegel's Dialectic of Desire and Recognition – Texts and Commentary*, Albany: State University of New York Press.

Luntz, F. 2007. *Words That Work – It's Not What you Say, It's What People Hear*, New York: Hyperion Press.

Lupton, N. (ed.) 2014. *Humanistic Perspectives on International Business and Management*, Basingstoke: Palgrave.

Lussier, R. N. & Sherman, H. 2014. *Business, Society, and Government Essentials: Strategy and Applied Ethics* (2nd ed.), New York: Routledge.

Macdonald, I. 2011. Cold, Cold, Warm: Autonomy, Intimacy and Maturity in Adorno, *Philosophy Social Criticism*, vol. 37, no. 6, pp. 669–689.

Macdonald, I. 2012. On the 'Undialectical': Normativity in Hegel, *Continental Philosophy Review*, vol. 45, no. 1, pp. 121–141.

Machiavelli, N. 1532. *The Prince* (transl. by Luigi Ricci; revised by E. R. P. Vincent, 1935), London: Oxford University Press.

MacIntyre, A. 1970. *Herbert Marcuse – An Exposition and a Polemic*, New York: Vicing Press.

MacIntyre, A. 1983. Why are the Problems of Business Ethics Insolvable?, in: Baumrin, B. & Freedman, B. (eds.) *Moral Responsibility and the Professions*, New York: Haven Publications.

Macky, K. (ed.) 2008. *Managing Human Resources: Contemporary Perspectives in New Zealand*. Sydney: McGraw Hill.

Maffettone, S. 2010. *Rawls – An Introduction*, Cambridge: Polity Press.

Magee, G. A. 2011. *The Hegel Dictionary*, London: Continuum Press.

Magnuson, J. 2008. *Mindful Economics: How the U.S. Economy Works, Why it Matters, and How it could be Different*, Toronto: Seven Stories Press.

Magnuson, J. 2013. *The Approaching Great Transformation: Toward a Livable Post Carbon Economy*, New York: Seven Stories Press.

Magretta, J. 2012. *What Management is – How It Works and Why It's Everyone's Business*, London: Profile.

Maier, C. 2005. *Hallo Laziness – Why Hard Work Doesn't Pay*, London: Orion Press.
Maihofer, W. 1974. Hegel's Prinzip des modernen Staates [Hegel's Principle of the Modern State], in: Riedel, M. (ed.) *Materialien zu Hegel's Rechtsphilosophie* [*Resources to Hegel's Philosophy of Right*], vol. 2, Frankfurt: Suhrkamp Press.
Maker, W. 1987. Introduction, in: Maker, W. (ed.) *Hegel on Economics and Freedom*, Macon: Mercer University Press.
Mandell, B. 2002. The Privatization of Everything, *New Politics*, vol. 9, no. 1. http://nova.wpunj.edu/newpolitics/issue33/bmande33.htm
Mander, J. 2001. The Rules of Corporate Behaviour, in: Goldsmith, E. & Mander, J. (eds.) *The Case against the Global Economy – And for a Turn towards Localisation*, London: Earthscan Press.
Mann, T. 1948. *Doctor Faustus: The Life of the German Composer, Adrian Leverkühn, as Told by a Friend* (transl. by Lowe-Porter), New York: A. A. Knopf.
Mant, A. 1977. *The Rise and Fall of the British Manager*, London: Macmillan.
March, J. G. & Simon, H. A. 1958. The Dysfunctions of Bureaucracy, in: Pugh, D. S. (eds.) *Organization Theory – Selected Readings*, Harmondsworth: Penguin Books.
Marchand, R. 1991. The Corporation Nobody Knew: Bruce Barton, Alfred Sloan, and the Founding of the General Motors "Family", *Business History Review*, vol. 65, no. 4, pp. 825–875.
Marchand, R. 1998. *Creating the Corporate Soul: The Rise of Public Relations and Corporate Imagery in American Big Business*, Berkeley: University of California Press.
Marcoux, A. M. 2000. *Business Ethics Gone Wrong*, Washington: www.cato.org.
Marcuse, H. 1941. *Reason and Revolution – Hegel and the Rise of Social Theory*, Boston (1961): Beacon.
Marcuse, H. 1964. *Industrialization and Capitalism in the Work of Max Weber*, republished in: Marcuse, H. 1968. *Negations – Essays in Critical Theory*, Boston: Beacon Press.
Marcuse, H. 1966. *One-Dimensional Man: Studies in the Ideology of Advanced Industrial Societies*, Boston: Beacon Press.
Marcuse, H. 1974. Die Jenenser Entwürfe der Hegelschen Sozialphilosophie [Hegel's Jena Conceptions of Social-Philosophy], in: Göhler, G. (ed.) *Georg Wilhelm Friedrich Hegel – Frühe Politische Systeme* [*Hegel's Early Political Systems*], Frankfurt: Ullstein Press.
Marglin, S. 1974. What Do Bosses Do? – The Origins and Functions of Hierarchy in Capitalist Production, *Review of Radical Political Economy*, vol. 6, no. 2, pp. 60–112.
Markell, P. 2003. *Bound by Recognition*, Princeton: Princeton University Press.
Martin, C. R. 2004. *Framed!: Labor and the Corporate Media*, Ithaca: ILR Press.
Martineau, W., Meer, N. & Thompson, S. 2012. Theory and Practice in the Politics of Recognition and Misrecognition, *Res Publica*, vol. 18, no. 1, pp. 1–9.
Marx, K. 1890. *Das Kapital – Kritik der politischen Ökonomie* [*Capital – A Critique of Political Economy*], Hamburg: 4th edited version by F. Engels, reprinted 1986: Berlin: Dietz-Press.
Marx, K. 1996. Critique on Hegel, in: O'Neill, J. (ed.) *Hegel's Dialectic of Desire and Recognition – Texts and Commentary*, Albany: State University of New York Press.
May, S., Cheney, G. & Roper, J. (eds.) 2007. *The Debate over Corporate Social Responsibility*, Oxford: Oxford University Press.
McCally, R. W. 2002. *Patterns of Management Power*, Westport: Quorum Books.

McCarthy, T. 1994. Kantian Constructivism and Reconstructivism: Rawls and Habermas in Dialogue, *Ethics*, vol. 105, no. 1, pp. 44–63.
McChesney, R. W. 2008. *The Political Economy of media: Enduring Issues, Emerging Dilemmas*, New York: Monthly Review Press.
McCurdy, C. W. 1975. Justice Field and the Jurisprudence of Government-Business Relations: Some Parameters of Laissez-Faire Constitutionalism, 1863–1897, *Journal of American History*, vol. 61, no. 4, pp. 970–1005.
McGregor, D. 1960. *The Human Side of Enterprise*, New York: McGraw-Hill.
McGregor, D. 2006. *The Human Side of Enterprise* (updated and with new commentary by Joel Cutcher-Gershenfeld), New York: McGraw-Hill.
McKee, A. 2014. *Management: A Focus on Leaders*, Boston: Pearson.
McKenna, C. D. 2006. *The World's Newest Profession: Management Consulting in the Twentieth Century*, New York: Cambridge University Press.
McKenna, G. & Feingold, S. (eds.) 2014. *Taking Sides – Clashing Views on Political Issues* (18th ed.), New York: McGraw-Hill.
McKenna, T. 2011. Hegelian Dialectics, *Critique*, vol. 39, no. 1, pp. 155–172.
McLaughlin, A. C. 1940. The Court, the Corporation, and Conkling, *American Historical Review*, vol. 46, no. 1, pp. 45–63.
McQueen, H. 2009. *Framework of Flesh – Builders' Labourers Battle for Health & Safety*, Canberra: Ginninderra Press.
Mead, G. H. 1934. *Mind, Self, and Society*, Chicago: University of Chicago Press.
Mele, D. 2011. *Management Ethics Placing Ethics at the Core of Good Management*, Basingstoke: Palgrave Macmillan.
Melman, S. 2001. *After Capitalism – From Managerialism to Workplace Democracy*, New York: Alfred Knopf.
Menke, C. 1992. On the Concept of Recognition: Hegel's Early Theory of Social Differentiation, *Praxis International*, vol. 12, no. 1, pp. 70–82.
Merrill, D. 2000. Hegel's Corporation and Associationalism: Democracy and the Economy, paper presented at the Political Studies Association, UK: *50th Annual Conference*, 10–13 April 2000, London, 22 pages.
Mesch, W. 2005. Sittlichkeit und Anerkennung in Hegels Rechtsphilosophie [Sittlicheit and Recognition in Hegel's Philosophy of Right], *Deutsche Zeitschrift für Philosophie*, vol. 53, no. 3, pp. 349–364.
Miles, R. E. & Snow, C. C. 1978. *Organisational Strategy, Structure & Process*, New York: McGraw-Hill.
Milgram, S. 1963. Behavioral Study of Obedience. *Journal of Abnormal and Social Psychology*, vol. 67, pp. 371–378.
Milgram, S. 1972. Group Pressure and Action Against a Person, in: Karlins, M. & Andrews, L. M. (eds.) *Man Controlled – Readings in the Psychology of Behavior Control*, New York: The Free Press.
Milgram, S. 1973. The Perils of Obedience, *Harpers Magazine*, no. 247, pp. 62–77.
Milgram, S. 1974. *Obedience to Authority*, New York: Harper and Row.
Milgram, S. 1992. *The Individual in a Social World: Essays and Experiments* (edited by John Sabini and Maury Silver, 2nd ed.), New York: McGraw-Hill.
Miller, L. M. 1984. *American Spirit: Visions of a New Corporate Culture*, New York: W. Morrow.
Mills, C. W. 1951. *White Collar: The American Middle Classes*, New York: Oxford University Press.
Mills, C. W. 1956. *The Power Elite*, Oxford: Oxford University Press.

Minkes, J. & Minkes, L. (eds.) 2008. *Corporate and White-Collar Crime*, London: Sage.

Mintzberg, H., Ahlstrand, B. & Lampel, J. 2009. *Strategy Safari: The Complete Guide through the wilds of strategic Management* (2nd ed.), Harlow: FT Prentice Hall.

Mirkinson, J. 2012. Rupert Murdoch at the Leveson Inquiry: Political Power a 'Myth', *The Huffington Post*, www.huffingtonpost.com, Posted: 04/25/2012 4:46 am; Updated: 04/25/2012 10:53 am.

Moggach, D. & Lledman, S-E. 1997. Hegel and the Enlightenment Project, *European Legacy*, vol. 2, no. 3, pp. 538–543.

Monbiot, G. 2008. *Bring on the Apocalypse – Six Arguments for Global Justice*, London: Atlantic Books.

Monk, R. 1997. *Just Managing*, Sydney: McGraw-Hill.

Moore, B. 1966. *Social Origins of Dictatorship and Democracy – Lord and Peasant in the Making of the Modern World*, Boston: Beacon Press.

Moore, M. 1989. *Roger and Me* (TV documentary), Hollywood: Warner Brothers.

Morgan, E. P. 2010. *What Really Happened to the 1960s: How Mass Media Culture Failed American Democracy*, Lawrence: University Press of Kansas.

Morgan, G. 1986. *Images of Organisations*, London: Sage.

Morgan, G. 1993. *Imaginization – The Art of Creative Management*, London: Sage.

Morse, G. 2004. Executive Psychopaths, *Harvard Business Review*, October 2004, pp. 20–21.

Mortiz, E. 1839. *Eine gegen Hegel gerichtete Anklage des Hochverrats, aus dessen Schriften beantwortet* [*An Indictment of Treason Directed against Hegel, Answered from His Writings*], Breslau: Ferdinand Hirt Press.

Moser, M. 2003. *Hegels Schüler C. L. Michelet: Recht und Geschichte jenseits der Schulteilung* [*Hegel's Student: C. L. Michelet: Right and History beyond Divisions*], Berlin: Duncker und Humblot Press.

Moyar, D. 2013. How the Good Obligates in Hegel's Conception of *Sittlichkeit*: A Response to Robert Stern's *Understanding Moral Obligation*, *Inquiry*, vol. 5, no. 6, pp. 584–605.

Mumby, D. 1997. The Problem of Hegemony: Reading Gramsci for Organisational Communication Studies, *Western Journal of Communication*, vol. 61, no. 4, pp. 343–375.

Mumby, D. 2001. Power and Politics, in: Jablin, F. & Putnam, L. (eds.) *The New Handbook of Organisational Communication – Advances in Theory, Research, and Methods*, London: Sage.

Murphy, J. B. 1993. *The Moral Economy of Labor – Aristotelian Themes in Economic Theory*, New Haven: Yale University Press.

Musch, R. 2011. *Demokratische Assoziation ohne Staat?*, Berlin: http://blogs.taz.de/blog

Nader, R. 1967. Business Crimes, *The New Republic*, 1 July 1967, pp. 7–8.

Nader, R. 2011. *Getting Steamed: To Overcome Corporatism, Build it Together to Win*, Monroe: Common Courage Press.

Nahm, K. 2008. *Hegels Begriff der Sittlichkeit in dessen Genese und in den Jenaer Systementwürfen* [*Hegel's Concept of Sittlichkeit and Its Genesis in the Jena System*] (Inaugural-Dissertation Zur Erlangung des akademischen Grades eines Doktors der Philosophie Ruhr-Universitat Bochum), Bochum: Ruhr-Unviersity (unpublished PhD).

Nakano, T. 2004. Hegel's Theory of Economic Nationalism: Political Economy in the Philosophy of Right, *European Journal of Economic Thought*, vol. 11, no. 1, pp. 33–52.

Nancy, J-L. 2002. *Hegel – The Relentlessness of the Negative*, Minneapolis: University of Minnesota Press.
Nederman, C. J. 1987. Sovereignty, War and the Corporation: Hegel on the Medieval Foundations of the Modern State, *Journal of Politics*, vol. 49, no. 2, pp. 500–520.
Negray, C. L. 2012. *Work Time*, Oxford: Polity Press.
Neschen, A. 2008. *Ethik und Ökonomie in Hegel's Philosophy und in Modernen Wirtschaftsethischen Entwürfen* [*Ethics and Economy in Hegel's Philosophy and in Modern Economical-Ethical Concepts*], Hamburg: Felix Meiner Verlag & Jaeschke, W. & Siep, L. (eds.) Hegel-Studien: Beiheft 49.
Ness, I. & Azzellini, D. (eds.) 2011. *Ours to Master and to Own: Workers' Control from the Commune to the Present*, Chicago: Haymarket Books.
Neuhouser, F. 2011. The Idea of Hegelian 'Science' of Society, in: Houlgate, S. & Baur, M. (eds.) *The Blackwell Companion to Hegel*, Oxford: Wiley-Blackwell.
Neumann, J. & Morgenstern, O. 1944. *Theory of Games and Economic Behaviour*, Princeton: Princeton University Press.
Newell, P. 2012. *Globalisation and the Environment – Capitalism, Ecology and Power*, Oxford: Polity Press.
Nicosia, F. R. & Huener, J. (eds.) 2004. *Business and Industry in Nazi Germany*, New York: Berghahn Books.
Nietzsche, F. 1880. *The Will to Power* (translated by Walter Kaufmann and R. J. Hollingsdale, 1968), New York: Random House.
Nietzsche, F. 1883. Thus *Spoke Zarathustra: A Book for All and None* (Also Sprach Zarathustra – *Ein Buch für Alle und Keinen*, ed. by Adrian Del Caro, Robert B. Pippin; transl. by Adrian Del Caro), Cambridge (2006): Cambridge University Press.
Niji, Y. 2014. Hegels Lehre von der Korporation [Hegel's Teachings on the Corporation], in: Arendt, A. (ed.) *Hegel-Jahrbuch 2014* [*Hegel Yearbook*], Berlin: deGruyter Press.
Noe, R. A., Gerhart, B. & Wright, P. M. 2015. *Human Resource Management: Gaining a Competitive Advantage* (9th ed.), New York: McGraw-Hill Education.
Norris, A. 2004. Beyond the Fury of Destruction: Hegel on Freedom, *Political Theory*, vol. 32, no. 3, pp. 409–418.
Northouse, P. G. 2011. *Leadership: Theory and Practice* (6th ed.), London: Sage.
Nowak, M. & Highfield, R. 2011. *Super Cooperators: Evolution, Altruism and Human Behaviour (or Why We Need Each Other to Succeed)*, London: Penguin Press.
Nussbaum, M. C. 2010. *Not for Profit: Why Democracy Needs the Humanities*, Princeton: Princeton University Press.
Nusser, K. H. 1970. Die Französische Revolution und Hegels Phänomenologie des Geistes [The French Revolution and Hegel's Phenomenology of Spirit], *Philosophisches Jahrbuch*, vol. 77, no. 2, pp. 276–296.
Nusser, K-H. 1981. Das Kriterium der Moralität und die sittliche Allgemeinheit. Zur Bestimmung von Moralität und Rechtsbegründung bei Kant und Hegel [Criteria of Morality and Common *Sittlichkeit*. Determining Morality and Legality in Hegel and Kant], *Zeitschrift für philosophische Forschung*, Sonderheft zum 150. Todestag von G. W. F. Hegel, vol. 35, no. 3–4, pp. 552–563.
O'Brian, K. 2012. How McDonald's Came Back Bigger Than Ever, *New York Times*, 4 May 2012.
O'Connell, D. J. 2005. *Children in the Global Sex Trade*, Oxford: Polity Press.

O'Connor, B. 2012. The Neo-Hegelian Theory of Freedom and the Limits of Emancipation, *European Journal of Philosophy*, vol. 20, no. 3, pp. 1–24.

O'Neill, J. 1996. Introduction: A Dialectival Genealogy of Self, Society, and Culture in and after Hegel, in: O'Neill, J. (ed.) *Hegel's Dialectic of Desire and Recognition – Texts and Commentary*, Albany: State University of New York Press.

Oade, A. 2009. *Managing Workplace Bullying: How to Identify, Respond to, and Manage Bullying Behaviour in the Workplace*, New York: Palgrave Macmillan.

Offe, C. & Wiesenthal, H. 1980. Two Logics of Collective Action: Theoretical Notes on Social Class and Organisational Form, in: Zeitlin, M. (ed.) *Political Power and Social Theory – A Research Annual*, vol. 1, Greenwich: JAI Press.

Orwell, G. 1948. *Nineteen Eighty-four*, London: Secker & Warburg.

Ottmann, H. H. 1981. Herr und Knecht bei Hegel. Bemerkungen zu einer mißverstandenen Dialektik [Hegel's Master and Servant: Comments on a Misunderstood Dialectics], *Zeitschrift für philosophische Forschung*, vol. 35, no. 3–4, pp. 365–384.

Ottow, R. 2001. Die Lehre von den Korporationen in der Rechtsphilosophie Hegels und ihre Fortschreibung durch Eduard Ganz als Beitrag zur Frage der Zivilgesellschaft, *Archiv für Rechts- und Sozialphilosophie*, vol. 87, no. 4, pp. 468–480.

Paauwe, J. 2009. HRM and Performance: Achievements, Methodological Issues and Prospects, *Journal of Management Studies*, vol. 46, no. 1, pp. 129–142.

Packard, V. O. 1959. *The Hidden Persuaders*, New York: McKay.

Packer, G. 2011. The Broken Contract – Inequality and American Decline, *Foreign Affairs*, vol. 90, no. 6, pp. 20–31.

Padgett, C. 2012. *Corporate Governance: Theory and Practice*, Houndmills: Palgrave Macmillan.

Painter-Morland, M. & ten Bos, R. (eds.) 2011. *Business Ethics and Continental Philosophy*, Cambridge: Cambridge University Press.

Palazzo, G. & Richter, U. 2005. CSR Business as Usual? The Case of the Tobacco Industry, *Journal of Business Ethics*, vol. 61, no. 4, pp. 387–401.

Palmer, D. 2006. Taking Stock of the Criteria We Use to Evaluate One Another's Work: ASQ 50 Years out, *Administrative Science Quarterly*, vol. 51, no. 4, pp. 535–559.

Pannokoek, A. 2010. *Workers Councils*, Seattle: CreateSpace Independent Publishing Platform – An Amazon Company.

Parker, M. 2002. *Against Management – Organisation in the Age of Managerialism*, Cambridge: Polity Press.

Parkinson, J. & Mansbridge, J. J. (eds.) 2012. *Deliberative Systems: Deliberative Democracy at the Large Scale*, Cambridge: Cambridge University Press.

Pascal, B. 1660. *Pensees – The Provincial Letters* (section 6, note 343), Garden City: Doubleday (1961), Chicago: Encyclopædia Britannica, Inc. (1990), London: Penguin Books (1995).

Patrick, G., Heraty, N. & Morley, M. J. 2011. *Human Resource Management in Ireland*, Dublin: Gill & Macmillan.

Patten, A. 1995. Hegel's Justification of Private Property, *History of Political Thought*, vol. XVI, no. 4, pp. 576–600.

Patten, A. 1999. *Hegel's Idea of Freedom*, Oxford: Oxford University Press.

Pearson, G. 2011. *The Road to Co-operation: Escaping the Bottom Line*, Burlington: Gower.

Peddle, D. 2000. Hegel's Political Idea: Civic Society: History, and Sittlichkeit, *Animus – The Canadian of Philosophy and Humanities*, vol. 5 (on Hegel), pp. 113–143.

Peet, R. 2003. *Unholy Trinity: The IMF, World Bank and WTO*, New York: Zed Books.

Pena, D. 2001. *Economic Barbarism and Managerialism*, Westport: Greenwood Press.

Penolidis, T. 2009. Unendlichkeit und Selbstbewusstsein – Bemerkungen zum Prozess von Bewusstsein und Selbstbewusstsein in Hegels Phänomenologie des Geistes [Infinity and Self-confidence – Remarks to the Process of Consciousness and Self-consciousness in Hegel's Phenomenology of Spirit], *Hegel-Studien – Beiheft 50*, Hamburg: Felix Meidner Press.

Peperzak, A. T. 1991. *Hegels praktische Philosophie: ein Kommentar zur enzyklopädischen Darstellung der menschlichen Freiheit und ihrer objektiven Verwirklichung* [*Hegel's Practical Philosophy: Comment on an Encyclopaedic Description of Human Freedom and Its Actualisation*], Stuttgart-Bad Cannstatt: Frommann-Holzboog Press.

Peperzak, A. T. 2001. *Modern Freedom – Hegel's Legal, Moral, and Political Philosophy*, Dordrecht: Kluwer Academic Publishers.

Pereboom, D. 2004. Living without Free Will: The Case for Hard Incompatibilism, in: Sample, R. et al. (eds.) *Philosophy – The Big Question*, Oxford: Blackwell.

Perlmutter, D. D. 1997. Manufacturing Visions of Society and History in Textbooks, *Journal of Communication*, vol. 47, no. 3, pp. 68–81.

Petit, T. A. 1961. Management Ideology: Myth and Reality, *California Management Review*, vol. 3, no. 2, pp. 95–103.

Petrick, J. A. & Quinn, J. F. 1997. *Management Ethics – Integrity at Work*, London: Sage.

Pfreundschuh, G. 1977. *Entstehung und Merkmale des frühen Rechtsstaats* [*Development and Concepts of Early States*], PhD Thesis at Speyer: Hochschule für Verwaltungswissenschaft.

Phillips, P. et al. (eds.) 2004. *Corporate Personhood Challenged – Censored 2005: The Top 25 Censored Stories*. Toronto: Seven Stories Press.

Piaget, J. 1928. *The Child's Conception of the World*, London: Routledge & Kegan.

Piaget, J. 1932. *The Moral Judgment of the Child*, London: Kegan Paul.

Piaget, J. 1951. *Psychology of Intelligence*, London: Routledge & Kegan Paul.

Pilapil, R. 2011. Phsychologization of Injustice? On Axel Honneth's Theory of Recognitive Justice, *Ethical Perspectives*, vol. 18, no. 1, pp. 79–106.

Pilger, J. 2001. *The New Rulers of the World* (DVD documentary), London: *Carlton* Television.

Pinkard, T. 2001. Tugend, Moral und Sittlichkeit – von Maximen zu Praktiken [Virtue, Morality and Ethics – From Maxims to Practice], *Deutsche Zeitschrift für Philosophie*, vol. 49, no. 1, pp. 65–87.

Pinkard, T. 2014. Hegel's Naturalismus und die Zweite Natur – Von Marx zu Hegel und zurück [Hegel's Naturalism and the Second Nature – From Marx to Hegel and Back], in: Jaeggi, R. & Loick, D. (eds.) *Nach Marx – Philosophie, Kritik, Praxis* [*After Marx, Philosophy, Critique, Praxis*] (2nd ed.), Frankfurt: Suhrkamp Press.

Pinto, J. K. 2016. *Project Management: Achieving Competitive Advantage* (4th ed.), Boston: Pearson.

Pippin, R. 2010. *Hegel and Self-Consciousness: Desire and Death in the Phenomenology of Spirit*, Princeton: Princeton University Press.

Piven, F. F. & Clowad, R. 1971. *Regulating the Poor: The Function of Public Welfare*, New York: Pantheon Books.

Plant, R. 1980. Economic and Social Integration in Hegel's Political Philosophy, in: Verene, D. P. (ed.) *Hegel's Social and Political Thought – The Philosophy of Objective Spirit*, Sussex: Harvester Press.

Plant, R. 2013. *Hegel*, London: Routledge.

Plesch, D. & Blankenburg, S. 2008. *How to Make Corporations Accountable*, London: Institute of Employment Rights.

Png, I. 2012. *Managerial Economics* (4th ed.), London: Routledge.

Pogge, T. 2007. *World Poverty and Human Rights* (2nd ed.), Cambridge: Polity Press.

Pogge, T. 2010. *Politics as Usual: What Lies behind the Pro-Poor Rhetoric*, Cambridge: Polity Press.

Pogge, T. & Horton, K. (eds.) 2008. *Global Ethics – Seminal Essays*, St Paul: Paragon House Press.

Pöggeler, O. 1961. Zur Deutung der Phänomenologie des Geistes [On the Interpretation of the Phenomenology of Spirit], *Hegel-Studien*, vol. 1, Bonn: Bouvier Press.

Poguntke, T. 1987. The Organization of a Participatory Party – The German Greens, *European Journal of Political Research*, vol. 15, no. 6, pp. 609–633.

Polanyi, K. 1944. *The Great Transformation – The Political and Economical Origins of our Time*, New York: Farrar & Rinehart.

Poole, S. 2006. *Unspeak*, London: Little, Brown.

Popper, K. P. 1945. *The Open Society and Its Enemies*, London: Routledge.

Porter, M. E. (ed.) 1986. *Competition in Global Industries*, Cambridge: Harvard Business School Press.

Porter, M. E. 1979. How Competitive Forces Shape Strategy, *Harvard Business Review*, March/April 1979.

Porter, M. E. 1980. *Competitive Strategy*, New York: Free Press.

Porter, M. E. 1985. *Competitive Advantage*, New York: Free Press.

Porter, M. E. 1998. *The Competitive Advantage of Nations*, New York: Free Press.

Porter, M. E. 1998a. *On Competition*, Cambridge: Harvard Business School.

Poundstone, W. 2012. *Are You Smart Enough to Work at Google?: Trick Questions, Zen-like Riddles, Insanely Difficult Puzzles, and Other Devious Interviewing Techniques You Need to Know to Get a Job Anywhere in the New Economy*, New York: Little, Brown and Company.

Powers, C. W. & Vogel, D. 1980. *Ethics in the Education of Business Managers*, Hastings-on-Hudson: The Hastings Centre.

Prahalad, C. K. & Hamel, G. 1990. The Core Competence of the Corporation, *Harvard Business Review*, May–June 1990, pp. 3–15.

Prescott, R. K. & Rothwell, W. J. 2012. *Encyclopedia of Human Resource Management – Key Topics and Issues*, vol. 1, San Francisco: Pfeiffer and imprint of Wiley & Sons.

Priddat, B. P. 1990. *Hegel als Ökonom* [*Hegel as Economist*], Volkswirtschaftliche Schriften No. 403, Berlin: Duncker & Humbolt Press.

Priddat, B. P. 2001. Naturalität und Geistigkeit in Hegels Kompatibilismus [Natur and the Spirit in Hegel Compatibilism], *Deutsche Zeitschrift für Philosopie*, vol. 49, no. 1, pp. 45–64.

Punch, M. 1996. *Dirty Business – Exploring Corporate Misconduct: Analysis and Cases*, London: Sage.

Punch, M. 2001. Management Studies and Researching Business Deviance, in: Malachowski, A. R. (ed.) *Business Ethics – Critical Perspectives on Business and Management*, London: Routledge.

Punch, M. 2008. The Organisation Did It – Individuals, Corporations and Crime, in: Minkes, J. & Minkes, L. (eds.) *Corporate and White-Collar Crime*, London: Sage.

Purtschert, P. 2008. Anerkennung als Kampf um Repräsentation. Hegel lesen mit Simone de Beauvoir und Frantz Fanon [Recognition as a Fight for Representation: Reading Hegel with Simone de Beauvoir and Frantz Fanon], *Deutsche Zeitschrift für Philosophie*, vol. 56, no. 6, pp. 923–933.

Purtschert, P. 2010. On the Limits of Spirit: Hegel's Racism Revisited, *Philosophy and Social Criticism*, vol. 36, no. 9, pp. 1939–1051.

Putterman, L. 1986. On Some Recent Explanations of Why Capital Hires Labor, in: Putterman, L. (ed.) *The Economic Nature of the Firm*, Cambridge: Cambridge University Press.

Quante, M. 2013. Recognition and Capital, *Ethical Theory and Moral Practice*, vol. 16, no. 4, pp. 713–727.

Quinn, T. K. 1953. *Giant Business: Threat to Democracy*, New York: Exposition Press.

Quittner, J. & Slatalla, M. 1998. *Speeding the Net: The Inside Story of Netscape and How It Challenged Microsoft*, New York: Atlantic Monthly Press.

Raden, M. H. 1968. *The Origins of the Movement for Workers' Councils in Germany 1918–1935* (with a foreword by Joe Thomas, translated [from the French] by M. H. and A. M.), London: Coptic Press.

Radkau, J. 2013. *The Age of Ecology*, Oxford: Polity Press.

Rae, G. 2012. Hegel, Alienation, and the Phenomenological Development of Consciousness, *International Journal of Philosophical Studies*, vol. 10, no. 1, pp. 23–42.

Raman, K. R. & Lipschutz, R. D. 2010. *Corporate Social Responsibility: Comparative Critiques*, Basingstoke: Palgrave Macmillan.

Rawls, J. 1972. *A Theory of Justice*, Cambridge: Harvard University Press.

Rawls, J. 1980. Kantian Constructivism in Moral Theory, *The Journal of Philosophy*, vol. 77, no. 9, pp. 515–572.

Rawls, J. 1993. *Political Liberalism*, New York: Columbia University Press.

Rawls, J. 1999. *The Law of Peoples*, Cambridge: Harvard University Press.

Rawls, J. 2001. *Justice as Fairness: A Restatement*, Cambridge: Belknap Press.

Reath, A. 2006. *Agency and Autonomy in Kant's Moral Theory*, Oxford: Clarendon Press.

Redding, P. 1996. *Hegel's Hermeneutics*, Ithaca: Cornell University Press.

Rees, S. & Rodley, G. (eds.) 1995. *The High Cost of Managerialism*, Sydney: Pluto Press.

Rehbein, K., Logsdon, J. M. & Van Bure, H. J. 2012. Corporate Responses to Shareholder Activists: Considering the Dialogue Alternative, *Journal of Business Ethics*, vol. 107 (Online only: www.springerlink.com).

Reich, R. 1992. *The Work of Nations – Preparing Ourselves for 21st Century Capitalism*, New York: Vintage Books.

Renault, E. 2013. Three Marxian Approaches to Recognition, *Ethical Theory and Moral Practice*, vol. 16, no. 4, pp. 699–711.

Rettig, B. 2014. *Hegels sittlicher Staat: Bedeutung und Aktualität* [*Hegel's Moral State: Meaning and Actuality*], Köln: Böhlau Verlag.

Rhodes, R. 2010. *Masters of Death: The SS-Einsatzgruppen and the Invention of the Holocaust*, New York: Vintage.

Riedel, M. 1969. *Studien zu Hegels Rechtsphilosophie* [*Studies on Hegel's Philosophy of Right*], Frankfurt: Suhrkamp Press.

Riedel, M. 1974. *Materialien zu Hegel's Rechtsphilosophie* [*Resources to Hegel's Philosophy of Right*], vol. 2, Frankfurt: Suhrkamp Press.

Riedel, M. 1974a. Hegel's Begriff der 'Bürgerlichen Gesellschaft' und das Problem seines geschichtlichen Ursprungs [Hegel's Concept of 'Civil Society' and the Problem of Its Historical Origin] in: Riedel, M. (ed.) *Materialien zu Hegel's Rechtsphilosophie*, Band 2 [*Resources of Hegel's Philosophy of Right*, vol. 2, Frankfurt: Suhrkamp Press.

Riedel, M. 1974b. Natur und Freiheit in Hegel's Rechtsphilosophie [Nature and Freedom in Hegel's Philosophy of Right], in: Riedel, M. (ed.) *Materialien zu Hegel's Rechtsphilosophie* [*Resources to Hegel's Philosophy of Right*], vol. 2, Frankfurt: Suhrkamp Press.

Riedel, M. 1974c. Die Rezeption der Nationalökonomie [The Reception of the Economy], in: Göhler, G. (ed.) *Georg Wilhelm Friedrich Hegel – Frühe politische Systeme* [*G W F Hegel – Early Political Systems*], Frankfurt: Uhlstein Press.

Riedel, M. 1974d. Die Rezeption der Nationalökonomie [The Adoption of Economics], in: Göhler, G. (ed.) *Georg Wilhelm Friedrich Hegel – Frühe Politische Systeme* [*Hegel's Early Political Systems*], Frankfurt: Ullstein Press.

Riedel, M. 1977. Eduard Gans als Schüler Hegels – Zur politischen Auslegung der Rechtsphilosophie [Eduard Gans as a Student of Hegel – On the Political Interpretation of the Philosophy of Right], http://hegel.net/pdf

Riedel, M. 1981. Eduard Gans als Schüler Hegels. Zur politischen Auslegung der Rechtsphilosophie [Eduard Gans as Hegel's Student. On the Interpretation of the Philosophy of Right], in: Riedel, M. (ed.) *Naturrecht und Universalrechtsgeschichte*, Stuttgart: Klett-Cotta Press.

Riedel, M. 2011. *Between Tradition and Revolution: The Hegelian Transformation of Political Philosophy*, Cambridge: Cambridge University Press.

Riley, P. 2001. Rousseau's General Will, in: Riley, P. (ed.) *Cambridge Companion to Rousseau*, Cambridge: Cambridge University Press, Cambridge Collections Online (accessed: 19 January 2013), http://cco.cambridge.org

Ritter, J. 1957. *Hegel und die Französische Revolution* [*Hegel and the French Revolution*], Köln: Westdeutscher Verlag.

Ritter, J. 1970. Moralität und Sittlichkeit, in: Fetscher, I. (ed.) *Hegel in der Sicht der neueren Forschung* [*Hegel from the Perspective of New Research*], Darmstadt: Wissenschaftliche Buchgesellschaft.

Ritter, J. 1974. Person und Eigentum. Zu Hegels 'Grundlinien der Philosophie des Rechts' §§ 34 bis 81 [Person and Property. On Hegel's Elements of Philosophy of Right §§ 34 to 81), in: Riedel, M. (ed.) *Materialien zu Hegel's Rechtsphilosophie* [*Resources to Hegel's Philosophy of Right*], vol. 2, Frankfurt: Suhrkamp Press.

Ritter, J. 1974a. Moralität und Sittlichkeit [Morality and Sittlichkeit], in: Riedel, M. (ed.) *Materialien zu Hegel's Rechtsphilosophie* [*Resources to Hegel's Philosophy of Right*], vol. 2, Frankfurt: Suhrkamp Press.

Ritter, J. 1974b. *Historisches Wörterbuch der Philosophie – vol. 3: G-H* [*Historical Dictionary of Philosophy*], Darmstadt: Wissenschaftliche Buchgesellschaft.

Ritz, D. 2001. *Defying Corporations, Defining Democracy: A Book of History & Strategy*, New York: Apex Press.

Ritz, D. 2007. Can Corporate Personhood Be Socially Responsible?, in: May, S. K. et al. (eds.) *The Debate over Corporate Social Responsibility*, Oxford: Oxford University Press.

Robins, N. 2006. *The Corporation that Changed the World: How the East India Company Shaped the Modern Multinational*. London: Pluto Press.

Robinson, W. I. 2014. *Global Capitalism and the Crisis of Humanity*, Cambridge: Cambridge University Press.

Rockmore, T. 1997. *Cognition – An Introduction to Hegel's Phenomenology of Spirit*, Berkeley: University of California Press.

Roelofs, J. 2003. *Foundations and Public Policy: The Mask of Pluralism*, Albany: State University of New York Press.

Roethlisberger, F. J. 1943. *Management and Morale*, Cambridge: Harvard University Press.

Rölli, M. 2013. Zur Aktualität der Moderne nach Hegel und Habermas [On the Actuality of Modernity in Hegel and Habermas], in: Arndt, M. (ed.) *Hegel-Jahrbuch 2013*, Berlin: deGruyter Press, pp. 297–303.

Römpp, G. 2008. *Hegel leicht gemacht – Eine Einführung in seine Philosophie [Hegel Made Easy – An Introduction to his Philosophy]*, Köln: Böhlau Press.

Rosenfeld, P. et al. 1995. *Impression Management in Organisations – Theory, Measures, Practice*, London: Routledge.

Rosenow, E. 1992. Bourgeois or Citoyen? The Democratic Concept of Man, *Educational Philosophy and Theory*, vol. 24, no. 1, pp. 44–50.

Rosenzweig, F. 1974. Die Entwicklung des Hegelschen Systems der Staatsphilosophie in Jena [The Development of Hegel's System of a Philosophy of the State during his Jena Period], in: Göhler, G. (ed.) *Georg Wilhelm Friedrich Hegel – Frühe Politische Systeme [Hegel's Early Political Systems]*, Frankfurt: Ullstein Press.

Rosoff, S., Pontell, H. & Tillman, R. 2009. *Profit without Honor: White-Collar Crime and the Looting of America* (5th ed.), Upper Saddle River: Prentice Hall.

Ross, A. 2009. *Nice Work If You can Get It: Life and Labor in Precarious Times*, New York: New York University Press.

Ross, N. 2008a. *On the Mechanism of Hegel's Social and Political Philosophy*, London: Routledge.

Ross, N. 2008b. Hegel on the Place of Corporations within Ethical Life, in: *Cutting-Edge Issues in Business Ethics*, vol. 24, Heidelberg: Springer Press & *Issues in Business Ethics*, vol. 24, pp. 47–58.

Rossington, B. 2014. England's £90 World Cup Shirt Made by Nike's Indonesian Workers Earning Just 30p an Hour, mirror.co.uk/news/uk; 5 April 2014.

Rössler, B. 2005. Arbeit, Annerkennung, Emanzipation [Labour, Recognition, Emancipation], *Deutsche Zeitschrift für Philosophie*, vol. 53, no. 3, pp. 389–413.

Rossouw, G. J. 2011. The Ethics of Corporate Governance in Global Perspective, in: Brink, A. (ed.) *Corporate Governance and Business Ethics*, Series: Ethical Economy, vol. 39, New York: Springer Press.

Rothkopf, D. J. 2012. *Power, Inc.: The Epic Rivalry between Big Business and Government – and the Reckoning that Lies Ahead*, New York: Farrar, Straus and Giroux.

Rousseau, J.-J. 1755. *Discourse on the Origins of Inequality* (second discourse); Polemics; and, Political Economy (edited by Roger D. Masters and Christopher Kelly & transl. by Judith R. Bush), Hanover: Published for Dartmouth College by University Press of New England (1992) & Mineola: Dover Publications (2004).

Rowbottom, J. 2010. *Democracy Distorted: Wealth, Influence and Democratic Politics*, Cambridge: Cambridge University Press.

Rowland, W. 2006. *Greed Inc – Why Corporations Rule our World*, New York: Arcade Publishing.

Ruda, F. 2011. *Hegel's Rubble – An Investigation into Hegel's Philosophy of Right*, London: Continuum.

Rummel, R. J. 1994. Power, Genocide, and Mass Murder, *Journal of Peace Research*, vol. 31, no. 1, pp. 1–10.

Rushkoff, D. 2011. *Life Inc: How Corporatism Conquered the World, and How We can Take It Back*, New York: Random House.

Sallaz, J. J. 2013. *Labour, Economy, and Society*, Oxford: Polity Press.

Salvendy, G. (ed.) 2012. *Handbook of Human Factors and Ergonomics* (4th ed.), Hoboken: Wiley.

Sample, R. et al. (eds.) 2004. *Philosophy – The Big Question*, Oxford: Blackwell.

Samson, D. & Daft, R. L. 2012. *Management* (4th Asia-Pacific ed.) Melbourne: Cengage.

Samson, D. & Daft, R. L. 2012a. *Fundamentals of Management* (4th Asia-Pacific ed.) Melbourne: Cengage.

Samuel, Y. 2010. *Organizational Pathology: Life and Death of Organizations*, New Brunswick: Transaction Publishers.

Sandbu, M. E. 2011. *Just Business – Arguments in Business Ethics*, Upper Saddle River: Pearson/Prentice-Hall.

Sandel, M. J. 1998. What Money Can't Buy: The Moral Limits of Markets, *The Tanner Lectures on Human Values*, Oxford: Brasenose College, 11–12 May 1998.

Sarakinsky, I. 1992. Reason, Freedom and History in Hegel, *Politikon*, vol. 19, no. 3, pp. 7–24.

Sartre, J. P. 1996. The Existence of Others, in: O'Neill, J. (ed.) *Hegel's Dialectic of Desire and Recognition – Texts and Commentary*, Albany: State University of New York Press.

Saunders, M. 2006. The Madness and Malady of Managerialism, *Quadrant*, 1 March, vol. 50, no. 2, pp. 9–17.

Sayama, K. 2004. *Die Geburt der bürgerlichen Gesellschaft: zur Entstehung von Hegels Sozialphilosophie* [*The Birth of Sittliche Corporations: On the Emergence of Hegel's Social Philosophy*], Berlin: Philo Press.

Schecter, D. 2010. *The Critique of Instrumental Reason from Weber to Habermas*, London: Continuum Press.

Schecter, D. 2013. *Critical Theory in the Twenty-First Century*, London & New York: Bloomsbury Academic.

Scherer, A. G. & Palazzo, G. 2007. Toward a Political Conception of Corporate Responsibility: Business and Society Seen from a Habermasian Perspective, *Academy of Management Review*, vol. 32, no. 4, pp. 1096–1120.

Schmidt am Busch, H-C. 2001. Arbeit zwischen Marx und Hegel – Andre Gorz' postkapitalistische Gesellschaftstheorie [Work between Marx and Hegel – Andre Gorz's Post-capitalist Society Theory], *Deutsche Zeitschrift für Philosophie*, vol. 49, no. 5, pp. 743–760.

Schmidt am Busch, H-C. 2002. *Hegels Begriff der Arbeit* [*Hegel's Concept of Work*], Berlin: Akademie-Press (published PhD thesis).

Schmidt am Busch, H-C. 2010. What Does it Mean to 'Make Oneself Into An Object?' In Defence of a Key Notion of Hegel's Theory of Action, in: Laitinen, A. & Sandis, C. (eds.) *Hegel on Action*, Basingstoke: Palgrave Macmillan.

Schmidt am Busch, H-C. 2011. The Legacy of Hegelian Philosophy and the Future of Critical Theory, Research Paper, Frankfurt: University of Frankfurt, Department of Sociology; Published in: Smith, N. H. & Deranty, J-P. (eds.). *New Philosophies of Labour*, Leiden: Brill Press.

Schmidt am Busch, H-C. 2011a. *Anerkennung als Prinzip der Kritischen Theorie* [*Recognition as a Principle of Critical Theory*], Berlin: DeGruyter Press.

Schmidt am Busch, H-C. 2013. Introduction to "Recognition" – A Special Issue of *Ethical Theory and Moral Practice*, vol. 16, no. 4, pp. 679–682.

Schmidt, S. 2007. *Hegels System der Sittlichkeit* [*Hegel's System of Sittlichkeit*], Berlin: Akademie-Verlag (Academia Press).

Schmitter, P. C. & Lehmbruch, G. (eds.) 1979. *Trends toward Corporatist Intermediation*, London: Sage.

Schneidereit, N. 2011. Hegels Begriff des sittlichen Staates und seine egalitaristischen Konsequenzen [Hegel's Concept of the Moral State and Its Egalitarian Consequences], *Archive für Rechts- und Sozialphilosophie*, vol. 97, no. 1, pp. 107–124.

Scholem, G. & Adorno, T. (eds.) 1994. *The Correspondence of Walter Benjamin, 1910–1940* (transl. by Manfred R. Jacobson and Evelyn M. Jacobson), Chicago: University of Chicago Press.

Schrijvers, J. 2004. *The Way of the Rat – A Survival Guide to Office Politics*, London: Cyan Books.

Schrijvers, J. 2005. *The Monday Morning Feeling – A Book of Comfort for Sufferers*, London: Marshall Cavendish.

Schumpeter, J. A. 1942. *Capitalism, Socialism, and Democracy*, New York: Harper & Brothers.

Schwartz, H. S. 1990. *Narcissistic Process and Corporate Decay – The Theory of the Organisational Ideal*, New York: New York University Press.

Schwartz, M. S. & Salia, D. 2012. Should Firms Go Beyond Profits? Milton Friedman versus Broad CSR, *Business and Society Review*, vol. 117, no. 1, pp. 1–31

Schweickart, D. 2002. *After Capitalism*, Lanham: Rowman & Littlefield.

Schweppenhäuser, H. 1970. Spekulative und negative Dialektik [Speculative and Negative Dialectics], in: Negt, O. (ed.) *Aktualität und Folgen der Philosophie Hegels* [*Actuality and Consequences of Hegel's Philosophy*], Frankfurt: Suhrkamp Press.

Schweppenhäuser, H. 1993. *Ethik nach Auschwitz – Adornos negative Moralphilosophie* [Ethics after Auschwitz – Adorno's Negative Moral Philosophy], Hamburg: Argument-Press.

Scott, J. 1997. *Corporate Business and Capitalist Classes*, Oxford: Oxford University Press.

Scott, W. G. & Hart, D. K. 1991. The Exhaustion of Managerialism, *Society*, vol. 28, no 3, pp. 39–48.

Searle, J. R. 1996. *The Construction of Social Reality*, London: Penguin Press.

Searle, J. R. 2007. *Freedom and Neurobiology: Reflections on Free Will, Language, and Political Power*, New York: Columbia University Press.

Seissl, T. 2013. *Revolutionäre Vernunft – Hegels ambivalentes Verhältnis zum Revolutionsgedanken* [*Revolutionary Reason – Hegel's Ambivalent Relationship to the Revolutionary Thinking*], Wien: Österreichisches Studienförderungswerk.

Selekman, B. M. 1959. *A Moral Philosophy for Management*, New York: McGraw-Hill.

Semler, R. 1989. Managing without Managers, *Harvard Businss Review*, September 1989.

Semler, R. 1993. *Maverick: The Success Story behind the World's Most Unusual Workplace*, New York: Warner Books.

Semler, R. 2004. *The Seven-Day Weekend: Changing the Way Work Works*, New York: Portfolio.

Senigaglia, C. 2013. Strukturen der Moderne und Inhalte der Globalisierung in Hegels Denken [The Structure of Modernity and the Content of Globalisation

in Hegel's Thought], in: Arndt, M. (ed.) *Hegel-Jahrbuch 2013*, Berlin: deGruyter Press, pp. 120–127.
Sennett, R. 2006. *The Culture of the New Capitalism*, New Haven: Yale University Press.
Sennett, R. 2012. *Together: The Rituals, Pleasures, and Politics of Cooperation*, New Haven: Yale University Press.
Sennett, R. & Cobb, J. 1972. *The Hidden Injuries of Class*, New York: Vintage Books.
Seymour-Smith, M. 1998. *The 100 Most Influential Books Ever Written: The History of Thought from Ancient Times to Today*, Secaucus: Carol Pub. Group.
Shah, S. 2006. *The Body Hunters: Testing new Drugs on the World's Poorest Patients*, New York: New Press.
Shaw, W. H. 2011. *Business Ethics – A Textbook with Cases* (7th ed.), Boston: Wadsworth.
Shaw, W. H. & Barry, V. 2010. *Moral Issues in Business*, Belmont: Wadsworth.
Sheehan, J. J. (ed.) 1973. *Industrialization and Industrial Labor in Nineteenth-Century Europe*, New York: Wiley.
Shelp, R. & Ehrbar, A. 2009. *Fallen Giant: The Amazing Story of Hank Greenberg and the History of AIG* (2nd ed.), Hoboken: Wiley.
Sheth, K. 2010. *Boys Without Names* (1st ed.), New York: Balzer + Bray.
Shipler, D. K. 2005. *The Working Poor: Invisible in America*, New York: Vintage Books.
Shipway, M. 1988. *Anti-parliamentary Communism: The Movement for Workers' Councils in Britain, 1917–45*, New York: St. Martin's Press.
Shleifer, A. & Vishny, R. W. 1997. A Survey of Corporate Governance, *Journal of Finance*, vol. 52, no. 2, pp. 737–783.
Shrivastava, P. 1986. Is Strategic Management Ideological? *Journal of Management*, vol. 12, no. 3, pp. 363–377.
Shuster, M. 2014. *Autonomy After Auschwitz – Adorno, German Idealism, and Modernity*, Chicago: Chicago University Press.
Sichler, R. 2010. Anerkennung im Kontext von Arbeit und Beruf [Recognition in the Context of Work and Profession], *Journal für Psychologie*, vol. 18, no. 2, pp. 1–38.
Siep, L. 1979. *Anerkennung als Prinzip der praktischen Philosophie – Untersuchungen zu Hegels Jenaer Philosophie des Geistes* [*Recognition as a Principle of Practical Philosophy – Studies on Hegel's Jena Philosophy of Mind*], Freiburg: Karl Alber Press.
Siep, L. 2004. Die Wirklichkeit des Guten [The Actualisation of the Good), in: Halbig, C., Quante, M. & Siep, L. (eds.) *Hegel's Erbe* [*Hegel's Heritage*], Frankfurt: Suhrkamp Press.
Siep, L. 2007. Hegel über Moralität und Wirklichkeit [Hegel on Morality and Reality], *Hegel-Studien*, vol. 42, pp. 11–30.
Siep, L. 2008. Anerkennung in der Phänomenologie des Geistes und in der Praktischen Philosophie der Gegenwart [Recognition in the Phenomenology of Spirit and in the Practical Philosophy of the Present], http://www.information-philosophie.de/
Silk, L. & Vogel, D. 1976. *Ethics and Profits – The Crisis of Confidence in American Business*, New York: Simon & Schuster.
Simon, H., Luby, F. & Bilstein, F. 2006. *Manage for Profit, Not for Market Share: A Guide to Greater Profits in Highly Competitive Markets*, Boston: Harvard Business School Press.
Sinderbrink, R. 2007. *Understanding Hegelianism*, Stocksfield: Acumen.
Singer, P. 1972. Famine, Affluence, and Morality, *Philosophy and Public Affairs*, vol. 1, no. 3, pp. 229–243.
Singer, P. 1978. The Fable of the Fox and the Unliberated Animals, *Ethics*, vol. 88, no. 2, pp. 119–125.

Singer, P. 1990. *Animal Liberation* (2nd ed.), New York: New York Review.
Singer, P. 1994. *The Oxford Reader on Ethics*, Oxford: Oxford University Press.
Singer, P. 2000. *Writings on an Ethical Life*, New York: Ecco Press.
Singer, P. 2007. All Animals are Equal, in: Shafer-Landau (ed.) *Ethical Theory*, Oxford: Blackwell.
Sirianni, C. 1982. *Workers Control and Socialist Democracy: The Soviet Experience*, London: NLB.
Sison, A. J. G. 2008. *Corporate Governance and Ethics – An Aristotelian Perspective*, Cheltham: Edward Elgar.
Sitrin, M. & Azzellini, D. 2014. *They can't Represent Us!: Reinventing Democracy from Greece to Occupy*, London: Verso.
Sitton, J. F. 1987. Hannah Arendt's Argument for Council Democracy, *Polity*, vol. 20, no. 1, pp. 80–100.
Skinner, B. F. 1983. *A Matter of Consequences*, New York: Knopf.
Smale, W. 2006. *Do Firms Really Need a Social Policy?*, London: BBC, http://news.bbc.co.uk/2/hi/business/6102108.stm
Smith, A. 1759. *The Theory of the Moral Sentiments*, www.adamsmith.org (250th anniversary edition, introduction by Amartya Sen, edited, with notes by Ryan Patrick Hanley, New York: Penguin Books, 2009).
Smith, A. 1776. *The Wealth of Nations* – Books I–III, London: Penguin Books (reprinted 1986).
Smith, A. A. 1985. Kant's Political Philosophy: Rechtsstaat or Council Democracy, *Review of Politics*, vol. 47, no. 2, pp. 253–280.
Smith, C. 2010. Go with the Flow: Labour Power Mobility and Labour Process Theory, in: Thompson, P. & Smith, C. (eds.) *Working Life – Renewing Labour Process Analysis*, Houndmills: Palgrave.
Smith, J. D. 2009. *Normative Theory and Business Ethics*, Lanham: Rowan & Littlefield Publishers.
Smith, S. B. 1989a. What is "Right" in Hegel's Philosophy of Right?, *American Political Science Review*, vol. 83, no. 1, pp. 3–18.
Smith, S. B. 1989b. *Hegel's Critique of Liberalism – Rights in Context*, Chicago: University of Chicago Press.
Snyder, T. 2010. *Bloodlands: Europe between Hitler and Stalin*, New York: Basic Books.
Soederberg, S. 2010. *Corporate Power and Ownership in Contemporary Capitalism: The Politics of Resistance and Domination*, London: Routledge.
Solomon, J. 2010. *Corporate Governance and Accountability* (3rd ed.), Chichester: Wiley.
Sondergergh, S. 2000. *Erin Brockovich*, wikipedia.org/wiki/Erin_Brockovich_(film).
Speight, A. 2008. *The Philosophy of Hegel*, Stocksfield: Acumen Publishing.
Spencer, H. 1880. *The Principles of Biology*, New York: Appleton & Co.
Steer, R. 2013. Karl Marx' Kapitalismuskritik und ihre anthropologischen Ursprünge [Karl Marx' Critiqu of Capitalism and Its Anthropological Origins], *Jahrbuch für Christliche Sozialwissenschaften*, issue 6, pp. 169–233 (www.jcsw.de).
Stengel, D. N. 2011. Managerial Economics: Concepts and Principles: Firm Competition and Market Structure, Cambridge: *Harvard Business Review*: hbr.org
Sternberg, E. 1997. The Defects of Stakeholder Theory, *Corporate Governance*, vol. 5, no. 1, pp. 3–10.
Steuart, J. 1770. *An Inquiry Into the Principles of Political Oeconomy: Being an Essay on the Science of Domestic Policy in Free Nations, in which are Particularly Considered Population, Agriculture, Trade, Industry, Money, Coin, Interest, Circulation, Banks,*

*Exchange, Public Credit, and Taxes, Volume 1*, Dublin: James Williams and Richard Moncrieffe.
Stewart, H. 2012. Super-Rich Hide $21 Trillion, *The Guardian Weekly*, 27 July 2012, vol. 187, no. 7, p. 18.
Stillman, P. G. 1980. Person, Property, and Civil Society in the Philosophy of Right, in: Verene, D. P. (ed.) *Hegel's Social and Political Thought – The Philosophy of Objective Spirit*, Sussex: Harvester Press.
Stohl, R. & Grillot, S. 2009. *The International Arms Trade*, Oxford: Polity Press.
Stone, A. 2005. *Petrified Intelligence: Nature in Hegel's Philosophy*, Albany: State University of New York Press.
Straubhaar, J., LaRose, R. & Davenport, L. 2011. *Media Now: Understanding Media, Culture, and Technology* (7th ed.), Boston: Wadsworth.
Strum, S. C., Lindburg, D. G. & Hamburg, D. (eds.) 1999. *The New Physical Anthropology: Science, Humanism, and Critical Reflection*, Upper Saddle River: Prentice Hall.
Sturmthal, A. F. 1964. *Workers Councils. A Study of Workplace Organization on Both Sides of the Iron Curtain*, Cambridge: Harvard University Press.
Styron, W. 1979. *Sophie's Choice – A Novel*, New York: Random House.
Suarez-Villa, L. 2012. *Technocapitalism: A Critical Perspective on Technological Innovation and Corporatism*, Philadelphia: Temple University Press.
Surowieki, J. 2013. Boom or Bubble?, *The New Yorker*, 27 May 2013, 3 pages.
Sutherland, E. H. 1949. *White Collar Crime*, New York: Dryden Press.
Svendsen, L. 2008. *A Philosophy of Fear*, Chicago: Chicago University Press.
Taleb, N. N. 2005. *Fooled by Randomness: The Hidden Role of Chance in Life and in the Markets* (2nd ed.), New York: Random House.
Tangian, A. 2009. Decent Work: Indexing European Working Conditions and Imposing Workplace Tax, *Transfer* (European Review of Labour and Research), vol. 15, no. 3–4, pp. 527–556.
Tangian, A. 2011. *Flexicurity and Political Philosophy*, New York: Nova Science Publishers.
Tassone, G. 2005. Amoral Adorno: Negative Dialectics Outside Ethics, *European Journal of Social Theory*, vol. 8, no. 3, pp. 251–267.
Taylor, C. 1975. *Hegel*, Cambridge: Cambridge University Press.
Taylor, C. 1985. The Concept of a Person, in: *Philosophical Papers. Volume 1*, Cambridge: Cambridge University Press.
Taylor, C. 1994. The Politics of Recognition, in: Taylor, C. (ed.) *Multiculturalism – Examining the Politics of Recognition*, Princeton: Princeton University Press.
Taylor, F. W. 1911. *The Principle of Scientific Management*, New York: Norton Press.
Thanem, T. 2011. *The Monstrous Organization*, London: Edward Elgar.
Theodosius, C. 2008. *Emotional Labour in Health Care: The Unmanaged Heart of Nursing*, Abingdon: Routledge.
Thibodeau, J. C. & Freier, D. 2014. *Auditing after Sarbanes-Oxley Auditing and Accounting Cases: Investigating Issues of Fraud and Professional Ethics* (4th ed.), New York: McGraw-Hill.
Thiele, L. P. 2013. *Sustainability*, Oxford: Polity Press.
Thompson, E. P. 1963. *The Making of the English Working Class*, London: Victor Gollancz.
Thompson, G. 2010. *Working in the Shadows: A Year of Doing the Jobs (most) Americans Won't Do*, New York: Nation Books.

Thompson, P. 2004. Brands, Boundaries and Bandwagons – Critical Reflections on Critical Management Studies, in: Fleedwood, S. & Ackroyd, S. (eds.) *Critical Realist Approach in Organisation and Management Studies* (pp. 54–71), London: Routledge.

Thompson, P. & Smith, C. (eds.), 2010. *Working Life – Renewing Labour Process Analysis*, Houndmills: Palgrave.

Thurow, L. C. 1980. *The Zero-Sum Society: Distribution and the Possibilities for Economic Change*, New York: Basic Books.

Timmerman, K. 2009. *Where am I Wearing?: A Global Tour to the Countries, Factories, and People that Make our Clothes*, Hoboken: Wiley.

Tocqueville, A. 1835. *De la démocratie en Amérique – Democracy in America* (transl. by Henry Reeve), London: Saunders & Otley (1835–1840).

Todorov, T. 1996. *Facing the Extreme: Moral Life in the Concentration Camps*, New York: Metropolitan Books.

Toews, J. E. 1980. *Hegelianism – The Path Toward Dialectical Humanism, 1805–1841*, Cambridge: Cambridge University Press.

Toffler, A. 1990. *Powershift: Knowledge, Wealth, and Violence at the Edge of the 21st Century*, New York: Bantam Books.

Tonn, C. 2004. *Eigentum und Selbstbewusstsein: Untersuchung einer Metapher by Kant und Hegel [Property & Self-consciousness: An Inquiry into a Kantian and Hegelian Metaphor]*, PhD Thesis at Bonn University's Faculty of Philosophy.

Townley, B. 1993. Foucault, Power/Knowledge, and Its Relevance for Human Resource Management, *Academy of Management Review*, vol. 18, no. 3, pp. 518–545.

Townley, B. 2005. Performance Appraisals and the Emergence of Management, in: Grey, C. & Willmott, H. (eds.) *Critical Management Studies*, Oxford: Oxford University Press.

Treptow, E. 1972. *Theorie und Praxis bei Hegel und den Junghegelianern [Theory and Praxis by Hegel and the Young Hegelians]*, Habilitation Thesis [Habilitationsschrift] at the Philosophical Faculty [Philosophischen Fakultät] at Ludwig-Maximilians-Universität München, Munch: unpublished (pdf-download: www.philosophie.uni-muenchen.de/lehreinheiten/...1/.../habil_treptow.pdf).

Trevino, L. K., Hartman, L. P. & Brown, M. 2000. Moral Person and Moral Manager: How Executives Develop a Reputation for Ethical Leadership, *California Management Review*, vol. 42, no. 4, pp. 128–142.

Trevino, L. K. & Nelson, K. A. 2011. *Managing Business Ethics – Straight Talk about How to Do It Right*, Hoboken: Wiley & Sons.

Triado, J. 1984. Corporatism, Democracy and Morality, *Thesis Eleven*, vol. 9, no. 1, pp. 33–51.

Tsoukas, H. & Chia, R. (eds.) 2011. *Philosophy and Organization Theory: Research in the Sociology of Organizations*, vol. 32, Bingley: Emerald Group Publishing.

Tuckman, A. 2005. Employment Struggles and the Commodification of Time: Marx and the Analysis of Working Time Flexibility, *Philosophy of Management*, vol. 5, no. 2, pp. 47–56.

Tugendhat, C. 1871. *The Multinationals*, London: Eyre and Spottiswoode.

Ugarriza, J. & Caluwaerts, D. 2014. *Democratic Deliberation in Deeply Divided Societies: From Conflict to Common Ground*, Basingstoke: Palgrave.

Upchurch, M. 2012. Neoliberal Globalization and Trade Unionism: Toward Radical Political Unionism?, *Critical Sociology*, vol. 38, no. 2, pp. 265–280.

Urban, G. (ed.) 2014. *Corporations and Citizenship*, Philadelphia: University of Pennsylvania Press.
USA. 2007. *Overseas Sweatshop Abuses, Their Impact on U.S. Workers, and the Need for Anti-sweatshop Legislation: Hearing Before the Subcommittee on Interstate Commerce, Trade, and Tourism of the Committee on Commerce, Science, and Transportation, United States Senate, One Hundred Tenth Congress, First Session, February 14, 2007*, Washington: U.S. G.P.O: For Sale by the Supt. of Docs., U.S. G.P.O., 2010.
Useem, M. 1990. Business Restructuring, Management Control, and Corporate Organization, *Theory and Society*, vol. 19, no. 6, pp. 681–707.
Utting, P. 2003. Promoting Development through Corporate Social Responsibility – Does it Work?, *Global Future*, Third Quarter, 1 September 2003; http://www.unrisd.org
Vallas, S. P. 2011. *Work – A Critique*, Oxford: Polity Press.
Vartenberg, T. E. 1981. Poverty and Class Structure in Hegel's Theory of Civil Society, *Philosophy and Social Criticism*, vol. 8, no. 2, pp. 169–182.
Villey, M. 1974. Das römische Recht in Hegels Rechtsphilosophie [The Roman Law in Hegel's Philosophy of Right], in: Riedel, M. (ed.) *Materialien zu Hegel's Rechtsphilosophie* [*Resources to Hegel's Philosophy of Right*], vol. 2, Frankfurt: Suhrkamp Press.
Virilio, P. 2012. *The Administration of Fear*, Cambridge: MIT Press.
Vishnu, G. 1984. *Industrial Democracy in India: A Sociological Study of Workers Participation in Management*, Allahabad: Chugh.
Vliet van, O. 2011. *Convergence and Europeanisation: The Political Economy of Social and Labour Market Policies*, Leiden: Leiden University Press.
Voiculescu, A. & Yanacopulos, H. 2011. *The Business of Human Rights – An Evolving Agenda for Corporate Responsibility*, London: Zed Books.
Voswinkel, S. 2001. *Anerkennung und Reputation* [*Recognition and Reputation*], Konstanz: UVK Press.
Wahl, A. 2011. *The Rise and Fall of the Welfare State*, London: Pluto Press.
Wallace, R. M. 1999. How Hegel Reconciles Private Freedom with Citizenship, *Journal of Political Philosophy*, vol. 7, no. 4, pp. 419–433.
Ward, H. F. 1924. *The Profit Motive, is it Indispensable to Industry?*, New York: League for Industrial Democracy.
Warren, B., Sampson, S. D. & McFee, E. 2011. Business Schools: Ethics, Assurance of Learning, and the Future, *Organization Management Journal*, vol. 8, no. 1–2, pp. 41–58.
Watkins, C. (ed.) 2011. *Child Labor and Sweatshops*, Detroit: Gale Cengage Learning.
Watson, D. 1997. *Against the Megamachine: Essays on Empire & Its Enemies*, Brooklyn: Autonomedia.
Watson, D. 2003. *Death Sentence – The Decay of Public Language*, Sydney: Knopf.
Weaver, G. R., Treviño, K. L. & Cochran, P. L. 1999. Corporate Ethics Practices in the Mid-1990's: An Empirical Study of the Fortune 1000, *Journal of Business Ethics*, vol. 18, no. 3, pp. 283–294.
Weber, M. 1924. *Economy and Society*, Berkeley: University of California Press (reprint in: Handel, M. (ed.) 2003. *The Sociology of Organizations – Classic, Contemporary and Critical Readings*, London: Sage).

Wellmer, A. 1991. *The Persistence of Modernity* (transl. by D. Midgley), Cambridge: MIT Press.

Wellmer, A. 1993. *Endspiele, Die unversöhnliche Moderne [End-Games the Uncompromising Modernity: Essays and Lectures]*, Frankfurt: Suhrkamp Press.

Wellmer, A. 1999. *Endspiele, Die unversöhnliche Moderne [End-Games the Uncompromising Modernity: Essays and Lectures]* (2nd ed.), Frankfurt: Suhrkamp Press.

Werhane, P. H. & Freeman, R. E. 2005. Corporate Responsibility, in: LaFollette, H. (ed.) *The Oxford Handbook of Practical Ethics*, Oxford: Oxford University Press.

Westphal, K. R. 1993. Hegel on Political Representation: Labourers, Corporations, and the Monarch, *The Owl of Minerva*, vol. 25, no. 1, pp. 111–116.

Westphal, K. R. 2002. Hegel's Standards of Political Legitimacy, *Jahrbuch für Recht und Ethik/Annual Review of Law and Ethics*, vol. 10, pp. 307–320.

Westphal, K. R. 2012. Hegel, in: Angier, T. (ed.) *Ethics – They Key Thinkers*, London: Blooksbury.

Westphal, M. 1992. *Hegel, Freedom, and Modernity*, Albany: State University of New York Press.

Whittington, R. 2001. *What is Strategy – And Does It Matter?* (2nd ed.), London: Routledge.

Whyte, W. H. 1961. *The Organisation Man*, Harmondsworth: Penguin.

Wicks, A. C. et al. 2010. *Business Ethics: A Managerial Approach*, Boston: Prentice Hall.

Wilde, O. 1892. *Lady Windermere's Fan*, New York: Collier Books (1962).

Wildt, A. 2005. Anerkennung in der Psychoanalyse [Recognition in Psychoanalysis], *Deutsche Zeitschrift für Philosophie*, vol. 53, no. 3, pp. 461–478.

Williams, C. A. & Zumbansen, P. (eds.) 2011. *The Embedded Firm: Corporate Governance, Labor, and Finance Capitalism*, Cambridge: Cambridge University Press.

Williams, R. R. 2011. Love, Recognition, Spirit: Hegel's Philosophy of Religion, in: Houlgate, S. & Baur, M. (eds.) *The Blackwell Companion to Hegel*, Oxford: Wiley-Blackwell.

Williamson, P. J. 1985. *Varieties of Corporatism: A Conceptual Discussion*, Cambridge: Cambridge University Press.

Willmott, H. 2011. Journal List Fetishism and the Perversion of Scholarship: Reactivity and the ABS List. *Organization*, vol. 18, no. 4, pp. 429–442.

Wilson, H. B. 1974. *Democracy and the Work Place*, Montréal: Black Rose Books.

Wiltermuth, S. & Flynn, F. 2013. Power, Moral Clarity, and Punishment in the Workplace, *Academy of Management Journal* (published online before print: 24 July 2012: www.amj.aom.org, manuscript forwarded by e-mail), 37 pages.

Winfield, R. D. 1983. Freedom as Interaction: Hegel's Resolution to the Dilemma of Liberal Theory, in: Stepelevich, L. S. & Lamb, D. (eds.) *Hegel's Philosophy of Action*, Atlantic Highlands: Humanities Press.

Winfield, R. D. 1984. Hegel's Challenge to the Modern Economy, in: Perkins, R. L. (ed.) *History and System – Hegel's Philosophy of History*, Albany: State University of New York Press.

Winfield, R. D. 1987. Hegel's Challenge to the Modern Economy, in: Maker, W. (ed.) *Hegel on Economics and Freedom*, Macon: Mercer University Press.

Winfield, R. D. 2011. Hegel's Solution to the Mind-Body Problem, in: Houlgate, S. & Baur, M. (eds.) *The Blackwell Companion to Hegel*, Oxford: Wiley-Blackwell.

Wischke, M. 1993. *Kritik der Ethik des Gehorsams – Zum Moralproblem bei Theodor W. Adorno* [*A Critique of the Ethics of Obedience – Theodor W. Adorno's Problems of Morality*], Frankfurt/New York: Peter Berg Press.

Wisdom, J. O. 1993. What was Hegel's Main Problem?, *Philosophy of the Social Sciences*, vol. 23, no. 4, pp. 411–425.

Wood, A. 1990. *Hegel's Ethical Thought*, Cambridge: Cambridge University Press.

Wood, A. W. 1972. The Marxian Critique of Justice, *Philosophy & Public Affairs*, vol. 1, no. 3, pp. 244–282.

Wood, A. W. 2011. Hegel's Political Philosophy, in: Houlgate, S. & Baur, M. (eds.) *The Blackwell Companion to Hegel*, Oxford: Wiley-Blackwell.

Young, S. 2004. *The Persuaders – Inside the Hidden Machine of Political Advertising*, Melbourne: Pluto Press.

Younge, G. 2007. Bush can Bury His Head, But can't Hide, *Guardian Weekly*, 24–30 August 2007, vol. 177, no. 10, p. 18.

Zambrana, R. 2012. Hegel's Legacy, *Southern Journal of Philosophy*, vol. 50, no. 2, pp. 273–284.

Zeitlin, M. 1974. Corporate Ownership and Control: The Large Corporation and the Capitalist Class, *American Journal of Sociology*, vol. 79, no. 5, pp. 1073–1119.

Zengotita, T. 2005. *Mediated – How the Media Shapes Your World and the Way You Live in It*, New York: Bloomsbury.

Zimbalist, A, 1975. The Limits of Work Humanisation, *Review of Radical Political Economics*, vol. 7, no. 2, pp. 50–59.

Zimmerman, D. 1981. Coercive Wage Offers, *Philosophy and Public Affairs*, vol. 10, pp. 121–145.

Žižek, S. 1993. *Tarrying with the Negative – Kant, Hegel, and the Critique of Ideology*, Durham: Duke University Press.

Žižek, S. 2012. *Less Than Nothing: Hegel and the Shadow of Dialectical Materialism*, London: Verso.

Žižek, S. 2014. *Absolute Recoil – Towards a New Foundation of Dialectical Materialism*, London: Verso.

Zolfagharieh, M. 2009. *G. F. W. Hegel – Die Theorie der Sittlichkeit – Die Akteure des sittlichen Staates* [*GWF Hegel – The Theory of Sittlichkeit – Actors of a Moral State*], Munich: Grin-Press.

Zurn, C. F. 2005. Schwerpunkt Anerkennung [Focusing on Recognition], *Deutsche Zeitschrift für Philosophie*, vol. 53, no. 3, pp. 377–387.

# Index

Printed and bound by CPI Group (UK) Ltd, Croydon, CR0 4YY